D1580569

THE LONGMAN HANDBOOK OF
EARLY MODERN EUROPE
1453–1763

THE LONGMAN HANDBOOK OF
EARLY MODERN EUROPE
1453–1763

Chris Cook

Philip Broadhead

An imprint of **Pearson Education**

Harlow, England · London · New York · Reading, Massachusetts · San Francisco · Toronto · Don Mills, Ontario · Sydney
Tokyo · Singapore · Hong Kong · Seoul · Taipei · Cape Town · Madrid · Mexico City · Amsterdam · Munich · Paris · Milan

Pearson Education Limited

Edinburgh Gate
Harlow
Essex CM20 2JE
England

and Associated Companies throughout the world

Visit us on the World Wide Web at:
www.pearsoneduc.com

First published 2001

ISBN 0-582-38217-3

British Library Cataloguing-in-Publication Data
A catalogue record for this book is available from the British Library

Library of Congress Cataloging-in-Publication Data
A catalog record for this book is available from the Library of Congress

Set by 35 in 10/12pt New Baskerville
Printed in Malaysia,LSP

CONTENTS

LIST OF MAPS

PREFACE

The *Longman Handbook of Early Modern Europe, 1453–1763* has been designed to cover the major aspects of European history between the fall of Constantinople in 1453 and the Treaty of Paris of 1763. Its main focus is on the subjects most studied by students at advanced level, and it provides a comprehensive survey of such topics as the Renaissance, Reformation, Imperial Spain, the Revolt of the Netherlands, the Thirty Years' War and the Enlightenment. Sections on political, military and diplomatic events are supplemented with information on social, economic and cultural developments. The book concentrates on the major developments which took place in Western Europe, but there is also coverage of the Baltic lands, Russia, the Ottoman Empire and the Voyages of Discovery.

Readers may wish to refer to titles in the *Longman Companion* series when seeking more detailed coverage of certain issues discussed here. These include Mark Greengrass, *The Longman Companion to the European Reformation*; Stella Fletcher, *The Longman Companion to Renaissance Europe*. For reasons of space only limited coverage of events in the British Isles is given in this volume, and readers may wish to consult Rosemary O'Day, *The Longman Companion to the Tudor Age*, and John Wroughton, *The Longman Companion to the Stuart Age, 1603–1714*.

To assist students coming new to the period there are chronologies, a wide-ranging glossary and brief biographies of the major figures. To help those who wish to study the topics in more detail, there is an extensive bibliography, including specimen essay questions.

ACKNOWLEDGEMENTS

We are grateful to the following for permission to reproduce copyright material:

Table of infant mortality rate in Fiesole (Tuscany) 1621–61, Table of mortality in selected Italian cities during plague epidemics in 1630–31 and 1656–57 and Table of exports of silver to Asia by the Dutch East India Company (Verenigde Oostindische Compagnie) in kilogrammes of fine silver, 1602–1769 from C. Cipolla, *Before the Industrial Revolution: European Society and Economy, 1000–1700, 3rd Edition*, 1993, Routledge, reprinted by permission of Taylor & Francis; Table showing the size of London's population of aliens from R. Finlay, *Population and Metropolis: The Demography of London 1580–1650* (1981) by permission of Cambridge University Press; Tables entitled 'Exports of manufacturers from England 1699–1754' (in £000s) and 'Values of English re-exports 1699/1701 and 1772/74 (in £000s sterling)' from R. Davis, 'English Foreign Trade, 1700–1774', *Economic History Review*, 2nd series, Vol. XV (1962–63) by permission of Blackwell Publishers; Table of imports into Europe, 1591–1600 (annual averages) from P. Kriedte, *Peasants, Landlords and Merchant Capitalists: Europe and the World Economy 1500–1800* (1980 English translation; Leamington Spa, Berg, 1983) by permission of Van den Hoeck & Kuprocht, Gottingen, Germany.

While every effort has been made to trace the owners of copyright material, in a few cases this has proved impossible and we take this opportunity to offer our apologies to any copyright holders whose rights we may have unwittingly infringed.

POLITICAL HISTORY

HEADS OF STATE

Anjou

French Royal Dukes

1434–80	René I (Good King René)
1480–81	Charles II*

* After his death, the duchy of Anjou was incorporated into the kingdom of France.

Aragon

After the protracted civil war of the reign of King Juan II (1458–79), the crowns of Aragon and Castile were united in 1469 by the marriage of Ferdinand II (ruler 1479–1516) and Isabella of Castile.

Austria

After 1273, the Habsburg dynasty had ruled Austria as part of the Holy Roman Empire (see p. 8).

Austrian Netherlands

See under The Netherlands, p. 11.

Bavaria

Dukes (Electors from 1623) (House of Wittelsbach)

1467–1508	Albert IV*
1508–50	William IV
1550–79	Albert V
1579–97	William V
1597–1651	Maximilian I (created Elector in 1623)
1651–79	Ferdinand Maria
1679–1726	Maximilian II Emanuel
1726–45	Charles Albert I
1745–77	Maximilian III

* From 1460 to 1467, co-ruler with Sigismund; after 1505, Duke of All Bavaria.

Bohemia

Elected Kings

Before 1627 kings were elected. Thereafter kingship became hereditary. Note: All Kings of Bohemia, except Frederick, Elector Palatine, were also Kings of Hungary.

The Monarchy

1440–57	Ladislas
1457–71	George Poděbrady (his rule was threatened by Matthias Corvinus)
(1469–78	Matthias Corvinus)
1471–1516	Ladislas II (son of Casimir IV of Poland)
1516–26	Louis II (killed at battle of Mohács)
1526–64	Ferdinand I (also Holy Roman Emperor)
1564–76	Maximilian II (recognised as King)
1576–1611	Rudolf (Rudolf II of Austria)
1611–17	Matthias II (Matthias of Austria)
1617–19	Ferdinand II (deposed in August 1619)
1619–20	Frederick (the Elector Palatine) (fled in November 1620)
1620–37	Ferdinand II (again)

Subsequently the ruler of Austria reigned as King of Bohemia until the collapse of the Austro-Hungarian Empire in 1918.

Brandenburg

Dukes of Prussia

1525–68	Albert of Hohenzollern
1568–1618	Albert II Frederick (regency under George Frederick of Ansbach, 1578–1603 and then the Elector of Brandenburg)

Electors of Brandenburg (Dukes of Prussia) (Hohenzollern)

1535–77	Joachim II
1577–98	Johann Georg
1598–1608	Joachim Frederick
1608–19	Johann Sigismund
1619–40	George William
1640–88	Frederick William (the 'Great Elector')
1688–1713	Frederick III (became King Frederick I in Prussia in 1701)

For rulers after 1701, see under Prussia, p. 14.

Brittany

Dukes (House of Montfort)

1405–57	Peter II
1457–58	Arthur III (Arthur of Richemont)
1458–88	Francis II
1488–1514	Anne

The duchy of Brittany was incorporated into the kingdom of France as a result of Anne's marriages to Charles VIII (1491) and Louis XII (1499).

Burgundy

Dukes (House of Valois)

1419–67	Philip ('the Good')
1467–77	Charles ('the Bold')
1477–82*	Mary (she ruled with her husband Maximilian I, Archduke of Austria and Holy Roman Emperor)

* In 1482, the duchy of Burgundy (but not the county of Burgundy and Mary's other imperial territories) was incorporated into kingdom of France.

Byzantium

Emperors (House of Palaeologus)

The last Emperor was Constantine XI Palaeologus, *de facto* ruler from early 1449 to 29 May 1453 when Constantinople fell to the Ottomans.

Castile and León

Kings and Queens

1406–54	Juan II
1454–74	Enrique IV
1474–1504	Isabella I ('the Catholic')
1504–16	Juana ('the Mad') (she ruled jointly with her husband Philip the Fair from November 1504 to August 1506. Nominally Queen thereafter)
1516–56	Charles I (Emperor Charles V)

See under Spain thereafter, p. 17.

Denmark* (with Norway)

Kings (House of Oldenburg)

1448–81	Christian I
1481–1513	Hans

1513–23	Christian II (deposed)
1523–33	Frederick I (interregnum and civil war)
1534–59	Christian III (known as 'Father of the People')
1559–96	Frederick II
1596–1648	Christian IV
1648–70	Frederick III
1670–99	Christian V
1699–1730	Frederick IV
1730–46	Christian VI
1746–66	Frederick V

* Until 1523, Denmark also ruled Sweden, under the 1397 Union of Kalmar.

England

Kings and Queens

House of York

1461–83	Edward IV
1483	Edward V
1483–85	Richard III

House of Tudor

1485–1509	Henry VII
1509–47	Henry VIII
1547–53	Edward VI
1553–58	Mary
1558–1603	Elizabeth I

House of Stuart

1603–25	James I
1625–49	Charles I

Commonwealth

1649–53	Long Parliament

Protectorate

1653–58	Oliver Cromwell
1658–59	Richard Cromwell

Stuart Restoration

1660–85	Charles II
1685–88	James II

House of Orange

1689–1702	William III
(1689–94	William III and Mary II)

House of Stuart

1702–14   Anne

House of Hanover

1714–27   George I
1727–60   George II
1760–1820 George III

Florence

Heads of the Medici Family (Dukes of Florence from 1537 and Grand Dukes of Tuscany from 1569)

1429–64   Cosimo (the 'father of his country')
1464–69   Piero
1469–92   Lorenzo ('the Magnificent')
1492–94   Piero

From 1494 to 1512 the Medici were exiled from Florence.

1512–13   Giovanni (later Pope Leo X)
1513   Giuliano
1513–19   Lorenzo (grandson of Lorenzo the Magnificent)
1519–31   Giulio (later Pope Clement VII)

From 1527 to 1530 the Medici were exiled from Florence.

1531–37   Alessandro
1537–74   Cosimo I (from 1569 Grand Duke of Tuscany)
1574–87   Francesco I
1587–1609 Ferdinando I
1609–21   Cosimo II
1621–70   Ferdinando II
1670–1723 Cosimo III
1723–37   Gian Gastone

House of Lorraine-Habsburg

1737–65   Francis II

France

Kings
House of Valois

1422–61   Charles VII
1461–83   Louis XI
1483–98   Charles VIII

7

1498–1515	Louis XII
1515–47	Francis I
1547–59	Henry II
1559–60	Francis II
1560–74	Charles IX
1574–89	Henry III (assassinated)

House of Bourbon

1589–1610	Henry IV (assassinated)
1610–43	Louis XIII
1643–1715	Louis XIV
1715–74	Louis XV

Genoa

Ruled by the Doges (who changed office every two years after 1531). However, Genoa was frequently under foreign rule (for example, France, 1458–64, 1499–1512, 1515–22, and Milan, 1464–78, 1488–99).

Granada

The dynasty of Nasrid rulers of Granada ended with the fall of the city of Granada in 1492 to the Christian forces of Ferdinand and Isabella. The last Muslim ruler was Muhammad XII (1486–92).

Holy Roman Empire

Emperors (House of Habsburg)

1440–93	Frederick III
1493–1519	Maximilian I
1519–56	Charles V (abdicated) (died 1558)
1556–64	Ferdinand I
1564–76	Maximilian II
1576–1612	Rudolf II
1612–19	Matthias
1619–37	Ferdinand II
1637–57	Ferdinand III
1658–1705	Leopold I
1705–11	Joseph I
1711–40	Charles VI
1740–42	Disputed succession
1742–45	Charles VII of Bavaria
1745–65	Francis I

Imperial elections were conducted by the Golden Bull (1356) of Emperor Charles IV (died 1378). The seven members of the electoral college were:

1 Archbishop of Trier
2 Archbishop of Cologne
3 King of Bohemia
4 Count Palatine of the Rhine
5 Duke of Saxony-Wittenberg
6 Margrave of Brandenburg
7 Archbishop of Mainz

Imperial Diets

From 1485 to 1663 (after which date the Diet met permanently in session at Ratisbon (Regensburg) until the dissolution of the Empire in 1806) the Imperial Diet met as follows:

1485	Frankfurt	1542	Nürnberg
1489	Frankfurt	1543	Nürnberg
1491	Nürnberg	1544	Speyer
1495	Worms	1545	Worms (removed to Ratisbon)
1496	Lindau (removed to Worms)	1547	Augsburg
1500	Augsburg	1555	Augsburg
1501	Nürnberg	1556	Ratisbon
1505	Cologne	1559	Augsburg
1507	Constance	1570	Speyer
1510	Augsburg	1576	Ratisbon
1512	Trier (removed to Cologne)	1582	Augsburg
1518	Augsburg	1594	Ratisbon
1521	Worms	1597	Ratisbon
1523	Nürnberg	1603	Ratisbon
1526	Speyer	1608	Ratisbon
1529	Speyer	1613	Ratisbon
1530	Augsburg	1623	Ratisbon
1532	Ratisbon	1630	Ratisbon
1541	Ratisbon	1640	Ratisbon
1542	Speyer	1653	Ratisbon

Hungary

With the exception of the Elector Palatine, Frederick, all Kings of Hungary were also Kings of Bohemia (see p. 4). However, their regnal dates were frequently different. From 1526 (after the battle of Mohács) Hungary was split into three parts – part Ottoman, part ruled by John Zápolya, ruler of Transylvania, who was crowned as anti-king, and the rest by the Habsburgs.

1444–57	Ladislas
1458–90	Matthias Corvinus (House of Hunyadi)
1490–1516	Ladislas II (House of Jagiello)
1516–26	Louis II (House of Jagiello)

9

1526–64	Ferdinand I
1564–76	Maximilian
1576–1608	Rudolph
1608–17	Matthias II
1617–25	Ferdinand II
(1620–25)	Gabriel Bethlen (a rival king)
1625–47	Ferdinand III
1647–57	Ferdinand IV
1657–1705	Leopold I
1705–11	Joseph I
1712–40	Charles III
1740–80	Maria Theresa

Milan

Dukes (House of Sforza)

From 1450 to 1535 the duchy of Milan was ruled by the dukes of the House of Sforza. In 1535 Milan became an Imperial possession and was ruled by a succession of governors.

1450–66	Francesco
1466–76	Galeazzo Maria
1476–94	Gian Galeazzo II
1494–99	Ludovico
1499–1500	Milan was under French occupation
1500 (Feb.–Apr.)	Ludovico again
1500–12	Renewed French occupation
1512–15	Massimiliano
1515–21	Renewed French occupation
1521–24	Francesco II Maria
1524–25	Renewed French occupation
1525–29	Imperial occupation
1529–35	Francesco II Maria again (but as an Imperial vassal)

Muscovy

See under Russia, p. 14.

Naples

Naples was ruled by Aragonese kings from 1442 to 1516 and then by the Habsburgs (see p. 17 for Kings of Spain). In their absence, Naples was ruled by a long succession of viceroys. In 1714 it was transferred to Austria (from

1735, with Sicily, it formed the Kingdom of the Two Sicilies under the Spanish (Bourbon) younger line).

Navarre

In 1512 most of Upper (Spanish) Navarre was occupied by Aragon, leaving only a small French Basque kingdom to the north of the Pyrenees. Henry III of Navarre became King of France as Henry IV in 1589.

The Netherlands

Prior to 1477 the Netherlands was part of the duchy of Burgundy. It became part of the Habsburg domains with the marriage of Mary of Burgundy and the Emperor Maximilian I in 1477. The struggle for independence (known as the Revolt of the Netherlands) culminated in the establishment of a Dutch republic in 1579. For the United Provinces, see p. 19.

Rulers

1477–82	Mary of Burgundy
1482–94	Maximilian I (House of Habsburg)
1494–1506	Philip ('the Handsome')
1506–14	Maximilian I
1514–56	Charles V (House of Habsburg–Trastámara)
1556–98	Philip II

Regents of the Spanish Netherlands (from 1507 to 1621)

1507–30	Margaret of Austria, Duchess of Savoy
1531–55	Mary of Austria, Queen of Hungary
1555–59	Emmanuel Philibert, Duke of Savoy
1559–67	Margaret of Austria, Duchess of Parma
1567–73	Fernando Alvarez de Toledo, Duke of Alva
1573–76	Luis de Requesens y Zuñiga
1576–78	Don John of Austria
1578–92	Alexander Farnese, Duke of Parma
1592–94	Count Peter Ernest von Mansfeld
1594–95	Archduke Ernest of Austria
1595–96	Pedro Henriquez de Acevedo, Count of Fuentes
1596–1633	Archduke Albert of Austria and Infante Isabella*

* The Archduke Albert died in 1621. Isabella died in 1633.

Norway

After 1450 Norway was ruled as an integral part of the Kingdom of Denmark. See p. 5 for Kings of Denmark during this period.

Orléans

French Royal Dukes

1407–65   Charles
1465–98*   Louis II (became Louis XII of France, 1498–1515)

* In 1498 the duchy of Orléans was united with the crown of France.

Ottoman Empire

Sultans

1451–81   Mohammed II (Mehmed II, Mahomet II)
1481–1512   Bayezid II
1512–20   Selim I
1520–66   Suleiman II ('the Magnificent') (Süleyman)
1566–74   Selim II
1574–95   Murad III
1595–1603   Mohammed III (Mehmed III)
1603–1617   Ahmed I
1617–18   Mustafa I (deposed as mentally incapable of ruling)
1618–22   Osman II (assassinated)
1622–23   Mustafa I (restored)
1623–40   Murad IV
1640–48   Ibrahim
1648–87   Mohammed IV (Mehmed IV)
1687–91   Suleiman III
1691–95   Ahmed II
1695–1703   Mustafa II
1703–30   Ahmed III
1730–54   Mahmud I
1754–57   Osman III
1757–73   Mustafa III

The Papacy

Popes

1447–55   Nicholas V (Tommaso Parentucelli)
1455–58   Calixtus III (Alonso de Borgia)
1458–64   Pius II (Enea Silvio Piccolomini)
1464–71   Paul II (Pietro Barbo)
1471–84   Sixtus IV (Francesco della Rovere)
1484–92   Innocent VIII (Giovanni Battista Cibò)
1492–1503   Alexander VI (Rodrigo de Borgia)
1503   Pius III (Francesco Todeschini-Piccolomini)
1503–13   Julius II (Giuliano della Rovere)

1513–21	Leo X (Giovanni de Medici)
1522–23	Hadrian VI (Adrian Florensz Dedal)
1523–34	Clement VII (Giulio de Medici)
1534–49	Paul III (Alessandro Farnese)
1550–55	Julius III (Giovanni Maria Ciocchi del Monte)
1555	Marcellus II (Marcello Cervini)
1555–59	Paul IV (Gian Pietro Caraffa)
1559–65	Pius IV (Giovanni Angelo de Medici)
1566–72	Pius V (Antonio Michele Ghislieri)
1572–85	Gregory XIII (Ugo Boncampagni)
1585–90	Sixtus V (Felice Peretti)
1590	Urban VII (Giambattista Castagna)
1590–91	Gregory XIV (Niccolò Sfondrati)
1591	Innocent IX (Gian Antonio Facchinetti)
1592–1605	Clement VIII (Ippolito Aldobrandini)
1605	Leo XI (Alessandro de Medici)
1605–21	Paul V (Camillo Borghese)
1621–23	Gregory XV (Alessandro Ludovisi)
1623–44	Urban VIII (Maffeo Barberini)
1644–55	Innocent X (Giambattista Pamphili)
1655–67	Alexander VII (Fabio Chigi)
1667–69	Clement IX (Giulio Rospigliosi)
1670–76	Clement X (Emilio Altieri)
1676–89	Innocent XI (Benedetto Odescalchi)
1689–91	Alexander VIII (Pietro Ottoboni)
1691–1700	Innocent XII (Antonio Pignatelli)
1700–21	Clement XI (Giovanni Francesco Albani)
1721–24	Innocent XIII (Michelangelo dei Conti)
1724–30	Benedict XIII (Pietro Francesco Orsini)
1730–40	Clement XII (Lorenzo Corsini)
1740–58	Benedict XIV (Prospero Lambertini)
1758–69	Clement XIII (Carlo Rezzonico)

Poland-Lithuania

Elected Kings (Jagiellonian Dynasty, 1386–1572)

1447–92	Casimir IV
1492–1501	John Albert
1501–06	Alexander
1506–48	Sigismund I (Zygmunt I) Stary
1548–72	Sigismund II (Zygmunt II) August
1573–74	Henry of Valois (Duke of Anjou)
1575–86	Stephen (Stefan) Báthory (died 1586)
1587–1632	Sigismund III Vasa
1632–48	Ladislas IV Vasa

1648–68	John II Casimir
1669–73	Michael Wísnowiecki (died 1673)
1674–96	John III Sobieski
1697–1704	Augustus II (of Saxony)*
1704–09	Stanislaw I Leszczyński
1709–33	Augustus II (again)
1733	Stanislaw Leszczyński (he was twice elected, twice deposed)
1733–63	Augustus III
1764–95	Stanislaw Poniatowski** (the last King of Poland)

* The abdication was confirmed in 1706 by the Treaty of Altranstadt.
** The first Partition of Poland took place in 1772.

Portugal

Kings (House of Avis until Spanish occupation in 1580)

1438–81	Alfonso V
1481–95	John II (João)
1495–1521	Manuel I ('the Fortunate')
1521–57	John III (João)
1557–78	Sebastian (Sebastião)
1578–80	Henry (Henrique) (deposed)

After 1580, Portugal was ruled by the Spanish Kings until 1640.

1580–98	Philip I (Philip II of Spain)
1598–1621	Philip II (Philip III of Spain)
1621–40	Philip III (Philip IV of Spain)

House of Braganza

1640–56	John IV ('the Fortunate')
1656–83	Alfonso VI
1683–1706	Pedro II
1706–50	John V
1750–77	Joseph

Prussia

Kings

1701–13	Frederick I
1713–40	Frederick William I
1740–86	Frederick II

For the period before 1701, see under Brandenburg, p. 4.

Russia

From 1462, with the accession of Ivan the Great, the former Grand Princes of Muscovy (Moscow) take the title Tsar of Russia. The House of Riúrik ruled until 1598, then briefly the House of Godunov (1598–1605) and, after the 'Time of Troubles', the House of Romanov from 1613.

(1425–62)   Basil II ('the Blind')

Tsars

1462–1505	Ivan III ('the Great') (House of Riúrik)
1505–33	Basil III (Vasily III)
1533–84	Ivan IV ('the Terrible')
1584–98	Theodore I (Fedor I)
1598–1605	Boris Godunov (House of Godunov)
(1605–13	The 'Time of Troubles')
1605	Fedor II Godunov
1605–06	Dmitri
1606–10	Vasily Shuiskii
(1610–13	Interregnum)
1613–45	Michael (House of Romanov)
1645–76	Alexis I
1676–82	Theodore II
1682–1725	Peter I ('the Great') (co-ruler with Ivan V under the Regency of Sophia, 1682–89)
1725–27	Catherine I
1727–30	Peter II
1730–40	Anna
1740–41	Ivan VI (deposed)
1741–62	Elizabeth
1762	Peter III (murdered)
1762–96	Catherine II ('the Great')

Sardinia

The Kingdom of Sardinia was established by the Savoy Dynasty during the period 1718 to 1720.

Kings

1718–30	Victor Amadeus II (abdicated)
1730–73	Charles Emmanuel III

Savoy-Piedmont

Dukes (from 1416)

1451–65	Louis
1465–72	Amédée IX
1472–82	Philibert I
1482–89	Charles I
1489–96	Charles II

1496–97	Philip II
1497–1504	Philibert II
1504–33	Charles III
1533–80	Emmanuel Philibert
1580–1630	Charles Emmanuel
1630–37	Victor Amadeus I
1637–38	Francis Hyacinth
1638–75	Charles Emmanuel II
1675–1730	Victor Amadeus II (King of Sicily, 1713–20)*

* Savoy was merged in the newly-formed Kingdom of Sardinia, 1718–20.

Saxony

In August 1485 the duchy of Saxony was divided into two halves: the eastern (Albertine) half and the western (Ernestine) half.

Ernestine Saxony
Electors

1486–1525	Frederick III ('the Wise')
1525–32	John ('the Constant', 'the Steadfast')
1532–47	John Frederick II ('the Magnanimous')

In May 1547 the Electorship passed to the Albertine line.

Albertine Saxony
Dukes (Electors from 1547)

1485–1500	Albert III
1500–39	George ('the Rich', 'the Bearded')
1539–41	Henry
1541–53	Moritz (Maurice)
1553–86	Augustus
1586–91	Christian
1591–1611	Christian II
1611–56	John George I
1656–80	John George II
1680–91	John George III
1691–94	John George IV
1694–1733	Frederick Augustus I
1733–63	Frederick Augustus II

Scotland

Kings and Queens (House of Stuart)

1437–60	James II
1460–88	James III

1488–1513 James IV
1513–42 James V
(1543–60 Regency of Mary of Guise)
1561–66 Mary ('Queen of Scots')
1566–1625 James VI (James I of England from 1603)

Sicily

In 1409 Sicily was united with the crown of Aragon (and from 1512 with Spain). In 1713 Sicily was transferred, as a kingdom, to Savoy. In 1720 it passed to Austria.

Spain

Houses of Aragon and Castile (the Catholic Kings)

1474–1504 Isabella of Castile*
1479–1516 Ferdinand II of Aragon*

* The marriage of Ferdinand and Isabella in 1469 established the Kingdom of Spain.

Spanish Habsburgs (post 1516)

1516–56 Charles I (Emperor Charles V) (abdicated 1556)
1556–98 Philip II
1598–1621 Philip III
1621–65 Philip IV
1665–1700 Charles II

Spanish Bourbons

1700–46 Philip V of Anjou*
1746–59 Ferdinand VI
1759–88 Charles III

* Louis I during 1724.

The Spanish Netherlands

See under The Netherlands, p. 11.

Sweden

Prior to 1523 Sweden was ruled by Denmark under the Union of Kalmar. Thereafter it was ruled by the Vasa Dynasty.

Regents

1470–1503   Sten Sture
1503–12   Svante Nilsson
1512–20   Sten Sture (the Younger)

Kings

1523–60   Gustavus I Vasa
1560–68   Erik XIV (deposed; died 1577)
1569–92   John III
1592–99   Sigismund III (deposed)
1604–11   Charles IX (Regent from 1600)
1611–32   Gustavus II Adolphus
1632–54   Christina (abdicated)
1654–60   Charles X Gustavus
1660–97   Charles XI
1697–1718   Charles XII
1718–19   Ulrika Eleonora (vacated the throne in favour of her husband)
1719–51   Frederick I
1751–71   Frederick Adolphus

Transylvania

Until 1526, Transylvania was united with Hungary. It was independent from 1526 until 1691, then dependent on Austria until 1713. In 1764 it was created a Grand Duchy. There were often rival kings and disputed claims. Many of the dates below can only be approximate.

1526–40   John I Zápolya (anti-King of Hungary)
1540–71   John II Sigismund Zápolya
1571–75   Stephen I Báthory (King of Poland, 1576)
(1576–81   Regency of Christopher Báthory)
1581–98   Sigismund II Báthory
1598–99   Andrew Báthory
1600–04   Emperor Rudolf II[1]
1604–06   Stephen II Boczai
1607–08   Sigismund III Rákóczy
1608–13   Gabriel Báthory
1613–29   Gabriel Bethlen (Bethlen Gábor)
1629   Catharine of Brandenburg[2]
1630–48   George I Rákóczy
1648–60   George II Rákóczy[3]
1661–63   John Kemenyi
1663–90   Michael I Apaffy
1690–91   Michael II Apaffy[4]

In 1691 Emperor Leopold I became ruler but he was not recognised until 1694.

[1] Rival claimant in 1601–02 was Sigismund Báthory and in 1603 Mozes Székhely.
[2] Stephen Bethlen was her rival.
[3] Rival claimants from 1658 to 1661 were Francis Rhedey and Achatius Boczai.
[4] The rival claimant was Emeric Tokoly (Imre Tököly).

Tuscany

Created as a Grand Duchy in 1569 for Cosimo de Medici, Duke of Florence (see p. 7), the Grand Duchy remained in Medici hands until 1737. It then passed to the Duke of Lorraine, husband of Maria Theresa.

United Provinces

After the long struggle against Habsburg rule, the Dutch Republic was established in 1579 and Prince William of Orange became the first Stadtholder (see p. 235).

1579–84	William ('the Silent') (assassinated)
1584–1625	Maurice of Nassau
1625–47	Frederick Henry
1647–50	William II

From November 1650 to July 1672 the post was vacant. Jan de Witt exercised much power.

1672–1702	William III (also King of England)

From March 1702 to May 1747 the post of Stadtholder was vacant.

1747–51	William IV
1751–95*	William V (deposed)

* In 1795 William V was deposed and the country was under French occupation.

Venice

The head of state was the Doge, elected to his post for life. Only one Doge in the entire history of the Venetian Republic was deposed, most died in office.

Doges

1423–57	Francesco Foscari	1473–74	Nicolò Marcello
1457–62	Pasquale Malipiero	1474–76	Pietro Mocenigo
1462–71	Cristoforo Moro	1476–78	Andrea Vendramin
1471–73	Nicolò Tron	1478–85	Giovanni Mocenigo

19

1485–86	Marco Barbarigo	1625–29	Giovanni Corner I
1486–1501	Agostino Barbarigo	1630–31	Nicolò Contarini
1501–21	Leonardo Loredan	1631–46	Francesco Erizzo
1521–23	Antonio Grimani	1646–55	Francesco Molin
1523–38	Andrea Gritti	1655–56	Carlo Contarini
1539–45	Pietro Lando	1656	Francesco Corner
1545–53	Francesco Donà	1656–58	Bertucci Valier
1553–54	Marcantonio Trevisan	1658–59	Giovanni Pesaro
1554–56	Francesco Venier	1659–75	Domenico Contarini
1556–59	Lorenzo Priuli	1675–76	Nicolò Sagredo
1559–67	Girolamo Priuli	1676–84	Alvise Contarini
1567–70	Pietro Loredan	1684–88	Marcantonio Giustinian
1570–77	Alvise Mocenigo I	1688–94	Francesco Morosini
1577–78	Sebastiano Venier	1694–1700	Silvestro Valier
1578–85	Nicolò da Ponte	1700–09	Alvise Mocenigo II
1585–95	Pasquale Cicogna	1709–22	Giovanni Corner II
1595–1605	Marino Grimani	1722–32	Alvise Mocenigo III
1606–12	Leonardo Donà	1732–35	Carlo Ruzzini
1612–15	Marcantonio Memmo	1735–41	Alvise Pisani
1615–18	Giovanni Bembo	1741–52	Pietro Grimani
1618	Nicolò Donà	1752–62	Francesco Loredan
1618–23	Antonio Priuli	1762–63	Marco Foscarini
1623–24	Francesco Contarini	1763–78	Alvise Mocenigo IV

POLITICAL CHRONOLOGIES

FRANCE

The Growth of Royal Power, 1453–1515

1453	French defeat English at Castillon; the end of the Hundred Years War (only Calais and the Channel Islands remain as English possessions).
1456–61	The Dauphin remains at the Court of Burgundy.
1459	French protest at the policy of Pius II towards Naples.
1461	Death of Charles VII (July); accession of Louis XI.
	Pragmatic Sanction is abolished by Louis (Nov.).
1462	*Parlement* of Bordeaux is established.
	Aquisition of Rousillon and Cerdagne as a result of the support given to John of Aragon against Castile.
1463	Somme towns recovered. Treaty at Hesdin with Edward IV.
	Anger at papal policy leads to the restoration of the Pragmatic Sanction.
1464	Louis assumes government of Normandy.
	John of Calabria joins the nobles against Louis XI.
1465	War of the League of Public Weal. Indecisive battle of Montlhéry (July) is followed by the Treaty of Conflans (Oct.).
1466	Normandy is annexed to the French crown. The sack of Dinant by Philip the Good (Philippe le Bon) of Burgundy.
1467	Death of Philip the Good (June). Charles the Bold (Charles le Téméraire) becomes Duke of Burgundy.
1468	Estates-General meet at Tours. Louis is forced to give Brie and Champagne to the Duke of Berry, not the Duke of Normandy (Oct.). Treaty of Peronne with Charles the Bold, Duke of Burgundy.
1469	Charles the Bold acquires Alsace, Ferrette and the Breisgau. Louis gives Guienne to Charles de Berry.
1470	Burgundian possessions in Picardy are attacked by the Constable, Saint-Pol.
1472	Death of Charles de Berry, Duke of Guienne. Beauvais is besieged by Charles the Bold after a new League is formed against Louis.

Charles the Bold is deserted by Philip de Commines (who joins Louis). Treaty with the King of Aragon.

1473   Charles the Bold plans a Burgundian kingdom. Burgundy temporarily gains Lorraine. Death of Count of Armagnac after intrigues against Louis.

1474   Anti-Burgundian alliance of Louis XI and Frederick III. Franche-Comté is invaded. Revolt of Alsace against Burgundy.

1475   Burgundy and the Swiss enter a period of hostility. Edward IV of England invades Picardy. Charles the Bold fails to support Edward because of his pre-occupation with Lorraine. Edward signs the Treaty of Pecquigny. Charles the Bold takes Nancy. Execution of Saint-Pol (Dec.).

1476   Burgundy is defeated by the Swiss and René of Lorraine at Grandson and Morat. Burgundian cause is also abandoned by René of Provence.

1477   Death of Charles the Bold during an attack on Nancy (Jan.). French successes include the retaking of Picardy and the occupation of Artois, Burgundy and Franche-Comté. Mary, daughter of Charles the Bold, marries Archduke Maximilian (son of Frederick III). Treaty of Pecquigny is extended.

1478   A brief truce between Louis XI and Maximilian is quickly broken. Louis XI attempts mediation (through Commines) between Florence and Papacy but is unsuccessful. A treaty with Castile bolsters Isabella.

1479   Maximilian defeats Louis at Guinegate (Aug.) but war continues.

1480   Anjou is reunited with French crown following the death of René of Provence (July). Bar is occupied by Louis.

1481   Death of Charles of Provence (Dec.), leaving Louis as his heir. Angevin lands revert to the French crown.

1482   Death of Mary of Burgundy (Mar.). Louis XI and Maximilian reach an agreement at the Treaty of Arras (Dec.). Mary's daughter, Margaret, is to marry the Dauphin of France.

1483   Betrothal contract of the Dauphin to marry Margaret of Austria is ratified. Death of Louis (30 Aug.) is followed by the Regency of Anne of Beaujeu (1483–91), sister of Charles VIII (who is aged 13 on accession).

1484   Estates-General meet at Tours.

1485   Revolt of the League of the great nobles, led by Orléans and Brittany ('La Guerre folle').

1488   The Regent wins St Aubin (July). The League is overthrown. Brittany makes the Treaty of Sablé. Death of Duke Francis of Brittany (Sept.).

1489	Brittany secures the Treaty of Radon for military assistance from England.
1490	Proxy marriage to be arranged between Anne of Brittany and Archduke Maximilian (but fails to happen).
1491	Personal rule of Charles VIII. Charles marries Anne of Brittany (Dec.). This marriage unites the last major fief to the French crown.
1492	Charles secures protection at home by the Treaty of Étaples with England (Nov.).
1493	Charles cedes territory to buy off potential enemies. Roussillon and Cerdagne are ceded to Ferdinand of Aragon, Franche-Comté and Artois to the new Emperor, Maximilian (following the death of Frederick III).
1494	First French invasion of Italy by Charles VIII. Charles enters Florence (17 Nov.). The Florentine Republic is re-established. Charles enters Rome.
1495	After his conquest of Naples (Feb.), Charles VIII is faced by the League of Venice, uniting his opponents against him. Treaty of Vercelli with Ludovico Sforza (Oct.). Charles leaves Italy (Nov.).
1496	French are defeated in the south of Italy. French garrison at Naples surrenders.
1498	Death of Charles VIII (7 Apr.), ending the direct line of the House of Valois. Accession of Louis XII (Louis of Orléans). The Treaty of Étaples is confirmed (July). Treaty of Marcoussis is signed with Spain (Aug.).
1499	Marriage of Louis XII to Charles's widow, Anne of Brittany following the annulment of his marriage to Jeanne de France (daughter of Louis XI). Milan is occupied by France and Venice (Oct.).
1500	Defeat of Ludovico Sforza's attempts to reconquer Milan. Treaty of Granada partitions Naples between Louis XII and Ferdinand of Aragon.
1501	Frederick of Naples surrenders Naples to Louis XII.
1502	Franco-Spanish conflict in Naples.
1503	Defeat of the French in Naples. French defeats at Cerignola (Apr.) and Garigliano (Dec.).
1504	Treaty of Blois (see p. 143) ends conflict with Spain.
1505	Marriage of Germaine de Foix, niece of Louis XII, and Ferdinand of Spain.
1506	Assembly of Notables at Tours disavows clauses of the Blois treaty. François of Angoulême is betrothed to Claude (daughter of Louis XII and Anne of Brittany).

1507	Savona Agreement of Louis and Ferdinand to sell Pisa to Florence (sale completed in 1509). Genoa is captured and annexed to France.
1508	League of Cambrai forms against Venice (see p. 143). Louis XII, Ferdinand and Maximilian I unite.
1509	French defeat of Venice at Agnadello (May) is followed by the hostility of Pope Julius II and Louis.
1510	Death of Cardinal Georges d'Amboise (principal minister of Louis XII). Papacy is attacked at the Synod of Tours.
1511	Holy League is formed against the French (see p. 143) to drive them out of Italy.
1512	French victory at the battle of Ravenna. Death of Gaston de Foix. Northern Italy is abandoned by French. Navarre is overrun by Ferdinand of Spain.
1513	Alliance of France with Venice. Battle of Novara thwarts a French attempt to recover Milan. The French are defeated at Thérouanne by Henry VIII of England. France promotes the schismatic Council of Pisa. Peace with Spain (Apr.) and the Papacy (Dec.).
1514	Death of Anne of Brittany (Jan.). Marriage of Claude (daughter of Louis XII) to François of Angoulême. Death of Louis XII (31 Dec.). François succeeds the French throne (Francis I) in 1515.

The Reign of Francis I

1515	Accession of Francis I (following the death of Louis XII on 31 December 1514). Duprat is made Chancellor. Invasion of Italy and victory at Marignano (Sept.) (see p. 119). Swiss power in Northern Italy is broken.
1516	Concordat of Bologna with the Papacy (see p. 143). Treaty of Noyon with Charles (King of Spain). Treaty of Freiburg with Swiss Cantons (known as 'the Perpetual Peace').
1518	Despite strong opposition, the *Parlement* of Paris is forced to register the Concordat of Bologna. Heir to the French throne is born.
1519	Birth of Henry, second son of Francis I (31 Mar.); birth of Catherine de Medici (13 Apr.). Unsuccessful candidature of Francis I for election as Holy Roman Emperor. France joins a league against the Turks.
1520	Meeting of Henry VIII of England with Francis I at the Field of the Cloth of Gold (May).
1521	Lutheranism is condemned by the Sorbonne. Start of a long rivalry between the French royal house and the Habsburgs. The French overrun Navarre.

24

1522	Defeat of French forces under Lautrec at La Bicocca (see p. 120). England declares war on France. Franco-Scottish alliance is formed.
1523	First burning of a Protestant in Paris. The Constable, Charles of Bourbon, signs a treaty with Charles V and Henry VIII. Invasion of France fails.
1524	Defeat of Admiral Bonnivet in Milan. Francis I enters Milan. Imperialists invade France, capturing Aix and besieging Marseilles.
1525	Defeat and capture of Francis I at Pavia. Louise of Savoy becomes Regent. *Parlement* leads the repression of Protestants.
1526	Burgundy is surrendered by the Treaty of Madrid. The French king is released in exchange for his sons. Francis I helps to organise the League of Cognac (see p. 143).
1527	Rome is sacked by the Imperialists. Invasion of Italy and siege of Naples by Lautrec.
1528	The French are deserted by the Genoese admiral, Andrea Doria. Death of Lautrec. French army is defeated at Aversa. The French secure trading concessions in Egypt.
1529	Louis de Berquin is executed. French under Saint-Pol are defeated at Landriano in Northern Italy. Popular rising in Lyons (*rebeine*). Treaty of Cambrai (July). France retains Burgundy, abandoning Italy.
1530	Establishment of the Collège de France. Francis marries Eleanor of Portugal.
1531	French alliance with John I Zápolya of Hungary.
1532	Francis I associates himself with the German Protestant princes of the Schmalkaldic League. Anglo-French alliance at Boulogne (Oct.).
1533	Francis I meets Pope Clement VII at Marseilles (Oct.–Nov.). Marriage of Catherine de Medici to Henry, Duke of Orléans (future Henry II) (27 Oct.).
1534	Francis intrigues with the German princes; allies with Suleiman the Magnificent. The 'Affair of the Placards' at Amboise turns Francis I against the Protestant reformers.
1535	Dispute with Emperor Charles following the death of Francesco II Maria Sforza of Milan. Francis I invades Savoy.
1536	Turin is occupied by the French. Provence is invaded by Charles V (who later withdraws). Death of the Dauphin, Francis (10 Aug.) who is succeeded as Dauphin by his brother Henry.
1537	The French invade Artois. Hostilities in Italy are suspended after papal mediation.

25

1538	The Truce of Nice (18 June) between Charles V and Francis I. The Duke of Savoy loses all his territory, except Savoy. Meeting of Francis I and Charles V at Aigues-Mortes. Anne de Montmorency becomes Constable. Expulsion of Calvin from Geneva.
1539	Treaty of Toledo concludes marriages between the House of Bourbon and the House of Habsburg. Charles V crosses France (on Francis's invitation) to subdue the Revolt of Ghent.
1540	Edict of Fontainebleau. The Vaudois are massacred in Provence. Charles V and Francis I enter Paris.
1541	Renewal of the war against Charles V (July), the *casus belli* being the assassination of the French envoy to the Ottomans in Milan. Disgrace of Montmorency.
1542	French armies attack Charles V in the Netherlands, Roussillon and Piedmont.
1543	France is faced by the alliance of Emperor Charles V and Henry VIII of England. Picardy is invaded by Henry VIII, Champagne by Charles V.
1544	Imperialists and the Swiss Cantons are defeated at Cerisola (Apr.). Devastation of Mérindol and Cabrières. Francis (the future Francis II) is borne to the Dauphin Henry and Catherine de Medici. The Peace of Crépy (see p. 144) (Sept.) ends the war.
1545	Massacre of the Vaudois in Provence (Apr.). Birth of Catherine's daughter Elisabeth (future wife of Philip II of Spain) (2 Apr.).
1546	Execution of Etienne Dolet and the Meaux reformers. Henry VIII promises to return Boulogne after eight years.
1547	Death of Francis I (31 Mar.). Accession of Henry II. Montmorency returns to influence. Establishment of *Chambre Ardente*. Stricter controls over printed books are decreed by the Edict of Fontainebleau (Dec.).
1548	Henry II enters Lyons (Sept.). Beginning of the major revolts in the provinces (protests over the introduction of the *gabelle*). Montmorency crushes the revolt.
1549	Death of Margaret of Angoulême (sister of Francis I and a protector of the humanist reformers).
1550	Birth of Charles-Maximilian (the future Charles IX) (June). France gains Boulogne by Treaty with England.
1551	Edict of Châteaubriant (the first comprehensive statute to deal with heresy) (June). Birth of the future Henry III (Sept.). Alliance of Henry II and Maurice of Saxony (who had joined the Protestant princes).
1552	Treaty of Chambord (Jan.). France at war with Charles V. Occupation of Metz, Toul and Verdun bishoprics by Henry II. Guise holds Metz against Charles V.

1553	Death of Maurice of Saxony. Continuation of Habsburg–Valois hostilities.
1554	Invasion and devastation of part of the Netherlands by Henry II. Guise and Coligny win battle of Renty.
1555	Beginning of the evangelisation of France by the Genevan Company of Pastors.
1556	Truce of Vaucelles with Charles V (Feb.).
1557	Tougher penalties against heretics under the Edict of Compiègne (July). Expedition of the Constable, the Duke of Guise to Italy. Alba retires to Naples. Battle of Saint-Quentin (Aug.). The Constable is defeated and captured. Protestant riot of the Rue St Jacques in Paris (Sept.).
1558	Calais (the last English possession in France) is conquered by Guise (Jan.). Marriage of the Dauphin, Francis, and Mary, Queen of Scots (Apr.).
1559	French monarchy is bankrupt. Peace of Cateau-Cambrésis (Apr.) (for details, see p. 144). Secret national synod of reformed churches meets in Paris (May). Marriage of Elizabeth of Valois (daughter of Henry II and Catherine de Medici) to Philip II of Spain (June). Accidental death of Henry II (July). Accession of Francis II (under the government of the Duke of Guise and the Cardinal of Lorraine).

The Wars of Religion, 1562–98

See 'The Reformation and Civil War in France', pp. 166–70 in Section Three.

The Age of Richelieu, 1610–43

1610	Henry IV is assassinated by Ravaillac (14 May). He is succeeded by Louis XIII (aged eight) under the Regency of Marie de Medici. Concini influences royal policy.
1612	Louis XIII is to marry the Infanta of Spain; the King of Spain's son is to marry Louis' sister.
1614	First civil war headed by Prince de Condé. Marie de Medici and Condé come to terms in the Treaty of St Ménehould (May). Proclamation of Louis XIII's majority and the opening of Estates-General (Oct.). Marie de Medici is kept under house arrest at Blois.
1615	Second civil war. Condé and the princes unite with the Huguenots. The marriage of Louis XIII to Anne of Austria (Nov.) marks a new foreign policy alignment.
1616	Louis XIII and Condé conclude the Peace of Loudon (May). Concini ministry is in power. Richelieu is appointed Minister for War (Nov.). The King and Luynes plot to overthrow Concini.

1617	Assassination of Concini (Apr.). Luynes is now the favourite (until 1621). Villeroy and Jeannin return to office. Richelieu is dismissed.
1618	Exile of Richelieu to Avignon (Apr.). Publication of his *Instruction du Chrétien*.
1619	Conflict between Marie de Medici (who had escaped from Blois) and Louis XIII (Feb.–Apr.) ends with Treaty of Angoulême (Apr.).
1620	Second war between Louis XIII and his mother. The nobles (Mayenne, Longueville, Vendôme) revolt against the government. Treaty of Angers follows the success of the royal troops. Louis XIII annexes Béarn to France (Oct.).
1621	Assembly of La Rochelle under Rohan and Soubise. Louis XIII fights the Huguenots. Death of Luynes (Dec.). Struggle of Condé and Marie de Medici. Uprising of La Vieuville.
1622	Royalist successes against the Huguenots are followed by the Treaty of Montpellier (Oct.) (see p. 146). Richelieu is created a cardinal (Sept.).
1623	See of Luçon is renounced by Richelieu. *Parlement* of Paris complains of the maladministration of the country.
1624	Rapid rise of Richelieu; enters Council of State (Apr.); La Vieuville is dismissed and Richelieu becomes First Minister (Aug.). Papal garrisons are expelled from the Valtelline by French–Swiss forces.
1625	Mazarin becomes Captain in the Papal Army. Rising of the Huguenots under Soubise. Total defeat of Soubise (Sept.) and his escape to England.
1626	Peace of La Rochelle is concluded with the Huguenots (Feb.). France and Spain sign the Treaty of Monçon (Mar.). Arrest (Apr.) and execution of Henri de Talleyrand, marquis de Chalais (Aug.) following his failed conspiracy against the government of Richelieu. Assembly of Notables meets in Paris (Dec.). Richelieu puts forward a plan of reform.
1627	Richelieu is appointed Superintendant-General of Commerce and Navigation (Feb.). A Franco-Spanish alliance is concluded (Mar.). The siege of La Rochelle begins (Sept.). The Duke of Nevers claims succession after the death of the Duke of Mantua.
1628	Casale is besieged by Spain (May.) The fall of La Rochelle (Oct.) marks a new step towards royal despotism.
1629	*Code Michau* is published. Piedmont is invaded by the French (Mar.). Edict of Alais (June). Richelieu is appointed the king's Lieutenant-General in Italy.

1630	Richelieu and Mazarin meet at Lyons (Jan.). The French capture Pinerolo (Mar.). Memorandum by Richelieu on Italian policy (Apr.). Illness of Louis XIII (Sept.). The Treaty of Regensburg is signed (Oct.). Truce of Casale is agreed with Spain (Oct.). 'Day of Dupes' sees the triumph of Richelieu and the fall of Michel Marillac de Fayet, his rival (10–11 Nov.).
1631	Under the Treaty of Bärwalde, France is to give supplies to Sweden for six years (Jan.). Triumph for Richelieu in the Treaty of Cherasco (Apr.), which ends the War of the Mantuan Succession. Intrigues against Richelieu by the exiled Marie de Medici and Gaston, Duke of Orléans, continue.
1632	Treaty of Vic with Lorraine (Jan.). Execution of Marillac (May). The Orléans and Montmorency (Governor of Languedoc) revolt ends with the execution of Montmorency and the flight of Gaston of Orléans to the Spanish Netherlands.
1633	League of Heilbronn is formed (see p. 146). France occupies Lorraine (Sept.) and invades Alsace.
1634	Battle of Nordlingen (see p. 127). Louis XIII and Gaston of Orléans agree the Peace of Écouen (Oct.).
1635	*Académie française* is founded (Jan.). Oxenstierna visits Louis XIII. War is declared on Spain (May). There are disturbances and unrest in Bordeaux and Périgueux.
1636	*Croquant* rebellion (see p. 127). Loss (Aug.) and subsequent recapture of Corbie (Nov.).
1637	Defeat of the *Croquants* at La Sauvetât (June). Beginning of the conquest of Artois. Spaniards are driven back after invading Languedoc.
1638	Birth of the Dauphin (the future Louis XIV) (Sept.). Defeat of the French at Fuenterrabía (Sept.). Death of Father Joseph (Dec.).
1639	Hesdin falls to France (June). The *nu-pieds* revolt in Normandy (for details, see p. 127). There are disturbances in Rouen.
1640	France occupies Alsace and Christina of Savoy is restored to Turin. The alliance of France and Catalonia follows the Catalan revolt (see p. 128).
1641	The Spanish invade France. An edict is promulgated, insisting on the immediate registration by *Parlement* of all royal edicts. The conspiracy of the Count of Soissons is suppressed (July).
1642	Death of Marie de Medici (in Cologne) (July). Perpignan is occupied by the French (Sept.). Cinq-Mars and De Thou are executed after crushing the conspiracy (Sept.). Death of Richelieu (4 Dec.). France invades Spain but fails to take Tarragona.

1643   Mazarin becomes godfather of the Dauphin. Death of Louis XIII and the accession of Louis XIV (May) followed by a major French victory over the Spanish at Rocroi (19 May).

Mazarin and the Fronde

1643   Death of Louis XIII. Accession of Louis XIV (14 May). Queen Anne becomes sole Regent and Mazarin is chosen as First Minister (Louis XIII's arrangements for the Regency Council are overturned by the *Parlement*).

French victory over the Spanish at Rocroi (19 May).

Plot of the *Importants* is suppressed (Sept.). There are numerous peasant risings.

1644   The *toisée* (see p. 265) is imposed (Mar.).

The French take Gravelines but lose Lérida.

Defeat of the Bavarians at Freiburg by Turenne (July).

1645   The Imperialists are defeated by Turenne and the Prince de Condé at Nördlingen. Baltic Sound is opened to French trade (Nov.). A growing rift between *Parlement* and the crown leads to the imprisonment of extremist members of *Parlement*.

1646   Duties on goods entering Paris are imposed by the crown. The French take Piombino and Porto Longone (Oct.).

1647   France and Bavaria sign the Treaty of Ulm (Mar.). French armies are hit by mutinies. Serious illness of Louis XIV (Nov.).

1648   Defiance of Omer Talon at *lit de justice*. The insurrection of the Fronde (see p. 129) becomes serious. Condé defeats the Spanish at the battle of Lens (Aug.). Barricades go up in Paris after the arrest of Blancmesnil and Broussel. The Peace of Westphalia (see p. 146) brings French gains.

1649   Siege of Paris (Jan.–Apr.). The Court leaves Paris (Jan.). The first Fronde ends with the Treaty of Rueil, but there are continuing conflicts in parts of France (civil war in Guienne, a siege of Aix by Alais).

1650   The princes (Condé, Conti and Longueville) are arrested by Mazarin (Jan.). Siege of Bordeaux and Peace of Bordeaux (Oct.). Turenne is defeated by a royalist army at Rethel (Dec.).

1651   The princes are liberated (Jan.). Mazarin is exiled (Feb.). Rebellion of Condé, after a break with Conti. The majority of Louis XIV begins (Sept.). Châteauneuf becomes Chief Minister. Condé is attainted by *Parlement* for high treason.

1652   Return of Mazarin (Jan.); dismissal of Châteauneuf. Victory of Turenne at the battle of Jargeau (Mar.). Condé defeats a royal army at Bléneau and enters Paris (Apr.). The *Ormée* coup in

Bordeaux (July). The French are expelled from Catalonia. Second exile of Mazarin (Aug.). Paris is recovered by Louis XIV (Oct.). Triumph for Louis XIV amid popular acclaim. Retz is arrested (Dec.).

1653   Return of Mazarin from his second exile (Feb.). The Spanish in Flanders are joined by Condé. Bordeaux surrenders to royal authority (Aug.) which ends the provincial Fronde. Fouquet and Servien are appointed Superintendants of Finance. Denunciation of Jansenists by the Papacy.

1654   Coronation of Louis XIV at Rheims (June). Escape of Cardinal Retz from prison (Aug.). Arras is relieved by Turenne (Aug.).

1655   *Parlement* is forbidden by Louis to obstruct royal edicts. There are French military successes: Saint-Guillain is taken (Aug.). A commercial treaty is concluded with Protector Cromwell.

1656   The French army is defeated by Condé at Valenciennes. Mazarin and Orléans are reconciled (Aug.). Start of the *Lettres provinciales* of Pascal.

1658   Battle of the Dunes (June). The Spanish (and Condé) are defeated by Turenne and the English.

1659   Renunciation of Marie Mancini by Louis XIV. France and Spain sign the Peace of the Pyrenees (Nov.) (for details, see p. 147).

1660   Marriage of Louis XIV and Maria Theresa, the Infanta of Spain (June). An earlier visit to Toulon led to reconciliation with Condé. Royal sovereignty is recognised by the district of Orange. Death of Gaston, Duke of Orléans.

1661   Death of Mazarin (9 Mar.).

France under Louis XIV

1661   Death of Mazarin (Mar.). Marriage of Philip of Orléans, brother of Louis, and Henrietta, sister of Charles II of England (Apr.). Arrest and fall of Fouquet. Colbert becomes a leading minister in France (Sept.). Birth of Louis, the Dauphin (Nov.).

1662   Treaty of Paris with the United Provinces (Apr.). Dunkirk is bought back from England (Nov.). Famine and discontent are widespread. The Boulonnais revolt. The French Ambassador and the Pope quarrel in Rome.

1663   Avignon and the Comtat Venaissin are seized from the Papacy. Colbert makes major improvements in finance, commerce and colonial affairs. An alliance with the League of the Rhine continues (Jan.).

1664   New trading companies are established (e.g. the East and West India Companies and the Company of the West). The League of the Rhine and treaties with Sweden and Brandenburg are renewed. Gremonville becomes Ambassador to Vienna (until 1672). Port Royal is closed.

1665   The Council of Commerce is reorganised. Colbert becomes Controller-General (Dec.). Inauguration of industrial reforms. The French suppress the Barbary Pirates.

1666   The French declare war on England (Jan.) (see p. 132). Persecution of the Huguenots begins a series of emigrations.

1667   Death of Anne of Austria (the King's mother). The League of the Rhine is renewed. Beginning of the War of Devolution (for details, see p. 133) followed by the conquest of the Netherlands. Construction of the Canal du Midi in Languedoc begins (completed 1684).

1668   A secret Treaty of Partition is agreed with the Emperor to divide the Spanish Empire (Jan.). The Peace of Aix-la-Chapelle between Louis XIV and Spain leads to the acquisition of twelve fortified towns on the eastern frontier.

1669   Colbert becomes Minister of the Marine, Commerce, Colonies and the Royal Buildings. A continuing series of alliances is made by Louis.

1670   A defensive alliance between France and Bavaria is agreed (Feb.). There follows the three-year treaty with Sweden (May) and the secret Treaty of Dover between Louis XIV and Charles II of England (May) (see p. 148). Lorraine is occupied by the French army (Sept.). Revolt in the Vivarais.

1672   Beginning of Dutch War (6 Apr.) (to 1678). The French cross the Rhine at Tolhuys (June). Postal services are farmed out to private contractors. Turenne secures military victories.

1673   Royal edict suppresses the right of the *Parlement* of Paris to make remonstrances until after the registration of royal edicts. The Great Elector makes peace, ending the first Coalition against France. A new anti-French coalition is formed between the Empire, United Provinces, Lorraine and Spain.

1674   Opening of the campaign in Lorraine. The reconquest of Franche-Comté is completed. Turenne continues his series of military victories (for example, Sinsheim in June).

1675   Death of Turenne (26 July) destroys hopes of a victorious campaign. Créquy and his army capitulate at Saarbrücken (Sept.). Condé retires to Chantilly (Dec.), ending his military career.

1677   Louis XIV and Duke of Orléans secure victories in the north (for example, at Valenciennes, Cambrai, St Omer). Victories of Créquy.

1678   Louis XIV takes Ghent and Ypres. Beginning of the quarrel with Pope Innocent XI over the *régale* (see p. 261).

1679	The Peace of Nijmegen (see p. 148) results in French gains. Establishment of the '*Chambres de Réunion*' in the major cities along the Rhine, to claim territories and annex them.
1680	French sovereignty in Upper and Lower Alsace is claimed by the *Chambres de Réunion* in Breisach. Edicts are issued against the Huguenots. The persecution of the Jansenists continues.
1681	Casale is bought from Mantua. Strasbourg is seized by French troops. Luxembourg is besieged. Large numbers of Huguenots emigrate from the north and west.
1682	Louis XIV's Declaration of Four Articles is endorsed by an assembly of the French clergy (see p. 251). Siege of Luxembourg is lifted.
1683	Death of Colbert (Sept.). Le Peletier is made chief Finance Minister. Death of Louis XIV's wife, Maria Theresa. Bombardment of Algiers. Spain declares war to prevent reunions.
1684	Marriage in secret of Louis and Madame de Maintenon. Occupation of Luxembourg (June). Truce of Ratisbon ends war in the Spanish Netherlands. Arrival of the embassy from Siam (Thailand).
1685	Revocation of the Edict of Nantes (Oct.) (see p. 248) and the Edict of Fontainebleau. Death of Le Tellier. Bombardment of Tunis.
1686	League of Augsburg is formed against Louis XIV. College of St Cyr is established by Madame de Maintenon. Death of the great Condé (Dec.).
1687	Hostility with Pope Innocent XI results in the occupation of Avignon (in October 1688).
1688	War of the League of Augsburg (the Nine Years War) (see p. 136), and the subsequent devastation of the Rhineland. Bombardment of Algiers is renewed.
1689	Pontchartrain succeeds Le Peletier as Controller-General of Finances. Revolt in the Cévennes (*Enfants de Dieu*).
1690	Restoration of Avignon (seized in 1663) to the Papacy (Nov.). Pontchartrain succeeds Seignélay as Minister of Marine.
1693	Reconciliation of the Gallican Church with the Papacy (see p. 251). Widespread famine in France.
1695	Death of Marshal of France, the Duke of Luxembourg.
1696	Torcy becomes Minister of Foreign Affairs on the death of Colbert de Croissy.
1697	The Nine Years' War is ended by the Peace of Ryswick (see p. 148).

1698	After negotiations by Tallard, the first Partition Treaty is agreed (see p. 149) with maritime powers. Mission of Marquis d'Harcourt in Spain.
1699	Rapid promotion of Chamillart to be Controller-General of Finances. Numerous offices follow. Fénélon banished from court.
1700	Second Partition Treaty is signed (Mar.).
1701	The War Department is now also under the control of Chamillart. French troops occupy the barrier fortresses of Luxembourg, Mons, Charleroi as well as Ostend. A Grand Alliance develops against Louis. Villeroy is defeated at Chiari.
1702	War of the Spanish Succession. Villeroy is captured at Cremona (Feb.). Villars defeats the Imperialists at Friedlingen (Oct.). Outbreak of the Camisard (*Enfants de Dieu*) revolt in Cévennes (see p. 249).
1703	The French are driven out of the Electorate of Cologne following the victories of Marlborough. The defection of the Duke of Savoy seriously hinders the French in Italy.
1704	Revolt in the Cévennes is largely put down by Villars. Disastrous French defeat at the battle of Blenheim (2 Aug.). Tallard and much of his army are taken prisoner.
1705	Jansenism is condemned in the Papal Bull *Vineam domini*. Amelot is despatched to Spain to plan the government of Spain, according to the wishes of Louis XIV.
1706	Battle of Ramillies results in the loss of the Netherlands.
1707	Publication of *Dîme Royal* by Vauban on the reform of taxation. There is a hostile reaction from Louis XIV.
1708	Desmarets becomes Controller-General. There are French reverses at Oudenarde and Lille.
1709	Famine and hardship result from the harsh winter of 1708/09. Amelot is recalled from Spain (Apr.). Voyson takes over administration of the war. Battle of Malplaquet is lost by Villars (31 Aug.).
1710	Infamous destruction of the Jansenist convent at Port-Royal by soldiers. Institution of a new tax, the *dixième*.
1711	Death of the Dauphin, then of Louis' eldest grandson (Louis, Duke of Burgundy) (1712). Camisard rising is finally quelled. Fresh proposals for peace from Louis XIV.
1712	Utrecht Congress opens. Claim to French throne is renounced by Philip V of Spain. English truce with France.
1713	Peace of Utrecht (for details, see p. 149) results in the formal registration of the renunciation by the Dukes of Berry and Orléans of their claims to the Spanish throne.

1714	Louis legitimises his bastard offspring in his last will. There is peace with the Empire. *Parlement* is compelled to register the Papal Bull *Unigenitus.*
1715	End of 72-year reign of Louis XIV with his death aged 76 (1 Sept.). Beginning of reign of Louis XV (the five-year-old great-grandson of Louis XIV). The Regency is assumed by the Duke of Orléans.

France under Louis XV 1715–74

1715	Death of Louis XIV (1 Sept.). Succession of five-year-old Louis XV (great-grandson of Louis XIV). The Regency is assumed by the Duke of Orléans. The government is in the hands of seven councils (under the Duke of Orléans and the Council of Regency).
1716	Foundation of the *Banque Générale* by John Law. Chamber of Justice is founded to help attack financial venality. A secret treaty is signed with Prussia (Sept.).
1717	Triple Alliance of France, England and Holland is formed (this is a major reversal of traditional French support for English Jacobites and an apparent diplomatic revolution). Formation of Mississippi Company (*Compagnie d'Occident*). Convention of Amsterdam with France, Russia and Prussia (Campredon becomes the first permanent Ambassador to Russia).
1718	*Banque Générale* becomes the *Banque Royale.* D'Argenson rises to power. The Councils are suppressed; Dubois becomes Foreign Minister. Imprisonment of the Duke of Maine follows the Cellanare conspiracy.
1719	Death of Madame de Maintenon (Apr.).
1720	Exile of the *Parlement* of Paris to Pontoise. John Law briefly becomes Controller-General of Finances before financial collapse forces his flight (Dec.).
1721	Torcy loses influence (Oct.). Dubois is created a cardinal.
1723	Regency ends as Louis XV attains his majority. Dubois briefly First Minister (Feb.–Aug.) before his death. The Duke of Orléans briefly succeeds (till his death in December) and then the Duke of Bourbon.
1725	Louis XV marries Marie Leszczyński (daughter of exiled King of Poland) having angered Spain by dismissing the Spanish Infanta. Treaty of Hanover is signed (see p. 151).
1726	Duke of Bourbon is overthrown by Fleury who succeeds him as First Minister. Serious illness of Louis XV.
1727	France declines to join English attack on Spain. Renewal of 1714 Secret Treaty with Bavaria (to support the Elector's claim

to the Imperial throne). Anti-English Chauvelin becomes Foreign Secretary.

1728   Congress of Soissons (June 1728–July 1729).

1729   Treaty of Seville is signed (see p. 151). Franco-Spanish Alliance replaces Austro-Spanish Alliance. Birth of the Dauphin (Sept.).

1730   Climax of the struggle between the Jesuits and the Jansenists (see p. 254).

1731   The Paris *Parlement* decrees that temporal power is to be independent of all other power (and clergy are to be under crown jurisdiction). The decree is annulled by Fleury in a crown versus *Parlement* clash.

1732   Strength of anti-English party grows. A truce between the Court and *Parlement* is achieved. *Parlement* declares a *lit de justice.* Temporary exile of 139 magistrates but they are recalled as war in Europe approaches.

1733   Louis XV seeks to place Stanislaw Leszczyński on the Polish throne following the death of the Polish King Augustus II (Feb.). Treaty of Turin with Sardinia. The Family Compact is signed (see p. 151). France declares war on Austria (Oct.) following aid given to the Elector of Saxony.

1734   Victories for France in the Austrian War (see p. 139). Lorraine is occupied. Success at Parma (June) and Guastalla (Sept.).

1735   Preliminaries of the Peace of Vienna are agreed (see p. 151).

1737   Fall of pro-war Chauvelin (Feb.) after clashes with Fleury. Orry, the Controller-General, institutes the *corvée* (see p. 246) throughout France.

1738   The French offer to mediate in the Austro-Turkish War, with Fleury aiming to detach Austria from an alliance with Russia. Definitive Treaty of Vienna is signed.

1739   Secret Treaty between France and Austria (Jan.). House of Sulzbach is granted the disputed duchies for two years after the death of the Elector Palatine. Villeneuve secures the Treaty of Belgrade (see p. 152), a French diplomatic *coup.*

1740   Growth of the war party under Belle Isle.

1741   French treaties with Bavaria (May) and Prussia (June).

1742   French influence in Russia declines.

1743   More aggressive foreign policy follows the death of Cardinal Fleury. The French are defeated at Dettingen. Second Family Compact with Spain is signed (Oct.).

1744   Amelot is succeeded as Foreign Minister by Marquis d'Argenson (Nov.).

1745	Louis XV's mistress, Madame de Pompadour, is installed at Versailles – a recognition of her influence. Saxe defeats the Duke of Cumberland at Fontenoy (May).
1746	Victory of Saxe at Raucoux (Oct.) over Charles of Lorraine.
1747	D'Argenson is succeeded as Foreign Minister by Puysieulx.
1748	Peace of Aix-la-Chapelle (Oct.) is greeted with much unpopularity in France (see p. 153).
1749	Machault is frustrated by clerical opposition in his attempt to impose a tax of one-twentieth (the *vingtième*, see p. 266).
1750	Death of Marshal Saxe.
1751	Saint Contest succeeds Puysieulx as Foreign Minister.
1752	Temporal possessions of the Archbishop of Paris are seized by the *Parlement* of Paris.
1753	Paris *Parlement* is exiled by Louis XV.
1754	Birth of the future Louis XVI (28 Aug.). *Parlement* is recalled in the face of potential civil war in Paris. Rouillé succeeds Saint Contest as Minister of Foreign Affairs.
1755	Temporary success of the Count de Broglie's mission in Poland: Augustus III supports the French cause. Policy is destroyed by the 1756 Treaty of Westminster.
1756	Renewal of religious struggle between the *Parlement* and the Church. Diplomatic revolution (see p. 247) is inaugurated by the various Treaties of Versailles with Austria. Beginning of Seven Years War (see p. 140). Coercion of Paris *Parlement* by Louis XV fails to end continuing struggle.
1757	Execution of Damiens after a failed assassination attempt on Louis XV. Second Treaty of Versailles with Austria in which Prussia is to be partitioned. Defeat of the Duke of Cumberland at Hastenbeck (July) is followed by the Convention of Kloster-Seven (Sept.). Total defeat of French at Rossbach (Nov.).
1758	Rise of Choiseul, who becomes Minister of Foreign Affairs in 1759. Defeat of the French army at Creveld by Ferdinand of Brunswick (June).
1759	French military fortunes end in total defeat at the battle of Minden (1 Aug.). Naval defeats for the Toulon fleet and then the Brest fleet in Quiberon Bay. Colonial disasters include the death of Montcalm at the battle of Quebec.
1760	French power in India is lost after defeat at Wandewash. All of Canada is in English hands.
1761	The Third Family Compact (see p. 153) between France and Spain is agreed (Aug.).
1762	Publication of *Du Contrat Social* by Jean-Jacques Rousseau.

| 1763 | England and France sign the Treaty of Paris (see p. 153). Freedom of trade in corn is established (May). |

ITALY

Late Renaissance Italy

1454	Ravenna is conquered by Venice. Milan and Venice conclude the Treaty of Lodi.
1455	Formation of the Italian League.
1458	The *Cento* (Council of One Hundred) is established in Florence as a permanent legislative body with powers over taxation and the hiring of troops. It replaces the earlier Councils of the Two Hundred and One Hundred and Thirty-one (created in 1411).
1458	Angevins and Aragonese fight a war of succession (until 1464).
1461	Beginning of the disastrous Venetian War against the Ottoman Empire.
1464	Death of Cosimo de Medici. Succession of Piero in Florence.
1466	Venice takes Athens.
1469	Lorenzo the Magnificent takes charge of Florence following the brief reign of Cosimo's son, Piero. Birth of Machiavelli.
1470	Defeat of Venice by the Ottomans at Negroponte.
1471	Authority of the *Signoria* in Florence is weakened by the growing power of the *Cento*, whose authority now extends to foreign affairs and taxation.
1475	Cyprus is taken by Venice.
1477	End of the Venetian War against the Ottoman Turks.
1478	Failure of the conspiracy of Francesco and Jacopo Pazzi (encouraged by Pope Sixtus IV) against the Medici. Florence is placed under edict by Sixtus. Florence, Venice and Milan go to war with the Papacy, Siena and Naples.
1480	Advent to power of Lodovico Sforza in Milan. Peace is negotiated by Lorenzo the Magnificent with a papal accord. A period of tranquility ensues. Establishment of the *Consiglio de'Settanta* (Council of Seventy) which prevents the *Signoria* initiating legislation and narrows the numbers involved in decision-making.
1483	Consecration of Sistine Chapel in Rome. Excommunication of Venice.
1486	Start of the Barons' War in Naples.
1489	Dominican Fra Girolamo Savonarola begins to attract a following in Florence with his preaching. Construction of the villa of Lorenzo at Poggio a Caiano.

38

1492	Death of Lorenzo. His eldest son, Piero, takes over his position in Florence (he dies in 1503).
1494	Charles VIII of France invades Italy, enters Florence and expels the Medici. Broadly-based republican constitution, supported by Savonarola, is formed: it has a new 3,000-member *Consiglio Maggiore* (Great Council), the *Consiglio degli Ottanta* (Council of Eighty) and a ten-man foreign affairs magistracy. It is the most democratic constitution in Florentine history. Anti-Jewish legislation is promulgated in Florence (where Jews have been tolerated since the return of Cosimo de Medici in 1434).
1495	Charles VIII of France enters Naples (Feb.). As a result of French successes (Mar.), the League of Venice is formed (comprising Aragon, Venice and the Empire). Elections are introduced in Florence following the abandonment of scrutinies.
1496	The French retreat after the Aragonese victory at Atella. The French garrison at Naples surrenders.
1497	France and Aragon agree to partition Naples. Circumnavigation of the Cape by Vasco da Gama (following the earlier voyage of Columbus to the Caribbean) leads to the long-term decline of Venice.
1498	Savonarola and two fellow Dominicans convicted of heresy (at the instigation of Pope Alexander VI) are burnt at the stake in the Piazza della Signoria in Florence. A period of chaos ensues.
1499	Cesare Borgia begins the capture of Romagna. Second French invasion. Milan is occupied. Government crisis in Florence over taxation required to recover Pisa.
1500	Louis XII lays dynastic claim to Milan. He gains the support of Florence, Venice and the Papacy. French victory over Sforza at Novara (Apr.) is followed by the capture of Milan. Sforza is captured and banished from Milan. Treaty of Granada agrees joint action by France and Aragon against Naples (Nov.).
1501	Louis XII of France and Ferdinand, King of Aragon, capture and partition Naples.
1502	The *Gonfaloniere di Giustizia* (Standard-bearer of Justice) is head of government under a new compromise constitution in Florence. Piero Soderini is appointed.
1503	Disputes between France and Aragon lead to French defeat at the battle of Garigliano. Naples is under Ferdinand of Aragon's control.
1504	France recognises Ferdinand's claim to Naples. Sicily and Naples are now ruled by Spain until 1713 as the Kingdom of the Two Sicilies. Michelangelo and Leonardo da Vinci are commissioned to paint frescoes on the walls of the council chamber in Florence.

1506	Foundation stone of St Peter's in Rome is laid by Pope Julius II.
1508	Formation of the League of Cambrai (France, the Empire and Aragon) against Venice (Dec.). Sistine Chapel ceiling is painted by Michelangelo.
1509	Important French victory over Venice at Agnadello (May). Surrender and reconquest of Pisa by Florence.
1510	Spanish-held Kingdom of Naples orders the expulsion of many Jews.
1511	Reaction against French successes leads to the formation of the Holy League (comprising Aragon, Venice and the Papacy) (Oct.). Subsequently, the anti-French alliance is joined by Henry VIII of England and the Emperor.
1512	Costly French victory at the battle of Ravenna (Apr.). The French withdraw from northern Italy. Pro-Medici papal forces reinstate the Medici in Florence. Soderini flees to Dalmatia. Prato is sacked.
1513	Third French invasion of Italy. French defeat at Novara leads to their withdrawal from Italy and the loss of Milan. Election of Cardinal Giovanni de Medici (son of Lorenzo the Magnificent) as Pope Leo X. This reinforces papal control in Florence; Medici power in Florence is stronger than ever before.
1515	Fourth French Italian invasion (following the accession of Francis I). The French are victorious at Marignano and occupy Milan. Pope Leo X enters Florence in triumph.
1516	Treaty of Noyon (Aug.) confirms French and Spanish possessions in Milan and Naples, respectively. Venetian Jews are ordered to live in a ghetto.
1519	Cardinal Giulio de Medici is created Archbishop of Florence (effectively its governor). Birth of Cosimo de Medici, later first Grand Duke of Tuscany.
1521	The French are driven from Milan by Imperial troops. Papal Bull *Decet Romanum Pontificem* excommunicates Luther (Jan.). Death of Pope Leo X (Dec.).
1522	Election of Pope Hadrian VI (Jan.). The French are defeated at Bicocca.
1523	Death of Hadrian VI (Sept.). Election of Cardinal Giulio de Medici as Pope Clement VII.
1524	The French are defeated in Milan. An army of recovery is headed by Francis I.
1525	Battle of Pavia. Total French defeat and capture of Francis I.
1526	Francis I and Pope Clement VII form the League of Cognac. Francis surrenders his claims to Milan, Naples and Genoa by the Treaty of Madrid (Jan.).

1527	Fifth French invasion of Italy. Imperial troops of Emperor Charles V defeat the French forces and sack Rome (May). The Medici are expelled from Florence and the Republican constitution of 1494 is restored. Expulsion of Jews from Florence (after toleration since 1512 under the Medici). French army of recovery is despatched to besiege Naples.
1528	Defeat of French forces at Aversa.
1529	Peace is established between the Emperor and the Pope under the Treaty of Barcelona (June). Charles V is confirmed in possession of Naples, and the Papacy retains recent gains in central and northern Italy. Emperor and the Papacy besiege Florence in the Medici's cause. The French are defeated at Landriano (June). Peace is achieved between Charles V and Francis I at the Treaty of Cambrai. All territorial claims in Italy and Flanders are renounced by Francis. Claims to Burgundian lands in France are abandoned by Charles.
1530	Surrender of Florence and the fall of the Republic (Aug.). The illegitimate Alessandro de Medici is declared head of government in Florence and is subsequently created Duke of the Florentine Republic in 1531. Combined papal and Imperial forces ensure the surrender of Florence. Charles V is summoned to the Bologna Conference (Nov. 1529–Feb. 1530).
1532	Machiavelli's *Il Principe* is first published (posthumously).
1533	Charles V returns to Italy. The Second Bologna Conference.
1534	Death of Pope Clement VII (Sept.). Election of Pope Paul III.
1535	Death of Francesco Sforza in Milan provokes a new succession dispute between France and the Emperor. Charles V returns to Italy.
1536	Sixth French invasion of Italy. Turin is occupied by French troops who also overrun part of the Duchy of Savoy.
1537	Assassination of Duke Alessandro by his cousin, Lorenzino. Cosimo de Medici is nominated as head of government by the ruling circle in Florence and is subsequently confirmed as Duke of Tuscany by Charles V. He rules until 1574.
1545	Opening of Council of Trent (see p. 181). Piero Luigi Farnese is made Duke of Parma.
1549	Death of Pope Paul III. Election of Julius III (in 1550).
1552	Expulsion of the Spanish garrison from Siena. The French invade a seventh time following an invitation to enter Siena.
1553	Corsica is invaded by the French.
1555	Death of Pope Julius III. Election of Pope Marcellus II (only a brief pontificate) is followed by the election of Paul IV. Siena is captured by Imperial and Florentine troops.

| 1559 | Treaty of Cateau-Cambrésis (see p. 144) sees the final French withdrawal from Italy. |

Italy under Spanish Domination, 1559–1713

1559	Emmanuel Philibert becomes Duke of Savoy.
1560	Construction of the Uffizi, the state offices, in Florence.
1569	Title of Grand Duke of Tuscany is bestowed on Cosimo by Pope Pius V.
1571	Major defeat of the Ottoman naval threat at the battle of Lepanto (see p. 123).
1574	Death of Grand Duke Cosimo in Florence.
1587	Death of Grand Duke Francesco, succeeded by his brother, Cardinal Ferdinando.
1593	Free port of Livorno, established by Cosimo I, is opened to all immigrants.
1595	Charles Borromeo becomes Archbishop of Milan.
1597	Annexation of Ferrara by Pope Clement VIII.
1606	Interdict is placed on Venice by Pope Paul V, but is ignored with contempt by Venice.
1609	Death of Grand Duke Ferdinando I, who is succeeded by his son, Cosimo II.
1612–17	Monferrato and Valtellina Wars.
1618	Outbreak of the Thirty Years' War.
1621	Succession of Ferdinando II Medici in Tuscany (he assumes power in 1628).
1627–31	Second War of Monferrato.
1630	Sack of Mantua.
1631	Pope Urban VIII annexes Urbino.
1633	Condemnation of Galileo in Rome.
1638	Charles Emmanuel II (a minor) accedes in Piedmont-Savoy.
1641	Beginning of the War of Castro between the Papacy and the Duke of Parma, supported by Venice, Modena and Tuscany.
1644	War of Castro ends with the Peace of Ferrara.
1647	Revolt in Naples against Spanish rule (July). Leader of revolt, Masaniello, is assassinated (16 July). Military expedition under Don John of Austria is sent to restore Spanish authority (Oct.).
1648	Spanish power is restored in Naples by Don John of Austria (Apr.). Charles Emmanel II assumes government in Piedmont-Savoy.
1651	Venetian naval victory over Turks at Scio.

1667	Clement IX succeeds Alexander VII as Pope.
1669	Candia is taken from Venice by the Turks.
1670	Succession of Cosimo III in Tuscany.
1674	Revolt in Messina.
1683	Part of Morea is recovered by Venice.
1684	Genoa is bombarded by the French fleet.
1691	Duke Victor Amadeus of Piedmont-Savoy invades Dauphiné.
1694	Treaty is signed between Victor Amadeus and Louis XIV. Louis gains Savoy, Nice, Casale and Pignerolo.
1701	Beginning of the War of the Spanish Succession (see p. 137).
1706	At the battle of Turin the French are defeated by Prince Eugène and are expelled from Piedmont. Piedmont makes territorial gains in Lombardy.
1707	Spanish rule ends as Naples is captured by Austrian forces.
1713	The Peace of Utrecht (see p. 149) marks the end of Spanish domination and sees the partition of Italy: Lombardy passes to Austrian control; Naples remains under Austrian rule; Sicily is ceded to Piedmont by Spain and Victor Amadeus secures the title of King.

Italy in the Eighteenth Century

1714	Venice goes to war with the Ottoman Empire.
1715	Expulsion of Venice from Morea by the Turks.
1717	Reorganisation of the Council of State in Piedmont-Savoy.
1718	Sicily is recaptured by Spain (July). By the Peace of Passarowitz Venice retains Corfu, Morea is ceded to the Ottomans. Don Carlos (the son of the King of Spain) is chosen by leading European powers to succeed eventually to the Grand Duchy of Tuscany.
1720	Under the Peace of Cambrai, Piedmont becomes Piedmont-Sardinia. Sardinia is gained in exchange for Sicily. Austria gains possession of Sicily.
1723	New royal constitution is established in Piedmont (revised again in 1729). Death of Grand Duke Cosimo III in Florence (he is succeeded by his childless son, Gian Gastone, the last Medici Grand Duke).
1730	Abdication of Victor Amadeus II of Piedmont in favour of his son, Charles Emmanuel III. Administrative reforms take place in Piedmont.

1732	Don Carlos of Bourbon becomes Duke of Parma. Don Carlos is crowned Charles II of Naples.
1733	Piedmont joins France and Spain in the League of Turin against Austria.
1734	Naples is reconquered by the Spanish army under Don Carlos.
1735	Peace preliminaries at Vienna. Don Carlos of Spain is to receive Naples and Sicily. Francis of Lorraine is promised Tuscany once the Medici line dies out. This is confirmed at the 1748 Treaty of Aix-la-Chapelle (see p. 153). Piedmont receives Tortonese and the remainder of Novarese.
1737	Death, without an heir, of the last Medici Grand Duke, Gian Gastone. Tuscan Grand Duchy passes to the House of Lorraine, thus initiating an era of enlightened rule under Francis of Lorraine (husband of Maria Theresa). Reforms in administration, agriculture (draining of the Valdichiana) and of religious foundations follow.
1739	Tribunals in Sicily are reformed by Bernardo Tanucci but the hostility of the nobility forces the abandonment of reforms in 1744.
1742	Anti-Spanish alliance of Charles Emmanuel III of Piedmont with Austria (Feb.).
1743	Piedmont allies with Austria and Britain at the Treaty of Worms to expel the Bourbons from Italy (Sept.).
1745	French and Spanish armies overrun Lombardy.
1746	Defeat for French and Spanish forces at the battle of Piacenza (June). They are driven out of Lombardy and Sardinia by Austria and Piedmont.
1748	Peace of Aix-la-Chapelle (Oct.): Piedmont makes territorial gains from Austria.
1755	Genoa sells Corsica to France. Beltrame Cristiani reforms the provincial and local administration in Lombardy.
1757	Last symbol of Spanish influence, the Council of Italy, is abolished. Lombardy is under increasingly tight Austrian control.
1758	Pompero Neri becomes the chief minister in the Grand Duchy of Tuscany (until 1777).
1759	Frederick IV (son of Charles III of Spain) accedes in Sicily-Naples.

THE NETHERLANDS

The Revolt of the Netherlands

For chronologies of the background and course of the Revolt, see p. 170.

The Rise of the Dutch Republic

1618	Synod of Dordrecht (Dort). Outbreak of the Thirty Years' War (see separate chronology, p. 126).
1619	Trial and execution of the Advocate, Oldenbarneveldt. The rise of Dutch power in the Indies (see p. 200). Anglo-Dutch rivalry becomes an Anglo-Dutch alliance.
1620	Pilgrim Fathers leave Holland.
1621	War with Spain is resumed. Foundation of the Dutch West India Company (see also p. 200).
1625	Death of Stadtholder Maurice. He is succeeded by his brother, Frederick Henry. Breda is recaptured by the Spanish.
1628	Piet Heyn captures the Spanish Silver Fleet off the coast of Cuba (Sept). 'sHertogenbosch is captured by the Dutch; unsuccessful Spanish siege of Bergen-op-Zoom.
1637	Frederick Henry recaptures Breda.
1639	Spanish fleet is destroyed by Martin Tromp in the battle of the Downs (Oct.).
1641	Marriage of William (son of Frederick Henry) to Mary, daughter of Charles I of England.
1644	Dutch naval expeditions to the Baltic (forcing the passage of the Sound).
1647	Death of Frederick Henry. He is succeeded as Stadtholder of five provinces by his son, William II.
1648	Treaty of Münster at last recognises the complete independence of the United Provinces (Jan.). River Scheldt is to remain closed. The comprehensive Treaty of Westphalia is signed (Oct.) (see p. 146).
1650	William II attempts to capture Amsterdam. This is followed soon after by his death (6 Nov.) and the birth of a son (later William III) (14 Nov.). The first 'Stadtholderless period' (except in Groningen and Friesland) follows (also known as the period of True Freedom).
1651	Delegates from all provinces meet in the Great Assembly. A decision is made to continue to enforce the 1619 Synod of Dort. Holland (and four other provinces) leave the post of Stadtholder vacant.
1652	Outbreak of the first Anglo-Dutch War (see p. 130).
1653	Johan de Witt becomes Grand Pensionary in Holland (until 1672), following the death of Adrian Pauw.
1654	Treaty of Westminster concludes the first Anglo-Dutch War (Apr.). Navigation Acts are recognised by the Dutch.

45

1656	Hostilities commence with Portugal resulting from colonial rivalries in the East Indies and Brazil.
1661	Settlement of the colonial disputes with Portugal. Ceylon and Macassar are retained, but the United Provinces surrender claims to Brazil.
1664	Colonial and naval clashes with England begin to escalate.
1665	Second Anglo-Dutch War (for details, see p. 132).
1667	Treaty of Breda concludes the second Anglo-Dutch War. Louis XIV invades the Spanish Netherlands during the 'War of Devolution'. Office of Stadtholder is abolished (Aug.).
1668	Formation of the Triple Alliance of the Dutch Republic, England and Sweden (Jan.). De Witt is re-elected Grand Pensionary with doubled salary.
1669	Death of Rembrandt.
1670	Secret Treaty of Dover. The Dutch are threatened by a joint attack by Charles II of England and Louis XIV of France.
1672	William III is appointed Captain-General (Feb.). Outbreak of third Anglo-Dutch War; French army invades United Provinces (see p. 134). Assassination attempt on Johan de Witt fails (June). The de Witt brothers are murdered at The Hague (Aug.). Re-establishment of the Stadtholdership in favour of William III.
1673	William III drives French troops out of the United Provinces.
1674	Treaty of Westminster ends the Third Anglo-Dutch War. Holland and Zeeland make the Stadtholdership hereditary in the Orange male line.
1676	Death of Admiral de Ruyter (Apr.).
1677	Renewed Dutch naval intervention in the Baltic. Marriage of William III to Mary, daughter of James, Duke of York (Nov.).
1678	Frist Treaty of Nijmegen ends war with France (restoration of Maastricht to Holland).
1679	Death of John Maurice of Nassau-Siegen and Joost van den Vondel.
1682	Beginning of the subjugation of Bantam in Java.
1685	Large-scale immigration of Huguenots to Holland from France follows the revocation of the Edict of Nantes. James II succeeds to the throne in England.
1686	William III forms an anti-French alliance (with Austria, Brandenburg, other smaller German states, Spain and Sweden).
1688	William III invades England following an invitation by leading Whigs and Tories (Nov.) (see p. 136). Death of Fagel, the Grand Pensionary.

1689	William and Mary become King and Queen of England (Feb.). Beginning of the War of the League of Augsburg (see p. 136).
1691	William III returns to Holland to coordinate the Alliance (Jan.).
1694	Death of William's wife, Mary (Dec.).
1696	Return of William III to Holland (to aid the campaign against French).
1697	Treaty of Ryswick (Ryswijk) ends the War of the League of Augsburg (see p. 148).
1701	Formation of the 'Grand Alliance' against France.
1702	Death of William III. Beginning of the second 'Stadtholderless period' (until 1747). War of the Spanish Succession begins (until 1713).
1711	Death of John William of Nassau.
1713	Treaty of Utrecht ends the War of the Spanish Succession (see p. 149).
1715	Dutch gain the right to man fortresses of Namur, Ypres and Tournai under the Barrier Treaty with Austria.
1716	Meeting of Great Assembly (Nov. 1716–Sept. 1717).
1720	Death of Heinsius (Aug.). Isaak van Hoornbeek becomes Grand Pensionary. Outbreak of popular disturbances in Amsterdam.
1722	William IV of Orange becomes Stadtholder of Drenthe and Gelderland (but Holland, Zeeland and Utrecht confirm government without a stadtholder in 1723).
1727	Death of Isaak von Hoornbeek. Van Slingelandt becomes Grand Pensionary.
1729	William IV assumes the Stadtholdership of Groningen, Drenthe and Gelderland on coming of age.
1731	William IV also becomes Stadtholder of Friesland. Treaty of Vienna, by which the Dutch recognise the Pragmatic Sanction. Ostend East India Company is wound up.
1734	Marriage of William IV to Anne, eldest daughter of George II of England.
1737	Van der Heim becomes Grand Pensionary, following the death of van Slingelandt in December 1736.
1743	States-General commit a force of 20,000 (commanded by Prince Maurice of Nassau-Ouwerkerk) to the aid of Maria Theresa (June).
1745	Alliance with England, Saxony and Austria to support the Pragmatic Sanction.
1746	Gilles becomes Grand Pensionary on the death of Van der Heim.

1747	French military successes in Belgium and Dutch Flanders herald the proclamation of William IV as Stadtholder of Holland (May). (Shortly afterwards he becomes Stadtholder of Utrecht and Overijssel.) He is appointed Captain and Admiral General of the United Provinces (4 May). Offices become hereditary, first in Holland and later elsewhere in the House of Orange-Nassau.
1748	Abolition of revenue farming in Holland (June). Widespread reforms are forced upon the Amsterdam city council (Aug.). Under the Peace of Aix-la-Chapelle (see p. 153) France withdraws from the Austrian Netherlands. William IV is declared hereditary Stadtholder by the States-General.
1749	Enforced resignation of Gilles as Grand Pensionary. He is succeeded by Pieter Steyn (May). Duke of Brunswick-Wolfenbüttel introduces reforms in the army.
1751	Unexpected death of William IV. Anne of England becomes Regent for William V (a minor). Duke of Brunswick is appointed acting Captain-General.
1756	Seven Years' War begins. Dutch profit from neutrality but seaborne trade is disrupted.
1763	Financial panic in Amsterdam.

PRUSSIA

The Early Rise of Brandenburg-Prussia (to the death of the Great Elector)

The Origins of Prussia

Under the Golden Bull of Rimini (1226), the Order of the Teutonic Knights was authorised to rule the territory of the *Pruzzen*. In 1466, by the Second Peace of Thorn, the Grand Master of the Teutonic Order was compelled to swear fealty to Poland (see p. 142). In 1525, the Teutonic Order state was transformed into the temporal Duchy of Prussia.

1535	Joachim II Hector becomes Elector of Brandenburg.
1539	Protestant Reformation in Brandenburg.
1544	University of Königsberg is founded.
1577	Johann Georg becomes Elector of Brandenburg.
1598	Joachim Frederick becomes Elector of Brandenburg.
1608	Johann Sigismund (1572–1619) becomes Elector of Brandenburg.
1609	Elector of Brandenburg claims the Cleves-Jülich succession.
1613	Conversion of Elector Johann Sigismund to the Reformed Church.
1618	Johann Sigismund, Elector of Brandenburg, is invested with the duchy of East Prussia. The Thirty Years' War (see p. 126) begins.

1619	Death of Johann Sigismund. George William (1595–1640) becomes Elector.
1640	Accession of Frederick William (1620–88), the 'Great Elector'.
1648	Major territorial gains for Brandenburg-Prussia at the Treaty of Westphalia; Halberstadt, Magdeburg and Minden are acquired.
1651	Privy Council membership is revised to ensure the representation of all electoral territories.
1652	The Great Elector puts pressure on the Diet to make taxes permanent.
1653	The Constitution is promulgated, then the Diet is suspended (after voting the Elector revenue for six years).
1655	The First Northern War between Sweden and Poland begins when Brandenburg forces invade East Prussia to halt the advance of Swedish forces into its own territory (July).
1656	East Prussia becomes a fief of Charles X of Sweden under the Treaty of Königsberg (Jan.). Under the Treaty of Labiau, Sweden cedes Prussia to Brandenburg (Nov.).
1657	Suzerainty of Prussia is renounced by Sweden in favour of Brandenburg (Sept.). Brandenburg forms an alliance with the Danes against Charles X (Nov.).
1658	The Great Elector aids Denmark; Charles X is blockaded (Sept.).
1659	Military successes for the Great Elector; he captures towns in Swedish Pomerania and forces the Swedes from Prussia.
1660	End of the First Northern War. East Prussia is freed from Polish suzerainty by the Peace of Oliva. Prussia is now a sovereign state.
1661	Confrontation between Frederick William and the Prussian Diet. The obstinacy of the Diet is followed by its dismissal.
1662	Invasion of Königsberg ensures the submission of the Diet.
1666	Quadruple Alliance of Holland, Denmark, Lüneberg and Prussia is formed to maintain Dutch independence from France (Oct.). The new Treaty of Cleves with Neuburg leads to the partition of the disputed territory of Cleves-Jülich (under its terms the Elector receives Cleves, Mark and Ravensberg).
1667	Death of Electress of Brandenburg (June). The imposition of an excise tax on consumption aids the funding of the standing army (the money is collected by the General War Commissary).
1668	Marriage of the Great Elector and the widowed Duchess of Brunswick.
1669	Secret Franco-Prussian alliance is signed (Dec.).
1672	Anti-French alliance with Holland is signed (May). Execution of Colonel von Kalckstein, leader of Prussian opposition.

1673	A preliminary Prussian peace (the Treaty of Vossem) with France ends the anti-French coalition.
1674	The Great Elector rejoins the alliance against Louis XIV.
1675	French forces under Turenne defeat the Prussians at Colmer (Jan.). The Great Elector defeats Swedish forces at Fehrbellin (June).
1677	Further Prussian military successes against Sweden. Stettin (on the Baltic) is captured after a siege (Dec.).
1678	Retreat of Swedish forces to Riga following the fall of Rügen to the Prussians. Last Swedish possessions in Pomerania are captured (Nov.). Stralsund had been captured earlier (12 Oct.).
1679	Prussian conquests are returned to Sweden under the Treaty of St Germain-en-Laye.
1680	The territories of Archbishop of Magdeburg are secured by Prussia.
1681	Defensive alliances are formed with France (Jan.) and Sweden (under the Treaty of Finsterwalde) (Apr.).
1684	Huguenots are received in Brandenburg under the Edict of Potsdam.
1688	Death of the Great Elector (Apr.). Reign of Frederick III begins.

The Consolidation of Prussia, 1688–1763

1688	Accession of Elector Frederick III following the death of the Great Elector Frederick William (Apr.). Eberhard von Danckelmann becomes chief minister.
1689	Frederick William undertakes reforms to the administration, including the formation of the *Geheime Hofkammer* (Secret Court Chamber).
1694	Opening of the University of Halle. Schweibus is restored to Austria by Frederick III (Dec.).
1697	Peace of Ryswick (see p. 148). End of von Danckelmann's period as chief minister.
1698	Marching in step is introduced into the Prussian army by Leopold von Anhalt-Dessau.
1700	The Prussian Academy of Sciences is founded in Berlin by Gottfried Wilhelm von Leibniz.
1701	Frederick III obtains the title 'King in Prussia' from Emperor Leopold I (in return for future military and diplomatic support). Frederick III's coronation at Königsberg (Jan.). From this time Elector Frederick III becomes King Frederick I. Beginning of the War of Spanish Succession (see p. 137).
1702	Kolbe von Wartenberg begins period as key minister.

1707	Further Prussian territorial acquisitions include Neuchâtel, Tecklenburg and Valengrin. Signing of the 'Perpetual Alliance' with Sweden (for mutual support in case of aggression by a third party).
1711	End of the ministry of Kolbe von Wartenberg.
1713	Death of Frederick I. Accession of Frederick William I. Prussia is recognised as a kingdom by the Peace of Utrecht (see p. 149). General Finance Directory is established.
1714	Witch trials are abolished in Prussia.
1715	Prussia joins the Northern War. Western Pomerania and Stralsund are conquered (Dec.).
1717	General compulsory state education is introduced in Prussia.
1720	Stettin and part of western Pomerania are acquired at the end of the Northern War by the Peace of Stockholm.
1723	Foundation of the General Directory of War, Finance and Domains as the Supreme Administrative Authority.
1725	Prussian claim to Jülich-Berg is guaranteed, by Treaty of Herrenhausen, with England and France.
1726	Treaty of Wüsterhausen (Oct.). Prussia switches alliance to Austria (with the promise of military support), overturning the 1725 alliance with England and France.
1728	Treaty of Berlin (Dec.). Prussia guarantees the Pragmatic Sanction in return for the recognition by Emperor Charles VI of the Prussian claim to Jülich-Berg.
1730	Imprisonment of the Crown Prince after an attempt to escape (Aug.). His accomplice, von Katte, is executed. Prussia is divided into military cantons to expedite recruitment.
1731	Beginning of the repopulation of East Prussia after devastation by the plague (the new settlers are mainly Protestants from Salzburg).
1738	Appointment of Baron von Cocceji as the Minister of Justice (Feb.).
1740	Accession of Frederick II (Frederick the Great) following the death of Frederick William I (May). Accession of Maria Theresa (20 Oct.) is followed by the outbreak of the first Silesian War when Frederick invades (16 Dec.). (For details of the War of the Austrian Succession, see p. 139.) Torture is abolished in Brandenburg-Prussia. Religious toleration is established (as is some degree of press freedom).
1741	Franco-Prussian Treaty of Breslau (for partition of Habsburg lands) is signed (Jan.). Under the Treaty of Kleinschellendorf, Lower Silesia is ceded to Prussia by Maria Theresa.

51

1742	Victory for Prussia over Austria at Chotusitz (May). Prussian gains at the Peace of Berlin include Glatz and Silesia. Construction of the Elbe–Havel Canal.
1743	Completion of the Opera House in Berlin.
1744	Outbreak of the second Silesian War (Aug.) (see p. 139). Establishment of a cotton factory in Berlin. The Union of Frankfurt is formed with Bavaria, Hesse-Cassel and Elector Palatine (May). East Friesland is acquired following the death of its last prince.
1745	Silesia is acquired by Prussia under the Treaty of Dresden (Dec.) concluded with Austria and Saxony. Frederick II recognises Francis I (husband of Maria Theresa) as Emperor.
1746	Publication of Frederick II's *History of My Age* (written in French). Von Cocceji is appointed Grand Chancellor.
1748	Peace of Aix-la-Chapelle (see p. 153) ends the War of the Austrian Succession. The Prussian conquest of Silesia is recognised. A uniform judicial system is begun in Prussia (the *Codex Fredericanus*).
1750	Foundation of a porcelain factory in Berlin. Voltaire visits Frederick at Sans Souci.
1755	Death of von Cocceji.
1756	Treaty of Westminster with Britain guarantees the neutrality of Hanover. Beginning of the Seven Years' War (Aug.) following the invasion of Saxony by Frederick the Great (see p. 140). Prussia faces a coalition of Austria, France, Russia, Sweden and the Empire.
1757	Prussian forces are victorious at Rossbach (over the French) and Leuthen (over the Austrians).
1758	East Prussia is occupied by Russia.
1759	The Prussians are defeated at Kunersdorf.
1760	Russian and Austrian forces enter Berlin.
1762	Russia loses the desire to fight a war following the death of Empress Elizabeth. The new Tsar, Peter III, allies with Frederick.
1763	The acquisition of Silesia is confirmed by the Peace of Hubertusburg (see p. 153), ending the Seven Years' War. Compulsory schooling is introduced for 5–13 year olds under the General Education Act.

Postscript: The expansion of Prussia received a major success with the first partition of Poland in 1772. Poland ceded West Prussia (except for Danzig and Thorn), the Netze district and Ermland (in East Prussia). Frederick the Great took the title King of Prussia.

THE BALTIC

The Baltic Lands, 1520–1632

By the 1397 Union of Kalmar, Sweden was under Danish rule until the national uprising of 1520 following the 'Bloodbath of Stockholm'. With the Protestant Reformation in northern Europe, and the subsequent rise of Sweden, the Baltic became an area of greater significance for the general history of Europe after 1520.

1520	The 'Bloodbath of Stockholm' (the execution of Sten Sture's supporters) provokes a national uprising (the revolt of Sweden) under Gustavus Vasa, the expulsion of the Danes and the end of the Union of Kalmar.
1523	Gustavus I Vasa becomes King of Sweden (until 1560). Laurentius Andreae is appointed Chancellor.
1526	Disputes in both Denmark and Sweden between the Catholic clergy and the evangelicals. Beginnings of the Reformation.
1527	Lutheranism is introduced into Sweden; the property of the Catholic Church is transferred to the crown. Revolt among the Swedish peasants. Monasteries are secularised in Denmark.
1529	Swedish National Synod sits at Örebro: abolition of feast days and the modification of the Latin mass.
1533–34	Civil war in Denmark is won by the Protestant Duke Christian.
1536–37	Full Lutheran Reformation takes place in Denmark (it is completed by the 1537 church ordinances).
1539	*Riksdag* at Örebro establishes royal authority over the Church in Sweden.
1541	The 'Gustavus Vasa Bible' is published (in Swedish).
1560	Erik XIV becomes King of Sweden (until 1569). Reval seeks aid from Sweden and becomes a Swedish town.
1563	Start of the Seven Years' War in Scandinavia (to 1570).
1568	Erik XIV is deposed by John III in Sweden.
1581	Narva is captured by Swedish forces.
1592	Death of John III; Sigismund becomes King of Sweden (until 1599).
1594	Birth of Gustavus Adolphus (Dec.).
1595	Peace of Teusina between Russia and Sweden.
1600	The future Charles IX becomes Regent in Sweden.
1601	Livonia is invaded by Charles IX.
1604	Charles IX becomes King of Sweden (until 1611).
1605	Major defeat of the Swedes at Kirkholm.

1610	Charles IX intervenes in the 'Time of Troubles' in Russia.
1611	Gustavus II Adolphus (Gustav II Adolf) becomes King of Sweden (until 1632). His reign marks the beginning of Sweden's 'Age of Greatness' (1611–1718). Christian IV of Denmark declares war on Sweden (the 'War of Kalmar').
1612	The Accession Charter is imposed on Gustavus Adolphus. Axel Oxenstierna is appointed Chancellor (Jan.). Alienation of crown lands and revenues is revoked by proclamation (Nov.).
1613	Denmark and Sweden conclude the Treaty of Knärod (Jan.).
1614	A series of ordinances reforming judicial system is initiated.
1617	Peace of Stolbova is secured with Russia (see p. 146). Sweden acquires Ingria and south-west Karelia. Reform of the *Riksdag* regularises the procedure at Diets. Statute of Örebro is promulgated against Roman Catholic and Polish intrigues.
1618	Two-year Truce of Tolsburg is signed with Poland. Reorganisation of central government by the Chancery Ordinance; reorganisation of the Treasury as the first *collegium*. Towns statute is promulgated by Oxenstierna.
1619	Fourteen-year Truce of Deulinie with Russia is secured (Jan.). Foundation of the Swedish Trading Company.
1620	Ordinance for Military Personnel is drawn up. Local government reforms are also initiated. Marriage of Gustavus Adolphus and Maria Eleonora of Brandenburg.
1621	Resumption of war with Poland; Riga is taken. A charter is granted to Gothenburg. Gustavus Adolphus draws up the 'Articles of War'.
1624	Introduction of the Poor Law. The Agreement at Sjöaryd signals a Danish defeat after a renewed crisis. Uppsala University is endowed. England and Brandenburg propose a Protestant League.
1626	Swedish victory at Wallhof (Gustavus Adolphus transfers the seat of war to Prussia). Wallenstein is appointed Imperial Commander. Denmark suffers a decisive defeat at Lutter-am-Baremberg.
1627	Denmark (as well as much of Baltic coast) is overrun by Imperialists.
1628	A defensive alliance of Denmark and Sweden is formed. Sweden begins to collect tolls at Baltic harbours.
1629	Peace of Lübeck is signed by Christian IV of Denmark and the Emperor (June). Truce of Altmark between Sweden and Poland is signed (Sept.). It lasts for six years.
1630	Gustavus Adolphus lands in Pomerania (June). Diet of Regensburg meets (Aug.). Dismissal of Wallenstein from his command.

Magdeburg allies with Sweden (Aug.). 'Contingent Convention' with Hesse-Cassel is concluded (Nov.).

1631   Treaty of Bärwalde is signed between Sweden and France (Jan.). Convention of the German Protestant states meets at Leipzig (Feb.). Frankfurt-on-Oder is stormed by the forces of Gustavus Adolphus (Apr.). Magdeburg is stormed by Tilly (May), who subsequently invades Saxony (Aug.). Sweden–Saxony alliance is formed (Sept.). Battle of Breitenfeld (see p. 127). Gustavus Adolphus forces the capitulation of Mainz (Dec.).

1632   Tilly is fatally wounded (Apr.). Death of Gustavus Adolphus at the battle of Lützen (6 Nov.). Christina becomes Queen of Sweden (until her abdication in 1654).

The Eclipse of Sweden

1632   Death of Gustavus Adolphus at the battle of Lützen. Accession of Queen Christina. The basis of the League of Heilbronn emerges at the Ulm Congress of the four southern Circles.

1634   Diet accepts the Form of Government. Battle of Nördlingen ends in Swedish disaster (Aug.).

1635   Sweden adheres to the Peace of Prague (see p. 146).

1636   Oxenstierna returns to Sweden (July).

1654   Charles X Gustavus becomes King of Sweden (until 1660) when Queen Christina abdicates.

1658   Peace of Roskilde: Denmark cedes its southern provinces to Sweden.

1660   Charles XI becomes King of Sweden (until 1697).

1668   Lund University is inaugurated.

1676   Battle of Lund confirms Skåne as part of the Swedish kingdom.

1693   Charles XI acquires absolute power in Sweden by the Declaration of Sovereignty.

1697   Charles XII becomes King of Sweden (until 1718).

1700   Start of the Great Northern War (see p. 137). Russian forces are defeated by Swedish ones at the battle of Narva (see p. 137).

1709   Battle of Poltava ends in Swedish rout.

1718   Death of Charles XII at Fredriksten (Dec.). His death effectively ends the Great Northern War. Beginning of the Swedish 'Age of Liberty'.

1719   Charles XII's sister, Ulrika Eleonora, is elected Queen of Sweden but she vacates the throne in favour of her husband, Frederick I.

1721   Great Northern War ends by the Treaty of Nystad (see p. 151).

1731	Establishment of the Swedish East India Company.
1738	Arvid Horn resigns as Chancellor. Hat Party assumes office.
1741	Unsuccessful hostilities against Russia.
1751	Frederick Adolphus becomes King of Sweden (until 1771).
1756	Abortive coup by Court Party. Outbreak of the Seven Years' War (the Pomeranian War).
1757	The *Storskifte* (land reform) is promulgated.
1763	End of the Seven Years' War (see p. 140).

POLAND-LITHUANIA

Poland-Lithuania, 1454–1686

From 1385 to 1572 the term Jagiellonian Poland refers to the personal union of Poland and Lithuania.

1454	Thirteen Years War against the Teutonic Knights (see p. 117). Incorporation of Royal Prussia.
1466	Under the Second Peace of Thorn (Torún), the Grand Master of the Teutonic Order is forced to swear fealty to Poland. The Knights surrender their headquarters at Marienburg.
1474	First printing press in Cracow.
1493	Bicameral *Sejm* (parliament) established.
1494	Expulsion of Jews from Cracow.
1505	*Nihil Novi* statute is promulgated.
1506	Death of King Alexander. Reign of Sigismund (Zygmunt) I Stary begins.
1525	Teutonic Order is secularised. Albert of Hohenzollern pays homage to the King of Poland.
1529	First Lithuanian Statute is promulgated. Incorporation of Mazovia.
1547	First known book in the Lithuanian language is published.
1548	Death of Sigismund I. Reign of Sigismund II August begins.
1561	Incorporation of Livonia. Polish involvement in the Livonian Wars (see p. 122).
1562	The Piotrków *Sejm* and the Executionist Movement.
1563	Calvinist schism in Poland. Breakaway of the 'Arians'.
1564	First Jesuits arrive in Poland.
1569	Polish–Lithuanian Commonwealth (known as the *Rzeczpospolita*) is established by the Union of Lublin between the Kingdom of Poland and the Grand Duchy of Lithuania. Ukraine is transferred to Poland from Lithuania.

1573	Election of Henry Valois to the throne. The *Pacta Conventa* (see p. 258). Religious toleration is guaranteed by the Confederation of Warsaw.
1575	Reign of Stephen (Stefan) Báthory.
1578	Legal Tribunals are created.
1579	University of Vilnius is founded.
1584	Death of Jan Kochanowski.
1586	Polish seat of government is moved to Warsaw from Cracow. End of the reign of Stephen Báthory.
1587	Reign of Sigismund III Vasa begins.
1596	Creation of the Uniate Church in Poland–Lithuania by the Union of Brest.
1605	Poland intervenes during the 'Time of Troubles' in Russia (see p. 62).
1606	The *Rokosz* of Zebrzydowski.
1611	Moscow is occupied by Polish–Lithuanian forces.
1617	First Swedish War (lasts until 1629).
1620	Outbreak of war against the Ottoman Turks. Battle of Cecora.
1621	Battle of Chocim. End of the Turkish war.
1632	Reign of Ladislas (Wladyslaw) IV Vasa begins (until 1648).
1634	Peace of Polanów is signed with Russia.
1635	Orthodox hierarchy is re-established. Peace of Stuhmdorf is signed with Sweden.
1648	Death of Ladislas IV (May). Election of John II Casimir (Nov.). Polish army is defeated by Ukrainian Cossacks under Chmielnicki at Pitawce.
1649	Zborów Agreement with Cossacks (Aug.).
1651	Cossacks are defeated at the battle of Beresteczko (June).
1652	First use of *Liberum Veto* in the *Sejm*.
1654	Cossack recognition of Tsarist overlordship of the Ukraine provokes Russo-Polish War (see p. 130).
1655	Attempted union of Lithuania and Sweden by the Treaty of Kédainiai follows the Swedish invasion and conquest of Warsaw (Aug.) and Cracow (Oct.).
1656	Serfs are promised an improvement in their lot by the king.
1657	Poland relinquishes suzerainty over Prussia in return for the assistance of Brandenburg against Sweden.
1658	Expulsion of the Arians.
1659	War again with Russia over Ukraine.

1660	War with Sweden ends with the Treaty of Oliva. Poland gives up its claim to the Swedish throne while Sweden relinquishes its claims to territories in Poland.
1661	Reactionary nobles and gentry block the proposed reform to the *Sejm*.
1666	Suppression of the Lubomirski rebellion.
1667	Treaty of Andrusovo. Extensive Russian gains in Ukraine.
1668	Abdication of King John Casimir.
1669	Prolonged election to the throne ends when Michael Wísnowiecki becomes king. The outbreak of peasant rebellions in several parts of Poland.
1672	Ottoman invasion of Poland forces Poland to give up Podolia and the last Ukrainian territories (by the Treaty of Buczacz).
1673	Ottoman army is defeated by John Sobieski at Chocim (Khorzim).
1674	Election of John III Sobieski as king. He intrigues with France to recover territory in Ukraine and Poland.
1675	Treaty of Jaworów is signed with France.
1676	Peace with Ottoman Empire. The Treaty of Zurawno leaves Podolia divided. Some territory in Ukraine is returned to Poland.
1683	Siege of Vienna is lifted by the Polish army under King John III Sobieski – a high-water mark in Polish history.
1684	Poland joins the Holy League of Austria and Venice against the Ottomans.
1686	Russo-Polish alliance against Turks is concluded.

The Decline of Poland, 1696–1763

1696	Death of John III Sobieski (17 June). This is followed in 1697 by the election of the Elector Augustus of Saxony as King Augustus II. Reign of the Saxon Kings begins.
1699	Territorial gains for Poland by the Peace of Karlowitz (see p. 149). The partition of the Swedish Empire is planned by the signatories of the Treaty of Preobrazhenskoe.
1700	Outbreak of Great Northern War (see p. 137) follows the invasion of Livonia by Augustus II.
1701	Courland and Poland are invaded by Charles XII of Sweden to overthrow Augustus II.
1702	Warsaw is taken by Charles XII (May), followed by the Swedish capture of Cracow (July).
1704	Confederacy of Sandomierz is formed to support Augustus II (May). The 'Two Polands' are created with the election of a

Swedish-backed rival, King Stanislaw Leszczyński, in Warsaw (July). Alliance of Poland and Russia is concluded by the Treaty of Narva.

1706   Abdication of Augustus II by the Treaty of Altranstädt. Recognition of Stanislaw Leszczyński as king (Sept.).

1708   Widespread famine and plague.

1709   Augustus II returns to Poland after the defeat of Swedish forces at Poltava by the Russians. Subsequently, the General Assembly in Warsaw recognises Augustus II as king.

1713   Augustus II's position is strengthened by the stationing of Saxon troops in Poland.

1714   Rebellions begin (at first gentry-led), partly at presence of Saxon troops.

1715   Poland enters a new coalition against Sweden. Establishment of the General Confederation of Tarnogród which is directed at restraining royal power.

1716   Russian attempts at mediation under Dolgoruki (envoy of the Tsar). Dolgoruki is bolstered by the arrival of Russian troops.

1717   Russian compromise proposals (the Treaty of Warsaw) are approved by the 'Silent *Sejm*' (the 'Dumb *Sejm*', because no one is permitted to speak). Limits are placed on the number of Saxon troops to guard the king. Russia claims the right to guarantee the constitution.

1720   Russian troops (in occupation since 1716) withdraw from Poland. Russian treaties with Prussia and the Ottoman Empire secure the future free election of Polish kings.

1721   Great Northern War ends with the Treaty of Nystad (p. 151).

1724   The 'Tumult of Thorn'.

1733   Death of Augustus II (1 Feb.). Second election of Stanislaw Leszczyński. The Russians intervene and the War of the Polish Succession begins (Sept.). Election of Frederick Augustus II of Saxony as Augustus III of Poland (Oct.) (he is backed by Austria, Prussia and Russia).

1734   Siege and surrender of Danzig (after the flight of Leszczyński). The Familia (see p. 249) joins the party of Augustus III.

1735   Under the Preliminaries of Vienna, Stanislaw Leszczyński abdicates as king (Oct.).

1736   General recognition of Augustus III as King of Poland by the Pacification *Sejm* (June–July).

1738   Henry Brühl rises to political prominence as chief minister.

1740   War of the Austrian Succession begins.

1743   Anti-Prussian alliance is formed with Austria by Brühl.

1744	The Familia attempts to bring about reform at the Grodno *Sejm*. An alliance is formed with Russia in order to resist the territorial ambitions of Frederick the Great.
1754	The Familia breaks up the *Sejm* and enters into opposition.
1756	Polish neutrality during Seven Years' War is frequently abused by the belligerents.
1757	Parts of eastern Poland are occupied by Russian troops (to put pressure on East Prussia).
1763	The Familia plots a confederation to seize power. Death of Augustus III of Poland (Oct.).

Postscript: Some reforms were introduced by the Convocation *Sejm* of 1764–66, including limitations on the power of the *Liberum Veto* and the abolition of internal customs. The candidate of Catherine II of Russia, Stanislaw Poniatowski, was elected king on 7 September 1764. The first Partition of Poland took place in 1772. Poniatowski's reign ended in 1795.

RUSSIA

The Gathering of Russia, 1462–1533

1462	Beginning of the rule of Ivan III ('the Great') until his death in 1505.
1463	Principality of Yaroslavl is annexed by Moscow; conquest of the Mari Lands. Beginning of the limitations on the freedom of movement for peasants.
1470	Spread of Judaizer heresy throughout Novgorod.
1471	Novgorod is attacked by Moscow. Novgorod armies are beaten.
1472	Principality of Perm is annexed by Moscow. Marriage of Ivan III and Sophia Palaeologue (the niece of the last Byzantine emperor).
1474	Rostov is annexed by Moscow.
1475	Construction begins in the Kremlin of the Cathedral of the Assumption (*Uspensky Sobor*) (completed 1479).
1477	Novgorod is annexed by Moscow after a renewed attack.
1480	Ivan III overthrows the Mongol Tatar rule.
1484	Massacres in Novgorod (and again in 1489) and deportations deep into Russia.
1485	Tver is annexed by Moscow. Beginning of the construction of the new Kremlin in Moscow.
1489	Annexation of Vyatka.
1494	Closure of Hansa trading depot in Novgorod.

1497	Promulgation of the Code of Laws (*Sudebnik*) by Ivan III.
1503	Judaizer heresy is condemned by the Church Council. Conflict between pro- and anti-property factions in the Church.
1505	Basil III (Vasily III) succeeds Ivan III (until 1533).
1510	Annexation of Pskov is followed by mass deportations.
1514	Smolensk is annexed by Moscow.
1521	Metropolitan Varlaam is deposed by Basil III.
1525	Divorce of Basil III is authorised by Metropolitan Daniil.
1533	Rule of Ivan IV ('the Terrible'). Until 1538, Elena, mother of Ivan, is Regent.

Russia under Ivan the Terrible

1533	Rule of Ivan IV (under the Regency of his mother, Elena, until 1538).
1535	Edicts prohibit the further acquisition of land by the monasteries.
1547	Title of 'Tsar' is assumed by Ivan IV. Marriage and coronation. Major fire in Moscow.
1549	*Zemsky Sobor* (Landed Assembly) meets for the first time. The Council of Reconciliation is formed.
1550	*Sudebnik* (Code of Laws) is promulgated. Formation of the *streltsy*.
1551	Emergence of the *Stoglav* (Hundred Chapters) is followed during the 1550s by local government reforms and the formation of the first *prikazy*.
1552	Khanate of Kazan is annexed.
1553	The English, under Richard Chancellor, open up the northern sea route to Russia (followed in 1555 by the formation of the Muscovy Company in London).
1556	Russian conquest of Astrakhan. Russian colonisation of the steppe gathers speed.
1557	Beginning of Russian attempts to secure the Baltic coastline (the Livonian War, see p. 122).
1561	Disbandment of the Livonian Order.
1564	Printing of the first book in Moscow (by Ivan Fedorov). Flight of Kurbskii. The *Oprichnina* terror (lasting until 1572).
1565	Beginning of Ivan IV's 'reign of terror'.
1566	Land Assembly convenes to discuss the Livonian War.
1569	Poland and Lithuania merge in the Union of Lublin.
1570	Novgorod is razed and its inhabitants massacred.
1571–72	Moscow is sacked by the Crimean Tatars.
1572	Abolition of the *Oprichnina*.

1577	Expansion of commerce with the West is reflected in the opening of commercial ties with the Dutch.
1582	Conquest of Siberia follows the defeat of the Khanate of Sibir by Ermak.
1584	Death of Ivan the Terrible. Rule of Tsar Theodore I (Fedor). Archangel is founded.

Russia in Turmoil, 1587–1613

1587	Boris Godunov acts as Regent (until 1598).
1589	The Metropolitan is elevated to the rank of Patriarch. Beginning of the Patriarchate of Moscow.
1591	Prince Dmitri is murdered at Uglich.
1597	Nobility is given a five-year time limit to claim fugitive peasants.
1598	Riúrik dynasty ends. Coronation of Tsar Boris Godunov (rules until 1605).
1601	Further edicts limit the mobility of peasants. Start of a four-year period of major famine.
1605	Death of Boris Godunov, followed by the 'Time of Troubles' until 1613. Rule of the first False Dmitri (until 1606). Russia is threatened by Sweden and Poland.
1606	Revolt of Bolotnikov (lasts until 1607). Rule of Tsar Vasily Shuiskii.
1607	Rule of the second False Dmitri.
1610	Moscow is occupied by Polish forces (until 1612). Effective interregnum in Russia. Throne of Russia is offered to Polish Prince Ladislas.
1611	Beginning of a national uprising against the Poles. Novgorod is occupied by Sweden until 1617. Foundation of the militia under Pozharskii.
1613	Michael Romanov is elected Tsar by the *Zemsky Sobor.* Beginning of Romanov dynasty.

The Early Romanovs

1613	Michael Romanov is elected Tsar by the *Zemsky Sobor.* Beginning of the Romanov dynasty (until 1917 February Revolution).
1617	Novgorod is evacuated by the Swedes under the Peace of Stolbovo.
1619	Patriarch Filaret (Philaret) (father of Michael Romanov) is co-ruler until 1633.
1631	Kiev Academy is founded by the Metropolitan, Peter Mogila of Kiev.

1632	Early beginnings of industrialisation with the foundation of the Tula and Kashira iron foundries.
1637	Azov is conquered by the Don Cossacks.
1639	First Cossacks reach the Pacific coast.
1643	Sea of Okhotsk is reached by Peyarkov.
1645	Beginning of rule of Tsar Alexis (July) following the death of Tsar Michael.
1648	Uprising against Poland by the Ukrainian Cossacks. Rebellions in major towns (in protest at inflation and taxation). New Code of Laws (*sobornoye ulozheniye*) is issued by the *Zemsky Sobor* which legalises serfdom.
1649	Abolition of the trading privileges of the Muscovy Company.
1650	Rebellions in Novgorod and Pskov are crushed.
1652	Patriarch Nikon is elected to lead the Russian Orthodox Church. Programme of reforms begins. German settlement in Moscow is re-established. Founding of Irkutsk.
1653	Full meeting of *Zemsky Sobor* meets for the last time.
1654	The adoption of Patriarch Nikon's reforms by the Church Council leads to schism in the Orthodox Church. Cossacks of Ukraine swear allegiance to the Tsar. Outbreak of the Russo-Polish War over Ukraine (see p. 131).
1658	Nikon resigns his office as Patriarch and retires to the monastery of New Jerusalem.
1662	Moscow witnesses 'copper riots' (rapid inflation following the substitution of copper for silver in coins).
1663	Restoration of silver coinage.
1665	After continued disputes with the Tsar, Nikon is deposed by the Church Council (which retains his reforms). Confirmation of the *raskol* (schism) in Russian Orthodoxy. Postal service is established in Russia.
1667	Smolensk and Kiev are ceded to Russia from Poland by the Treaty of Andruszov. Promulgation of the New Commercial Code. Old Believers are condemned by the Church Council. Revolt of the Solovetsky Monastery. Outbreak of the peasant revolt of Stenka Razin in Ukraine and southern Russia (lasts until 1671).
1671	Suppression of revolt of Stenka Razin (followed by his execution).
1672	Birth of Peter the Great. Russian Embassies are established in most important West European states.
1676	Rule of Tsar Theodore II (Fedor Alexeyevich) (half-brother of Peter) following the death of Alexis. War with the Ottoman Empire (until 1680).

1680	End of Ottoman War.
1682	Death of Tsar Theodore II. Proclamation of Peter, younger son of Alexis, as Tsar by Patriarch Joachim. Revolt of the *streltsy* militia. Ivan (retarded son of Alexis) is proclaimed first Tsar (Ivan V) and Peter second Tsar (Peter I).

Russia under Peter the Great

1682	Death of Tsar Theodore II (Apr.). Peter is proclaimed Tsar. Revolt of the *streltsy* militia is led by Sophia. Ivan V and Peter I are crowned as joint tsars under the Regency of Sophia. Execution of Prince Ivan Khovansky. The abolition of the *mestnichestvo*. Real ruler of Russia is Golitsyn.
1684	Renewal of the treaty with Sweden (May). Formal persecution of the Old Believers is instituted.
1686	Treaty of 'Permanent Peace' with Poland. Russia enters the Holy League.
1687	First (unsuccessful) Crimean Tatar campaign. Mazepa becomes Hetman of Ukraine.
1689	Overthrow of the Regency of Sophia; exile of Golitsyn; Peter's mother, Natalia, becomes Regent. Treaty of Nerchinsk with China.
1690	Birth of Tsarevich Alexis. Death of Patriarch Joachim.
1693	Tsar Peter makes his first visit to Archangel and the White Sea.
1694	Death of Tsaritsa Natalia.
1695	First unsuccessful attack on Azov.
1696	Death of Ivan V. Peter becomes sole Tsar. Capture of Azov from the Turks.
1697–98	The 'Great Embassy' to Holland, Prussia, England and Austria. Authority over political crimes is vested in the *Preobrazhensky Prikaz*.
1698	Savage suppression of *streltsy* revolt.
1699	Industrialisation is reflected in the growth of metal production. Reorganisation of the army on Western European lines. Chamber of burgomasters is established.
1700	Peace with the Ottoman Empire and the cession of Azov. Outbreak of the Great Northern War (see p. 137). Russian defeat at Narva by Charles XII of Sweden. Abolition of the Patriarchate following the death of Patriarch Adrian. Law Code commission is established.
1701	Revenues of monasteries are to be acquired by the state (Monastery *Prikaz* is established). Navigation School is founded at Moscow.

1702	Russian victories at Hummeslhof and Nöteborg.
1703	St Petersburg is founded. Ingria and Livonia are conquered from Sweden. First Russian newspaper, *Vedomosti*, is launched.
1704	Death of Tsarevna Sophia. Russian victory at Narva. Admiralty yard is founded in St Petersburg.
1705	Extension of systematic recruiting for the army. Grodno is occupied. Uprising in Astrakhan.
1707	Charles XII of Sweden invades Russia. Russian 'scorched earth' policy. Cossack rising in the Don area. Moscow is replaced by St Petersburg as capital.
1708	Russian military victories under Menshikov; victory over the Swedes at Lesnaya. Ukraine is invaded by Charles XII. Local government reforms are promulgated (initial division of Russia into eight administrative provinces (*gubernii*) under an appointed governor).
1709	Major Russian victory at Poltava over Charles XII of Sweden. New Russo-Polish alliance and treaties with Denmark and Prussia.
1710	Livonia and Estonia are taken by Russia. Capture of Baltic fortresses. Census ordered. First national budget is introduced.
1711	War is renewed with the Ottoman Empire. Defeat on the Pruth. Surrender of Azov and Taganrog. Senate is replaced with a boyar *duma*. Most trading monopolies are abolished. Treaty with *hospodar* of Moldavia.
1712	Peter and Catherine are married.
1713	Peace with Ottoman Empire. Finnish campaign. Russia captures Helsinki.
1714	Law on Single Inheritance forbids the subdivision of estates. Reform of the civil service. Civil servants are now salaried and the *Kormleniya* is abolished. Compulsory elementary education system for sons of officials and landowners is introduced.
1715	Naval Academy is established in St Petersburg.
1716	Flight of Alexis (the Tsarevich) to Vienna and Naples following an ultimatum. Promulgation of the Military Code (*Ustav voinsky*). Peter meets the kings of Prussia and Denmark.
1717	New administrative colleges (nine in number) replace the *Prikazy*. Second journey of Peter to Western Europe.
1718	Execution of Alexis (son and heir of Peter). Double tax is imposed on the Old Believers. Provincial court system is established.
1719	Ending of the majority of state monopolies (salt remains a monopoly). New census is ordered.

1720	Promulgation of the Naval Code and the General Regulation reflect the increasing systemisation of the machinery of government.
1721	Great Northern War ends with the Treaty of Nystad (see p. 151). Peter takes the title of Emperor. Orthodox Patriarchate is abolished and replaced by the Holy Synod (which is subordinate to secular authority). Start of four years of crop failures. Ban on the sale of individual serfs.
1722	'Table of Ranks' is instituted (see p. 264). Start of war with Persia. Peter wins the right to nominate his successor (Law on Succession to the Throne). Office of Procurator-General is created.
1723	Imposition of a poll tax on all servile males. Russian gains in Caspian (including Baku and Derbent) are confirmed in a peace treaty.
1724	Catherine, Peter's second wife, is crowned as Empress. Heavy comprehensive import tariffs are introduced. First collection of the poll tax.
1725	Death of Peter the Great. Succession of Empress Catherine.

Russia after Peter the Great

1725	Death of Peter the Great. Rule of Empress Catherine (with the support of the Imperial Guard). Prince Menshikov is the leading figure in the government.
1726	Opening of the Academy of Sciences. Supreme Privy Council is established under the control of Menshikov and Golitsyn. Military alliance with Austria against the Ottoman Turks.
1727	Death of Catherine. Accession of Peter II, son of the Tsarevich Alexis.
1730	Death of Peter II. Rule of Empress Anna after a constitutional crisis (a failed attempt by the Supreme Privy Council to impose conditions on Anna). Repeal of the 1714 inheritance law.
1731	Re-establishment of the secret police leads to a reign of terror. Noble Cadet Corps is established. Ostermann and Count Biren, the German favourites, dominate the Cabinet.
1732	Russian claims to parts of Prussian territory are abandoned by the Treaty of Riascha.
1733	War of the Polish Succession (see p. 139).
1735	Outbreak of the Russo-Turkish War (until 1739). Powers of landowners over serfs are extended.
1736	Edict defining the limits of service to the state by the aristocracy, with provision for a family member to remain at home to manage the estate.

1737	Serfs are effectively deprived of the right to buy land.
1739	Treaty of Belgrade, under which Russia regains Azov, ends the Turkish War.
1740	Death of Empress Anna. Rule of Ivan VI (great-nephew of Anna) under the Regency of Count Biren. Subsequent palace coup is led by Field-Marshal Münnich. Anna Leopoldovna, mother of Ivan VI, is made Regent. Exile of Count Biren.
1741	Further palace coup. Ivan VI is deposed, the Regent Anna Leopoldovna is exiled. Elizabeth, daughter of Peter I and Catherine I, becomes Empress. The Cabinet is abolished and the Senate and colleges are restored. War with Sweden.
1743	Peace of Åbo ends the Swedish War. Territory in the south of Finland is acquired by Russia.
1744	Count Bestuzhev-Riumin rises to influence in foreign policy after becoming Chancellor. Abolition of death penalty.
1745	Marriage of Charles Peter (nephew of Elizabeth and heir to the throne) and Princess Sophia Augusta of Anhalt-Zerbst (the future Catherine the Great).
1746	Shuvalov becomes head of the secret police (later he becomes the favourite of Elizabeth).
1747	Russia agrees to support Austria and Britain in the War of the Austrian Succession.
1753	Internal customs are abolished. State Nobility Bank is established.
1754	Foundation of the University of Moscow. Commercial Bank is established in St Petersburg. Start of the construction of the Winter Palace.
1756	The 'Conference' (later the chief organ of government until its abolition in 1762) is set up. Russia signs the anti-Prussian Treaty of Versailles.
1757	Treaty with Austria for military cooperation against Prussia.
1758	East Prussia is seized by Russian forces. Arrest and disgrace of Bestuzhev-Riumin. New Chancellor is Count Vorontsov.
1760	Berlin is set alight by Russian forces.
1762	Peter III becomes Tsar on the death of Elizabeth. The Conference is abolished. Secret police is also abolished. The gentry are emancipated from state service (May). Peter is deposed and murdered; Catherine II (the Great) ascends the throne.
1763	Count Panin takes control of foreign affairs. Courland (a fief of Polish crown) is occupied.

THE OTTOMAN EMPIRE

The Rise of the Ottoman Empire

1453   Fall of Constantinople to the Ottoman Turks under Mohammed II (Mahomet II, Mehmed II) ends the Eastern Roman Empire (29 May). Fall of Pera.

1454   Ottoman peace with Venice (18 Apr.). Mohammed's first expedition to Serbia.

1455   Moldavia becomes an Ottoman tributary (Oct.). Mohammed's second Serbian expedition.

1456   Relief of Belgrade by Huniades' victory over the Turks (July). Ottomans conquer Athens.

1457   Victory of Iskander Beg (Scanderbeg) at Albulena.

1458–60 Greece falls under Ottoman rule.

1459   Crusade against Turks is declared by Pius II. Serbia is overrun by the Ottoman Turks.

1460   Conquest of the Morea is completed.

1461   Empire of Trebizond finally falls to the Ottomans.

1462   Wallachia is invaded by Mohammed II.

1463   War with Venice. Venice regains the Morea. Bosnia is invaded by Mohammed II. Death of the last Bosnian king, Stepan Tomasević.

1464   The Morea is reconquered by the Ottomans.

1465   Kroya, the capital of Albania, is besieged by the Turks.

1466   Ottoman campaign against Iskander Beg.

1467   Second Ottoman campaign by Mohammed II against Iskander Beg.

1468   Death of Iskander Beg (Jan.) from fever.

1469   Enos and New Phocaea are attacked by Venice.

1470   Euboea is conquered by Mohammed II.

1471   Coalition against the Ottomans includes the King of Cyprus, Venice and the Knights of St John.

1472   Pope Sixtus sends a fleet against the Ottomans.

1474   Siege of Scutari in Albania. Transylvania is raided by the Ottomans.

1475   Genoese colonies in the Crimea are conquered.

1476   Ottoman summer campaign against Moldavia.

1477   Lepanto is besieged; Venice is threatened by Ottoman raiders.

1478   Siege of Scutari (Albania) by Ottomans. Kroya surrenders. Ottoman raid into Friuli.

1479   Peace with Venice (Jan.). Transylvania and Hungary are raided.

1480	Ottoman capture of Otranto (on the Italian mainland) causes widespread panic. It is held by the Turks for a year.
1481	Death of Mohammed II. He is succeeded by Bayezid II. Ottomans in Otranto surrender (Sept.).
1484	Campaign against Moldavia by Bayezid. Start of the war with the Mamelukes of Egypt (lasts until 1491).
1496	Ottoman forces invade Montenegro. Moldavia is invaded by Albert of Poland (and the Polish-Hungarian alliance).
1497	War of the Ottomans with Poland (until 1499).
1499	War of the Ottomans with Venice (until 1503). Ottoman successes include the naval victory at Navarino in August and the conquest of Lepanto.
1500	Hungary declares war on the Turks.
1503	Ottomans secure peace with Venice (Aug.).
1511	Civil war in the Ottoman Empire.
1512	Forced abdication of Bayezid. Accession of Selim I who is raised to power by the Janissaries. Death of Bayezid (May).
1512–13	Execution of his brothers by Selim.
1514	Archipelago islands fall to the Turks.
1515	Syria is overrun by the Turks. Mutiny of the Janissaries (Feb.).
1516	Egypt falls to Ottoman control after the defeat of the Mamelukes.
1517	Mecca submits to the Ottomans.
1520	Accession of Suleiman II (Süleyman) ('the Magnificent') following the death of Selim.
1521	Belgrade falls to Suleiman (Aug.).
1522	Rhodes is conquered by Suleiman (Jan.).
1523	Ibrahim becomes Grand Vizier.
1524	Ottomans face revolt in Egypt.
1526	Major Ottoman victory over the Hungarians at Mohács (29 Aug.). Suleiman in Buda (Sept.). John Zápolya (Zápolyai) becomes King of Hungary (Nov.).
1527	Ferdinand of Austria arrives in Buda.
1528	Algiers is captured by the Knights of Malta.
1529	Suleiman captures Buda in his third campaign (Sept.). The first Ottoman siege of Vienna is repulsed (Oct.). Algiers becomes a vassal of the Ottomans.
1530	Buda is besieged by the Austrians (Dec.).
1532	Güns is captured in Suleiman's fourth campaign against Austria (Aug.). Coron is captured by Andrea Doria.

1533	Ottoman truce with the Holy Roman Empire. Khairredin Barbarossa (corsair leader) becomes Grand Admiral and conquers Tunis (Aug.). Coron is reconquered.
1534	Suleiman arrives in Baghdad.
1535	Ottoman fleet attacks Corfu.
1536	Execution of Grand Vizier Ibrahim.
1537	War with Venice. Ottomans raid Apulia (July) and lay siege to Corfu (Aug.).
1538	Major Ottoman naval victory at Prevesa (defeating the forces of the Pope, Venice and Charles V).
1539	Ottomans conquer Castelnuovo.
1540	Peace with Venice. Buda is besieged by the Austrians.
1541	Bad weather defeats Charles V's expedition against Algiers. Suleiman's campaign against Ferdinand of Austria. Annexation of most of Hungary by the Ottomans.
1543	Khairredin Barbarossa sacks Reggio (southern Italy) and captures Nice (southern France). Ottoman navy winters in Toulon.
1544	Ottoman conquest of Višegrad. Further conquests in western Hungary.
1545	Armistice is agreed between Suleiman and Ferdinand.
1547	Peace Treaty with the Ottomans (includes the Habsburgs, the Papacy, France and Venice). This paves the way for Suleiman's campaign against Persia in 1548.
1551	Ottomans capture Tripoli from the Knights of Malta; beginning of a strong Ottoman naval presence in the western Mediterranean. Ottomans renew activity in Transylvania.
1552	The Portuguese repulse the Ottomans at Hormuz.
1553	Execution of Suleiman's son, Mustafa.
1555	Ottomans conclude peace with Persia.
1556	Beginning of a period of continuous warfare against the Austrians in Hungary (until 1559).
1559	Civil war between Suleiman's sons (Selim and Bayezid).
1560	Djerba (an island off the North African coast) is captured by the Ottomans. Philip of Spain orders major naval constructions.
1561	Execution of Bayezid (Sept.).
1562	Ottoman peace with the Emperor Ferdinand is renewed (July).
1565	Siege of Malta (May–Sept.). Ottomans are forced to withdraw.
1566	Death of Suleiman during the siege of Szigetvár (6 Sept.). Accession of Selim II (24 Sept.). Occupation of Chios (taken from Genoa by the Ottomans).

Stagnation and Decline, 1566–1763

1566	Death of Suleiman the Magnificent. Accession of Selim II ('the Sot'). Chios taken from Genoa.
1568	Peace with the Holy Roman Empire renewed (Feb.).
1570	Tunis is captured. Conquest of Nicosia during the Cyprus expedition.
1571	Ottomans complete the conquest of Cyprus from Venice (Aug.). Naval battle of Lepanto, a major Christian victory (7 Oct.) (see p. 123).
1572	Muscovy is invaded by Devlet Giray. Tunis is captured by Don John of Austria (Oct.).
1573	Ottoman peace with Venice (Mar.); peace with the Holy Roman Empire renewed.
1574	Tunis is reconquered by the Ottoman Empire. Death of Selim II. Accession of Murad III.
1577	Peace is again renewed with the Holy Roman Empire.
1578	Grand Vizier Sokollu Mehmed is assassinated. Battle of Alcazar in Morocco (Aug.).
1579	Ottoman Treaty of Commerce with England is agreed.
1585	Persians under Shah Abbas drive out the Ottomans.
1587	Reversal of Ottoman incursions into Hungary.
1589	Mutiny of the Janissaries (Apr.).
1593	Start of the 'Great Hungarian War' (p. 124).
1594	Rebellion in Wallachia against Ottoman rule.
1595	Alliance against the Ottomans of the Habsburgs, Transylvania, Wallachia and Moldavia (Jan.). Death of Murad III. Accession of Mohammed (Mehmed) III (his nineteen brothers are strangled). Austrian advances (e.g. Višegrad) against the Ottomans.
1596	Hungarian campaign of Mohammed III.
1598	Austrians retake Raab (Mar.) and besiege Buda.
1599	Ottoman peace negotiations with Austrians. Ottomans conquer Kanisza (Sept.).
1601	Defeat of Archduke Ferdinand before Kanisza (Nov.).
1602	Buda is besieged by Archduke Matthias.
1603	Revolt of the *sipahis* (cavalrymen). Death of Mohammed III (Dec.). He is succeeded by Ahmed I.
1604	Ottomans are driven back by Shah Abbas in Erivan and Kars. Siege of Buda again by Archduke Matthias.
1605	Boczai is declared King of Hungary by the Ottomans. Gran falls to the Ottomans.

1606	Peace of Sitvatorok between the Austrians and the Ottomans. Constantinople is ravaged by a disastrous fire.
1617	Ahmed I is succeeded by a brief reign of Mustafa I (until 1618).
1618	Fourteen-year truce between Poland and the Ottoman Empire. Mustafa I is deposed and is succeeded by Osman II.
1622	Brief return of Mustafa I (until 1623).
1623	Murad IV succeeds Mustafa I. He rebuilds the empire and captures Erivan and Baghdad.
1637	War with the Cossacks; Cossacks take Azov.
1638	Ottomans defeat the Persians; Baghdad falls to the Ottomans.
1640	Murad IV is succeeded by the insane Ibrahim.
1645	Venetian Candia, capital of Crete, is under siege by the Ottomans.
1648	Ibrahim is deposed by the Janissaries. Mohammed (Mehmed, Mahomet) IV succeeds as sultan, reigning until 1687.
1656	Restoration of Ottoman discipline is begun by Grand Vizier Ahmet Koprulu. Venetians inflict naval defeat on the Ottomans (June).
1657	Venetians lose Tenedos and Lemnos to the Ottomans.
1660	Beginning of the reduction of Transylvania by the Ottoman Turks.
1661	Fazil Ahmed, son of Ahmet Koprulu, succeeds him as Grand Vizier (until his death in 1676).
1663	Ottomans declare war on the Holy Roman Empire (18 Apr.).
1664	Peace of Eisenburg between the Turks and the Holy Roman Empire (10 Aug.) following the Ottoman defeat at St Gotthard on the Raab (1 Aug.).
1667	Ottomans begin siege of Candia (May).
1669	Turks take Candia (Crete) from Venice (Sept.).
1672	Treaty of Buczácz; Poland cedes Podolia to the Ottomans (Oct.).
1676	Peace of Zurawno between Poland and the Ottoman Empire. Podolia is now divided.
1678	Emeric Tokoly (Imre Tököly) is active in Transylvania.
1681	Treaty of Radzin; Ottomans abandon most of Ukraine to Russia (Jan.).
1682	Tokoly is proclaimed King of Hungary by the Ottomans (Dec.).
1683	Alliance between Poland and the Emperor against the Turks (Mar.). Siege of Vienna by Mohammed IV; siege is relieved by John Sobieski of Poland and the Ottomans are routed (Sept.).

1684	Formation of Holy League (the Holy Roman Empire, Poland and Venice) against the Turks.
1686	Buda is taken by the Duke of Lorraine (Sept.) after 145 years of Ottoman occupation.
1687	Important victory over the Turks at the battle of Nagyharsány (near Mohács). Central Hungary comes under Austrian control and Transylvania is recovered. Suleiman III succeeds Mohammed IV as sultan.
1688	Belgrade is taken from the Turks by Imperial forces who overrun Bosnia, Serbia and Wallachia. Religious toleration is confirmed in Transylvania.
1689	Ottomans are defeated by Lewis of Baden at Nissa. Subjugation of Bulgaria.
1691	Ahmed II succeeds Suleiman III.
1695	Mustafa II becomes sultan.
1697	Turks are defeated at Zenta by Prince Eugene (11 Sept.).
1699	Peace of Carlowitz (Karlowitz) (26 Jan.). Ottomans lose the Peloponnese to Venice; Transylvania and Hungary, as far as the Danube, to Austria; Podolia and southern Ukraine to Poland; and Azov and lands north of the Dniester to Russia.
1703	Mustafa II is deposed by the Janissaries. Ahmed III becomes sultan.
1715	The Morea is retaken by the Ottomans.
1716	Turks are defeated at the battle of Peterwardein.
1718	Decline of Ottoman power is emphasised by the loss of Belgrade after the Peace of Passarowitz.
1720s	Start of period of active diplomacy. Ottoman Ambassadors are despatched to European capital cities.
1730	Mahmud I succeeds Ahmed III. Patrona rebellion in Constantinople against Western influence and taxation. Ibrahim Pasha, the Grand Vizier, is strangled.
1732	Peace of Erivan with Persia.
1735	Outbreak of war with Russia.
1737	Start of Austro-Turkish War.
1739	Peace of Belgrade with Austria. Belgrade is ceded to the Austrians. Russia, campaigning in Moldavia, signs a separate peace, ceding Azov.
1745	Defeat of the Turks at Kars.
1749	Wahabi insurrection against Ottoman rule.
1754	Osman III succeeds Mahmud I as sultan.
1757	Mustafa III succeeds Osman III as sultan (until 1773).

THE HOLY ROMAN EMPIRE

Germany before the Reformation

1452   Frederick III is crowned Holy Roman Emperor in Rome (Mar.). Austria, Hungary and Bohemia rise against the Emperor, who submits to their demands.

1454   Congress at Ratisbon (Regensburg) (Apr.–May) and Diet at Frankfurt (Dec.) discuss crusades.

1455   Proposals for reform of the Empire are put forward at the Neustadt Diet.

1457   Death of Ladislas Postumus (Dec.), King of Hungary and Bohemia and Duke of Austria.

1458   Lower Austria is secured by the Emperor; George Poděbrady (Podiebrad) becomes King of Bohemia, and Matthias Corvinus is elected King of Hungary.

1459   Poděbrady is invested by the Emperor (July). Struggle for the Archbishopric of Mainz between Diether of Isenburg and Adolf of Cleves.

1460   Discontent is widespread in the Empire. Plot to depose Emperor Frederick III.

1461   Emperor Frederick is attacked by his brother, Albert of Austria (Aug.). Diether of Isenburg is deposed from Mainz by Pope Pius II (Aug.). Adolf of Cleves is appointed.

1462   Uprising in Vienna. Frederick III cedes Lower Austria (including Vienna) to his brother Albert for eight years.

1463   Death of Albert of Austria. Except for Tyrol, all Austrian lands are regained by the Emperor. Peace between Matthias Corvinus and the Emperor is arranged by Pius II.

1464   Gradual pacification of the Holy Roman Empire. Death of Frederick II of Saxony whose lands are left to his sons, Ernest and Albert.

1465   League formed against George Poděbrady.

1466   Diet declares years 1466 to 1486 a period of public peace.

1467   Papal proposal for a crusade against Poděbrady is rejected.

1468   Beginning of a war against Poděbrady by Matthias Corvinus (brings war to Bohemia). Emperor is alarmed at the ambitions of Matthias Corvinus.

1469   Armistice (subsequently broken) between Matthias and Poděbrady (Apr.). War resumes. Matthias is crowned King of Bohemia by the papal legate.

1470   Corvinus and Poděbrady conclude a truce (July).

1471	Death of George Poděbrady (Mar.). Ladislas (son of Casimir IV of Poland) is elected king by the Bohemians.
1473	Emperor and Charles the Bold meet at Trier.
1474	Unsuccessful siege of Neuss by Charles the Bold (in support of Archbishop of Cologne). Opposition of Emperor Frederick to Charles the Bold. Victories of Corvinus over the Bohemians, Poles and Ottoman Turks.
1475	Marriage is proposed of Mary of Burgundy, daughter of Charles the Bold, and the Emperor's son, Maximilian.
1476	Victory of Morat. Bavaria is divided into three duchies until 1502. Palatinate goes to Philip, nephew of Frederick the Victorious.
1477	Marriage of Maximilian and Mary of Burgundy. Battle of Nancy is won by René of Lorraine with Swiss aid. Ladislas formally receives the Bohemian crown. Corvinus invades Austria, forcing the Emperor to accept humiliating terms.
1479	Hungary and Bohemia conclude the Treaty of Olmütz, while Hungary signs the Treaty of Brünn with Poland. Ladislas cedes Moravia, Silesia and Lusatia to Corvinus. French are defeated by Maximilian at Guinegate (Aug.). Ottoman defeats in Transylvania and in their advance on Germany.
1482	Death of Maximilian's wife (Mary of Burgundy) (Mar.).
1485	Vienna is captured by Matthias Corvinus. Division of Saxony into two lines (the Ernestine and Albertine), centred on Wittenberg and Dresden respectively.
1486	Ten-year Public Peace proclaimed by the Diet. Coronation of Maximilian as King of the Romans. Court of the Emperor is now entitled Imperial Chamber.
1488	Swabian League formed (see p. 142). Imprisonment of Maximilian in Bruges after local revolt.
1489	Treaty of Bruges with Maximilian ends its revolt (Oct.).
1490	Ladislas of Bohemia is elected King of Hungary on the death of Matthias Corvinus.
1491	Invasion of Hungary by Maximilian. Under the Treaty of Pressburg (Nov.), Hungary and Bohemia are to revert to the Emperor if Ladislas's male line fails.
1492	Albert of Bavaria submits and joins the Swabian League.
1493	Death of Frederick III (Aug.). Election of Maximilian I (Holy Roman Emperor until 1519). Peasant rebellion in the Black Forest area is suppressed.
1495	Perpetual Peace is declared at the Diet of Worms (May). Among numerous measures, private wars are outlawed, a general tax (the Common Penny) is imposed and a new Court of Appeal

(the Imperial Chamber) is established. The Court of Appeal eventually meets at Wetzlar.

1496   Marriage of Maximilian's son, Philip, and Juana (Joanna), subsequently heiress of the Spanish dominions. Failure of Maximilian's campaign in Italy.

1498   Frederick of Saxony becomes Grand Master of the Teutonic Order.

1499   Failure of Maximilian in the War of the Grisons. Defeat for Maximilian by the Treaty of Basle (see p. 143) and independence for the Swiss Confederation.

1500   The Diet of Augsburg. A Council of Regency is established to administer political affairs. Division of Germany into six Circles (Franconia, Bavaria, Swabia, Upper Rhine, Westphalia and Lower Saxony).

1502   Maximilian assumes the title of Emperor. Electors meet at Gelnhauen determined to maintain their rights. The *Bundschuh* (peasant revolt in the Bishopric of Speyer). University of Wittenberg is founded by the Prince Elector of Saxony.

1504   War of the Bavarian Succession. Maximilian defeats Rupert, Count Palatine and seizes his lands.

1505   Diet of Cologne demonstrates Maximilian's strength following the deaths of the Electors of Trier and Mainz in the previous year.

1506   Death of Maximilian's son, Philip, in Spain (Sept.).

1507   Margaret, daughter of Maximilian, becomes Governor of the Netherlands. Diet of Constance re-establishes the Imperial Chamber. Diet recognises a system of territorial taxation (the Roll).

1508   Maximilian's unsuccessful expedition against Venice. He subsequently joins League of Cambrai.

1509   Padua is retaken by Venice. Maximilian leaves Italy.

1511   Teutonic Knights elect Albert of Brandenburg as Grand Master.

1512   Holy League (see p. 143) is joined by Maximilian and the Swiss, who invade Italy. Diet at Cologne forms hereditary dominions of Maximilian and the Electors into ten Circles: Austria, Burgundy, Upper Saxony with Brandenburg, Lower Saxony, Franconia, Swabia, Bavaria, Westphalia, Upper Rhine and Lower Rhine.

1513   Treaty between Maximilian, Henry VIII of England, Ferdinand of Aragon and the Papacy.

1514   Suppression of the 'Poor Conrad' peasant revolt in Württemberg. (Revolt of the Hungarian peasantry, who had enlisted for a crusade against the Ottoman Turks, is defeated by John Zápolya in July 1514.)

1515   Habsburg dynastic marriage plans include betrothal of Mary (Maximilian's granddaughter) to Louis, the heir of Hungary and Bohemia. Maximilian's grandson, Ferdinand, is betrothed to Anna, sister of Louis.

1516   Death of Ladislas (King of Poland, Hungary and Bohemia) (Mar.). Succession of his son Louis (1516–26). Failure of Maximilian's Italian expedition.

1517   Publication of Luther's Ninety-Five Theses. (See pp. 159–61 for subsequent events leading to the Reformation.)

1519   Death of Maximilian (Jan.). Charles of Spain, the grandson of Maximilian, inherits Austria.

Charles V, 1519–56

1519   Death of Maximilian (Jan.). His grandson, Charles of Spain, inherits Austria. Expulsion from his lands of Ulrich of Württemberg. Habsburgs administer his lands.

1520   Charles V visits England.

1521   Diet of Worms (Jan.–May). The appearance of Luther, where he is declared a heretic. Diet of Worms reconstitutes the Imperial Chamber and re-establishes the Council of Regency, which governs Germany during Charles's absence. Treaty between Charles V and the Pope (see p. 143).

1522   Diet of Nürnberg (Nov. 1522–Feb. 1523) is dominated by proposed legislation to regulate the Empire's economic life and institutions. Arguments and counter-arguments over the enforcement of the condemnation of Luther. Reaction against Zwickau prophets. Beginning of the Knights' War (see p. 121).

1523   Death of Ulrich von Hutten. Capture of the castle of Landstuhl is followed by the death of Franz von Sickingen and the end of the Knights' War. Death of the Imperialist General Colonna (Dec.).

1524   Beginning of Peasant Revolt in Germany and elsewhere (for details, see p. 121). Diet of Nürnberg orders that the Edict of Worms be executed as far as possible and calls for a General Council. Imperialist invasion of southern France ends in failure.

1525   Death of Elector of Saxony (Frederick the Wise). Suppression of peasant revolt (see p. 121). Prussia is secularised by Albert of Brandenburg. League of Dessau is formed by the Catholic electors. Mastery of Italy is achieved by Charles V at Pavia.

1526   Charles V marries Isabella of Portugal (Mar.). League of Torgau is formed (see p. 143). Diet of Speyer. There are rival royal claimants in Bohemia as both Archduke Ferdinand and John Zápolya are elected king.

1527   Charles V is preoccupied with Italy following the 'sack of Rome' by Imperial troops. Charles V's reconquest of Italy. Treaty with the Papacy (Nov.). Ferdinand of Austria is crowned King of Bohemia. Conflict in Bohemia with Zápolya (who is defeated at Tokay).

1528   Treaties by Zápolya with the Ottomans (Feb.) and France (Oct.).

1529   Siege of Vienna by Suleiman awakens national feeling in Germany. The Emperor signs the Treaty of Barcelona with the Papacy. Second Diet of Speyer proposes to overturn the Edict of 1526 and return to the Edict of Worms. Term 'Protestant' is used of the minority reformers (from their 19 July 'protest').

1530   Coronation of Charles V at Bologna (Feb.). Diet of Augsburg is held (Apr.–Sept.) in the presence of Emperor Charles V: 'Articles of Torgau' and 'Confession of Augsburg'. Reorganisation of the Imperial Chamber (Nov.). Initial formation of the Protestant League of Schmalkalden (Dec.).

1531   Adherents to Schmalkaldic League rapidly grow. League completes its organisation (Dec.). Truce (then renewed conflict) in Bohemia with Zápolya.

1532   Ottoman threat forces Charles V to agree to the Religious Peace of Nürnberg (the Nürnberg Interim) (July). Death of the Elector of Saxony who is succeeded by his son John Frederick (Aug.). Criminal law is reformed by the Diet of Ratisbon (Regensburg).

1533   First Austrian–Ottoman peace treaty (between Ferdinand and Suleiman) (June).

1534   Philip of Hesse and League forces seize Württemberg, restoring Duke Ulrich (by the Treaty of Cadan) and ousting Habsburg influence in south-west Germany. Anabaptist excesses in Münster (see p. 174).

1535   Charles V captures Tunis. Ferocious suppression of the Münster anabaptists. Death of the Catholic Joachim I of Brandenburg. The succeeding Elector, Joachim II, is a moderate Catholic but John of Brandenburg-Neumark adopts Protestantism.

1536   Greater doctrinal agreement between the Lutherans and the South German Zwinglians is achieved by the Concord of Wittenberg. Charles V is involved with the seizure of Tunis and disaster in France.

1537   Rebellion by Ghent over impost levied by Charles V's Regent of the Netherlands, Mary, Queen of Hungary.

1538   Formation of the (Catholic) Holy League of Nürnberg. Treaty of Charles V and Ferdinand of Austria with Zápolya. Ferdinand is to receive Hungary on Zápolya's death.

1539   Charles V agrees a truce with the League under the Frankfurt Interim. Death of George, Duke of (Albertine) Saxony who is succeeded by his Protestant brother, Henry.

1540   Passage of Charles V through France. Destruction of the liberties of Ghent and ruin of its commercial prosperity. Death of Zápolya, leaving a son, John Sigismund.

1541   Attempted religious compromise at Diet of Ratisbon (Regensburg). Death of Henry, Duke of Saxony. Dukedom goes to Moritz. Disastrous expedition by Charles V against Algiers.

1542   Forcible conversion of the duchy of Brunswick-Wolfenbüttel to Protestantism strengthens the League in northern Germany. Withdrawal of Moritz, Duke of Saxony, from the Schmalkaldic League. Ottoman advances alarm the Diet of Speyer. Turks are attacked by Joachim II of Brandenburg.

1543   Charles forces the submission of Cleves (having travelled from Spain via Italy). Cleves cedes Gelderland and Zutphen (Aug.).

1544   Opening of the Diet of Speyer (Feb.). Supplies are voted to fight the Turks and French. Invasion of Champagne by Charles V.

1545   Diet of Worms moves to Ratisbon (Regensburg) (June).

1546   Death of Martin Luther (Feb.). Diet of Ratisbon (June). Philip of Hesse and other Protestants are placed under an Imperial ban. Outbreak of the Schmalkaldic War. Moritz of Saxony allies with Charles V (June). Early surrender of Ulm, Frankfurt, Strasbourg and Elector Palatine to Imperial forces.

1547   Defeat of the Schmalkaldic League at Mühlberg (24 Apr.). Moritz of Saxony wins the Electorate. Philip of Hesse is imprisoned at Halle (June). Catholic Imperial League is formed in the autumn. Main participants include the Emperor, Ferdinand, Moritz of Saxony and the Duke of Bavaria. The 'armed diet' of Augsburg is in session. Charles V is at the pinnacle of his power. Reconstitution of the Imperial Chamber. Organisation of the Military Treasury and the Netherlands is formed into an (Imperial) Circle. Deposition of Hermann von Wied, Archbishop of Cologne, for having permitted the introduction of Protestantism.

1548   The 'Augsburg Interim' (15 May). Charles V's attempt at a temporary compromise settlement of the religious issue. However, it is subsequently rejected by many Protestants, led by the city of Magdeburg.

1549   Charles V in the Netherlands.

1552   Protestant League of Saxony emerges (including the Elector of Saxony, the Landgrave of Hesse and other Protestant princes allied to Henry II of France). Augsburg is taken by Moritz of Saxony. Near-capture of Charles V is followed by the Treaty of Passau, giving Lutherans the freedom to exercise their religion and releasing the rulers of Saxony and Hesse.

1553	Defeat of Albert of Brandenburg at Sievershausen (also death of Moritz).
1555	The Religious Peace of Augsburg (see p. 144).
1556	Charles V resigns the crown of Spain to Philip and abdicates.

The Empire after 1556

1556	Ferdinand I's claim to Imperial throne is not recognised by Pope Paul IV. Jesuit College is founded at Vienna by Ferdinand.
1559	Death of Isabella of Hungary. Her son, John Sigismund, seeks the royal title and war ensues.
1560	Ferdinand's title to the Imperial throne is recognised by Pius IV. Protestants refuse Ferdinand's invitation to attend the Council of Trent.
1562	Maximilian is elected King of the Romans and is crowned as Ferdinand's heir to Bohemia. Peace of Ferdinand with Ottomans (for eight years).
1563	Poland acknowledges the right of the Elector of Brandenburg and his male heirs to the succession in Ducal Prussia.
1564	Death of Ferdinand (July). Maximilian II inherits Austria, Bohemia and Hungary. Ferdinand is bequeathed the Tyrol and other provinces, Charles receives Carinthia, Styria and Carniola. Formation of the Catholic League of Landsberg by the Duke of Bavaria, supported by various bishops.
1566	Publication of the ban of the Empire on the Duke of Saxe-Gotha.
1567	Maximilian signs a truce with the Ottomans (following death of Suleiman in 1566). Gotha is taken by the Elector of Saxony, Augustus.
1568	Prussia becomes an hereditary dukedom of the Hohenzollern dynasty. Increasing friendship of Maximilian and Philip II hastens a Catholic reaction.
1571	Death of John Sigismund of Hungary. Maximilian gains his possessions (but Stephen Báthory is elected *voivode* of Transylvania).
1573	Restoration of Catholicism in Fulda.
1574	Meeting of Maximilian with Henry III in Vienna.
1575	John Casimir, brother of the Elector Palatine, supports the Huguenots in France.
1576	Death of Maximilian II, who is succeeded by Rudolf. Principality of Fulda is invaded by the Bishop of Wurzburg to prevent its Lutheran secularisation (June). Archduke Maximilian of Habsburg prepares to contest the crown of Poland.

1578	Suppression of Protestantism in Vienna. Rapid advance of the Counter-Reformation in southern Germany.
1579	Albert of Bavaria dies. He is succeeded by Duke William (until 1597). Bavaria becomes leading centre of Catholic Reformation.
1580	Death of the Elector Palatine, Louis (Ludwig) VI. He is succeeded by Frederick IV, who permits Calvinism to become firmly established.
1581	Promulgation of an ordinance against Protestants in Bohemia (remains unenforced until 1602).
1582	Friction in the Imperial Diet over the rights of the bishoprics of Magdeburg and Aachen.
1583	Deposition by Pope Gregory XIII of the Calvinist Gebhard, Archbishop of Cologne, who had married Agnes of Mansfeld and attempted to retain his see. Gebhard is not supported by the Lutherans. Ernest of Bavaria is elected to the archbishopric.
1585	New problems over the potential secularisation of the bishoprics of Paderborn and Osnabrück.
1586	Christian, Duke of Saxony, creates unrest by attempting to secure toleration for Calvinists in his duchy.
1588	Defeat of Maximilian (half-brother of Rudolf) in Silesia. Maximilian's candidature for the Polish throne ends. Maximilian is ransomed by Rudolf (the Poles force the cession of the county of Zips).
1589	Gebhard of Cologne abandons his struggle with the Pope.
1591	Calvinism is put down in Saxony after Christian II succeeds to the throne. The twelve-year-old Archduke Ferdinand succeeds to the Archduchy of Styria.
1592	Archduke Ernest moves from Hungary to be governor of the Netherlands. Contested succession in Cleves-Jülich (see p. 244).
1593	Outbreak of war with the Ottoman Empire.
1595	Ottoman disasters (after a virtual stalemate in 1594). Death of Archduke Ernest.
1596	Imperial forces are defeated by the Turks under Mohammed III at Keresztes (Oct.). Ferdinand of Styria begins religious persecution.
1597	Maximilian becomes Duke of Bavaria (until 1651).
1598	Imperialist victories over the Ottomans. Accession of Joachim Frederick in Brandenburg is followed by the ascendancy of Calvinism. Re-Catholicisation of the imperial city of Aachen is bitterly disputed.
1602	Rudolf begins the persecution of Protestants in Bohemia and Hungary.

1603	Revolt in Transylvania against Rudolf.
1605	Stephen Boczai is proclaimed ruler of Hungary and Transylvania.
1606	Treaty is concluded between Archduke Matthias and Stephen Boczai (June). Later, toleration is granted to the Lutherans and Calvinists in 1608. Crucial meeting of the Habsburg Archdukes acknowledges Matthias as head of the House. Peace of Sitvatorok with Ottoman Empire (Nov.).
1607	Crisis over the Imperial city of Donauwörth, which is re-Catholicised after military occupation by Maximilian of Bavaria by the order of the Imperial Council.
1608	Rudolf resigns all his territories except Bohemia and Tyrol (June). Formation of the Protestant Evangelical Union at Anhausen (near Nördlingen) (May). Its main supporters are the Elector Palatine, the Count of Neuberg and the Duke of Württemberg, together with the rulers of Ansbach, Kulmbach and Baden-Durlach. Calvinism is established in Brandenburg by Johann Sigismund following the death of Joachim Frederick.
1609	Formation of the Catholic League (July). The main supporters were the bishops of Würzburg, Augsburg, Regensburg and Constance. They were later joined by the bishops of Speyer, Worms, Bamberg, Cologne, Trier and Mainz. Crisis over the death of William, Duke of Cleves. Both the Elector of Brandenburg and the son of the Duke of Neuberg claim the succession. Bohemia is granted a Royal Charter allowing freedom of conscience.
1610	Accession of Frederick V as Elector Palatine. Jülich is temporarily seized by Archduke Leopold (Feb.) before he is forced out. Upper Austria is laid waste by mercenaries of Archduke Leopold.
1611	Transfer of the Bohemian crown to Matthias. John George, the new Elector of Saxony, heads the Lutherans.
1612	Emperor Rudolf is deposed. Death of Rudolf (20 Jan.). Treaty between Protestant Union and Frederick V, the Elector Palatine.
1613	Matthias is refused aid by the Diet in his war against the Ottomans. Alliance of the Protestant Union with the United Provinces. Rise of Gabriel Bethlen (Bethlen-Gábor) in Transylvania.
1614	Despatch of Spanish troops to intervene in the religious disturbances in Mülheim and Aachen. The Cleves-Jülich dispute is temporarily resolved by the Convention of Xanten.
1615	Treaty with the Ottoman Empire, while Austria is at war with Venice.
1616	Archdukes Maximilian and Albert renounce their claims to the Empire in favour of Ferdinand of Styria.

1617   Ferdinand is recognised as heir to the Bohemian throne by the Bohemian Estates and is elected King of Hungary. French mediation ends hostilities between Ferdinand and Venice.

1618   Revolt in Bohemia (May). The 'Defenestration of Prague', as Martinitz and Slawata are thrown out of window, opens the Thirty Years' War (see pp. 126–7). Death of Albert II Frederick, Duke of Prussia, without heirs. The Elector of Brandenburg acquires his dominions.

1619   Death of Matthias (20 Mar.).

Germany and the Thirty Years' War

1617   Ferdinand II is crowned in Hungary and Bohemia. The 'Defenestration of Prague' marks the beginning of the Thirty Years' War (for survey see pp. 126–7).

1619   Matthias dies. Ferdinand becomes Emperor. Bohemian estates elect Elector Palatine (Frederick), having deposed Ferdinand (Aug.). Frederick is crowned (Oct.). Death of Johann Sigismund of Brandenburg. Gabriel Bethlen besieges Vienna.

1620   Agreement of Mulhausen (between the Catholic League and the Protestant Evangelical Union) (Mar.). Battle of the White Mountain destroys Frederick's cause in Bohemia (Nov.). Submission of Prague. Ferdinand secretly gives Upper Palatinate and its electoral title to Maximilian of Bavaria.

1621   Dissolution of the Protestant Evangelical Union. Succession Treaty under Emperor Ferdinand II.

1622   Peace concluded between the Emperor and Gabriel Bethlen (Jan.). Victory of Tilly at Wimpfen (May) and subsequently at Höchst.

1623   Frederick is stripped of the Palatinate and is put under the ban of the Empire. Electoral title is formally given to Maximilian of Bavaria. Second defeat for Christian of Brunswick by Tilly (at battle of Stadtlohn) (Aug.).

1624   Habsburgs consolidate their military predominance in Germany.

1625   Christian IV of Denmark is elected chief of the Lower Saxony Circle (after Saxony raises forces for him). Entry of Tilly into Lower Saxony and the start of the Danish War. Wallenstein enters the dioceses of Halberstadt and Magdeburg.

1626   Swedish victory at Wallhof (Gustavus II Adolphus transfers the seat of war to Prussia). Wallenstein is appointed Imperial Commander. Wallenstein defeats Mansfeld at the bridge of Dessau. Subsequent death of Mansfeld. Denmark suffers a decisive defeat at Lutter at the hands of Tilly. Death of Christian of Brunswick.

1627	Denmark (as well as much of Baltic coast) is overrun by Imperialists. Wallenstein (now created Duke of Friedland) achieves the submission of the whole of Silesia. Preponderance of Wallenstein. Gabriel Bethlen is isolated by the treaty between the Emperor and the Ottomans. Imperial troops are victorious over Baden at Heiligenhafen. The *Verneuerte Landesordnung* (New Constitution) is established in Bohemia and Moravia.
1628	Defensive alliance of Denmark and Sweden. Sweden begins to collect tolls at Baltic harbours. Duchy of Mecklenburg is confiscated by the Emperor and placed under Wallenstein's control. Wallenstein assumes the title 'Admiral of the Baltic'. As a defensive measure against Swedish attack, Wallenstein takes Wismar, blockades Rostock and occupies Pomerania. Failure of Wallenstein at Stralsund (Aug.) marks a turning point in the war.
1629	Failure of Tilly at Glückstadt (Jan). Emperor issues the Edict of Restitution (see p. 248) (Mar.). Peace of Lübeck is signed by Christian IV of Denmark and the Emperor (June). Truce of Altmark (for six years) between Sweden and Poland is signed (Sept.).
1630	Landing of Gustavus II Adolphus in Pomerania (June). Diet of Ratisbon meets (Aug.). Dismissal of Wallenstein from his command. Magdeburg allies with Sweden (Aug.). 'Contingent Convention' of Sweden with Hesse-Cassel (Nov.). Prince George Rákóczy is elected Prince of Transylvania.
1631	Treaty of Bärwalde between Sweden and France (Jan.). Leipzig Convention of the German Protestant states (Feb.). Frankfurt-on-Oder is stormed by the forces of Gustavus Adolphus (Apr.). Magdeburg is stormed and sacked by Tilly (May). Tilly subsequently invades Saxony (Aug.). Sweden–Saxony alliance is agreed (Sept.). Major victory for Gustavus Adolphus at the battle of Breitenfeld. Gustavus Adolphus forces the capitulation of Mainz (Dec.).
1632	Tilly is fatally wounded at the battle of the Rain. Wallenstein is reinstated to command the Imperial troops; the Saxons are forced out of Bohemia. Death of Gustavus Adolphus at the battle of Lützen (16 Nov.) despite the defeat of Wallenstein. Christina becomes Queen of Sweden (until 1654). Basis of League of Heilbronn emerges at the Ulm Congress of the four southern Circles.
1633	Negotiations of Wallenstein with Saxony (June) and later Oxenstierna (Aug.). Formation of League of Heilbronn.
1634	The assassination of Wallenstein at Eger (Feb.). Diet accepts the Form of Government. Battle of Nördlingen ends in a Swedish disaster (Aug.). Renewed alliance between the two branches of the Habsburgs.

1635	Philipsburg is taken from the French by Imperial forces (Jan.). Sweden adheres to the Peace of Prague (see p. 146) between John George of Saxony and the Emperor (May).
1636	Oxenstierna returns to Sweden (July). Swedes, led by Banér, defeat the Saxons at Wittstock (Oct.).
1637	Death of Ferdinand II (Feb.). Ferdinand III becomes Emperor. Sweden fights to retain its position in Pomerania.
1638	Fall of Breisach to Bernard of Saxe-Weimar, a key turning point in French fortunes.
1639	Death of Bernard of Saxe-Weimar (July). The French take Alsace.
1640	Succession of Frederick William, 'the Great Elector', on the death of George William, Elector of Brandenburg. The Swedes withdraw from Bohemia.
1641	Ratisbon (Regensburg) is attacked by Banér. Emperor narrowly avoids capture (Jan.). Truce between Sweden and Brandenburg (June). Victory by Guébriant over Imperial forces at Wolfenbüttel (June). Peace preliminaries are agreed at Hamburg (Dec.).
1642	Imperial forces suffer a succession of defeats: by Torstenson at Schweidnitz (May) and Leipzig (Nov.); by Guébriant at Kempten (Jan.).
1643	Peace Congress of Münster is formally opened (July).
1644	French envoys arrive at Münster. Torstenson outmanoeuvres Gallas who loses most of his forces after retreating to Magdeburg. Invasion of Hungary by Rákóczy.
1645	Torstenson defeats the Austrians at Jankowitz. The French advance on Vienna is thwarted by the resistance of Mercy at Nördlingen.
1646	Prague falls to the Swedes under Königsmark. Invasion of Bavaria persuades its Elector to seek a truce. Dispute between the Great Elector and Pfalz-Neuburg.
1647	Resumption of the struggle by Maximilian of Bavaria and the Elector of Cologne. Wrangel moves back into Westphalia.
1648	Treaty of Westphalia (see p. 146) concludes the Thirty Years' War.

The Empire after 1648

1648	Signing of the Treaty of Westphalia (Oct.) (see p. 146).
1650	Turenne aids Archduke Leopold in Flanders against the French but is defeated at Rethel (Dec.)
1651	Catholic and Protestant Leagues are formed (see p. 147) to carry out the implementation of the Peace of Westphalia.

1653	Diet at Ratisbon (Regensburg) (presided over by Emperor) confirms the provisions of the Treaty of Westphalia.
1656	Ferdinand III supports Poland against Sweden.
1657	Death of Ferdinand III (Apr.). Imperial throne is vacant until 1658. Poland and Brandenburg sign the Treaty of Wehlau, by which Brandenburg is to acquire Prussia (Sept.). Offensive alliance of the Great Elector and Denmark (Nov.).
1658	Election of Leopold I as Holy Roman Emperor after a sixteen-month interregnum (July). Formation of the League of the Rhine (Aug.).
1660	Renewal of the League of the Rhine for three years.
1663	War against Ottoman Turks. Neuhausel falls and an invasion of Germany is threatened. Sittings of the Imperial Diet at Ratisbon are made permanent. Marriage of Leopold and the Spanish Infanta, Margaret, is arranged.
1664	Peace of Vasvár with the Turks, following Imperial successes. Start of a Perpetual 'Diet' in Germany.
1665	Unsuccessful invasion of the United Provinces by the bishop of Münster. Foundation of Kiel University.
1671	Saxony, Mainz, Trier and Denmark remain neutral while Louis XIV attacks Holland.
1672	Alliance of the Emperor with Brandenburg after fears of the extension of French power (June). Treaty of Leopold with the United Provinces (Oct.).
1673	Conference of Cologne. Second coalition against France of Leopold, Lorraine, Spain and the Netherlands. Bonn is captured by Montecuccoli. Cologne and Münster make peace.
1674	Empire declares war on France at the Diet of Ratisbon (May). Denmark and Elector Palatine join the coalition, followed by the Dukes of Brunswick and Lüneburg (June). Empire joins Spain and Holland in a new triple alliance against France. Forces of the Great Elector are active on the Rhine.
1675	Dispute following the death of the Duke of Liegnitz without heirs. Emperor seizes Liegnitz, Brieg and Wohlau (despite the claims of the Great Elector) and incorporates them into Bohemia. Swedes are defeated by the Great Elector at Fehrbellin (June).
1676	Recovery of Philippsburg for the Imperial cause.
1679	Emperor Leopold makes peace with Sweden (Feb.).
1680	John George III succeeds to the duchy of Saxony on death of John George II. He supports the general arming of Germany to counteract the designs of Louis XIV. Alliance of the Bishop of Münster with France (Dec.).

86

1681	Defensive treaty is formed between Saxony and Brandenburg. Leopold faces the French entry into Casale and Strasbourg (Oct.) and an Ottoman intrusion into Styria. Congress meets at Frankfurt-am-Main.
1682	Leopold joins the emerging League of Augsburg. He is followed in June by the other German states, including Saxony, Bavaria and Hesse-Cassel.
1684	Emperor agrees to a twenty-year cease-fire in the Truce of Ratisbon because of his preoccupation with the Turkish war.
1685	Beginning of the dispute between the Empire and France over the Palatinate.
1686	The Emperor, Elector Palatine, Duke of Saxony and various Imperial Circles become part of the League of Augsburg (July).
1687	League of Augsburg is joined by the Dukes of Bavaria and Savoy.
1688	Death of the Great Elector. The French invade the Palatinate.
1689	Following the devastation of the Palatinate, the Imperial Diet declares war (Feb.). Ratification of the League of Augsburg at Vienna (May) (eventually becoming Grand Alliance). Treaties of the Emperor with the Dutch and with the Elector of Bavaria. The allies gain military success against French. Imperial Chamber is fixed at Wetzlar.
1690	Turks make major advances in Bulgaria and capture Belgrade. The French plunder Aachen and Liège as the Emperor is distracted in the East.
1691	Turkish threat is removed by Baden's total victory at Szalankenen (Aug.). All of Transylvania falls to the Imperial forces.
1692	Hanover is created a ninth Electorate by the Emperor in return for a perpetual alliance. Command of the Imperial forces is given to Louis of Baden. Grosswardein is captured from the Turks.
1693	French troops destroy much of the Rhineland.
1695	Formal renewal of the Grand Alliance. Namur falls to the allies.
1697	Saxony sells some territory to Prussia. Augustus of Saxony becomes King of Poland.
1698	Death of Ernest Augustus, first Elector of Hanover. He is succeeded by George Louis (later George I).
1699	Peace of Carlowitz (Karlowitz) ends wars against the Ottomans.
1700	Emperor refuses to accept the Second Treaty of Partition. Agreement, in principle, that the Elector of Brandenburg shall be granted his request to take the title of King. 'Crown Treaty' of Brandenburg is agreed to support the Habsburgs.
1701	Elector of Brandenburg is crowned King Frederick I in Prussia (see also p. 50). Revolt in Transylvania of Francis Rákóczy.

Electors of Bavaria and Cologne side with France when Prussian troops are despatched to the Rhine.

1702   Imperial troops take Landau (June).

1703   Ulm is taken by the Elector of Bavaria; Bonn is captured by the Duke of Marlborough. Bavarian plans are disrupted by the Tyrolese rising. Revolt in Hungary by Francis II Rákóczy. Treaty between Prussia and Sweden.

1704   Triumph of the Duke of Marlborough at Blenheim. Bavaria is subsequently overrun and the Elector flees to France. Marlborough visits Berlin to resolve outstanding issues.

1705   Death of Emperor Leopold (May). He is succeeded by his son, Joseph I. France aids Francis II Rákóczy. Marlborough is again sent to Berlin, this time to retain Frederick I of Prussia in the Grand Alliance.

1706   'Year of Victory' for forces of the Grand Alliance. Victories of Ramillies (May) and Turin (Sept.). The ban of the Empire is proclaimed on the Electors of Bavaria and Cologne (Apr.). Marriage of the Crown Prince of Prussia and Sophia Dorothea, daughter of George of Hanover.

1707   Military disasters befall the Grand Alliance. Empire secures peace with Naples (Joseph I proclaimed King). Archduke Charles is invested with Milan. Charles XII of Sweden is all-powerful in Germany. Prussia–Sweden alliance is formed.

1708   Victory for the Imperialists over Rákóczy and the Hungarians. Hanover is successful in its claim to a vote in the Electoral College. Emperor claims a reversion of the estates of the Duke of Mantua.

1709   Victories for Marlborough and Prince Eugene at Malplaquet (Sept.) and Mons (Oct.).

1710   The neutrality of Pomerania is proclaimed. Francis II Rákóczy is overthrown in Hungary. This is followed by his withdrawal.

1711   Death of the Emperor Joseph (17 Apr.). Austria and Hungary conclude the Treaty of Szatmár, securing for the Habsburgs the hereditary crown of Hungary, but the liberties of the Magyars are protected. Archduke Charles is elected Emperor (Dec.).

1712   Emperor Charles VI is crowned King of Hungary at Pressburg. The ban of the Empire on the Electors of Bavaria and Cologne is effectively withdrawn.

1713   Frederick William I succeeds Frederick I in Prussia. The Russians take Stettin. Prussia, Poland and Russia agree the Sequestration Treaty. Pragmatic Sanction (see p. 260) is brought forward to determine the Austrian succession by Charles VI. Emperor leans towards peace as Austria loses Landau and Freiburg to the French.

1714	Bavaria and France form a secret treaty (France is to support the Elector of Bavaria if he is a candidate for the Imperial throne).
1714	Treaty of Baden (Sept.), by which the Empire accepts the earlier Treaty of Rastatt between Austria and France (Mar.).
1715	Offensive Alliance of Prussia with Denmark, Hanover, Saxony and Poland is formed. It is subsequently joined by Russia (Nov.). Treaty of Denmark and Hanover (Bremen and Verden are ceded to Hanover). Prussia takes Stralsund in the Northern War. Wider war threatens.
1716	Prussia secures all of western Pomerania. Ottoman forces are defeated by the Empire at Peterwardein (Aug.) and Temesvar. Last Ottoman possessions in Hungary are lost. Death of Leopold, only son of Charles VI (Nov.).
1717	Charles VI orders Peter the Great to remove his troops from the Empire. Prince Eugene enjoys military success in the Balkans. He wins the battle of Belgrade (Aug.).
1718	Congress of Passarowitz is opened (see p. 150). Charles VI joins the Triple Alliance, which henceforth becomes the Quadruple Alliance.
1719	Charles VI begins to form the Ostend East India Company. Marriage of Princess Josepha and the Elector of Bavaria.
1720	Charles VI secures Sicily. Territorial acquisitions are secured by Prussia at the Treaty of Stockholm with Sweden (gains include Stettin, the islands of Usedom and Wollin, and Pomerania between the Oder and the Peene). In a treaty between Hanover and Sweden, Hanover obtains Bremen and Verden.
1722	National Diet of Hungary agrees to the Pragmatic Sanction.
1724	Compact of mutual support between the Electors of Bavaria and the Palatinate.
1726	Austro-Prussian Treaty of Wüsterhausen (Oct.).
1728	Secret Treaty of Berlin between Charles VI and Frederick William (Dec.). Prussia guarantees the Pragmatic Sanction in return for Charles VI's rights on Berg and Ravenstein.
1731	Imperial troops enter Parma following the death of the duke. Second Treaty of Vienna is signed by Austria, Spain and Britain.
1732	Pragmatic Sanction is accepted by the Diet of Ratisbon. The Electors of Saxony and Bavaria and the Count Palatine refuse to guarantee it (Jan.).
1733	War of the Polish Succession. Charles VI calls upon Frederick William of Prussia to supply a 10,000 troop contingent.
1736	Marriage of Maria Theresa and the Duke of Lorraine (Feb.). Death of Prince Eugene (Apr.). Bartenstein rises to power in Vienna.

1737	Ottomans retake Nissa. Kaunitz enters Imperial service.
1738	Further Ottoman military success at Orsova. Charles VI is eager to secure an early peace with the Turks. Definitive Treaty of Vienna is signed (Nov.).
1739	Treaties between Austria and France (Jan.) over the Jülich-Berg successions, between Prussia and France (Apr.) and between Austria and the Ottomans (Treaty of Belgrade, see p. 152).
1740	Death of Frederick William I of Prussia (May). He is succeeded by Frederick II ('the Great'). Emperor Charles VI also dies (Oct.). Beginning of the War of the Austrian Succession when Silesia is invaded by Frederick the Great (16 Dec.).
1741	Battle of Mollwitz (Apr.). Prussia controls Lower Silesia. Maria Theresa receives the Hungarian crown. Frederick allies with France after negotiations with Maria Theresa fail. 'Insurrection' is decreed by the Hungarian Diet. Treaty of Kleinschellendorf between Prussia and Austria (Oct.) is short-lived. Saxony allies with France (Sept.). Prussia, Saxony and Bavaria sign a treaty to partition Austria. Prague falls to the Allies. Glatz is occupied by Prussia.
1742	Linz is retaken for Maria Theresa (Jan.). Charles Albert of Bavaria is elected as Emperor (Jan.) and is subsequently crowned Charles VII (Feb.). First Silesian War ends with the Treaty of Berlin (July). Prussia and Poland withdraw from the coalition against Maria Theresa. Silesia is ceded by Maria Theresa. Death of Zinzendorf. Uhlefeld becomes Chancellor of Austria.
1743	Coronation of Maria Theresa at Prague (Apr.). Under the Convention of Niederschönfeld (June) most of Bavaria is handed over to Austria for the duration of the war.
1744	Frederick the Great forms the Union of Frankfurt (see p. 152). Second Silesian War begins (Aug.). Prague falls to Prussia. *Rapprochement* takes place between Austria and Russia.
1745	Death of Charles VII (Jan.). Election of Grand Duke Francis as Emperor (Sept.). By the Treaty of Warsaw, Austria and Saxony partition Prussia. Treaty of Füssen between Austria and Bavaria (see pp. 152–3). Year of military setbacks for Austria. Treaty of Dresden with Prussia ends the Second Silesian War. Death of Austrian Chancellor Stahremberg.
1746	Decisive Austrian victory at Piacenza. Treaty of St Petersburg (see p. 153).
1748	End of the War of the Austrian Succession. Congress meets at Aix-la-Chapelle.
1751	Empire recognises Prussian title to Silesia.

1756	Outbreak of the Seven Years' War with an attack on Saxony by Frederick the Great (29 Aug.) (for details see p. 140). Both Prussia and Austria claim victory at Lobositz (Oct.). Fall of Pirna (Oct.).
1757	Empire declares war on Frederick (Jan.). Austria and Russia renew the Treaty of Alliance (Feb.). Bohemia is invaded by Frederick, who wins the battle of Prague (May) but loses at Kollin (June). Prussian victories at Rossbach (Nov.) and Leuthen (Dec.).
1758	The Prussians suffer a reverse at the hands of the Austrians at Hochkirch.
1759	The Prussians are defeated by the Russians at Kay. Ferdinand of Brunswick wins a decisive victory over the French at Linden.
1760	Defeat of the Prussians at Landshut (June) leaves Silesia open to the Austrians. The Austrians are defeated at Torgau (Nov.).
1761	Frederick's position worsens dramatically.
1762	Accession of Peter III in Russia saves Frederick (Jan.). Peace between Prussia and Russia (5 May) and Prussia and Sweden (22 May). Austrians are defeated by Prussia at Burkersdorf (July).
1763	Prussia and Austria sign the Treaty of Hubertusburg (Feb.) (see p. 153).

THE AUSTRIAN MONARCHY

The Habsburg Lands, 1521–1618

1521	The Treaty of Worms between Charles V and Ferdinand I resolves Ferdinand's regency in the Lower Austrian duchies. First Hungarian campaign of Suleiman the Magnificent.
1522	The Treaty of Brussels confirms the separation of the Spanish and Austrian lines of the Habsburg dynasty and Ferdinand's rule in all Austrian lands.
1526	Second Hungarian campaign led by Suleiman. Death of Louis II of Hungary and Bohemia in the battle of Mohács. Ferdinand is elected King of Bohemia (Oct.) and King of Hungary (Nov.). Ottoman forces control much of central Hungary. Ottomans reach Buda (Sept.) and cross to western Hungary.
1527	Ferdinand is elected King of Croatia (Jan.).
1529	First siege of Vienna by the Ottoman Turks under Suleiman the Magnificent during his third Hungarian campaign (29 Sept.). Brief siege ends (Oct.).
1532	Fourth campaign of Suleiman to Inner Austria.

91

1533	Truce between the Habsburgs and the Ottomans determines the borders between 'royal' Hungary and the Ottoman central and eastern parts.
1541	Buda becomes a pashalic in the Ottoman Empire.
1544	Further Ottoman attacks in western Hungary.
1547	Five-year truce is secured between Ferdinand and Suleiman.
1551	Outbreak of ten years of intermittent challenges to Ottoman supremacy in Transylvania.
1554	Ferdinand I indicates that the hereditary lands of the Habsburgs are to be divided after his death.
1562	Ferdinand renews the 1547 truce. Tribute is paid to Suleiman. Transylvania remains a Turkish vassal state.
1564	Death of Ferdinand I. He is succeeded by Maximilian II.
1566	Final campaign of Suleiman to Belgrade. Gyula and Szigetvar in western Transylvania are captured by the Ottomans.
1568	Maximilian II makes concessions to the Protestant noble estates in Upper and Lower Austria. Habsburg–Ottoman truce is renewed.
1576	Death of Maximilian II. Rudolf II becomes Emperor. Beginning of the Counter-Reformation in the hereditary Austrian lands.
1587–93	Border incursions by the Ottomans against Hungary and Inner Austria.
1593	The 'Long War' (also called the Great Hungarian War) begins in Transylvania (until 1606) (see p. 124).
1595	Archduke Ferdinand (the future Emperor Ferdinand II) assumes rule in Inner Austria.
1606	Treaties of Vienna (between Boczai, Prince of Transylvania, and the Empire) and Sitvatorok (with the Ottoman Empire).
1608	Matthias becomes King of Hungary and ruler of Archduchy of Austria and Moravia.
1609	The '*Majestätsbrief*' (Letter of Majesty) of Rudolf II. Major concessions are granted to the Protestant nobles and royal towns in Bohemia.
1612	Death of Rudolf. Accession of Matthias as Emperor.
1613	Gabriel Bethlen (Bethlen Gábor) becomes Prince of Transylvania (until 1629).
1614	General Diet meets in Linz.
1615	General Diet meets in Prague.
1617	Ferdinand II is elected King of Hungary and Bohemia.
1618	The 'Defenestration of Prague' marks the beginning of the Thirty Years' War (see pp. 126–7).

The Habsburg Empire after 1648

1648	Habsburg Emperor recognises the independence of the German states at the Peace of Westphalia (see p. 146).
1656	Bohemia elects Archduke Leopold as King.
1657	Death of Emperor Ferdinand III. Leopold I becomes King of Hungary and, in the following year, Holy Roman Emperor.
1660	Beginning of the reduction of Transylvania by the Ottoman Turks.
1663	Beginning of the unsuccessful war with the Ottomans over the question of Transylvania.
1664	Peace of Vasvár with the Turks (Aug.) recognises the continued Ottoman overlordship of Transylvania.
1666	Conspiracy of the Hungarian magnates.
1668	Leopold I signs a treaty for the future partition of the Spanish Empire.
1669	The 'Nádasdy conspiracy' is betrayed.
1670	Birth of Zinzendorf (subsequently Austrian Chancellor).
1671	Execution of Nádasdy, Zrinyi and Frangepán after rising in Hungary.
1673	Suspension of the Hungarian constitution (Leopold declares war on France).
1675	Death of Duke George William (last Piast of Lower Silesia). Seizure of Liegnitz, Brieg and Wohlau by Leopold.
1678	Emeric Tokoly (Imre Tököly) is active in Transylvania.
1681	Effective restoration of the Hungarian constitution at the Diet of Odenburg. Office of Palatine is restored, and the traditional privileges of the Magyar nobility and religious freedom for the northern Hungarian Protestants are recognised.
1682	Tokoly is proclaimed King of Hungary by the Ottomans (Dec.).
1683	Invasion of the Habsburg Empire by Ottoman forces. Second Turkish War of Leopold I. Second siege of Vienna by Ottoman forces. The famous relief of Vienna by King John Sobieski of Poland and Duke Charles of Lorraine.
1684	Formation of the Holy League of Linz against the Turks (Mar.). The League comprises Austria, Poland and Venice. Reconquest of Hungary begins.
1686	Buda is taken by the Duke of Lorraine (Sept.) after 145 years of Ottoman occupation.
1687	Important victory over the Turks at the battle of Nagyharsány (near Mohács). Central Hungary comes under Austrian control and Transylvania is recovered. Diet of Hungary at Pressburg recognises the hereditary Habsburg succession in the male line.

1688	Belgrade is taken from the Turks by Imperial forces who overrun Bosnia, Serbia and Wallachia. Religious toleration in Transylvania is confirmed.
1689	Ottomans are defeated by Louis of Baden at Nissa. Subjugation of Bulgaria. The 'Bloody Assizes' of Eperjes take place against the Magyar collaborators with the Turks (and against the Protestants).
1690–91	The Diploma Leopoldinum for the Serbs of Hungary and Transylvania is issued.
1697	The Turks are defeated at the battle of Zenta by Prince Eugene (11 Sept.).
1699	Peace of Carlowitz (Karlowitz) with the Turks (see p. 149).
1700	Death of Charles II of Spain leads to the War of the Spanish Succession (p. 137).
1701	The War of the Spanish Succession diverts the Habsburgs towards a struggle against Louis XIV. The Grand Alliance is formed.
1703	Rebellion in Hungary is led by Francis II Rákóczy. Mutual Succession Pact (*Pactum Mutuae Successionis*) is signed by the sons of Leopold I. First regular Viennese daily newspaper (*Wienerische Diarium*) is launched.
1704	Rákóczy is elected Prince of Transylvania.
1705	Death of Emperor Leopold I (May). He is succeeded by his son, Joseph I.
1709	The *Konferenz* is established to coordinate the work of the central government committees.
1711	Death of Joseph I (Apr.). He is succeeded by Charles VI. Hungarian rebellion ends with the Peace of Szatmár (May). Traditional Hungarian constitution is confirmed by Charles VI. Charles VI is elected Holy Roman Emperor (Oct.).
1712	Under provisions agreed at Diet of Pozsony, the separation of the Hungarian and Austrian Chanceries is agreed. The nobles secure a continued exemption from direct taxation. Standing army is to be established.
1713	Pragmatic Sanction is issued by Charles VI (19 Apr.). Peace of Utrecht (see p. 149).
1714	Peace of Rastatt (see p. 150). Charles acquires the Spanish Netherlands, but renounces the Spanish succession. Austria retains Lombardy, Naples and Sardinia.
1716	Renewal of the war against the Ottoman Empire (Apr.).
1717	Maria Theresa is born (May). Recapture of Belgrade from the Turks (Aug.). All financial institutions of the Empire are placed under the *Finanzkonferenz*.

1718	Treaty of Passarowitz results in significant Austrian gains (see p. 150). Austria joins the Quadruple Alliance.
1719	Spanish troops are expelled from Sicily by the Austrians (June).
1720	Acquisition of Sicily from Savoy in exchange for Sardinia at Treaty of The Hague (Feb.). Estates of Austria and Bohemia accept the Pragmatic Sanction.
1721	Estate of Croatia accepts the Pragmatic Sanction.
1722	Pragmatic Sanction is accepted by the Hungarian Diet in return for a constitutional guarantee. Patent approved for the Ostend Company (the Austrian East India Company). Major administrative reforms in Prussia (see separate chronology, p. 51).
1724	Proclamation by Charles VI of the Pragmatic Sanction (all territories of the Empire having given their assent) (Dec.). Electors of Bavaria and the Palatinate sign a mutual support compact.
1725	Austria and Spain sign the Treaty of Vienna (see p. 151). Charles VI renounces his claim to Spain. Pragmatic Sanction is recognised. Ostend Company secures privileges in Spanish ports.
1726	Russia accepts the Pragmatic Sanction. Austria joins Russia in an alliance against the Ottoman Turks (Aug.). Treaty of Wüsterhausen with Prussia (Oct.) whereby Prussia recognises the Pragmatic Sanction.
1731	Treaty of Vienna (July). Britain and the United Provinces recognise the Pragmatic Sanction. Charles VI suppresses the Ostend Company.
1732	Recognition of the Pragmatic Sanction by the Imperial Diet.
1733	Beginning of the War of the Polish Succession. Saxony ratifies its acceptance of the Pragmatic Sanction.
1734	Major defeats for Austria in Italy begin. Eventual loss of Naples and Sicily to Spain.
1735	End of the War of the Polish Succession (not formally ended until 1738 Treaty of Vienna). Charles VI loses Naples.
1736	Marriage of Maria Theresa to Francis Stephen of Lorraine (Feb.). (Francis is compelled to exchange Lorraine for Tuscany). Death of Prince Eugene.
1737	Austro-Turkish War (arising from the 1735 Russo-Turkish War).
1738	Definitive (Third) Treaty of Vienna (see p. 152). Austria gains French recognition of the Pragmatic Sanction. Austria makes other gains in Italy, but also loses Naples and Sicily.
1739	Peace of Belgrade (see p. 152). Austria loses Serbia and Belgrade.

The Rule of Maria Theresa

Maria Theresa was born in 1717, the eldest daughter of Emperor Charles VI and Elisabeth Christina of Brunswick-Wolfenbüttel. In 1736 she married Prince Francis Stephen of Lorraine, Grand Duke of Tuscany.

1740	Death of Emperor Charles VI (20 Oct.); Maria Theresa becomes ruler (Nov.). Succession is not accepted by Bavaria, Saxony and Spain. Invasion of Silesia by Frederick II of Prussia (Dec.).
1741	Austrian forces are defeated by the Prussians at Mollwitz (Apr.). Maria Theresa is crowned Queen of Hungary (June). Treaty of Hanover with England. The succession of Maria Theresa is challenged by Elector Charles Albert of Bavaria who invades Austria with French support (July). Successful appeal of Maria Theresa to the Hungarians (Sept.). The fall of Prague (Nov.). Elector Charles Albert is crowned King of Bohemia (Dec.). Commerce Directory is established for all of the Habsburg lands.
1742	Elector Charles Albert is crowned Emperor Charles VII at Frankfurt (Feb.). Munich taken by Khevenhüller for Austria (Feb.). Prussia withdraws from the war, keeping most of Silesia, under the Treaty of Breslau (June). Count Uhlefeld succeeds Zinzendorf as Chancellor (Sept.). The Court Chancery is divided into the Court and the State Chancery. Prague is recaptured by the Austrians (Dec.). Bohemia and Upper Austria are reconquered by the Austrians.
1743	Coronation of Maria Theresa as Queen of Bohemia (Apr.). Count Haugwitz becomes the State Chancellor (until 1761). Bavaria is under Austrian rule.
1744	France declares war on Austria (Apr.). Frederick II of Prussia renews his attack (May). Bohemia is invaded, leading to the capture of Prague.
1745	Death of Emperor Charles VII (Jan.). Peace of Füssen with Bavaria. Coronation of Francis of Lorraine as Holy Roman Emperor (Francis I) (Oct.). Under the Treaty of Dresden (signed by Austria and Prussia), Silesia is ceded to Prussia (Dec.) but the Pragmatic Sanction is recognised.
1746	Beginning of a decade of administrative reforms (the 'First Reform Period'), under the influence of Haugwitz. Alliance with Russia in order to recover Silesia.
1748	Treaty of Aix-la-Chapelle (see p. 153) ends the War of the Austrian Succession. Austria recovers the Netherlands.
1749	Major administrative reforms. A centralised *Directorium in Publicis et Cameralibus* is established. Reform of the universities. Local government in Bohemia is also reformed: the nobility and clergy are now subject to direct taxation.

1750	Count Kaunitz is appointed Ambassador in Paris.
1753	Count Kaunitz becomes Chancellor of State. Single tariff system for all Bohemian lands is imposed.
1754	Chair of Natural Law is established at the University of Vienna.
1755	Collapse of plans for a diplomatic alliance with Britain paves the way for closer ties with France.
1756	Start of the Seven Years' War with the invasion of Saxony by Prussia (Sept.). 'Diplomatic Revolution' sees Austria, France and Russia allied against England and Prussia (the Treaty of Versailles had ended Habsburg–Bourbon enmity) (see p. 153). Limits are imposed on the labour services (*robot*) owed by peasants in Slavonia.
1757	Austria declares war against Prussia; the Prussians invade Bohemia. The battle of Prague. The victory of Count Daun at Kolin saves Bohemia for Austria. Second Treaty of Versailles with France agrees the partition of Prussia (May).
1759	Frederick II is defeated by the Russians at Kunersdorf. Austro-Russian army captures Dresden (Aug.).
1760	Fortress of Glatz is taken back from Prussia (July).
1761	The Council of State (*Staatsrat*) is established to coordinate all internal affairs. Financial constraints reduce the strength of the Austrian armies.
1762	The Austrian ally, Russia, withdraws from war against Prussia following the death of Empress Elizabeth. Abolition of the *Directorium*. Its functions are assigned to the Court Treasury and the newly created Austro-Bohemian Chancery.
1763	Peace of Hubertusberg ends the Seven Years' War (Feb.) (see p. 153). The *status quo antebellum* is restored. A poll tax is introduced.

Postscript: In August 1765, Emperor Francis I died. Joseph II became Emperor and co-regent. The major events of the rest of the reign of Maria Theresa included the promulgation of the Legal Code in 1767, the marriage of Marie Antoinette to the Dauphin of France in 1770, the first partition of Poland in August 1772, the new era of domestic reforms from 1773 to 1780, and the outbreak of the War of the Bavarian Succession. Maria Theresa died in November 1780.

SPAIN

The Making of Spanish Absolutism

1453	The Constable of Castile, Alvaro de Luna (effective ruler since 1431) is executed at Valladolid by the order of Juan II.

1462	Catalan civil war. Cities and nobles unite against the King. Treaty of Olite (between France and Aragon) ensures the succession to the throne of Navarre.
1469	Marriage of Ferdinand of Aragon and Isabella of Castile.
1471	Siege of Barcelona begins (it ends in 1472, marking the end of the civil war).
1472	Catalan privileges are confirmed in the Capitulation of Pedralbes.
1473	Perpignan is taken from France (the French retake it two years later).
1474	Death of Enrique IV of Castile (Isabella's half-brother). Start of civil war in Castile (see p. 117 for details).
1475	Concord of Segovia (Ferdinand has equal powers in Castile to Isabella). Burgos surrenders to Isabella (Jan.).
1476	Battle of Toro (Isabella's supporters defeat Juana's followers) (Mar.). Founding of the *Santa Hermandad* (Apr.).
1478	Papal Bull authorises the appointment of Inquisitors in Castile and Aragon.
1479	Civil war ends in Castile. Ferdinand II becomes King of Aragon following the death of his father. Spain is now seen as 'united' with the union of the crowns of Aragon and Castile.
1480	Inquisitors are first appointed to Castile. Mass exodus of the *conversos*. Central Council of Finance is established.
1481	Isabella and Ferdinand rule jointly in both kingdoms. The first *auto-de-fé* (see p. 241) at Seville.
1482	Beginning of the final war against the last Moorish stronghold of Granada (see p. 118). The Tribunal of the Inquisition is established at Córdoba.
1483	Expulsion of Jews from the diocese of Seville and the city of Cadiz. Extension of the Inquisition to Aragon.
1485	Protectorate over Navarre is secured by Ferdinand of Aragon.
1486	The *Sentencia de Guadalupe* frees peasants in Aragon in exchange for payments to the crown (Apr.).
1487	Ferdinand takes over the Grand Mastership of the Military Order of Calatrava (this is followed by Alcántara in 1494 and Santiago in 1499).
1489	Anti-French Treaty of Medina del Campo with England is agreed (see p. 142). Central Council of Military Orders is established.
1492	Fall of Granada heralds the conclusion of the War of Reconquest (for details, see p. 118). Mass exodus of Moors following an edict requiring all Moors to be baptised or leave (Mar.). Voyage of Columbus (Aug.) results in the discovery of the New World.

1493	Papal Bull *Dudum Sequidem* proposes the division of the newly-discovered lands between Castile and Portugal. Territories of Rousillon and Cerdagne are returned to Aragon under the Treaty of Barcelona with France.
1494	Treaty of Tordesillas is signed between Spain and Portugal (see p. 142). A formal claim to the crown of Naples is made by Ferdinand (to protect Sardinia and Sicily). Alexander VI grants Ferdinand and Isabella the title of 'the Catholic Kings'.
1495	Ferdinand of Aragon joins the Holy League against France (Mar.).
1496	Marriage of Philip the Fair and the Infanta Juana (Joanna), daughter of Ferdinand and Isabella (Oct.).
1497	Melilla (on the North African coast) is occupied by an expedition led by the Duke of Medina Sidonia.
1499	Compulsory conversion of *Mudejars* (Castilian Muslims) of Granada leads to a revolt (which is put down in March 1500). The term 'Moriscos' for Christianised Moors comes into use.
1500	Birth of the future Charles V at Ghent. Treaty of Granada (Ferdinand and Charles VIII of France plot the partition of Naples).
1501	Papal Bull *Eximiae Devotionis* grants to the crown of Castile all tithes levied in the territories of the New World.
1502	*Casa de la Contratación* (for the control of all trade with overseas possessions) is founded at Seville. Enforced baptism of the *Mudejars* after a revolt in the Alpujarra around Granada.
1504	Death of Isabella, Queen of Castile. Cardinal Jiménez (Ximenes) is appointed Regent of Castile. A Spanish force under Gonzalo de Córdoba drives the French out of Naples.
1505	Under the Treaty of Blois, Ferdinand redirects policy towards France following his marriage to Germaine de Foix (niece of Louis XII of France). Beginning of the military successes in North Africa with the capture of Mers el Kebir. Acquisition of Naples.
1506	Death of Philip the Fair. Madness of Queen Juana of Castile. Ferdinand secures recognition as Regent of Castile. Appointment of Guillaume de Croy, Seigneur de Chièvres, as Governor of Flanders.
1508	Papal Bull *Universalis Ecclesiae Regimini* gives the crown of Castile power to make ecclesiastical appointments in its New World possessions. University of Alcalá is founded by Cardinal Jiménez.
1509	Marriage of Catherine of Aragon and Henry VIII, King of England.
1510	Capture of Tripoli in North Africa.

1511	Ferdinand of Aragon joins the Holy League against France.
1512	Navarre is attacked by Ferdinand and its Spanish territories are seized while the French forces are preoccupied in Italy.
1515	Navarre is transferred to the crown of Castile. The majority of the Archduke Charles is proclaimed.

The Reign of Charles V

1517	Arrival of Charles in Spain. Meeting at Tordesillas with his mother (Juana) and youngest sister (Catherine) (Nov.). Death of Cardinal Jiménez (Nov.).
1518	Charles visits Catalonia. Nomination of Gattinara as Grand Chancellor of Burgundy.
1519	Succession struggle between Charles V and Francis I for the Empire following death of Maximilian I (12 Jan.). Charles is elected unanimously at Frankfurt (June). Confrontation with Estates of Catalonia. Start of the unrest with the beginning of a later revolt in Castile (*Communeros*) and Aragon (*Germanía*) (see p. 120).
1520	Laws of Burgos are promulgated for the protection of Indians in the New World. Departure of Charles from Spain (May) with Adrian of Utrecht as Regent. *Communeros* form the Holy Junta (29 June). Recognition of the *Germanía* of Valencia.
1521	Defeat of the *Communeros* near Villalar (Apr.). Execution of Juan de Padilla. Revolt of the *Germanía* ends with military defeats (July). First ban on Lutheran books entering Spain.
1522	Adrian of Utrecht (tutor of Charles V) is elected Pope Hadrian VI. The Spanish defeat the French at La Bicocca. Genoa is captured by Pescara and Colonna. Revolution (followed by terror) in Majorca.
1523	Peace is re-established in Majorca; execution of Joannot Colom.
1524	Edict of the Inquisitor General against the *alumbrados* (see p. 240).
1525	Imperialist victory at Pavia (see p. 119). Charles V creates the Council of the Indies.
1526	Peace of Madrid between Charles V and Francis I. Marriage of Charles V and the Infanta, Isabella of Portugal. War with France (and allies in the League of Cognac).
1527	Birth of the Infante Philip (future Philip II of Spain).
1528	Financial agreement (with the Welsers of Augsburg) on the development of Venezuela.
1530	Imperial coronation at Bologna; Charles V is crowned by the Pope. Death of Grand Chancellor, Gattinara. Empress Isabella

promulgates a decree forbidding the enslavement of local peoples in New World.

1531   Queen Mary of Hungary is nominated as Regent of the Low Countries.

1533   Death of Ariosto.

1535   Expedition of Charles V against Khairredin Barbarossa (corsair leader). Victory at the battle of La Goletta. Capture of Tunis and the liberation of Christian slaves.

1536   War with France is renewed (Francis I forms an alliance with the Ottomans).

1538   Armistice of Nice between Charles V and Francis I. The two rulers meet at Aigues-Mortes.

1539   Death of Empress Isabella.

1541   Charles V's expedition against Algiers turns into failure.

1542   Charles V (with support from England) is faced with a fourth war with France, whose allies include Denmark, Cleves and the Ottomans. New Laws to protect local peoples in the New World are promulgated.

1543   Infante Philip is nominated as Regent of Spain and is married to Infanta Maria of Portugal. There is crisis in the Low Countries following French advances. Meeting in Busseto of Charles V and Pope Paul III.

1544   Charles V has some military success against France following financial support from the Diet of Speyer. Peace of Crépy, by which Francis I relinquishes his claims to the Burgundian and Italian possessions of the Habsburgs.

1545   Birth of Philip's son, Don Carlos. Death of the Infanta Maria.

1546   Charles V in Ratisbon (Regensburg). The Danube campaign follows.

1547   Victory of Charles V in the Elbe campaign leads to the defeat of Saxony. Deaths of Francis I and Henry VIII. Council of Trent moves to Bologna.

1554   Kingdom of Naples is ceded by Charles V to his son, Philip. Philip marries Mary, Queen of England.

1555   Death of Queen Juana (Charles V's mother). Religious Peace of Augsburg (see p. 184). Charles V transfers the government of the Low Countries to Philip.

1556   Abdication of Charles V. Retirement of Charles V to a house on the land of the Convent of St Jeronimo de Yuste. Succession of Philip II to the crown of Spain, Italy, the Low Countries and the Spanish overseas empire.

Postscript: Charles V died in September 1558 and his body was moved to a crypt in the Escorial by Philip II in 1574.

Spain under Philip II

1556	Abdication of Charles V in Spain and the Empire. Ferdinand I becomes Emperor. Philip II inherits Spain, the Netherlands, Italy and the overseas possessions. Pope Paul IV declares war on Philip and Charles.
1557	Spanish victory over the French forces at St Quentin and Gravelines. Paul IV is forced to make peace with Spain. First 'decree of bankruptcy'. There is a wave of show trials against Protestants and *alumbrados*.
1559	Peace of Cateau-Cambrésis between France and Spain (see p. 144). Philip II returns to Spain. 'General Visitation' is conducted for the Spanish possessions in Italy. The Archbishop of Toledo is arrested on charges of heresy.
1560	Second 'decree of bankruptcy'. Philip II launches an unsuccessful attack on Djerba (North Africa).
1561	Philip moves the Court to Madrid.
1563	Philip in Aragon (until 1564).
1566	Outbreak of rebellion in the Netherlands (see p. 123).
1568	Revolt of the Moriscos of Granada (see p. 122). Arrest and death of Don Carlos, Philip's son and heir.
1569	Publication of *Nueva Recopilación*.
1571	End of the Morisco revolt. Spain occupies Finale. Spain joins the Holy League (see p. 145). Victory of Lepanto over the Turks (see p. 123).
1572	Professors at Salamanca University are arrested on charges of heresy.
1573	Spain briefly recaptures Tunis. Finale surrenders to the Imperial Commissioners.
1574	Turks recapture Tunis from Spain.
1575	Third 'decree of bankruptcy'.
1576	Spanish authority in the Netherlands collapses (see p. 123).
1578	One-year truce is agreed with the Turks (it is later extended for a second year).
1580	Further truce between Spain and the Turks. Philip II conquers Portugal after claiming the succession following the death of Henry I of Portugal. Philip stays in Portugal until 1583.
1581	Act of Abjuration of seven of the northern provinces of the Netherlands from Philip II. A three-year truce is agreed with the Ottoman Turks.

1582	The Azores campaign against the Portuguese claimant, Dom Antonio.
1583	Philip II returns from Portugal to Castile. The Terceira campaign.
1584	Final truce with the Turks. Alliance between Philip II and the Duke of Guise's Holy League (the Treaty of Joinville).
1585	Revolt in Naples. Philip is in Aragon (until 1586). Galicia and the Cape Verde Islands are raided by Francis Drake. Infanta Catalina marries the Duke of Savoy.
1586	Preparations begin for the Armada; Spanish coast is blockaded by John Hawkins.
1587	Drake's raid on Cadiz.
1588	The failure of the Spanish Armada (see p. 124).
1589	English raid on Corunna and Portugal.
1590	Castile votes the *millones* tax.
1591	The revolt of Aragon.
1592	Philip visits Old Castile and Aragon.
1593	Growing unrest in Portugal leads to violence at Alemtejo and Beja.
1595	France declares war on Spain (lasts until 1598).
1596	Spain faces an alliance of France, England and the United Provinces. An Anglo-Dutch fleet sacks Cadiz. A second Spanish Armada is driven back. Spain aids Irish rebels (see p. 124). Fourth 'decree of bankruptcy'.
1597	Third unsuccessful Spanish Armada sails.
1598	Peace of Vervins with France (see p. 145).

The Decline of Spain, 1598–1700

1598	Death of Philip II. Accession of Philip III.
1599	Philip III marries Margaret of Austria.
1601	Spanish expeditionary force lands in Kinsale (Ireland) but is driven out in 1602. Beginning of the siege of Ostend.
1604	Ostend falls to the Spaniards after a three-year siege (Sept.). Spain concludes the Peace of Westminster with England.
1609	Decree of expulsion is promulgated against the Moriscos (4 Jan.). A mass exodus, mainly from Valencia and Aragon, follows. A twelve-year truce is concluded between Spain and the United Provinces (it expires in 1621).
1614	War between Spain and the duchy of Savoy.
1615	Don Philip, the Infante of Spain, marries Elizabeth of France (Nov.).

1617	Ferdinand of Austria cedes Alsace and Finale to Spain. The war with Savoy ends.
1618	Retirement of Lerma (Oct.) after opposition to Habsburg policy.
1620	Philip III decides to aid Austria. Spanish troops enter the Palatinate.
1621	Death of Philip III (Mar.). Accession of Philip IV. Zúñiga, the main advocate of an aggressive foreign policy, becomes Chief Minister. War with the United Provinces is renewed following the expiry of the twelve-year truce (Apr.).
1628	Spanish treasure fleet is captured by the Dutch.
1629	War of the Mantuan Succession. The Spaniards besiege Casale; the Imperialists besiege Mantua. The Dutch press Spain in the southern Netherlands.
1630	Treaty of Madrid ends war with England (Nov.).
1633	Spanish Netherlands fall under the direct government of Spain after an attempted revolt following the death of the Infanta Isabella.
1635	Spanish abduction of the Elector of Trier leads to war with France.
1639	The Catalans defend Roussillon against the French (July). Spanish fleet is destroyed in The Downs.
1640	Revolt of Catalonia against Spain (see p. 128). Independence of Portugal under John IV of Braganza is proclaimed after revolution (see p. 110).
1643	The fall of Olivares. He is succeeded by Don Luis de Haro. The French are forced to retire into Catalonia by the Spanish army.
1644	Continuing Spanish military successes. The French are driven out of Aragon.
1645	Death of Olivares (June).
1648	Spanish power is restored in Naples.
1652	The revolt in Catalonia is suppressed by Don Juan José of Austria (the son of Philip IV).
1658	The Portuguese secure victory over the Spaniards near Elvas.
1661	Birth of the future Charles II of Spain (Nov.).
1663	Portuguese victory over the Spaniards. Retirement of Don Juan José of Austria from command of the Spanish forces.
1665	Victory of Villaviciosa over Spanish forces secures Portuguese independence. Death of Philip IV (Sept.) and succession of the infant Charles II. Father Nithard becomes First Minister.
1668	Peace with Portugal (Feb.). Independence of Portugal is recognised by Spain.

1669	Resignation of Father Nithard.
1671	Alliance with United Provinces (Dec.).
1675	Duquesne defeats the Spanish in the Mediterranean.
1676	Political revolution in Madrid. The Queen Mother, Mariana of Austria, is overthrown and Don Juan José, the natural son of Philip IV, takes over government. Pro-French influence dominates.
1677	Don Juan José attempts to reform Spanish government.
1679	Death in Madrid of Don Juan José (Dec.). Restoration of the Queen Mother (and Austrian influence). Marriage of Charles II to Maria Luisa of Orléans.
1680	Charles II appoints the Duke of Medinaceli as First Minister (Feb.). The Spanish are frustrated at the annexations of Louis XIV.
1683	Spain declares war on France (Dec.).
1684	Rise of the influence of the Count of Oropesa, who is appointed President of the Council of Castile.
1685	Count Oropesa succeeds the Duke of Medinaceli as First Minister (Apr.). Renewal of the alliance with Austria.
1689	Death of Queen Maria Luisa (Feb.). Charles II marries Mariana of Neuburg, the sister of Emperor Leopold of Austria.
1690	Spain joins the Grand Alliance (June).
1691	Spanish military defeats are followed by the resignation of the Count of Oropesa. Queen Mariana rules in the name of Charles II who is physically and mentally feeble.
1693	The government of the Spanish regions is divided among four nobles (the '*planta de gobierno*') by Charles II.
1694	English fleet saves Barcelona.
1696	No effective government in Spain following the effective end of *planta de gobierno*. Spain agrees a treaty with Portugal.
1697	Treaty of Ryswick (see p. 148) restores Spanish territory in the Netherlands and the Caribbean.
1698	First Partition Treaty divides the Spanish Empire (Oct.) (see p. 149). Charles II leaves his possessions to Joseph Ferdinand of Bavaria.
1699	Death of Joseph Ferdinand of Bavaria.
1700	In the second will of Charles II, the Spanish dominions are bequeathed to Philip of Anjou, grandson of Louis XIV (Oct.). Death of Charles II. Philip of Anjou is proclaimed Philip V (Nov.).

Bourbon Spain, 1700–63

1700	Death of Charles II (Oct.) having bequeathed his kingdom to Philip, Duke of Anjou, who is proclaimed Philip V of Spain. Creation of the *Junta de Gobierno*.
1701	Inauguration of the Bourbon dynasty as Philip V enters Madrid (Feb.). He is recognised by England, the United Provinces, Savoy, Portugal and the key German princes. The pro-French Cardinal Portocarrero becomes chief adviser. On the insistence of Louis XIV, a treaty with Portugal cedes Spanish claims in South America. Marriage of Philip V and Maria Luisa of Savoy.
1702	Arrival of Philip V in Naples (Apr.) He joins an army in Lombardy. Last meeting of the Cortes of Aragon begins (Apr.).
1703	Archduke Charles of Austria is proclaimed King Charles III of Spain in Madrid. In the War of the Spanish Succession, Portugal defects to the English–Austrian cause. Spain is abandoned by Piedmont-Savoy.
1704	Gibraltar falls to the English. Compulsory military service is introduced in Spain.
1705	Barcelona is captured by the Earl of Peterborough (Oct.). Valencia, Catalonia and many smaller Aragonese towns recognise Charles III as King. Cardinal Portocarrero is dismissed as royal adviser. Princess d'Orsini returns to Madrid.
1706	Galway enters Madrid. The high-water mark of allied success as allied forces also conquer the Spanish Netherlands.
1707	British forces are defeated at Almanza. The traditional laws of Aragon and Valencia are abolished by Philip V.
1708	Pope Clement XI is forced to recognise Charles III as King of Spain and grant him the investiture of Naples and Sicily.
1709	Recall of Michel Amelot (French Ambassador and effective Chief Minister of Spain). The Duke of Medinaceli leads the government.
1710	Arrest of Medinaceli for treason. The allies are victorious at Saragossa. The forces of Charles III are defeated at Villaviciosa (Dec.).
1711	Philip V enters Saragossa in triumph. Death of the Habsburg Emperor, Joseph. Archduke Charles becomes Emperor Charles VI.
1712	Philip V renounces the French throne.
1713	Philip V acknowledges the Duke of Savoy as his heir in the event of his line failing. Gibraltar and Minorca are ceded to Britain (as well as a grant of *asiento*) (Feb.). The Peace of Utrecht is signed (for details, see p. 149). Administrative reforms of Orry imposed by Philip V.

1714	Death of the Queen of Spain, Maria Luisa of Savoy. The fall of Barcelona guarantees Philip's supremacy in Catalonia (Sept.). Philip marries Elizabeth Farnese (16 Sept.). Alberoni becomes Chief Minister. Expulsion of Princess d'Orsini from Spain marks the independence of Spanish policy from France (Dec.).
1715	Peace is concluded between Spain and Portugal (Feb.) (Second Peace of Utrecht). Spain gains control of the Balearic islands. Philip V regains Majorca (July). Cellamare becomes the new Spanish Ambassador to France.
1716	The power of the crown increases with the re-establishment of royal government in Catalonia under the New Plan (Jan.).
1717	Alberoni is created a Cardinal. Sardinia falls to Spanish assault (Aug.).
1718	Sicily falls to Spanish forces (June), prompting the formation of an anti-Spanish Quadruple Alliance (July). A major naval defeat for Spain off Cape Passaro by English Admiral Byng (Aug.). The King of Sicily becomes King of Sardinia (Nov.). Spain is faced with an English declaration of war (Dec.).
1719	French army invades Catalonia; English seize Vigo in Galicia. The Austrians expel Spaniards from Sicily. The fall (and exile) of Cardinal Alberoni (Dec.).
1720	Negotiations lead to a treaty between Spain and the Quadruple Alliance (Jan.). Philip V renounces his claims to Italy (on condition that the sons of Elizabeth Farnese succeed to the duchies of Parma-Piacenza and Tuscany). Charles VI renounces his claims to Spain, but acquires Sicily from Spain.
1721	Mutual defence and marriage alliance is concluded with France at the Treaty of Madrid (Mar.).
1723	Philip V recognises the right of the last of the Medici line to succeed in Tuscany after the death of the Grand Duke (1 Nov.).
1724	Confusion in Spanish royal house: Philip V abdicates in favour of his eldest son, Don Louis of Asturias (Jan.). This is followed shortly by the death of Louis I (31 Aug.) and Philip V returns as king (Sept.). Rapid rise in influence of Baron Ripperdá.
1725	Relations with France abruptly worsen following the breakdown of the marriage engagement of Louis XV and the Spanish Infanta, Maria Ana (Mar.). But Spain and Austria are reconciled by the Treaty of Vienna (negotiated by Ripperdá) (Nov.). Triumphal return for Ripperdá who becomes Chief Minister (Dec.).
1726	Fall of Ripperdá (May). He is succeeded by José Patiño, 'the Colbert of Spain'.
1727	Hostilities begin against Britain. Attempted blockade of Gibraltar. Retirement of Philip V after nervous depression. Queen Elizabeth Farnese rules in his place.

1728	War with England ends by the Convention of Pardo (Feb.). Escape of Ripperdá from Spain.
1729	Spain signs the Treaty of Seville with England and France (Oct.) (see p. 151). There is a double marriage between the Spanish and Portuguese royal houses.
1731	Death of the Duke of Parma. Succession of Philip V's son, Don Carlos. Spanish troops occupy the duchies of Parma and Piacenza. War over the duchies is averted by the Treaty of Vienna.
1733	Spain forms the League of Turin with France and Piedmont-Sardinia (Sept.). First Bourbon Family Compact (Nov.) (see p. 151).
1734	Don Carlos conquers Naples (May) and Sicily (Aug.–Sept.).
1735	Orbitello and other Tuscan ports are taken by Spain. Mantua is besieged. Don Carlos is crowned Charles III of Naples. Peace preliminaries are agreed at Vienna (Oct.). Naples and Sicily are to be retained by Charles III, but not to be united with Spain under one crown.
1736	Anglo-Spanish disputes are settled by the Convention of Pardo (e.g. over the *asiento*) (Jan.). Death of José Patiño, the Chief Minister, ending a scheme to develop Spanish naval power. He is succeeded by Laquadra. Britain declares war on Spain, alleging violations of the Convention of Pardo (Oct.).
1739	Spain declares war on England (Aug.). Marriage of Don Philip and Marie Louise Elisabeth of France.
1741	Rapid rise to ministerial power of José del Campillo. Spanish troops land in Tuscany (Dec.).
1742	English naval mastery of the Mediterranean forces Neapolitan troops to withdraw from the Spanish army, ending hopes of a Spanish kingdom of Lombardy. France and Spain agree to a Second Family Compact (Gibraltar is promised to Spain; Don Philip is to have Milan, Parma and Piacenza).
1743	Rise of Marqués de Ensenada to become Chief Minister.
1745	French and Spanish forces enter Madrid.
1746	The Spanish are defeated in Italy at the battle of Piacenza (July). Death of Philip V (9 July), who is succeeded by Ferdinand VI, the only surviving son of his first marriage. José de Carvajal becomes Secretary of State.
1749	Ferdinand VI, adopting a peace policy, detaches himself from the Family Compact with France.
1751	Spain and Portugal agree to a treaty to settle old colonial claims.
1753	Concordat of Ferdinand VI with the Papacy. Ferdinand asserts the right of the crown to appoint candidates to all important

benefices, reduces the number of papal presentations and regulates the introduction of Bulls.

1759   Death of Ferdinand VI and accession of Don Carlos (Charles III) to the Spanish throne (Aug.).

1762   Havana (in Cuba) is captured by the British from Spain. Spanish invasion of Portugal. Braganza and Almeida are seized.

1763   Peace of Paris with England (see p. 153). Peace between Spain and Portugal.

PORTUGAL

Portugal and its Empire, 1453–1581

1452   Papal Bull, *Dum Diversas*, grants to the crown of Portugal the lands, property and persons of all the unbelievers whom they encountered on their voyages.

1455   Portugal is granted a monopoly by the Papal Bull *Romanus Pontifex* over all the lands, sea routes and trade in regions already explored or still to be discovered. This is followed in 1456 with the granting of spiritual jurisdiction in the Bull *Inter Caetera*.

1460   Death of Henry the Navigator. The Portuguese reach present-day Senegal.

1470s   Portuguese exploration of West African coast (see p. 193).

1487   Bartholomew Diaz rounds the·Cape of Good Hope.

1494   Treaty of Tordesillas divides New World (see p. 142).

1495–1521   Reign of Dom Manuel I ('the Fortunate'). Manuel and the Royal Council decide to continue seeking a maritime route to Asia.

1497   Sea route to India is opened up by Vasco da Gama. Expulsion of Jews from Portugal creates a mass exodus to North Africa and Portuguese-held Brazil.

1500   Brazil is 'discovered' by Cabral and claimed for Portugal.

1509   Battle of Diu. Naval victory of Francisco de Almeida gives Portugal command of the Indian Ocean.

1510   Portuguese fort at Goa is established by Afonso de Albuquerque, thus beginning Portuguese hegemony in south Asia.

1511   Malacca outpost is established.

1513   The Portuguese reach China.

1515   Ormuz has a Portuguese fort.

1521   Accession of John (João) III on the death of Manuel.

1531   Inquisition is established in Portugal.

1536	A second Papal Bull is decreed to enforce the Inquisition (a third one follows in 1547).
1557	The Portuguese acquire Macao on the coast of China. Death of John III who is succeeded by Sebastian (Sebastião).
1570s	There are increasing signs of a collapse in the economy.
1578	Disastrous Moroccan expedition results in defeat at the battle of Alcácer-Quibir (the 'Battle of the Three Kings') and the death of Sebastian and many of the nobility. Accession of Cardinal Henry (Henrique).
1580	Death of Cardinal Henry without heirs. Philip II of Spain defeats rivals to the Portuguese throne at the battle of Alcântara. Beginning of a period of Spanish occupation with the union of the crowns of Spain and Portugal in the person of Philip II.
1581	Philip of Spain is crowned King of Portugal.

For Portugal from 1581 to 1640 see under Spain, pp. 102–3.

Restoration and the Second Empire, 1640–1763

1640	Restoration of Portuguese independence following an uprising of 1 December when the Duchess of Mantua is deposed as Governor. Duke of Braganza takes the throne as John IV. War of independence from Spain continues.
1654	The Dutch are expelled by force from their conquests in Brazil and Angola. Portugal agrees a treaty with England.
1656	Succession of Alfonso VI following the death of John IV (Nov.). Queen Mother Luisa serves as Regent.
1659	An invading Spanish force is defeated at Elvas.
1661	Ceylon is ceded to the Netherlands by treaty (Aug.).
1662	Marriage of Catherine of Braganza and Charles II of England (May) under an Anglo-Portuguese alliance. England pledges to defend Portugal. Tangier is ceded. Alfonso VI takes control of government and Queen Luisa is dismissed as Regent. Rise to power of Count Castelo-Melhor.
1665	Independence of Portugal is assured following Spanish defeats at Montes Claros and then at Villaviciosa.
1667	Alfonso VI dismisses Castelo-Melhor (Sept.) but then loses power to his brother Pedro, who becomes Prince Regent (Nov.) (a move later backed by the Cortes).
1668	Treaty of Lisbon. Spain accepts Portuguese independence, ending the 28-year 'War of Restoration' (Feb.).
1703	Methuen Treaty is signed: a major agreement on commerce and trade between England and Portugal.

1706	Death of Pedro II begins the long reign of John (João) V (until 1750). Discovery of vast gold and diamond wealth in Brazil.
1708	Marriage of Emperor Joseph I's daughter (sister of Charles VI) and John V.
1715	War between Portugal and Spain ends with the second Peace of Utrecht.
1729	Double marriage alliance with Spain.
1735	Diplomatic rift with Spain.
1736	Reorganisation of the ministerial team. There are now three Secretaries of State.
1747	Death of Cardinal da Mota (Chief Minister).
1749	Rise to power of Frei Gaspar da Encarnacão as Chief Minister.
1750	Death of John V. Accession of Joseph (José) who rules until 1777. Pombal becomes Chief Minister (until 1777 when he is dismissed by Queen Maria I).
1751	Pombal reduces the power of the Inquisition in Portugal.
1755	The great earthquake hits Lisbon.
1758	Pombal attacks the Jesuits. A conspiracy is discovered against King Joseph after he is wounded.
1759	Expulsion of the Jesuits from Portugal (Sept.).
1761	Confiscation of Jesuit property in Portugal (Feb.).
1762	Portugal is invaded by Spain. Braganza and Almeida are seized.

ENGLAND

Reformation and Religious Change in Early Modern England

See chronology in Section Three, pp. 177–9.

WARFARE AND DIPLOMACY

THE MILITARY REVOLUTION

The concept of a 'military revolution' in early modern Europe was first put forward by Professor Michael Roberts in 1956. The idea of a 'military revolution' during the century after 1550 centred round four main propositions:

1. the revolution in military tactics (i.e. the arrow and musket replaced the lance and pike, marking the end of the feudal knights);
2. the major growth in the size of armed forces;
3. the strategic reforms to back up such forces with appropriate logistics (e.g. the campaigns of Gustavus Adolphus);
4. the increasing devastation wrought on society in general by war (e.g. the Thirty Years' War).

Despite criticisms of the scale of the 'military revolution', the concept still remains useful.

Chronology of Key Events[1]

1450s	Matchlock musket is developed.
1490s	Development of the rifled barrel.
1492	Conquest of Granada demonstrates the effectiveness of siege guns.
1494	French invasion of Italy with 18,000 men and 40 siege guns acts as a catalyst for military change.
1512	The devastating effect of gunfire on pikemen is seen at Ravenna (and later at Marignano in 1515 and La Bicocca in 1522).
1515	Civitavecchia is the first full artillery fortress (the '*trace italienne*').
1519	The devastating conquest of the Aztecs by Cortés and the conquistadores (completed in 1521).
1537	The science of ballistics is developed by Niccolò Tartaglia.
1590s	Volley fire and drill training are first developed by the army of the United Provinces.
1599	Count John of Nassau begins work on a new method of advanced military training: the illustrated drill manual.
1607	First illustrated drill book is published by Jacques de Gheyn.

---

[1] Principal Source: *Cambridge Illustrated History of Warfare* (Cambridge: Cambridge University Press, 1995).

1616	Count John of Nassau opens a military academy (*Schola Militaris*) under Johan Jakob von Wallhausen at Siegen.
1618	Outbreak of Thirty Years' War.
***c.* 1620**	Invention of the flintlock musket.
1631	Battle of Breitenfeld demonstrates the superiority of the Swedish military system (Sept.).
1632–45	The superiority of the Swedish military system is confirmed at Lützen (1632), Wittstock (1636), Breitenfeld II (1642) and Jankov (1646).
1690	Socket bayonet is now found in general use.

MAJOR WARS AND REBELLIONS

1453 The Siege of Constantinople

In May 1453 Constantinople, the capital of the Byzantine (or Eastern Roman) Empire, finally fell to the Ottoman Turks. The city had been besieged by Mohammed with 80,000 men since February. The last Byzantine Emperor, Constantine XI, died defending the city. Following the fall of Constantinople, the Ottomans rapidly seized control of the Balkans (see pp. 68–73).

1454–66 The Thirteen Years' War

A conflict in which the Poles supported a revolt against the Teutonic Order (see p. 264). Casimir of Poland won an important military victory (September 1462). The war saw major Polish gains at the Peace of Thorn (see p. 142).

1455–87 The Wars of the Roses

The prolonged dynastic conflict in England between the Lancastrians (red rose) and the Yorkists (white rose). The war began with the first battle at St Albans in 1455. The first Yorkist king, Edward IV, was proclaimed in 1461 (to be followed briefly by his son Edward V and then by his brother Richard III). The decisive year was 1485, when Henry Tudor landed at Milford Haven on 7 August and reached Shrewsbury unopposed. King Richard was killed at the battle of Bosworth Field near Leicester on 22 August after treachery in the ranks of his army by the Stanleys and the Earl of Northumberland. In 1487 a Yorkist pretender, Lambert Simnel, was also defeated.

1465 The War of the Public Weal

A conflict in France in which many of the nobles, led by Philip of Burgundy and including the dukes of Brittany, Anjou and Bourbon, and the king's brother Charles de France, revolted against Louis XI. The conflict developed from Louis' dismissal of his father's ministers and his reaction to their policies. An inconclusive battle was fought at Montlhéry (July). The war was ended by the Treaty of Conflans (5 October).

1474–79 The Castilian War of Succession

The war, fought over the accession to the throne after the death of Enrique IV, was marked by the Portuguese invasion of Castile. Castile responded by developing its own naval capacity. The rival claimants to the throne were Enrique's IV's sister (Isabella, the wife of Prince Ferdinand of Aragon) and Joan (the dubiously legitimate daughter of Henry who was married to Alfonso V of Portugal). Ferdinand's victory over the Portuguese at Toro (1476) ensured his ultimate success.

1482–92 The Conquest of Granada

The last struggle of Christians and Muslims in Spain had begun with a raid on Zahara by the King of Granada in December 1481. In response, the Spaniards seized Alhama. This, in turn, was invested. Intermittent warfare continued for ten years. Loja was captured in 1486, followed by Spanish success at Málaga (May–August 1487). With the capture of the fortresses of Baza and Almeria (1489), Granada was isolated. The final siege, culminating in the surrender by Boabdil of the last Moorish stronghold in Spain, lasted from April 1491 to January 1492.

1488–1559 The Anglo-French Invasions

English intervention in France continued on numerous occasions during this period. Thus, in February 1488, a body of volunteers was sent to aid the Bretons, but the English envoy was not well received and Henry VII renewed the truce with France. In October 1492 Henry VII crossed to Calais and besieged Boulogne, but by the Treaty of Etaples in November he ended the campaign in return for a financial settlement.

The first of Henry VIII's three invasions took place in 1513, capturing the towns of Therouanne and Tournai. The French cavalry were defeated at the battle of the Spurs. A second invasion in 1523 into Picardy ended when the army, demoralised by hunger and frostbite, retreated in December to Calais. In February 1544 Henry secretly agreed to a military alliance with the Emperor, by which they would join forces on the Marne in August 1544 for the 'Enterprise of Paris'. Boulogne was captured, but at the Peace of Ardres in 1546 Henry agreed to surrender the town in return for an indemnity. Boulogne was in fact given up in 1550 after a brief French campaign.

In June 1557 England declared war on France and in July 7,000 men under the Earl of Pembroke crossed the Channel to assist the Spanish besieging St Quentin. A relieving army was routed in August. However, the French attacked Calais, the last English possession in France, on 1 January 1558, and it was forced to surrender on the 8th.

1489–1601 The Tudor Rebellions

Despite the Tudor victory at Bosworth and the defeat of Lambert Simnel in 1487, numerous threats emerged to disturb the Tudor succession. These included the Yorkshire rising of 1489, the Perkin Warbeck impersonation of 1495–97, the Cornish rebellion of 1497 in protest against taxation to pay for the Scottish War and the 1525 rebellion against Wolsey's 'Amicable Grant'. Other significant rebellions included the 1536 Pilgrimage of Grace (marking general hostility to religious innovation), the 1549 Western Rebellion (principally against the new Prayer Book), Kett's Rebellion (also of 1549, in protest against enclosures and gentry exploitation) and Wyatt's Rebellion of 1554. Two serious rebellions in Elizabeth's reign were the rebellion of the Northern Earls in 1569 and Essex's Rebellion in 1601. See also under Ireland, pp. 124–5.

1494–1559 The Habsburg–Valois Wars

The long series of wars, initiated by the invasion of Italy by Charles VIII of France in pursuit of dynastic claims to Naples. The wars, which at first were fought mainly in Italy, later spread north. Among the causes of the conflict were mutual dynastic rivalries, numerous territorial disputes (e.g. Burgundy, Milan, Naples, Cerdagne and Roussillon) and the internal ambitions of the feuding Italian states. The main landmarks in the conflict were:

1494–95   The invasion of Charles VIII of France in support of his somewhat remote claim to Naples, which he secured on 22 February 1495, but which led to his enemies uniting against him in the Holy League of Venice. Charles was forced to retreat after the inconclusive battle of Fornovo.

1499–1505   The invasion of Louis XII of France in support of his claim to Milan, which he secured on 6 October 1499. After the French victory of Novara (8 April 1500), French rule in Milan was recognised by Emperor Maximilian I in the first Treaty of Blois. Naples was then partitioned with Ferdinand of Aragon by the Treaty of Granada (1500). Subsequent quarrels led to the French defeats at Cerignalo (April 1503) and the River Garigliano (December 1503). By the second Treaty of Blois (1504), French claims to Naples were renounced.

1508–14   The French formed the League of Cambrai to attack Venice, which resulted in a French triumph at Agnadello (14 May 1509). This in turn produced an anti-French alliance (the Holy League). The French suffered reverses at Ravenna (April 1512) and Novara (June 1513), and France itself was invaded. Divisions among the loose anti-French alliance enabled Louis to make separate peace treaties despite French military reverses at the battle of the Spurs, in August 1513.

1515–16   The first invasion of Italy by Francis I secured a major victory at Marignano (September 1515). French success was confirmed in the Concordat of Bologna (August 1516).

119

1521–26	Fearing the potential encirclement of France, war was declared by Francis I on 22 April 1521. The French were defeated at La Bicocca (24 June 1522). A major French defeat occurred at Pavia (February 1525). Francis was taken prisoner and forced to sign the Treaty of Madrid.
1526–29	After breaking the Treaty of Madrid and forming the League of Cognac, as well as concluding a close alliance with Henry VIII, Francis invaded Italy under Lautrec. A total defeat of the French at Aversa (28 August 1528) was followed by the evacuation of Naples and Genoa.
1536–38	The disputed succession in Milan, following the death of Francesco Maria Sforza on 1 November 1535, led to a French invasion which took Turin (April 1536). In turn, Emperor Charles V invaded France. A ten-year truce (the Truce of Nice) was negotiated by Pope Paul III in 1538.
1542–44	This was a period of widespread conflict in Europe (though not Italy) between France and the Holy Roman Empire. France allied with the Ottomans, Charles V allied with Henry VIII of England. The conflict was resolved by the Treaty of Crépy, which was signed in September 1544 between Francis and Charles V (see p. 144).
1547–59	The final stage of the Habsburg–Valois conflict was concluded by the Treaty of Cateau-Cambrésis in April 1559 (see p. 144).

1513 The Anglo-Scottish War

Warfare between England and Scotland was a recurrent theme, particularly from 1513 to 1603. The 'Auld Alliance' of Scotland and France meant that hostilities between France and England precipitated invasions across the England–Scotland border. Thus James IV crossed the border on 22 August 1513 in an attempt to take advantage of English involvement in a war with his allies, the French. On 9 September, at the battle of Flodden, an English army of 26,000 led by the Earl of Surrey inflicted a crushing defeat on the Scots, who numbered 30–40,000. James IV himself was killed, along with many of the Scottish nobility. Further English expeditions took place in 1542, 1544, 1547 and 1560.

1521–23 The Revolt of the *Comunidades* and *Germanías*

With the revolt of the *Comunidades* (communities) of northern Castile, a strong radical element emerged from a complex welter of political and economic grievances. Rebel forces were defeated in April 1521 by Juan de Padilla at Villalar. Charles V issued a general pardon in 1522. There was also a parallel revolt of the *Germanías* (brotherhoods) in Valencia and Majorca. Peace was soon restored to Valencia (1522) and Mallorca (1523).

1522 The Knights' War

The uprising of the free imperial knights of the Holy Roman Empire, who were led by the mercenary captain Franz von Sickingen (1481–1523). The particular cause of the revolt was the law passed at the Diet of Worms which criminalised feuding between nobles of the Empire (although the knights had proved an unruly element in the Empire as recently as the 1510s). Mobilising themselves in Franconia and the Rhineland and with the support of Ulrich von Hutten, they moved against the bishops of Bamberg and Würzburg. They were soon defeated by the forces of the Swabian League (see p. 142).

1524–25 The Peasants' Revolt

The great peasants' revolt, although centred in Germany, principally in Swabia, Franconia and Thuringia, was not confined to Germany. The revolt drew on a long tradition of rural armed unrest (as in the 1494 *Bundschuh* rising) but had different roots and manifestations in different regions. The revolt first began in June 1524 in Stühlingen. It spread rapidly to Lake Constance and the Black Forest before engulfing much of Alsace, the Rhineland, northern Switzerland, Saxony, Austria, Swabia and Franconia. The original Twelve Articles were drawn up at Memmingen. The rebel forces at Mühlhausen, involving Thomas Müntzer, were defeated in May at the battle of Frankenhausen. The revolt in Alsace and the upper Rhineland was crushed at Saverne (May 1525).

1546–47, 1552 The Schmalkaldic Wars

These wars were between the Schmalkaldic League (see p. 144) and the Emperor Charles V. The League had been established by the Protestant German princes to defend their faith against the re-introduction of Catholicism. The Emperor had been forced in 1544 to give recognition to the League. However, the Emperor secured the alliance of the Duke of Bavaria and the Protestant Duke Moritz of Saxony (with the promise of the electoral title). Despite the greater forces at the disposal of the Schmalkaldic League, the invasion of Electoral Saxony by Duke Moritz split their forces. In April 1547 the Schmalkaldic League was destroyed at the battle of Mühlberg and Elector John Frederick of Saxony was captured. Philip of Hesse also surrendered.

The second Schmalkaldic War broke out in 1552. The Protestant princes, now led by Duke Moritz of Saxony and enjoying the support of Henry II of

France, resisted the Emperor. Despite a French invasion of Metz, Toul and Verdun, military stalemate ensued.

1557–62 The Livonian War

The name given to the struggle waged by Ivan IV of Muscovy to secure a Russian coastline on the Baltic. The sustained (but unsuccessful) effort involved Poland and Sweden. The conflict was renewed in 1577.

1562–98 The French Wars of Religion

This great series of conflicts convulsed France from 1562 until it was settled in 1598 by the Edict of Nantes. The conflict is usually divided into the following eight phases (for further details, see pp. 166–9).

1. First Civil War (Apr. 1562–Mar. 1563)   Ended by the Edict of Amboise.
2. Second Civil War (Sept. 1567–Mar. 1568)   Ended by the Peace of Longjumeau.
3. Third Civil War (Oct. 1568–Aug. 1570)   Ended by the Peace of Saint-Germain.
4. Fourth Civil War (Sept. 1572–July 1573)   Ended by the Edict of Boulogne.
5. Fifth Civil War (Sept. 1574–May 1576)   Ended by the Edict of Beaulieu or the Peace of Monsieur.
6. Sixth Civil War (Apr. 1577–Sept. 1577)   Ended by the Peace of Bergerac.
7. Seventh Civil War (Apr. 1580–Nov. 1580)   Ended by the Peace of Fleix.
8. Wars of the League (Aug. 1585–Mar. 1598)   Ended by the Edict of Nantes.

1563–70 The Seven Years' War of the North

The conflict between Sweden on the one side and Denmark, Lübeck and Poland on the other. An early Swedish naval victory at Götland (1564) was briefly followed by the occupation of Trondheim. The Swedes failed to follow up these successes and, after Eric XIV was deposed by John III, Sweden concluded a peace in 1570.

1568–71 The Revolt of the Moriscos

Persecution of those Muslims who had converted to Christianity (Moriscos) continued in Spain. A major uprising ensued in the Alpujarra region in 1568. In March 1569 Don John of Austria was given command of the troops suppressing the revolt, which was quelled by 1571. An estimated 300,000 Moriscos were later expelled *en masse* from 1609 to 1614.

1568–1648 The Revolt of the Netherlands

Hostility in the Spanish Netherlands to Imperial rule (and particularly Imperial taxation) had a long history. Thus, in 1540, the urban revolt of Ghent took place over fiscal matters and traditional liberties. It was ruthlessly crushed by the Emperor Charles V. Growing hostility by the nobility, and the spread of Protestantism, led to Spanish repression. A premature military revolt was easily suppressed, but the Duke of Alba's severity only served to encourage rather than crush revolt.

The revolt gained its first success with the capture of Brill (1 April 1572). A succession of other towns came over to the rebel cause (as at Gouda, Dordrecht, Leiden, Hoorn and Haarlem). The Spaniards responded by seizing and plundering Malines (in the south) and Zutphen and Naarden (in the north). Haarlem was retaken after a long siege. Alkmaar held out. Most significant was the celebrated failure of the seige of Leiden. Henceforth Spanish troops were never again to force their way into Holland. In the south the Pacification of Ghent was followed by the 'Spanish fury' in Antwerp (November 1576). The Union of Utrecht of 23 January 1579 effectively marked the birth of the Dutch Republic. From 1579 to the truce of 1612 an effective stalemate existed (see pp. 170–2).

From the 1570s England became increasingly embroiled in the conflict. Under the treaty signed on 10 August 1585, England was to send 5,000 foot and 1,000 horse to the Netherlands and to garrison Flushing and Brill. The forces crossed the Channel in December under the Earl of Leicester. English troops fought in the Netherlands throughout the 1590s and assisted the Dutch at the victories of Turnhout (24 January 1597) and Nieuport (2 July 1600) and in the defence of Ostend (1601).

Following the Twelve Years Truce (1609–21), war resumed with the Dutch under Maurice's leadership. In 1625 the Dutch cause suffered a major reverse with the fall of the fortress of Breda on the southern frontier to the Spaniards (it followed shortly after the death of Maurice). Under Frederick Henry (Maurice's half-brother) the Dutch victories resumed, culminating in the fall of Maastricht, the capture off Cuba of the Spanish silver fleet by Piet Heyn and the naval victory over the Spanish in the Downs by Martin Tromp. The 80-year war with Spain was eventually concluded at the Treaty of Westphalia (see p. 146) which acknowledged Dutch independence.

1571 The Battle of Lepanto

The epic naval victory of the allied Christian fleet, under the command of Don John of Austria, over the Ottoman Turks on 8 October 1571. Pope Pius V had established the Holy League in 1570 in response to the Ottoman siege of Famagusta on Cyprus. The assembled Christian fleet consisted of 108 Venetian galleys, 81 Spanish galleys and a further 32 galleys from smaller allies. There were six giant Venetian galleasses. Advancing in four squadrons against the Ottoman fleet, after a four-hour engagement the Christian forces secured a resounding victory, capturing 117 galleys and thousands of prisoners. The battle was of greater value in terms of morale than practicality, as Cyprus was surrendered by Venice to the Turks in 1573 and Ottoman naval losses were soon made good. However, the victory (recorded in paintings by Titian and Tintoretto) seemed to symbolise the end of the Ottoman threat.

1588 The Spanish Armada

The great attempt by Philip of Spain to invade England. Preparations for the Armada had been disrupted by Drake's raid on Cadiz in 1587. Drake sailed from Plymouth on 12 April 1587 and in an attack on Cadiz (19–20 April) did much damage to the preparations of the Spanish Armada. He cruised off the Spanish coast and captured a rich Portuguese convoy off the Azores, before returning to Plymouth on 26 June. The Armada itself, consisting of 130 ships and 27,000 men, sailed in May 1588 under the command of the Duke of Medina Sidonia, who had orders to link up with Parma in the Netherlands and escort his 17,000 veterans across the Channel. The Spanish were sighted off the Lizard on 19 July. On 28 July fireships were sent among the Spanish fleet at anchor off Calais paving the way for the decisive battle of Gravelines the following day. The Armada fled round the north of the British Isles, and reached Spain with possibly sixty of its ships lost in September 1589. A further Spanish invasion was launched when, in October 1596, the Governor of Castile sailed from Ferrol with over 100 ships and 16,000 men intended for the conquest of England. However, the fleet was dispersed by a gale off Finisterre. Another attempt in 1597 also failed.

1593–1606 The Great Hungarian War

The 13-year war against the Ottoman Turks, which featured a complex series of arduous military campaigns, was provoked by a revolt in the Ottoman-dominated Balkan provinces of Moldavia, Wallachia and Transylvania. The uprising in Moldavia and Wallachia prompted Polish intervention while the Austrian Habsburgs fomented the Transylvania revolt. Most of the war centred around sieges of key fortresses on the Danube. Under the November 1606 peace, the Emperor made a final 'gift' to the Sultan in return for no further tribute. Essentially, the frontier dividing Hungary was reinforced.

1594 The Irish Rebellions

Rebellion against English rule resulted in numerous uprisings in Ireland. During the reign of Elizabeth I alone, four major rebellions took place – that of Shane O'Neill (1559–66), the Fitzmaurice confederacy in Munster (1569–72), the Desmond Rebellion (1579–83), and Tyrone's Rebellion (1594–1603). The last was the most serious and necessitated the sending of large numbers of English troops to Ireland. In September 1601 a Spanish fleet with 4,000 men occupied Kinsale, but the Irish and Spanish were routed on 24 December. Tyrone finally submitted on 30 March 1603.

1600–11, 1617–29 The Polish-Swedish Wars

The war begun by Sweden in 1600 was in essence a continuation of the earlier Livonian Wars of 1557–71 and 1579–82 (see p. 122). In 1600, most of Estonia and Livonia was quickly seized by Sweden until a successful counter-attack by Hetman Jan Karol Chodkiewicz drove them back. A new Swedish offensive occurred in 1604, when the new King, Charles IX, marched on Riga. The Swedish adventure was abruptly ended by Chodkiewicz and the Polish heavy cavalry at Kitchholm. Heavy Swedish losses at Kitchholm effectively ended the main fighting and a truce was concluded in 1611. In 1617, under Gustavus Adolphus, conflict was renewed when Poland was already at war with Russia and Turkey. Livonia's Baltic Coast was quickly regained by Gustavus Adolphus. Attacking again in 1619, Riga was captured in September 1621. After a further armistice, more Swedish gains followed in 1626. Despite the intervention of the Holy Roman Emperor to aid the Poles, Sweden remained firmly in control of the Baltic littoral. After a long war of sieges and manoeuvres, peace was concluded in 1629 (to free Gustavus Adolphus to enter the Thirty Years' War).

1609–18, 1632–34 The Russo-Polish Wars

With Russia engulfed in its 'Time of Troubles' (see p. 62), Sigismund III of Poland invaded Russia to claim the crown himself. Smolensk valiantly held out against the Polish advance. The Russian attempt to relieve Smolensk, led by Vasily Shuiskii, suffered a major defeat on the battlefield of Klushine (4 July 1610). The Poles under Hetman Stanislaw Zolkiewski went on to enter Moscow (October) and Smolensk also finally surrendered (November). A popular uprising under Prince Pazhatsky reconquered Moscow. As the national uprising spread over northern and eastern Russia, the Poles withdrew, their encircled garrison in Moscow having been massacred after their surrender. From 1613 to 1617 only intermittent border clashes occurred, but in 1617 the Poles again invaded, this time commanded by Hetman Chodkiewicz. Repulsed at the gates of Moscow, the peace treaty of 1618 recognised the Polish conquest of Smolensk. War resumed in 1632 when Russia attempted to retake Smolensk, which was relieved by King Ladislas IV and the Russians under Boris Shein were in turn besieged. Shein surrendered in February 1634, but was executed on his return to Moscow. Peace in 1634 left Poland in possession of its 1609–11 conquests, but Polish claims to the Russian throne were abandoned.

1614–21 The Polish-Turkish War

Polish support for revolts in Ottoman-held Moldavia and Wallachia, and constant raids by Polish Cossacks, led to war with the Turks in 1614. With Poland already at war with Russia, the Ottoman armies laid waste the Polish Ukraine. Poland secured a much-needed victory under Hetman Stanislaw Zolkiewski at Jassy in Moldavia in September 1620. This prompted a massive Ottoman military response, leading to the destruction of Zolkiewski's army at Cecora (December 1620). The battle of Khotin (September 1621) saw a 75,000-strong Polish army inflict 30,000 losses on a vastly larger Ottoman army. Following this battle, a truce was declared. Although the *status quo* was restored, other conflicts between Poland and the Ottomans would soon begin (see p. 133).

1618–48 The Thirty Years' War

This great conflict engulfed Europe for three decades prior to the Peace of Westphalia. It began as a rebellion in May 1618 in Bohemia, gradually spreading throughout the Austrian Monarchy and the Holy Roman Empire. It soon involved Denmark, France, Sweden and Spain. The conflict can be divided into the following six phases:

1. The Bohemian War, 1618–20

This ended in the defeat of the rebels and Frederick V at the battle of the White Mountain by the forces of the Emperor and the Duke of Bavaria.

2. The Palatinate War, 1621–23

This saw the conquest of the Upper Palatinate by Bavaria and of the Rhenish Palatinate by Spain and Bavaria. At the same time, the Revolt of the Netherlands was renewed against Spain following the twelve-year truce.

3. The Danish War, 1624–29

This witnessed the defeat of the anti-Habsburg coalition, organised by the Netherlands under the leadership of Denmark. The Imperialists were successful. The armies of Wallenstein and Bavaria saw the defeat of the Danes at Lutter (1626) and the subsequent Treaty of Lübeck (1629).

4. Imperial supremacy and fall, 1629

The victories of the Imperialists were rapidly lost through such factors as Wallenstein's ambitions towards military dominance and the ill-conceived Edict of Restitution (see p. 248), the aggressive Catholicism of which provoked the Ratisbon (Regensburg) meeting of the Electors and the dismissal of Wallenstein.

5. The Swedish War, 1630–35

Under Gustavus Adolphus, Sweden invaded northern Germany, aided by French subsidies. With their Protestant allies, Sweden defeated the Imperialists at Breitenfeld, subsequently conquering south-west Germany and occupying Bavaria. Wallenstein was recalled by the Emperor. Wallenstein was defeated at Lützen, but Gustavus Adolphus was killed. The German Protestants were then organised into the League of Heilbronn, but were defeated at Nördlingen. The war became increasingly international.

6. The Franco-Habsburg War, 1635–48

This war involved the French conflict against Spain, which was fought in north Italy and along the Rhine as well as against Spain itself. It also saw the Dutch war against Spain in the southern Netherlands, as well as the Swedish-French gains on the Rhine (including Breisach) and north Germany, the Swedish invasions of Bohemia and Moravia and the Franco-Swedish attempt to push to Vienna. The war was concluded with the eventual Peace of Westphalia (see p. 146).

1625–30 The Huguenot Rebellion

The repressive measures of Cardinal Richelieu, who was determined to suppress any possible Protestant threat, led to the Huguenot Rebellion of 1625. With their strength centred on La Rochelle, the Huguenots were led by Duke Henry of Rohan and his brother Soubise. The Huguenot fleet (under Soubise) was defeated by Duke Henry of Montmorency, the High Admiral of France, and La Rochelle was progressively blockaded. English forces, under the Duke of Buckingham, twice attempted to relieve La Rochelle (with unsuccessful expeditions in 1627 and 1628, leading to English losses of 4,000 men). These failures made the fall of La Rochelle inevitable. The Huguenot stronghold finally surrendered on 29 October 1628 (with a mere 5,400 people still alive from a pre-war population of 28,000). In 1629, the Huguenots under Rohan in Languedoc were defeated by Montmorency and by 1630 the revolt was crushed, thus freeing France to enter the Thirty Years' War.

1636–39 The Peasant Rebellions in France

The peasantry of south-west France rose in revolt in 1636 as a result of incessant financial demands by the crown and the need for recruits to fight in the French armies in Germany. The insurgency, numbering perhaps 40,000 *croquants*, was strongest around Périgord. The main *croquant* force was heavily defeated by the Duke of La Vallette at La Sauvetat on 1 June 1637. A further rebellion, against taxation and royal absolutism, arose among the salt workers of Normandy (the *nu-pieds*) in 1639. The rebels (loosely grouped as the 'Army of the Suffering') were defeated by regular French troops at Avrance in December 1639. A further peasant revolt (the Torrébens

127

Rebellion) took place in Brittany. The 15,000 rebels, led by Sebastian Le Balp, were soon defeated.

1638–40 The Bishops' Wars

The hostilities arose between England and Scotland, resulting from the attempt of Charles I to impose Anglicanism and the Episcopacy on the Scots. An army was raised by the Scots and in 1638 war broke out. Charles raised an army to oppose them but did not have the finance to pay his troops. As a result, he was forced to sign the Treaty of Berwick in June 1638 but he refused to agree to the abolition of the Episcopacy in Scotland. The Short Parliament refused Charles money. However, armed with a benevolence, and with further aid from the Irish parliament, war was resumed although the discipline and morale of the army was poor and it was routed near Newcastle. On 26 October 1640 Charles signed the Treaty of Ripon which was virtually a surrender.

1640–52 The Revolt of Catalonia

The rising was provoked by the attempt of Olivares to force provinces other than Castile to provide for the needs of Spain. Rejected by the Catalan *cortés* as an attack on their constitutional liberties (*fueros*), rebellion broke out in May 1640, partly because of the excesses of the Spanish army billeted in Catalonia. On 7 June 1640 the Viceroy was assassinated while attempting to escape. Initially begun by the nobility and bourgeoisie, the peasants then turned against the leaders of the revolt, who in turn handed Catalonia over to France. A reaction to French absolutism led to divisions among an increasingly leaderless revolution. Gradually, Spanish rule was restored (with France being preoccupied with the Frondes). In May 1652 Barcelona finally surrendered.

1641 The War of Castro

The brief war between the Papacy, under Urban VIII, and the Italian princes. It was significant for the disruption it caused to Richelieu's Italian policy.

1642–48 The English Civil Wars

The greatest internal conflict in English history, between the Royalists (supporting Charles I) and the Parliamentarians, arose as a result of the growth of royal power. Hostilities finally began in 1642 when Charles raised the royal standard at Nottingham. The battle of Edgehill in October 1642 was largely inconclusive. The Royalist strategy centred on taking London, but they were frustrated at Newbury. In 1643 Parliament allied with the Scots in the Solemn League and Covenant. With this new ally, Parliament inflicted defeat on the Royalists in 1644 at Marston Moor. This was a setback for the Royalists who in 1643 had achieved some success at the second battle of Newbury. Parliament was strengthened further in 1645 with the creation of the New Model Army and victories at Naseby and Langport followed. In May 1646 the surrender of Charles to the Scots at Newark marked the end of the first Civil War (the Royalist stronghold of Oxford fell in June). An uneasy peace lasted from June 1646 to April 1648.

War resumed when Charles, now armed with a secret alliance with the Scots to establish Presbyterianism in England, was aided by a Scots invasion of England in April 1648. But he was defeated at the battle of Preston in August 1648. Charles was executed on 30 January 1649. Hostilities continued in Ireland (1649–51) and Scotland (1650–51) with risings in favour of Charles I.

1645–70 The Venetian-Ottoman Conflict

This long conflict (sometimes called the Candian War) centred on the Otto-man struggle to control Crete and involved an epic 21-year siege of the island. In August 1645 the Turks captured Canea and in 1646 Retino. The siege of Crete (Candia) began in 1645. Early Venetian naval victories against the Ottomans (in 1649 and 1656) prompted a major expansion of the Turk-ish navy. Ottoman naval success at the Dardanelles in 1657 led to their regaining control of the Aegean in 1658 and the intensification of the siege of Crete in 1666. A French relieving force failed and the Venetian com-mander, General Morosini, finally surrendered on 27 September 1669. The 1670 peace saw Venice lose nearly all of Crete and much of Dalmatia and the Aegean Islands.

1647–48 The Revolt of Naples

The revolt of the Neapolitan peasants, nominally led by Masaniello, took place against oppressive Spanish rule. The revolt, sparked by an additional tax on fruit, began with riots in July 1647. The authorities lost control, the property of the nobility suffered widespread destruction, and the Viceroy hurriedly agreed to a truce. Masaniello was eventually assassinated, but tur-moil continued and a short-lived republic was declared. A large Spanish force crushed the rebellion in 1648. The real leader of the revolt was the populist lawyer, Giulio Genoino.

1648–53 The Wars of the Fronde

The conflict consisted of two civil wars (1648–49 and 1650–53) which racked France after 1648. There was much support among both nobility and the ordinary people against the use of royal prerogative and the burden of taxation under Richelieu and Mazarin. The initial outbreak caused the Court to vacate Paris in 1648 as unrest and rioting continued in the capital. In January 1649 civil war broke out, the rebels having the support of many nobles. Paris was besieged by the Great Condé (January–February 1649) until threat of Spanish intervention produced a truce (Peace of Rueil, March 1649). The brief alliance of Condé and Mazarin collapsed, leading to the second Fronde (the Fronde of the Princes). After Condé's imprisonment, leadership of the Fronde passed to Turenne, but he was defeated at Champ .Blanc (October 1650). The civil war was renewed in September 1651 following the release of the princes in February 1651. Chaos caused by the rival armies of Condé and Turenne engulfed Paris. The rebellion, however, finally collapsed. Louis XIV returned to Paris on 21 October 1652 and Mazarin in February 1653, by which time Condé had joined the Spaniards but to no avail. By August 1653 the Fronde was finally over. The Frondes had constituted the most dangerous revolt ever seen during the *ancien régime* against royal authority.

1648–54 The Cossack Rising

The major rebellion of the Cossacks and peasants of Ukraine under the leadership of the Hetman Bogdan Chmielnicki. In alliance with the Crimean Khan, Chmielnicki inflicted a series of defeats in 1648–49 on the Polish king, John II Casimir (e.g. Zolte Wody, Korsun). A temporary truce at Zborów was followed by a major Polish victory at the battle of Beresteczko (June 1651). Peace at the Treaty of Biala Cerkew (June 1651) was ignored by Chmielnicki, who placed Ukraine under Tsarist protection, thus ensuring a long conflict between Russia and Poland. The Cossack Rising was noted for extreme cruelty and bloody, anti-semitic pogroms, which claimed 150,000 Jewish lives.

1652–54 The First Anglo-Dutch War

Partly as a result of naval rivalry and commercial competition over trade with the East Indies, and partly as a result of the October 1651 Navigation Act, which had struck a blow at the Dutch carrying trade, friction between the two countries ran high. In 1652 the English claim to the right of salute in the Channel led to an action off Dover (19 May) between the fleets under Blake and Martin Tromp. The Dutch retired, losing two ships. At the battle of Kentish Knock (28 September), Blake, with 68 ships, defeated a Dutch fleet of 57 ships led by Tromp and Cornelis de Witt. Other English naval victories followed (e.g. the battle of Scheveningen (31 July 1653)). A twelve-hour battle between fleets of 130 vessels ended in the complete defeat of the Dutch, who lost 30 ships. Tromp was killed and the Dutch fleet took refuge in Texel. Peace was made by the 1654 Treaty of Westminster (see p. 147).

130

1653–59 The Franco-Spanish War

The Peace of Westphalia (see p. 146) had ended French hostilities against the Holy Roman Empire, but war with Spain continued. Paris was threatened in 1653 by an invasion from Spain led by Condé (now a Spanish commander). The French were successful at Arras in August 1654 but were defeated at Lalenciennes (July 1656). The war against Spain was joined by England under Cromwell in 1655. An expedition of 38 ships and 6,000 men was sent to capture Hispaniola (this failed, but Jamaica was occupied). By a treaty of 23 March 1657 with France, England agreed to provide 6,000 men, in French pay, and a fleet, and France an army of 20,000 for operations in Flanders. Mardyck was captured from the Spanish in the autumn. Blake destroyed eleven Spanish ships in an attack on Santa Cruz (20 April). In 1658, at the battle of the Dunes (14 June), French and English forces defeated the Spanish army. Dunkirk surrendered and was ceded to England (Charles II sold it to Louis XIV in 1662). The Peace of the Pyrenees (7 November 1659) ended the war between France and Spain (see p. 147).

1654–56, 1658–67 The Russo-Polish Wars

The offer by the Cossack leader, Bogdan Chmielnicki, to put Ukraine under Russian power in return for aid against Poland, led to the Russo-Polish conflict. Smolensk (lost by the Russians in 1611) was quickly retaken as Polish Lithuania was attacked and conquered up to the River Beresina. Kiev in Ukraine fell, while the Cossacks took revenge by massacring Poles. But a Polish counter-attack was successful at Okhmatov in January 1655. In spring 1655 Russia (helped by the Swedish attack on the Poles that began the First Northern War) resumed the offensive. Success swiftly followed until Poland was aided by the support of the Crimean khan who invaded Ukraine and captured Chmielnicki, thus forcing a Russian withdrawal. A Russo-Polish Truce came about in November 1656 – the prelude to Russia changing sides to enter the First Northern War *against* Sweden. Gaining no success against Sweden, Tsar Alexis resumed the war against Poland. An invasion of Ukraine met with a heavy defeat at Konotop in July 1659 at the hands of the Ukrainian Hetman John Wykowski. With Poland now at peace with Sweden, Polish forces expelled Russian forces from Lithuania, with futher military successes in 1660 at Lubar and Slobodyszcze. These defeats ended the struggle by Chmielnicki to free the Cossacks of Ukraine from Polish rule. After six more years of intermittent frontier fighting, the 1667 Treaty of Andruszov ended the war. Ukraine was divided between Russia and Poland along the River Dnieper while Russia regained Smolensk and Kiev.

1655–60 The First Northern War

One of several conflicts designed to enlarge Sweden's territory along the southern Baltic littoral. In July 1655 Charles X of Sweden declared war on

Poland, which itself was facing war against Russia (see above) and internal division. Swedish success followed swiftly. Warsaw (August) and Cracow (October) fell to the Swedes. Following renewed Swedish victories in 1656, including a major victory at the battle of Warsaw in July 1656, a coalition of Denmark, the Holy Roman Empire and Russia was formed to aid Poland. When Poland renounced its sovereignty of Prussia under the Treaty of Wehlau in favour of Brandenburg, Brandenburg switched allegiance to join Poland. The Swedes withdrew from Poland and hostilities centred on Denmark. Copenhagen withstood a long siege (August 1658–October 1659). Fortunes then changed. A Dutch fleet helped relieve Copenhagen, the Danes defeated the Swedes at Nyborg (November 1659) and on 13 February 1660 Charles X died. Peace was then concluded by the Treaty of Oliva (see p. 147), under which Sweden acquired Livonia.

1661–68 The Portuguese-Spanish War

Although Portugal had regained its independence (lost in 1580) from Spain in November 1640, repeated attempts were made after 1640 to reconquer it. One such attempt was defeated by the Portuguese (with French and English help) at the battle of Montijo (near Badajoz) on 26 May 1644. Under Philip IV, Don Juan José was despatched in 1661 with substantial forces. Despite overrunning Alentejo province, Spanish defeats followed – on 8 June 1663 at Ameixal and later at Montes Claras and Villaviciosa.

1664–89, 1708 The Barbary Wars

Numerous attempts were made by such maritime powers as England and France to end the ravages of the North African corsairs on vulnerable shipping in the Mediterranean. A French expedition against Djidjelli was defeated in 1664, while in 1669 Algiers (the corsair capital) was blockaded by an English fleet. Despite Algiers seeking peace in 1670, conflict soon resumed. French vessels shelled Algiers in 1682 (and again in 1683). Tripoli, Tunis and Algiers were bombarded in 1688. In 1689 Algiers requested peace terms. The conflict, however, never died away. In 1708 Oran was taken from the Spaniards in a major Barbary victory.

1665–67 The Second Anglo-Dutch War

Conflict between England and Holland, which resulted from commercial rivalry, the English seizure of New Amsterdam and the attack on Dutch slaving ports in West Africa, was renewed in March 1665. Although an English fleet defeated the Dutch off Lowestoft (June 1665), the war widened when France entered the conflict against England (which had earlier declared war on Denmark). The naval war saw mixed fortunes until a Dutch fleet burnt

Sheerness and entered the Medway (June 1667). This gave urgency to England's desire for peace which was subsequently concluded at the Treaty of Breda in July 1667 (see p. 147).

1667–68 The War of Devolution

The first (albeit relatively minor) of the expansionist wars waged by Louis XIV. It was based on the claim, following the death of his father-in-law Philip IV of Spain, of the inheritance right of devolution over the Spanish Netherlands. On 24 May 1667 Turenne invaded the Spanish Netherlands. Much of Flanders was quickly subdued. Rapid French success prompted the formation of an Anglo-Dutch-Swedish Triple Alliance against Louis XIV. However Louis, now armed with a secret treaty to partition the Spanish empire if Charles II died without heirs, was willing to make peace. The subsequent Treaty of Aix-la-Chapelle (May 1668) restored Franche-Comté to Spain.

1670–71 The Cossack Revolt

The great rebellion of the Cossacks, led by Stenka Razin, against the Tsar. Tsaritsyn quickly fell and a 10,000-strong Cossack force took Astrakhan. As the rebellion grew, a two-pronged Cossack invasion was mounted along the Volga and Don. On the Volga, the rebels were halted at Simbirsk. On the Don, the Cossacks were defeated at Korotoyak. A Russian counter-offensive succeeded in defeating and capturing Razin in April 1671. He was subsequently tortured and executed (June 1671). Finally, Astrakhan, the last remaining city in rebel hands, was taken by Prince Miloslavsky in November 1671. An estimated 100,000 people were killed in the rebellion.

1671–76 The Polish-Turkish War

With the refusal of the Ukrainian Cossack leader Peter Doroshenke to accept Polish suzerainty, and when Poland refused to cede Ukraine to the Ottomans, Sultan Mohammed IV declared war in December 1671. Kamienic was besieged in August 1672 (with its entire garrison blowing itself up) and the following month Lublin fell. Following these defeats, and with civil war threatening, Poland signed the Treaty of Buczácz in October 1672. War resumed under John Sobieski when the Polish diet refused to ratify the treaty, which had surrendered Podolia and western Ukraine. Under Sobieski's leadership, the Ottomans were heavily defeated at Khotin (Chocim) in November 1673. A general Ottoman withdrawal from Poland followed, while Sobieski was elected the new King of Poland. A second Ottoman invasion was then checked at the battle of Lvov (August 1675). A third and final Ottoman invasion (with 200,000 forces) failed to take the fortified Polish positions at Zorawno (September–October 1676). With this effective stalemate, terms were agreed at the Treaty of Zorawno in October. Most of the Ottoman Polish conquests were surrendered, Podolia was divided and western Ukraine was formally returned to Poland.

1672–74 The Third Anglo-Dutch War

Under the secret Treaty of Dover (22 May 1670) Charles II agreed to support French operations against Holland in return for a large subsidy. On 17 March 1672 England declared war on the Dutch. An English naval victory at Southwold Bay (27 May 1672) was followed a year later by Dutch success at the battle of Schoonveldt Channel (28 May 1673) when the allied fleet was driven off as it attacked the Dutch coastal anchorage. At the battle of Texel on 11 August 1673, De Ruyter successfully escorted an East Indies convoy and the allies were unable to carry out their plans for a descent on Holland. The inconclusive conflict was ended by the Treaty of Westminster on 19 February 1674.

1672–78 The Franco-Dutch War

In May 1672 French forces invaded the Netherlands, quickly conquering southern Holland and even threatening Amsterdam. The French were fortified in the knowledge that Holland had been isolated from her normal allies by a series of treaties (the secret Treaty of Dover with England in June 1670, other treaties with Sweden, Cologne and Münster). Faced with the French advance, Holland concluded alliances with Leopold I, Frederick William of Brandenburg (who quickly made the separate Treaty of Vossem with Louis XIV in June 1673) and eventually Christian V of Denmark (1674). Louis XIV then redirected his attack towards Franche-Comté and the Spanish Netherlands. A series of French successes followed – Valenciennes in March 1677, and the capture of Ghent and Ypres in 1678. Earlier, France had won naval successes in the Mediterranean. The war was settled by the Treaties of Nijmegen in September 1678 and February 1679 (see p. 148). Separately, Denmark restored her conquests from Sweden by the Peace of Fontainebleau (September 1679) and the Elector of Brandenburg restored his Swedish conquests by the Treaty of St Germain-en-Laye (June 1679).

1678–81, 1695–1700 The Russo-Turkish Wars

The expansion of Russia towards the Black Sea, and the onset of the prolonged decline of the Ottoman Empire led to a series of wars from the late seventeenth century onwards. In the first war, which devastated the battleground of Ukraine from 1678 to 1681, a stalemate emerged. War was renewed in 1695 when Tsar Peter sent a 31,000-strong army in an unsuccessful attempt to take Azov. Returning in 1696, and now armed with a navy, Peter took Azov on 28 July 1696. The war was ended by a truce in 1700.

1682, 1698 The *Streltsy* Rebellions

The *streltsy* (see p. 263) had risen to considerable strength in seventeenth-century Russia. With 22 regiments (each comprising 1,000 men), they rose in revolt in May 1682, following the death of Tsar Alexis, at the perceived threat to their position by the boyars (see p. 243). Their rebellion, which was accompanied by massacres of the boyars, placed Sophia in power as Regent of the ten-year-old Peter. Eventually Peter took his place on the throne and the boyars once again rose in influence. A new *streltsy* rebellion (of 2,000 men from four regiments) was put down by a 4,000-strong force under the boyar Alexis Shein. The *streltsy* were then mercilessly crushed, in an orgy of torture and execution. Ensuring they never rose again, the last 16 regiments of the *streltsy* were disbanded.

1682–99 The Habsburg-Ottoman War

Once again this latest conflict in the series of wars between the Habsburg and Ottoman Empires was centred on Hungary, where Magyar rebels, led by Emeric Tokoly (Imre Tököly), had staged an uprising in 1678 to break free from Habsburg rule. Virtually defeated, Tokoly appealed for Ottoman assistance. A major Ottoman army (reaching 200,000 strong when forces from Transylvania under Prince Michael Apafi joined) was despatched under Grand Vizier Kara Mustafa in March 1683. In response, the Habsburgs concluded an alliance with King John Sobieski of Poland. The Ottomans conquered Upper Hungary and besieged Vienna in June 1683 until they were forced to retreat by the arrival of Sobieski in August. The Ottomans, now demoralised, subsequently lost Gran, much of northern Hungary, then Pest, Buda and even Belgrade in September 1688. When Austria seemed all-conquering, the Ottomans launched a speedy comeback after 1689, reconquering Serbia. However, the Habsburgs successfully held the Turks and the battle of Szalánkemen (1691) was followed by the Habsburgs gaining control of Transylvania. In 1697 the Turks were totally routed by Prince Eugene of Savoy at the battle of Zenta. Peace was concluded by the Treaty of Carlowitz (Karlowitz) in January 1699 (see p. 149).

1684 The Conquest of Luxembourg

An expansionist French military invasion was launched against Luxembourg in 1684. After an easy victory over the Spanish defending forces (at a cost of 2,500 French casualties), France held Luxembourg until its return to Spain under the 1697 Treaty of Ryswick (Ryswijk).

1688–89 The Glorious Revolution

The climax of the events in England which began with the accession of the Catholic James II (1633–1701) on 6 February 1685 and which eventually led to his exile and the accession to the throne of his daughter, Mary (1662–94) and her husband William of Orange (1650–1702). James's unconstitutional rule and pro-Catholicism led seven leading members of the Lords to invite William to invade England. As William prepared, James frantically tried to rescind his previous policies, but to no avail. On 5 November 1688 William landed at Torbay with 11,000 infantry and 4,000 cavalry. The English peerage and gentry rallied to him. James was allowed to flee to France and William and Mary became joint sovereigns after accepting the Declaration of Rights and the Bill of Rights.

1689–91 The War of the English Succession

The attempt of James II to regain the throne and Louis XIV's desire to distract Wiliam III from the war in Flanders are known as the War of the English Succession. James II's attempt to regain his throne began with his landing in Ireland in March 1689. The subsequent siege of Londonderry (April–July 1689) and his defeat at the battle of the Boyne (1 July 1690) by William followed. James fled to France, although fighting continued in Ireland until the battle of Aughrim on 12 July 1691 finally put an end to James II's ambitions.

1688–97 The War of the League of Augsburg

Faced with the policy of territorial aggrandisement pursued by Louis XIV (the concept of *réunion*), an anti-French alliance had been formed of the Emperor Leopold I, Spain, Bavaria and various Circles of the Empire (the 1686 League of Augsburg). During the War of the League of Augsburg (or War of the Palatinate Succession as it was also known), the alliance was joined by England, Savoy and the United Provinces (giving the War a third alternative name as the War of the Grand Alliance).

The war was precipitated by the French invasion of the Rhenish Palatinate on 24 September 1688. The war extended far beyond the Rhineland (the Palatinate itself was devastated by French troops during 1689). The war was fought to a large degree at sea, in the American colonies (where it was known as King William's War) and in lesser theatres, such as French support for Catholic rebels in Ireland. The naval conflict resulted in an allied victory at La Hogue (May 1692) but on land the allies were defeated at Steenkerke (August 1692) and Neerwinden (July 1693). The French were successful in Savoy (1690) and Nice (1691) and took Barcelona in 1697, but were thwarted by allied naval domination from further gains. Savoy and France agreed terms in 1696. Peace was eventually agreed at Ryswick (see p. 148) when

William III was recognised as King of England and all territories taken since the 1678 Treaty of Nijmegen were restored.

1700–21 The Great Northern War

The war was waged between Sweden under Charles XII and a coalition of Russia (under Peter the Great), Denmark, Saxony, Poland and eventually Prussia and Hanover. All were opposed to Swedish dominance in the Baltic. In April 1700 Denmark opened the first phase of the war by invading Schleswig, while Livonia was invaded by the Saxon forces of Augustus II (Augustus the Strong) (June 1700). A swift military response by Sweden (embracing a landing near Copenhagen) knocked Denmark out of the war at the Treaty of Travendal in August 1700. The military success of Sweden continued at Narva (20 November 1700) over the Russians and Riga (June 1701) over the Saxon troops. Courland was annexed after a further Swedish victory at Dunamunde (July 1701). Cracow soon followed (July 1702) and eventually Augustus II was forced to make peace at Altranstädt in September 1706. The war changed quite dramatically when, following the Swedish invasion of Russia in January 1708, the Russians inflicted a major defeat on the invaders at Poltava in July 1709. Charles fled to Turkey. An Ottoman declaration of war on Russia was hurriedly settled by the Peace of the Pruth, leaving Charles feeling betrayed. Charles eventually returned to Sweden but was killed at Frederikshall in 1718 and Sweden's ambitions fell with him. A series of treaties ended the war: with Hanover in November 1719; with Prussia in February 1720; and with Denmark in July 1720. Sweden was forced to accept the Treaty of Nystad with Russia in 1721 (see p. 151).

1701–14 The War of the Spanish Succession

In November 1700, the childless Charles II of Spain died and Louis XIV's grandson became Philip V of Spain. The ensuing war for the Spanish crown was fought by the 'Grand Alliance' of the Emperor Leopold I and the major naval powers of Britain and Holland, later joined by Portugal and Savoy, against the forces of France. In February 1701 Philip of Anjou entered Madrid. The southern Spanish Netherlands was occupied by French troops, but after this French high point, in May 1704, the Archduke Charles entered Lisbon and was also proclaimed King of Spain. Portugal joined the Grand Alliance. The French (and their Bavarian allies) suffered a major defeat at the battle of Blenheim at the hands of the Duke of Marlborough and Prince Eugene (13 August 1704). In 1705 Barcelona was captured by the British and Charles III was recognised in Aragon, Catalonia and Valencia. Thereafter, French and Spanish troops won a series of victories (Almanza in 1707, Brihuega and Villaviciosa in 1710) before suffering defeats at Almenara and Saragossa, both in the summer of 1710. The changing fortunes of war had left all sides exhausted. Despite Bourbon control in Spain, elsewhere the allies held the upper hand and increasingly peace seemed the most desirable option. Negotiations began in January 1712 at Utrecht. The war was finally ended by the 1713 Peace of Utrecht (see p. 149) and the 1714 Peace of Rastatt (see p. 150).

1715, 1745 The Jacobite Rebellions

These were rebellions by the Scots in support of the Jacobite cause. The first rebellion came when the Earl of Mar raised the Stuart standard at Braemar on 6 September 1715. The rebellion faltered when Mar failed to dislodge the royal army under Argyll from Sheriffmuir, north of Stirling, on 13 November, and on the same day a Jacobite army surrendered at Preston. The Pretender landed in Scotland on 22 December, but as Argyll advanced the Jacobite army dispersed, and James sailed again for France on 5 February 1716.

Thirty years later, a further Jacobite rebellion took place. Prince Charles Edward, the Young Pretender, raised his standard at Glenfinnan on 19 August 1745. He occupied Edinburgh on 17 September and defeated a royalist army under Sir John Cope at Prestonpans on 20 September. On 31 October, Charles Edward led an army of 5,000 men south into England. The Jacobites reached Derby on 4 December, but their hopes of an English uprising were disappointed, and the decision to retreat was taken the following day. The rebellion had its last success with a victory at Falkirk on 17 January 1746, but on 16 April the Duke of Cumberland decisively defeated the Jacobites at Culloden, near Inverness. Charles Edward later escaped to France in September 1746.

1716–18 The Austro-Turkish War

The Ottomans, already in conflict with Venice since 1714, declared war on Austria in April 1716 after Emperor Charles VI had renewed his alliance with Venice. The Ottomans suffered major defeats at the hands of Prince Eugene – at Peterwardein in August 1716, followed by the loss of Temesvar, their last Hungarian stronghold, in October. In August 1717 Prince Eugene completed a successful campaign by taking Belgrade. The conflict was ended by the Treaty of Passarowitz in July 1718 (see p. 150), confirming the Austrian possession of Hungary. Venice lost the Morea.

1718–20 The War of the Quadruple Alliance

Following the Spanish occupation of Sardinia in November 1717 and Sicily in July 1718, the Quadruple Alliance was formed by France, Austria, Britain and Holland on 2 August 1718 to oppose Philip of Spain's designs on Italy and France. On 11 August 1718, Admiral Byng destroyed the Spanish fleet off Cape Passaro. The British fleet then supported Austrian operations in Sicily and carried out raids on the Galician coast in October 1719. The war was ended by the Treaty of The Hague on 17 February 1720, by which Philip gave up his claims. Fighting took place briefly between Spain and France and Britain in 1727 over the implementation of the terms of the Treaty of The Hague. The dispute over Philip's son's succession to the Italian duchies was resolved by the Treaty of Seville in November 1729, in which Charles's claims were recognised (see p. 151).

1733–38 The War of the Polish Succession

The war broke out after February 1733 as a result of the disputed election to the throne of Poland following the death of Augustus II. The rival candidates were Stanislaw Leszczyński, the father-in-law of Louis XV, who had been King of Poland from 1704 to 1709 (he was supported by France, Spain and Savoy-Sardinia). The other was Augustus III, the Elector of Saxony, who was supported by Austria and Russia. In Poland, a major Russian offensive, aided by Saxon troops, eventually secured Danzig in June 1734, although Stanislaw had fled. Elsewhere, France attacked Austrian possessions in Lorraine and Italy, defeating Austria at Parma on 29 June 1734. Subsequently, Austrian losses mounted rapidly in Italy until only Milan remained. The French had some success on the Upper Rhine, eventually taking Philippsburg. Despite its promise under the 1731 Treaty of Vienna, Britain under Walpole refused to aid the Emperor Charles VI. Although peace preliminaries were agreed in October 1735, prolonged negotiations preceded the definitive Treaty of Vienna of 18 November 1738. Augustus III secured the Polish throne. Important changes took place in Italy (see p. 152).

1736–39 The Austro-Russian-Turkish War

With war against the Persians over, and urged on by France to enter the war of the Polish Succession, the Turks found themselves faced with war against Russia in 1737. Russia (supported by the Emperor Charles VI) wanted revenge for the terms of the 1711 Treaty of Pruth and to retake Azov. Russian forces gained the advantage over the Turks in Moldavia, Ukraine and elsewhere, having taken Azov on 1 July 1736. Austria, alarmed at the prospect of Russian military success, signed the Treaty of Belgrade with the Turks, surrendering Serbia and Belgrade. Now isolated, Russia made its own Treaty of Nissa with the Ottomans in October 1739. Under its terms, the Russians agreed not to construct a Black Sea fleet and destroyed the fortifications of Azov.

1740–48 The War of the Austrian Succession

Colonial conflicts, and particularly the incident in which Captain Jenkins claimed to have had his ear cut off by a Spanish official, led Britain to declare war on Spain on 19 October 1739. This war became part of a wider European conflict when Frederick the Great of Prussia launched his campaign to seize Silesia from Maria Theresa of Austria on 16 December 1740. King George II, commanding in person an army of British, Hanoverian and Dutch troops in support of Maria Theresa, defeated the French at Dettingen on 27 June 1743. In May 1745 the French began an advance into the Austrian Netherlands, defeated the Duke of Cumberland at Fontenoy on 10 May and completed their conquest of Flanders. In 1747 the French invaded Holland and defeated the allies at Lauffeld on 2 July. At sea, Admiral Anson, who had carried out a circumnavigation and raided Spanish possessions from 1740 to 1744, defeated the French at the first battle of Finisterre on 3 May 1747. Admiral Hawke achieved a similar victory over a convoy escort in a second battle in October. In North America, Louisburg was captured from the French in June 1745, but in India, Madras was lost in September 1746. They were exchanged by the Treaty of Aix-la-Chapelle, signed on 18 October 1748, which brought the war in Europe to a close.

1741–43 The Russo-Swedish War (the War of the Hats)

In 1738 the Swedish 'Hats' (the pro-French party) (see p. 243) succeeded in overthrowing Horn and the 'Caps' (the anti-noble faction). Gyllenborg became head of government. In 1741, seeking to take advantage of the palace coup in Russia which had ousted Biren and to recapture the territories lost in the Great Northern War, Sweden attacked Russia. Russia responded forcibly and under the 1743 Treaty of Åbo acquired from Sweden the Finnish province of Kymmenegard.

1756–63 The Seven Years' War

Britain and France declared war on 17 May 1756, but the war in Europe began when Frederick the Great invaded Saxony in August, precipitating one of the greatest European wars of the eighteenth century. In 1757 a French army invaded Hanover and defeated the allies at Hastenbeck on 26 July. The Duke of Cumberland signed the Convention of Kloster-Seven on 8 September, disbanding his army, but this was repudiated after Frederick the Great's victory at Rossbach on 5 November 1757. Ferdinand of Brunswick took command of the allied army and Pitt began the payment of subsidies to Frederick the Great. On 1 August 1759 Ferdinand routed the French at Minden, and on 31 July 1760 saved Hanover by a victory at Warburg. While Prussia bore the brunt of the fighting in Europe, in North America Britain mounted a fourfold attack on the French in 1758. This culminated in Wolfe's victory before Quebec on 13 September 1759 and the capture of the city. On 8 September 1760 the Marquis de Vaudreuil surrendered Montreal and with it French Canada. French plans to invade England were disrupted by Admiral Boscawen's victory at Lagos Bay on 18 August 1759 and Hawke's victory at

Quiberon Bay on 20 November. A French expedition to Ireland surrendered at Kinsale in February 1760. Following the outbreak of war with Spain in January 1762, Britain seized Havana and Manila. The death of Empress Elizabeth of Russia on 5 January 1762 led to a peace treaty between Prussia and Russia on 5 May 1762. Britain, France, Spain and Portugal signed the Treaty of Paris on 10 February 1763, and Prussia, Austria and Saxony concluded the Treaty of Hubertusburg on 15 February.

TREATIES AND ALLIANCES

The following chronological list covers some of the more important treaties, alliances and congresses which students are likely to encounter. The myriad shifting alliances of individual countries, and some of the more important marriage settlements and commercial treaties, are to be found in the individual country chronologies.

1466   Second **Peace of Thorn** (Torun) ended the Thirteen Years' War (see p. 117). Much of Prussia was acquired by Poland. The Grand Master of the Teutonic Order was forced to accept nominal Polish overlordship.

1479   **Treaty of Alçacovas** (September) confirmed the Portuguese monopoly over the Guinea trade. Portuguese possession of Madeira, the Azores and Cape Verde was also confirmed. Only the Canaries remained with Castile.

1488   **Swabian League** founded in Germany (at Esslingen). It consisted not only of the Emperor Frederick III and 22 Imperial Cities but also of the Swabian knights' League of St George's Shield, and the bishops and princes of Tyrol, Württemberg, the Palatinate, Mainz, Trier, Baden, Hesse, Bavaria, Ansbach and Bayreuth. The League was governed by a federal council of three colleges of princes, cities and knights, calling upon an army of 13,000 men. The League was renewed in 1512, but was disbanded in 1534.

1489   **Treaty of Medina del Campo**, by which England and Aragon agreed to the marriage of Prince Arthur and the Infanta Catherine.

1494   **Treaty of Tordesillas**. The pact between Spain and Portugal which established a line of demarcation running through the Atlantic. Lands west of the line were reserved for Spain, those east of the line for Portugal. This treaty modified an earlier award (of 1493) by Pope Alexander VI which would have denied Portugal any lands in the western hemisphere. Under the Treaty of Tordesillas, Brazil was reserved for Portugal.

1495   **League of Venice** was an important alliance against France joined by the Emperor, Spain, Milan, Venice and Pope Alexander VI.

1496   **Magnus Intercursus**. The popular name for the commercial treaty between England and the Netherlands.

1499	**Treaty of Basle** ended the Grisons War between the Swiss and Emperor Maximilian and confirmed the independence of the Swiss Confederation from Imperial authority.
1504	**Treaty of Blois** ended the war between France and Spain. Claude (the daughter of Louis XII and Anne of Brittany) was betrothed to Archduke Charles (the grandson of Maximilian and Mary of Burgundy and of the dual monarchs Ferdinand and Isabella), with a promise to cede Brittany and Burgundy should Louis XII die without a son.
1508	**League of Cambrai** was an alliance of major powers in Italy against Venice.
1511	**The Holy League** was an alliance formed by Pope Julius II for the expulsion of the French from Italy.
1512	Alliance of Scotland and France, and of Maximilian I with Pope Julius II.
	Renewal of the Swabian League.
1514	Alliance of Henry VIII of England with Louis XII of France to establish peace and to arrange the marriage of Princess Mary.
1516	**Concordat of Bologna** between Francis I of France and Papacy (August). The convention replaced the Pragmatic Sanction of Bourges, which had been adopted at the Assembly of Bourges in 1438 but which had never been recognised by the Pope. The annates were re-established and the French king was given the right of nominating bishops.
	Treaty of Freiburg between France and the Swiss Cantons (also known as the 'Treaty of Perpetual Peace').
1520	Meeting of Henry VIII and Francis I at the **Field of the Cloth of Gold**.
1521	**Alliance of Bruges** between Henry VIII, Charles V and Pope Leo X for the expulsion of the French from Italy and for the suppression of heresy.
1522	**Alliance of Windsor** between Henry VIII and Charles V.
1524	**Catholic Alliance of Regensburg** (Ratisbon) (June) between Archduke Ferdinand, the Duke of Bavaria and various southern German ecclesiastical princes.
1525	**Catholic League of Dessau** (July) included Duke George of Saxony, Elector of Brandenburg and the Archbishop of Mainz.
1526	**Treaty of Madrid** (14 January) between Charles V and Francis I, by which Francis was released from captivity in return for the cession of Burgundy.
	League of Cognac and the Protestant **Alliance of Torgau**. The League of Cognac comprised France, Florence, Venice and

Milan. The Alliance of Torgau comprised the Elector of Saxony, the Landgrave of Hesse, the Prince of Mecklenburg, the Prince of Anhalt and the Prince of Brunswick-Lüneburg.

1529   Formation of Protestant **League of Speyer** which included the Elector of Saxony, the Landgrave of Hesse and the Count of Brandenburg-Ansbach.

1529   **Treaty of Cambrai**, by which Francis I renounced all claims to Italy, and all claims over Flanders and Artois. Charles V's right to succession to Gelderland was also recognised and Francis gave up Tournai.

1530   **First Conference of Bologna** between Charles V and Pope Clement VII.

1530–31   **League of Schmalkalden** marked the emergence of a Protestant League whose early adherents were the Elector of Saxony, the Landgrave of Hesse, the Counts of Anhalt and Mansfeld and the Duke of Brunswick-Lüneburg.

1536   Alliance of France with the Ottoman Turks. With the Turks threatening many outposts of Christianity in the eastern Mediterranean, the alliance scandalised Christian Europe.

1538   **Truce of Nice** between Charles V and Francis I.

1544   **Peace of Crépy** (September) between France and the Holy Roman Empire, by which all conquests since the Truce of Nice were to be given up. Francis gave up all claims to Naples, Flanders, Artois, Gelderland and Zutphen. Charles V promised his daughter Mary, or his niece, the second daughter of Ferdinand, as wife of the Duke of Orléans, the dowry to be the Netherlands and Franche-Comté or Milan. Charles gave up all claim to Burgundy and the Somme towns.

1546   **Peace of Ardres** (June) between England and France, by which Boulogne was restored (after eight years) to France.

1547   **Imperial League**. The Catholic alliance of King Ferdinand, the Emperor, the Duke of Bavaria and Moritz of Saxony.

League of Princes was formed to oppose Charles V.

1552   **League of Saxony** was the grouping of the princes led by the Elector of Saxony and the Landgrave of Hesse, in collaboration with King Henry II of France, against Charles V.

1555   The religious **Peace of Augsburg** recognised both Catholicism and Lutheranism as legitimate religions in the Holy Roman Empire. The peace also established the principle of *cuius regio, eius religio* (see p. 247).

1559   **Peace of Cateau-Cambrésis** (3 April). Among the provisions of this major settlement were: (1) the restoration of Savoy and Piedmont to Emmanuel Philibert with the exception of five places; (2) the mutual cession of French and Spanish conquests from each other; (3) the French retention of Calais for eight more years; and (4) the French retention of Saluzzo.

1562   **Treaty of Richmond** (September) between Elizabeth of England and Louis de Bourbon, Prince of Condé, for English assistance in the defence of Rouen and the occupation of Dieppe and Le Havre.

1563   **Pacification of Amboise**. The first Edict of Pacification in the French Wars of Religion. (For this and other edicts, see pp. 166–9.)

1564   **League of Landsberg**. A Catholic alliance of the Duke of Bavaria and various bishops.

1568   **Holy League**. An alliance against the Turks of Philip II of Spain, Venice and the Papacy.

1570   **Edict of St Germain**. A seminal edict in the French Wars of Religion, it aimed at restoring peace (see p. 167).

1571   **Triple Alliance** between the Papacy, Spain and Venice against the Turks.

1576   **Peace of Monsieur**. The most liberal edict of the French Wars of Religion, it allowed Protestants to practise their faith freely except in the vicinity of Paris (see p. 168).

1577   **Peace of Bergerac** (17 September) modified the Peace of Monsieur (see above and p. 168).

1579   **Union of Utrecht**. The union of the seven provinces of Holland, Zealand, Utrecht, Friesland, Gelderland, Groningen and Overijssel which laid the foundation of the United Provinces.

1585   **Treaty of Nemours** (7 July) rescinded all earlier edicts of pacification in the French Wars of Religion and banned the exercise of the Protestant faith.

1585   **Treaty of Nonsuch** (10 August) provided English aid to the United Provinces of the Netherlands. It was supplemented on 12 August 1585 and renewed on 16 August 1598.

1588   **Edict of Union**. Henry III of France agrees to the demands of Guise for upholding Catholicism in France.

1598   **Edict of Nantes** (April). The most famous edict of the French Wars of Religion, it gave the Huguenots liberty of conscience and certain concessions (see p. 169).

1598   **Peace of Vervins** (May) ended the French war with Spain. Spain restored all conquered territories except Cambrai.

1601   **Treaty of Lyons** between France and Savoy, by which France acquired Bresse and Bugey, Valromey and Gex.

1608   Foundation of the Protestant **Evangelical Union** (May). The union was agreed at Anhausen (near Nördlingen) and joined by the Elector Palatine, the Count of Neuberg, the Duke of Württemberg and the rulers of Ansbach, Kulmbach and Baden-Durlach.

1609   Formation of the **Catholic League** (July) followed the 1608 Evangelical Union. The Catholic League consisted of the Archduke Leopold and the Catholic Bishops of Würzburg, Augsburg, Ratisbon (Regensburg) and Konstanz (with many later signatories, including the Bishops of Worms, Cologne and Mainz).

1610   **Alliance of Brosolo** by which France and Savoy united against Milan.

1613   **Treaty of Knärod** ended the Swedish-Danish War. Sweden gained Kalmar. Elfsborg was retained by Denmark for six years (until redemption money was paid).

1617   **Peace of Stolbova** (February) between Sweden and Russia. Territorial gains by Sweden included Ingria and Karelia, including the key fortresses controlling Livonia and Finland.

1622   **Treaty of Montpellier** between the Huguenots and French crown, by which the Huguenots were compelled to accept the prohibition of all political meetings. Two 'safe towns' were left to the Huguenots – La Rochelle and Montauban. It confirmed the Edict of Nantes.

1631   **Treaty of Cherasco**, by which the French and Imperialist armies withdrew from Italy.

1633   **League (Union) of Heilbronn**. The alliance of Sweden and the German Protestants in the war against the Holy Roman Empire (it was signed at Heilbronn).

1635   **Peace of Prague**. The treaty between Emperor Ferdinand II and the Elector of Saxony, by which Saxony acquired Lusatia. It also recognised Lutheranism as the only privileged religion.

1648   **Peace of Westphalia** (October) was signed at Münster and Osnabrück between the Empire, France and Sweden. It incorporated the earlier peace (of January 1648) between Spain and the United Provinces. The main settlement of the Thirty Years' War, it provided for the recognition of the independence of the United Provinces and the Swiss Cantons, territorial gains at the expense of the Emperor in Germany by France, Sweden, Saxony and Brandenburg, and recognition of Lutherans and Calvinists. For many Princes and Imperial Cities it meant effective independence. Thus Germany was left as a patchwork of absolute monarchies in which the Catholic counter-reformation had failed to eradicate Protestantism. Among the victors, France gained the Austrian possessions of Upper and Lower Alsace, the Sundgau and Breisach, with Metz, Toul and Verdun, as well as prefecture over ten Imperial Cities in Alsace. Sweden got

Western Pomerania and several towns and islands. Brandenburg also made certain territorial acquisitions. Bavaria retained the electoral dignity, while a new electorate was created for the Elector Palatine.

1649   **Treaty of Rueil** ended the first Fronde in France (see p. 129).

1651   Formation of the **Catholic League** and the **Protestant League** to implement the Peace of Westphalia. Formed at Frankfurt, the Catholic League encompassed the three ecclesiastical electors, the Count Palatine, and the Bishop of Münster. It was joined later by the Circles of Swabia, Franconia and Lower Saxony. The Protestant League comprised Christina of Sweden, the Landgravine of Hesse, and the Duke of Brunswick-Lüneburg.

1652   **Alliance of Hildesheim**, formed by Sweden and the North German Protestants.

1654   **Treaty of Westminster** (5 April) by which the Dutch paid compensation for the Amboyna Massacre of 1623 and agreed to make annual payment to fish in English waters and to respect the Navigation Act and the English right of salute. The treaty ended the first Anglo-Dutch War.

1658   Formation of the **League of the Rhine** under French protection (2 August). Its members included the three ecclesiastical Electors together with Münster, Neuburg, Brunswick, Hesse-Cassel, Sweden, Bavaria and the King of France.

1659   **Peace of the Pyrenees** (November) between France and Spain was signed on the island of Bidassoa (near the Pyrenees). France gained Artois and a number of fortresses in Flanders, Hainault and Luxembourg, and most of Roussillon and Cerdagne. A marriage was arranged between Louis XIV and the Infanta of Spain, Maria Theresa, daughter of Philip IV. Spain resigned claims to Alsace and Prince de Condé was restored to his Governorship of Burgundy.

1660   **Peace of Oliva** between Brandenburg, Poland, Austria and Sweden which ended the First Northern War. John Casimir of Poland abandoned claims to the Swedish throne and Sweden acquired Livonia.

1667   **Treaty of Andruszov** (January) concluded the Thirteen Years' War between Russia and Poland (see p. 131). Under its terms, Poland gave up Kiev, Smolensk, Chernigov and some territory beyond the Dnieper.

          Peace of Breda between England and the United Provinces made certain commercial concessions to the Dutch. Acadia was surrendered to the French and Surinam to the Dutch, who accepted, however, English possession of the North American colonies.

147

| 1668 | **Peace of Aix-la-Chapelle** (May) between Louis XIV of France and Spain. |

1668   **Peace of Aix-la-Chapelle** (May) between Louis XIV of France and Spain.

1670   **Treaty of Dover** A secret treaty of 22 May 1670 between Charles II and Louis XIV of France. In return for French subsidies, Charles agreed to assist the French in their war against the Dutch. He also undertook to declare himself a Roman Catholic.

1674   **Triple Alliance** was an anti-French alliance concluded between the Emperor, Spain and the United Provinces but subsequently joined by the Pope and the Elector of Brandenburg.

1678/79   **Peace of Nijmegen** comprised two settlements: the first (a) between France and the United Provinces in August; and the second (b) between France and Spain in September.

       (a) France returned Maastricht and its dependencies to the United Provinces and Messina back to Spain. The Dutch received favourable commercial advantages and Colbert's hostile tariff was given up. William of Orange recovered Orange and his estates in the Spanish Netherlands, France, Franche-Comté and the Charolais.

       (b) France restored Charleroi, Binch, Ath, Oudenarde, Courtrai, Limburg and its Duchy, Ghent, Rodenhus, Leuze, St Ghislain and Puycerda in Catalonia to Spain but retained the strongholds of Valenciennes, Condé, Bouchain, Maubeuge, Cambrai, Saint Omer, Aire, Ypres, Warneton, Cassel and Franche-Comté.

       In a separate treaty with the Empire, France restored Philippsburg, but retained Freiburg (with passage across the Rhine at Breisach) and agreed to the restoration of the Duke of Lorraine under the conditions of 1659. He refused to accept these terms.

1684   **Holy League of Linz** was an alliance of the Empire, Poland and Venice against the Ottomans.

1686   **League of Augsburg** was an agreement uniting the Emperor, Sweden, Saxony, the Palatinate and Brandenburg against France.

1689   **First Grand Alliance** was the anti-French alliance formed between the Emperor Leopold I, Holland, England and Bavaria, and was joined later by Spain, Savoy and Saxony.

1697   **Treaty of Ryswick (Ryswijk)**, signed in a village in the province of South Holland, ended the War of the Grand Alliance. Under its terms, the Dutch Barrier was set up and Louis XIV recognised William III as King of England. France also agreed to return Luxembourg to Spain and key fortresses on the right bank of the Rhine, including Philippsburg and Breisach, to the Empire. Outside Europe, the Dutch restored Pondicherry to the French, and England and France mutually restored conquests in America.

1698   The **First Partition Treaty** was signed by England, France and Dutch Republic. Its main provisions were as follows: the Electoral Prince of Bavaria was to have Spain, the Spanish Netherlands and the Spanish possessions in the New World; the Dauphin was to have the Two Sicilies and the Tuscan ports of Porto Ercole, Porto San Stephano, Orbitello, Piombino, Finale and Guipuzcoa; the Archduke Charles was to have Milan.

1699   **Treaty of Carlowitz** ended the war of Austria, Russia, Poland and Venice against the Ottoman Turks. Under its terms, Austria obtained Hungary, except the Banat of Temesvár, Transylvania and the greater part of Slavonia and Croatia. Russia kept Azov. Poland recovered the territories in Podolia, lost to Mohammed IV. Venice restored all conquests north of the Isthmus of Corinth, but retained the Morea.

1700   **Second Partition Treaty**, ratified in March 1700, included the following main provisions: the Archduke Charles was to have Spain, the Spanish Netherlands and the Spanish possessions in South America; the Dauphin was to receive the Two Sicilies, the Tuscan ports of Guipuzcoa and Finale, and the Milanese, which would be exchanged for Lorraine.

1701   **Second Grand Alliance** was signed at The Hague by England, the Dutch Republic and the Emperor. Its two main strands were a call for the partition of the Spanish Empire and for the Dutch Barrier to be restored.

1703   **Anglo-Portuguese Treaty** (or **Methuen Treaty**) (May), by which Portugal joined the Grand Alliance. Savoy also joined the Grand Alliance in November 1703.

1707   **Union of England and Scotland** (May) created Great Britain.

        The '**Perpetual Alliance**' (August) was signed between Prussia and Sweden.

1711   **Treaty of the Pruth** (July) between Russia and Ottoman Empire, by which Peter the Great gave back Azov to the Turks, destroyed all Russian fortresses in Turkish territory and agreed that Charles XII of Sweden should be permitted to return. The treaty is sometimes referred to as the Treaty of Falczi.

1713   The **Treaty of Utrecht** was a major settlement concluded through several separate treaties between France on one side and Great Britain, Holland, Prussia, Savoy and Portugal on the other, and acceded to by Spain. With the subsequent treaties of Rastatt and Baden, it ended the War of the Spanish Succession. Among its clauses with Britain, Holland and Prussia were:

        1. France lost Newfoundland, Acadia and Hudson's Bay to England;

149

2. France promised to dismantle Dunkirk;
3. France retained Cape Breton and her share in the fisheries off the coast;
4. France recognised the Protestant succession in England;
5. A barrier was established between France and the United Provinces;
6. The Spanish Netherlands was given to Austria;
7. France regained Lille, Aire, Bethune, Saint Venant;
8. France recognised the royal title of the King of Prussia and his rights over Neufchâtel;
9. France established its claims to Orange;
10. France handed Upper Gelderland to Prussia. ·

Among other parts of the settlement, Spain ceded Gibraltar and Minorca to Britain and granted the *asiento*.

1714   **Peace of Rastatt** (March) between France and the Empire was supplemented by the **Treaty of Baden** (see below). France confirmed the Austrian possessions in Italy (Naples, part of Milan, Mantua and Sardinia). It secured the restoration of the Electors of Bavaria and Cologne to their territories and rights. The Duke of Savoy, Victor Amadeus, became King of Sicily. Strasbourg was retained by France.

Treaty of Baden between France and the Empire supplemented the Peace of Rastatt. The treaty confirmed French possession of Alsace and Strasbourg.

1716   **Treaty of Westminster** between Britain and the Empire by which Britain undertook to guarantee the Emperor's possessions (excluding his claim to Spain) and the Emperor guaranteed the Hanoverian succession.

1717   **Triple Alliance** (January) between Britain, France and the Netherlands was signed at The Hague and opposed Philip V's ambitions in France and Italy. This became the **Quadruple Alliance** after the accession of Austria on 2 August 1718.

Treaty of Amsterdam (August) between France, Russia and Prussia, by which Russia and Prussia guaranteed the Utrecht settlement and France promised mediation to seek an end to the Northern War.

1718   **Treaty of Passarowitz** (July) between Austria and the Ottoman Empire had the following provisions: Austria gained Belgrade, a strip of Serbia and the Banat of Temesvár; the Turks kept the Morea and engaged to give no help to Francis II Rákóczy; and Venice was confirmed in its possession of Corfu, Santa Maura and its conquests in Albania and Dalmatia. The treaty lasted for 25 years.

1720	**Treaty of The Hague** (17 February) ended the War of the Quadruple Alliance. The succession to Tuscany, Parma and Piacenza was confirmed for Charles, eldest son of Philip of Spain and Elizabeth Farnese. Philip renounced his claims in France and Italy. Sardinia was given to Victor Amadeus of Savoy. In exchange, Sicily was made over to Austria.
1721	**Treaty of Nystad** between Russia and Sweden, by which Livonia, Estonia, Ingria and parts of Karelia were acquired by Russia. Sweden retained most of Finland.
1725	**First Treaty of Vienna** (April) was signed between Spain and the Emperor. Under its terms, the Emperor confirmed the succession to Parma and Tuscany of Philip V's two sons, Spain guaranteed the Pragmatic Sanction and trading rights were conferred on the Ostend Company.
	Treaty of Hanover (3 September) created a defensive league between Britain, France and Prussia to counterbalance the alliance between Austria and Spain signed earlier in the year. The integrity of the three powers and the Prussian claim on Jülich were recognised.
1727	**Treaty of Paris** (31 May) between Austria and Britain, France and Prussia ended a brief conflict. A peace treaty with Spain was signed at the Pardo on 6 March 1728.
1729	**Treaty of Seville** (November) was a treaty of peace and friendship between Britain, France and Spain. Holland joined later. The treaty guaranteed the succession of Don Carlos to the Italian duchies. Spain, for its part, withdrew the privileges granted to the Ostend Company. A Franco-Spanish alliance replaced the Austro-Spanish alliance.
1731	**Second Treaty of Vienna** (22 July) was signed between Britain, Spain, the Netherlands and Austria. Britain and the Netherlands guaranteed the Pragmatic Sanction in return for which the Emperor suspended the Ostend East India Company.
1733	By the **Treaty of Turin** (September) France pledged itself to support the struggle of the Duke of Savoy to secure the Milanese from the Emperor.
1733	**First Bourbon Family Compact** (the **Treaty of the Escorial**) (was signed in November) by the two Bourbon powers, France and Spain. They mutually guaranteed each other's European and imperial possessions and joined forces in removing the power of the Emperor in Italy.
1735	Preliminary **Peace of Vienna** (October) ended the War of the Polish Succession. Its provisions were finally confirmed in the definitive **Treaty of Vienna** in November 1738.

1738   **Third Treaty of Vienna**. Following up the 1735 Peace Preliminaries, the treaty formally ended the War of the Polish Succession. Don Carlos became King of the Two Sicilies, the Duke of Savoy secured part of the Milanese and the Emperor received Parma and Piacenza. The former Duke of Lorraine was to inherit Tuscany after the death of the last Medici Grand Duke and Augustus III was confirmed as King of Poland. Stanislaw, who had renounced the crown of Poland but not the title in January 1736, received Lorraine and Bar, but both would revert to France on his death. Austria also gained French recognition of the Pragmatic Sanction.

1739   **Treaty of Belgrade**. Russia, Austria and the Ottoman Empire agreed peace through the clever mediation of Villeneuve and the French. Russia evacuated the Romanian principalities, the close connection of Austria and Russia was checked, both Russia and Austria sought a French alliance, and French influence was restored in Constantinople.

1741   In the (First) **Treaty of Breslau** (June) France agreed to support the seizure of Silesia by Prussia. In October 1741, under the **Treaty of Kleinschellendorf** between Prussia and Austria, Prussia temporarily withdrew from the First Silesian War.

1742   (Second) **Treaty of Breslau** brought the First Silesian War between Prussia and Austria to a close. Prussia received Upper and Lower Silesia as well as the county of Glatz from Maria Theresa.

1743   In the (Second) **Bourbon Family Compact** (**Treaty of Fontainebleau**) France committed itself to support Spain's territorial ambitions in the Italian peninsula. Meanwhile, under the secret articles of the **Treaty of Worms**, Maria Theresa, Britain and Sardinia plotted the expulsion of the Bourbons from Italy.

1743   **Treaty of Åbo** ended the Russo-Swedish War. Russia acquired southern Finland up to the River Kiümen.

1744   Formation of **Union of Frankfurt**. Frederick the Great aimed to prevent Bavaria from being absorbed by Austria. He was joined by the Emperor, the Elector Palatine and Hesse-Cassel. The Union agreed:

           1. The constitution of the Empire was to be restored;
           2. Maria Theresa was to give up Bavaria;
           3. Maria Theresa was to arrange a final peace.

1745   **Quadruple Alliance** against Prussia was signed at Warsaw by Austria, Britain, the Netherlands and Saxony on 8 January.

           Convention of Hanover between Britain and Prussia was signed on 26 August.

Peace of Füssen was signed by Austria and Bavaria. The latter renounced its claim to the Empire.

By the **Peace of Dresden** Austria confirmed Prussia in the possession of Silesia and Frederick recognised Maria Theresa's husband, Francis I, as Emperor. The treaty was signed by Prussia, Austria and Saxony in December.

1746   **Treaty of St Petersburg** was a defensive alliance of Austria and Russia against Prussia. It was also known as the 'Two Empresses' Treaty'.

1748   **Treaty of Aix-la-Chapelle**, ending the War of the Austrian Succession, was signed on 18 October by Britain, France and the Netherlands (and was subsequently accepted by Spain, Austria, Genoa and Sardinia by December). The succession of Maria Theresa was recognised, but Silesia was ceded to Prussia. Parma, Piacenza and Guastalla were ceded to Don Philip of Spain. France evacuated the Austrian Netherlands and restored the barrier fortresses to the Dutch. The succession of the House of Hanover in its German states and Great Britain was confirmed.

1752   **Treaty of Aranjuez** (14 June) between Austria, Sardinia and Spain guaranteed each other's Italian possessions.

1756   **First Treaty of Versailles** (May) represented a highly important reversal of French policy. France entered into a defensive alliance with Austria. Russia joined in December.

1757   **Second Treaty of Versailles** (May) was an offensive alliance between France and Austria which aimed at the partition of Prussia.

1761   **(Third) Family Compact** between the Bourbon powers of France and Spain guaranteed one another support in the widening colonial struggle against Britain.

1763   **Peace of Paris** (10 February) between France, Spain and Britain ended the Seven Years' War. France ceded Canada, Cape Breton Island, Granada and Senegal to Britain and also gave up Minorca in exchange for Belleisle. The Mississippi was recognised as the frontier between Louisiana and the British colonies. Britain restored Gorée in Africa, and all conquests in India to France. Spain ceded Florida to Britain, but received back all conquests in Cuba. In Europe, France and Britain were to retire from the war in Germany with France evacuating Hanover, Hesse and Prussia. In the same year, under the **Peace of Hubertusburg**, Silesia was finally ceded to Prussia by Austria.

RELIGION

RELIGIOUS LIFE IN EUROPE ON THE EVE OF THE REFORMATION

c. 1448	Johannes Gutenberg invents the process of printing using moveable type.
1454	Gutenberg prints copies of the Bible.
1469	Brethren of Common Life establish a school at Deventer. This is followed by several more schools, such as those at Utrecht, Groningen, Trier, and 'sHertogenbosch. Those educated by the Brethren include Erasmus and Luther.
1474	Pope Sixtus IV grants papal approval to the new order of Minims, founded by Francesco Paola. They follow strictly the rule of St Francis.
1475	Establishment of the Brotherhood of the Rosary in Cologne by the Dominican friar Jacob Sprenger. It aims to encourage the use of the rosary and rapidly spreads, attracting many members, especially women.
1476	Pope Sixtus IV rules that indulgences bought by the living can bring benefit to souls in Purgatory.
1478	So-called Cologne Bible is printed. It is one of the earliest illustrated printed Bibles.
1483	Appointment of Tomás de Torquemada as Inquisitor General in Spain. This is followed by an increase in the persecution of Jews and Jewish converts to Christianity (*conversos*).
1491	Girolamo Savonarola, a Dominican friar in Florence, begins preaching of the imminent purging of the Church, and the need for general repentance.
1494	Sebastian Brant publishes his *Ship of Fools* (*Narrenschiff*) in Basle. It is an indictment of the folly and worldliness of all sections of society.
1495	Cardinal Jiménez de Cisneros (Ximénez) is made Archbishop of Toledo and begins reforms within the Franciscan, Benedictine and Dominican Orders in Castile.
1497	Foundation of Oratory of Divine Love in Genoa. Composed largely of laymen, its members emphasise the importance of attendance at the sacraments, prayer and charitable work.
1498	Execution of Savonarola.

1499	Cardinal Jiménez begins forcing Muslims in Spain to convert to Christianity or face expulsion.
1502	Work begins on the Complutensian Polyglot Bible at Alcalá which, by providing parallel texts of Scripture in Hebrew, Greek and Latin, facilitates detailed biblical study. It is published in 1514.
1504	Erasmus publishes *Enchiridion Militis Christiani* (*The Manual of the Christian Soldier*).
1507	Pope Julius II grants an indulgence to raise money for the rebuilding of St Peter's Church in Rome.
1508	Erasmus publishes *In Praise of Folly*, an attack on corruption within the Church and on the role of monasticism.
1511	The Congregation of Windsheim (a group of monasteries and convents associated with the reforming aims of the *devotio moderna*) has grown to include 97 houses.
1512	Jacques Lefèvre d'Étaples publishes a commentary on the Epistles of St Paul. It was to influence subsequent evangelical thought.
	Fifth Lateran Council is summoned. It identifies the need for the reform of clerical education and discipline. It also criticizes the over-involvement of the Papacy in temporal matters.
1515	Appointment of Guillaume Briçonnet as Bishop of Meaux. As a humanist, he encourages the introduction of reforming measures in his diocese.
1516	Ulrich von Hutten and Crotus Rubeanus publish *Epistolae obscurorum virorum* (*The Letters of Obscure Men*), a satirical attack on the opponents of humanist scholars, particularly directed against those attacking the hebraist Johannes Reuchlin.
	Death of Abbot John Trithemius of Sponheim. An innovative scholar, he had done much to encourage the reform of Benedictine monasteries in North Germany.
1516	Erasmus publishes his edition of the New Testament in Greek (*Novum Instrumentum*).
1517	Division of the Franciscan Order into the Friars Minor and the Conventual Friars by Pope Leo X.
1518	Erasmus publishes *Julius Exclusus* (*Julius Excluded*), a satirical attack on the military exploits of Pope Julius II in Italy.

MARTIN LUTHER AND THE REFORMATION

1483	Martin Luther is born in Eisleben on 10 November.
1501	Luther enrols at the University of Erfurt.
1502	Luther graduates with the degree of bachelor of arts.
1505	He is awarded the degree of master of arts in January and prepares to study law. In September he abandons the idea of legal study and enters the house of the reformed Augustinians in Erfurt as a novice.
1507	Luther is ordained a priest.
1510	Luther travels to Rome to represent the reformed Augustinians of the Saxon province in a conflict within the order.
1511	He returns to Germany and moves to the Augustinian house in Wittenberg.
1512	Luther is awarded the degree of doctor of theology.
1513	He begins his first series of lectures on the Psalms to theology students at Wittenberg.
1515	He gives a series of lectures on St Paul's Epistle to the Romans. These indicate that Luther has already begun to question the teaching of the Church on how salvation is achieved. He criticises the belief that individuals can accumulate spiritual merit which will influence whether they are saved or damned.
1517	The Dominican Johann Tetzel begins selling indulgences in the area around Electoral Saxony.
	Luther produces his *Ninety Five Theses*. These were in Latin and were intended to stimulate a debate over what Luther considered to be false teaching concerning salvation and bogus claims for the power of the indulgences which had been made by Tetzel. Within a month, the *Theses* have been translated into German, printed and circulated throughout Germany, without the consent of Luther. They stimulate widespread interest and support.
1518	Luther is summoned to Rome to defend his criticisms of the Church. Following the intervention of his ruler (Elector Frederick the Wise of Saxony), Luther is allowed to present his case to the papal legate (Cardinal Cajetan) at the meeting of the Imperial Diet in Augsburg in October. At the meeting Cajetan rejects the justifications offered by Luther. He calls on

Frederick the Wise to hand over Luther to the ecclesiastical authorities, but Frederick refuses.

1519   Attempt by the papal envoy Karl von Miltitz to negotiate a compromise between Luther and the Papacy, but no real progress is made. In July a disputation is held at Leipzig between Luther and Johann Eck. Some views held by Luther are shown by Eck to have been previously condemned as being heretical by the Church. Luther insists that the authority of Scripture is paramount. In October, Luther begins to question the sacramental teaching of the Church in sermons on penance, baptism and the mass.

1520   Luther publishes *On the Power of Excommunication* (Jan.). In May he publishes *Treatise on Good Works*, in which he emphasises that amends for sins can be made only by faith in God's redeeming love, and not by human acts. In June he publishes *On the Papacy at Rome*, which challenges papal authority over the Church and its doctrine. Luther is threatened with excommunication by the Papal Bull *Exsurge Domine* if he refuses to recant. In August Luther publishes *Address to the Christian Nobility of the German Nation*, in which he describes the failings of the Church, and urges the Emperor and the secular authorities in Germany to support the introduction of religious reform. In September he publishes *The Babylonian Captivity of the Church*, in which he condemns the sacramental teaching of the Church for imposing a tyranny over the souls of the faithful. He also accuses the Papacy of being the Antichrist. In November he publishes *The Freedom of the Christian,* in which he shows that faith and not outward acts are of benefit to the soul, but that true Christians would freely wish to perform acts of love towards their neighbours. In December Luther publicly burns the Papal Bull *Exsurge Domine*, signalling his break with the Papacy.

1521   Luther is excommunicated by the Papal Bull *Decet Romanum Pontificem* (Jan.). Luther is summoned by Charles V to the Imperial Diet to be held at Worms (Mar.). He is granted a promise of safe conduct. Luther appears before the Imperial Diet at Worms and refuses to recant his works (Apr.). On his way home from the Diet, Luther is taken into protective custody by soldiers of Frederick the Wise. He is held at the fortress of the Wartburg until March 1522. Charles V declares Luther to be an outlaw by placing him under the ban of the Empire (May). In the Edict of Worms he declares his intention to root out all Lutheran teaching.

1522   While at the Wartburg Luther translates the New Testament into German. He publishes *A Sincere Admonition by Martin Luther to All Christians to Guard Against Insurrection and Rebellion* and

Temporal Authority: To What Extent It Should Be Obeyed, in which he expounds his view that each person is subject to two kingdoms, the kingdom of God and a secular kingdom. Secular government is to be obeyed in worldly matters, but should not attempt to constrain people in matters of religion. Rebellion is not justified by unchristian acts by rulers, but passive refusal to carry out unchristian commands is justified. In March Luther returns to Wittenberg from the Wartburg. He preaches against radical religious changes which have been introduced there under the influence of Karlstadt.

1523   Luther begins work on revising the form of worship in Wittenberg. He publishes *That Jesus Christ was Born a Jew*, expressing the hope that Jews would wish to become members of a Christian church which is based on evangelical teaching.

1524   Luther publishes *To the Councillors of All Cities in Germany That They Establish and Maintain Christian Schools*, emphasising the importance of education for boys and girls. Luther ceases to wear the habit of a friar.

1525   In April Luther publishes *An Admonition to Peace: A Reply to the Twelve Articles of the Peasants of Swabia*, in which he upbraids princes for their oppressive rule but insists that rebellion by subjects cannot be justified. In May, following the outbreak of violence and rebellion, Luther publishes *Against the Robbing and Murdering Hordes of Peasants*, in which he urges the German princes to put down the peasant rebellions by force. Luther marries Katharina von Bora, a former nun (June). In December he publishes *De servo arbitrio*, which responds to criticism, made by Erasmus, of Luther's denigration of the role of free will.

1527   Luther publishes his views on the eucharist in *That These Words of Christ, 'This Is My Body' Still Stand Firm Against Fanatics*.

1529   Luther and Zwingli meet at the Colloquy of Marburg, but are unable to agree over eucharistic teaching (Oct.).

1534   Luther publishes his translation of the entire Bible into German.

1540   Luther supports the bigamous marriage of Philip of Hesse.

1543   He publishes *On the Jews and Their Lies*, an intemperate call for the suppression of Jewish belief and for the expulsion of Jews from Germany.

1546   Luther dies in Eisleben on 18 February. He is buried in Wittenberg.

ZWINGLI AND THE REFORMATION
IN ZURICH

1484	Huldrych Zwingli is born in a village near Glarus in Switzerland (Jan.).
1498	Zwingli enrols at the University of Vienna.
1502	He enrols at the University of Basle.
1506	Zwingli obtains the degree of master of arts. He is made parish priest in Glarus. He continues humanist studies and is strongly influenced by the ideas of Erasmus.
1515	Zwingli accompanies Swiss mercenary troops to Italy and witnesses the heavy loss of life at the battle of Marignano. As a result he becomes an opponent of mercenary service.
1516	Zwingli is made people's priest at the pilgrimage church of Einsiedeln.
1518	He is made people's priest at the Great Minster in Zurich.
1519	Zwingli begins preaching sermons critical of abuses within the Church and of the moral failings of society.
1520	Under the influence of the writings of Erasmus, and probably also of those of Luther, Zwingli begins to develop his own evangelical teaching.
1522	Zwingli is present when a group of citizens eat meat during Lent, a time when the Church demands that people abstain from eating meat (Mar.). Zwingli publishes a defence of their defiance in *Regarding Freedom and Choice of Foods*. Zwingli secretly marries Anna Reinhart.
	With some other clerics in Zurich, he petitions the diocesan bishop for the abolition of clerical celibacy (July). In September he publishes *Of the Clarity and Certainty of the Words of God*, a brief introduction to evangelical study. Zwingli resigns as people's priest and is re-appointed by the city council as preacher (Oct.).
1523	First Disputation is held at the town hall in Zurich (Jan.). Zwingli prepares 67 theses for discussion of the main issues which separate evangelical teaching from that of the Roman Catholic Church. These include: the authority of the Papacy; the doctrine of the mass; the existence of Purgatory. The diocesan bishop (Hugo von Hohenlandenberg, Bishop of Constance) refuses to participate, allowing Zwingli to present his views

unchallenged and to consolidate his influence. In August he publishes *An Essay on the Canon of the Mass*, in which he attacks the belief that the mass was a re-enactment of the sacrifice of Christ. Second Zurich Disputation, in which Zwingli argues against the presence of religious images in churches (Oct.).

1524   The Zurich city council orders the removal of all images from churches (June). Some parents refuse to have their babies baptized (Aug.). Zwingli publishes *Who Is the Source of Sedition?*, in which he calls for reform to the system of tithing, urging that tithes be used only for their original purpose of supporting the work of the Church and the poor in the locality.

1525   Measures are established to eliminate begging in Zurich and to create a common fund for the relief of the poor. This is partly funded from the secularised revenues of the Church. Zwingli completes *On the True and the False Religion*, a statement of his views on evangelical beliefs. These include: justification by faith alone; a rejection of the mass; the need for infant baptism; the rejection of papal authority. In April the mass is abolished in Zurich and is replaced by a service in German. In May a marriage court (*Ehegericht*) is established to regulate all matters relating to marriage. Instruction in biblical studies and languages is established for the clergy in classes known as the 'Prophecy' (*Prophezei*).

1526   Zwingli publishes *A Clear Exposition of Christ's Last Supper*, in which he rejects belief in transubstantiation and insists that the bread and wine in the eucharist are symbolic. This leads to conflict with the Lutherans, who insist that Christ is present in the elements.

1527   Zwingli publishes *Refutation of the Tricks of the Anabaptists*. He meets Luther at the Colloquy of Marburg (Oct.), but is unable to come to an agreement with him over eucharistic teaching.

1530   Zwingli compiles his *Confession of Faith*.

1531   Zurich is at war with the catholic cantons in the Swiss Confederation. Death of Zwingli at the battle of Kappel.

CALVIN AND GENEVA

1509	John Calvin is born at Noyon in France.
1523	Calvin enrols in the arts faculty at the University of Paris.
1525–26	Calvin enrols at the University of Orléans to study law.
1531	He leaves Orléans as a licentiate in law and returns to Paris to resume his studies.
c. **1532**	Calvin develops an interest in evangelical theology.
1534	During a period of persecution of French Protestants, in the wake of the Affair of the Placards, Calvin flees from France and settles initially in Basle.
1535	Calvin completes the first edition of the *Institutes of the Christian Religion.*
1536	Religious reform is introduced in Geneva (May). In August Calvin passes through Geneva and is persuaded to stay and assist in the consolidation of the Reformation there. Calvin presents his *Confession of Faith* to the Genevan city council, which appoints him as preacher (Nov.).
1537	Calvin presents his 'Articles on the Government of the Church' to the council (Jan.). This seeks to impose reform on religious and moral life and is accepted with some alterations by the council.
1538	Opposition grows in Geneva to Calvin and his attempts to impose reform. Calvin is ordered to leave Geneva (Apr.). He moves to Strasbourg.
1539	Publication of the second edition of the *Institutes of the Christian Religion.*
1540	Supporters of Calvin regain influence within the council and summon him back to Geneva to establish order and discipline within the church. Some civic leaders believe that Geneva needs a strong Protestant identity in order to survive prolonged conflict with its former bishop and the neighbouring territory of Savoy.
1541	Calvin returns to Geneva. His *Ecclesiastical Ordinances for the Church of Geneva* are accepted by the city council. It is established that the church will be run by a consistory, composed of pastors and elders of the church. The consistory has responsibility for upholding religious and moral discipline among the servants

of the church and the wider community, although the council insists that the work and the powers of the consistory should in no way impair its own authority. This becomes the model for church government in Calvinist churches throughout Europe.

1546   Pierre Ameaux, a playing-card maker whose business has suffered as a result of the reform of morality, is accused of slandering Calvin. He is forced to perform public penance, and this, along with other similar incidents, prompts riots by opponents of Calvin.

1547   Council approves Calvin's plans for visitations of rural parishes controlled by Geneva, to ensure that catholic observance is eradicated. Opposition in Geneva to Calvin and the 'French' influence coalesces around Ami Perrin, in a faction known as the 'Libertin'. Perrin is removed from his position on the council.

1549   Increasing numbers of French Huguenots flee to Geneva from the late 1540s. This leads to anxiety among the citizens and some on the council of being overwhelmed by religious migrants.

1550   Establishment of annual household visitations by members of the consistory to examine people on matters of religion.

1551   Council receives suggestions from Calvin aimed at punishing swearing and blasphemy.

1553   Michael Servetus, a Spanish intellectual, is arrested in Geneva on account of his antitrinitarian writings. He is sentenced by the council to be burnt at the stake, despite an attempt by Calvin to intervene and have the sentence changed to execution – the less barbaric punishment favoured by Calvin.

1555   Election of council which strongly supports Calvin's reforms.

Measures are passed allowing increased numbers of refugees to obtain citizen status. These changes prompt riots led by Perrin and the 'Libertin' faction. The riots are put down and the 'Libertin' leaders are punished by exile or execution. This marks the triumph of Calvin and his supporters over their opponents in the city.

1559   Establishment of the Genevan Academy to train pastors. Publication of the fifth edition of the *Institutes of the Christian Religion*, the definitive version of Calvin's teaching.

1564   Death of Calvin (May).

THE REFORMATION AND CIVIL WAR IN FRANCE

1520	Lutheran teaching is condemned as heretical by the theology faculty of the University of Paris.
1520s–30s	Occasional persecution of evangelical supporters in France by Francis I and the *Parlement* of Paris.
1534	The Affair of the Placards (Oct.). Evangelical supporters in Paris and in other towns secretly put up posters denouncing the clergy and the mass. This angers and alarms Francis I, who instigates a campaign against heresy, including the execution of heretics and measures for censorship. Many evangelicals (including Calvin) flee abroad.
1540s–50s	Secret Huguenot conventicles are established in many parts of France. In many cases they are in touch with Calvin and his supporters in Geneva. Huguenots gain significant support from among the French nobility.
1551	Edict of Châteaubriant aimed at eliminating heresy in France.
1559	Death of Henry II (July). His successor, Francis II, is a minor, and his government is dominated by the strongly Catholic Duke of Guise.
1560	Tumult of Amboise (Mar.), an attempted coup by Huguenots led by Prince de Condé. It aimed at wresting control over government from the Guise faction, but ended in failure. Death of Francis II (Dec.), who is succeeded by his brother Charles IX. His mother (Catherine de Medici) becomes Regent, and in seeking to bolster the authority of the monarchy, attempts to achieve a settlement between the Huguenots and Catholics.
1561	Colloquy of Poissy is organised by Catherine de Medici and attended by leading theologians, including Théodore de Bèze, representing the Calvinists, and Diego Laínez, the head of the Jesuits. Despite long discussions, a compromise proved to be unobtainable. The failure of the Colloquy was followed by a growth of support for Huguenots and an increase in their militancy.
1562	Outbreak of the first civil war. Forces of the Duke of Guise attack a Huguenot congregation at Vassy and kill 74 worshippers (Mar.). Huguenots seize control of several cities. Inconclusive battle of Dreux (Dec.).

1563	Assassination of the Duke of Guise (Feb.). Pacification of Amboise (Mar.) grants limited rights of worship for Huguenots. They are allowed to worship in the following places: on the lands of Huguenot nobles who control higher jurisdiction; in the households of Huguenot nobles who do not control higher jurisdiction; in cities where Huguenots were already established; in one city in each *bailliage*.
1564	Charles IX and Catherine de Medici undertake a royal progress through the realm.
1567	Outbreak of the second civil war. The fear of Huguenots that Spain intends to intervene on the side of French Catholics prompts them to seize some cities and attempt to capture the king (Sept.). Battle of St Denis destroys an attempt by the Huguenot forces to blockade Paris (Nov.).
1568	Pacification of Longjumeau (Mar.). Restores the terms of the Pacification of Amboise of 1563. Outbreak of the third civil war. In September Charles IX issues secret orders for the arrest of the Huguenot leaders, the Prince de Condé and Admiral de Coligny, but both elude capture. Huguenot forces gather, including German mercenary forces.
1569	Battle of Jarnac (Mar.), during which Condé is killed and the Huguenot army is defeated. Defeat of the Huguenot army under Coligny at the battle of Montcour (Oct.).
1570	Huguenots defeat the royal army at the battle of Arnay-le-Duc (June). Pacification of St Germain (Aug.) restores the right of worship to Huguenots in places where it had existed at the beginning of the war. It also allows Catholic worship in places where it had ceased.
1571	Protracted negotiations between the Duke of Anjou (the brother of the king) and Elizabeth I, over the possibility of a marriage alliance.
1572	Outbreak of the fourth civil war. Marriage of Huguenot leader Henry of Navarre to Marguerite de Valois (sister of the king) (Aug.). The celebrations bring many Huguenot leaders to Paris. An attempted assassination of Coligny fails (22 Aug.). Catherine de Medici may have been implicated in this plot as she was concerned about the growth of Coligny's influence over the king. In particular, she feared he might persuade Charles to intervene against Spain in favour of Protestant rebels in the Netherlands. She convinces the king that Coligny poses a dangerous influence. Massacre of St Bartholomew's Day (24 Aug.). Plans to kill Huguenot leaders gathered in Paris spill over into a more general massacre of Huguenots in Paris and elsewhere in France. The collusion of the king and Catherine de Medici

in the instigation of the massacre prompts several communities, which were dominated by Huguenots, to refuse to accept royal authority.

1573 Edict of Boulogne (July) limits Huguenot worship to the towns of La Rochelle, Montauban and Nîmes. Calvinist leader, de Bèze, writes *The Rights of Magistrates Over Their Subjects*, which criticises arbitrary and tyrannical royal actions and says magistrates are justified in acting to overthrow tyrannical kings.

1574 Outbreak of the fifth civil war. Many Huguenots refuse to accept the terms of the Edict of Boulogne. Their military strength grows in southern France and they are joined by some moderate Catholic 'malcontents'. Death of Charles IX, who is succeeded by his brother, Henry III (May).

1576 Peace of Monsieur (Peace of Beaulieu) (May). Huguenot worship is allowed in France, except in the vicinity of Paris. Huguenot judges are to try cases involving Huguenots.

1577 Estates-General, meeting at Blois, declares the intention of imposing Catholicism on France. (Meeting of Estates-General commenced in 1576.) Several military skirmishes, especially in southern France, take place in August and September. In October the Peace of Bergerac restores the rights of worship of Huguenots and Catholics. Huguenot judges are established in every *Parlement*. Huguenots are allowed to garrison eight strongholds.

1580 Outbreak of the seventh civil war. Few significant military actions are fought and the Peace of Fleix (Nov.) ends the conflict.

1586 Outbreak of the War of the League. As Henry III had no direct heir, the Catholic League, led by the Guise faction, feared that the crown would pass to Henry of Navarre, whose religious allegiances were unpredictable, and who was widely believed to favour the Huguenots.

1587 German and Swiss mercenary soldiers enter France to aid the Huguenots. The forces of Henry of Navarre defeat royal troops at Coutras (Oct.). Heavy losses are inflicted on German mercenaries at Vomory. Henry III is placed under heavy pressure by the Catholic League to end toleration of Huguenot worship.

1588 Day of the Barricades (12 May), in which the Duke of Guise (leader of the Catholic League) enters Paris to be greeted by shows of support. Henry III flees the capital rather than fall under the domination of the Guise. Henry III agrees to the demands of the Duke of Guise over religion and the succession to the throne (July). Assassination of the Duke of Guise and the Cardinal de Guise on the orders of the king (23 Dec.). Other leaders of the Catholic League are arrested.

1589   Supporters of the League in Paris and some other towns rebel against royal authority (Jan.). Henry III is mortally wounded in an assassination attempt (July). The Cardinal de Bourbon is accepted as king by the League. Henry of Navarre (the rightful heir) begins a military campaign to secure the crown.

1590   Henry defeats League forces at the battle of Ivry (Mar.).

1593   Estates-General, formed from supporters of the League, meets in Paris and begins to consider the problem of the succession. There is alarm at the attempt by the Spanish to press the claim of Infanta Isabella of Spain (daughter of Philip II and Eliza-beth, daughter of Henry II of France) to the French crown. Estates-General declares that it accepts the Salic Law (which acknowledges only male claimants) as the only way of deciding the succession. This is an acceptance of the claim of Henry of Navarre. Henry renounces his Huguenot beliefs and attends mass (July). This makes it possible for Catholics to accept him as King (Henry IV).

1594   Coronation of Henry IV. Triumphal entry of Henry into Paris. Expulsion of the Jesuits from France.

1595   France declares war on Spain.

1596   Calais is captured by the Spanish. Meeting of Assembly of Not-ables in Rouen.

1597   Amiens is captured by Spanish forces.

1598   Catholic League's opposition to Henry IV ends throughout France. Edict of Nantes restores Catholic worship to all parts of France (Apr.). Huguenot worship is permitted in the following places: on the lands of all Huguenot nobles with the right of higher jurisdiction; in towns where it had taken place in 1596 and 1597; in all places where it had been allowed under the Peace of Bergerac (1577); in some places by the special consent of the king. *Parlements* are to have Catholic and Huguenot judges. Huguenots are allowed to maintain 84 strongholds (*places de sûreté*). Treaty of Vervins ends the war with Spain.

REFORMATION AND REVOLT IN
THE NETHERLANDS

1520	The writings of Luther are first translated into Dutch.
1523	Two Augustinians are burnt in Brussels for their support of Luther. Support for religious reform continues to grow.
1529	Edicts (Placards) to suppress heresy are published by Charles V.
1530	Formation of some Anabaptist congregations in the Netherlands.
1531	Anabaptist followers of Melchior Hoffman make converts in Amsterdam and elsewhere.
1534	Following persecution, many Dutch followers of Hoffman flee to Münster.
1544	Repression of religious dissent by Charles V increases.
1556	Abdication of Charles V. He is succeeded by his son Philip II.
1559	Philip II introduces measures for the creation of fourteen additional dioceses in the Netherlands, under the overall control of the Archbishop of Mechelen. There are also measures to improve the effectiveness of the inquisition in the Netherlands.
1562	Opposition to plans for the reform of bishoprics, led by the local nobility, grows. The main target of the protests is Philip's minister in the Netherlands, Cardinal Granvelle.
1564	Granvelle is removed from office.
1565	Letters from the Segovia Woods, in which Philip II refuses to make any concessions to the opponents of his religious changes (Oct.). A league of nobles forms to press Philip for concessions.
1566	The Regent of the Netherlands (Margaret of Parma) rejects a petition calling for the abolition of the inquisition. The activity of Calvinist preachers, who find growing support, increases. A second petition is sent to the Regent calling for restrictions on Protestant worship to be removed. There are outbreaks of acts of iconoclasm throughout the Netherlands (Aug.). Regent makes an agreement with the leaders of the opposition (William of Orange, Count Egmont and Count Hoorne) to grant limited rights of toleration, but requires an end to the iconoclasm. The continuation of iconoclasm persuades Philip II of the need to use force to restore Catholicism and his authority.
1567	William of Orange flees into exile. Duke of Alva is sent to the Netherlands with 10,000 Spanish troops. Alva forms the

Council of Troubles (Council of Blood) and takes control of the government.

1568 Attempted invasion of the Netherlands by exiles led by Orange fails. Egmont and Hoorne are arrested and executed for treason.

1569 The demand for new taxation raises considerable opposition to Alva's rule, especially the Tenth Penny (a 10 per cent sales tax).

1572 Unable to gain the consent of the States-General for the new taxes, Alva decides to impose them using force. Resistance to these measures is encountered, especially in the provinces of Flanders and Brabant. The Sea Beggars, a group of Protestant exiles and opponents of the Alva government, land at Brill and begin an invasion of the Netherlands (Apr.). Many towns in the provinces of Holland and Zeeland soon fall to them. In July William of Orange, who is declared Stadtholder of Holland, invades.

1573 Alva's troops re-capture Haarlem. Alva is replaced by Requesens as Governor General of the Netherlands.

1574 Leiden is besieged by Spanish troops but is saved by the breaching of the dykes, flooding the area around the town and cutting the supply lines of the Spanish.

1575 The provinces of Holland and Zeeland accept William of Orange as sovereign in place of Philip II. Representatives of Requesens and the states of Holland and Zeeland meet at Breda to discuss peace. Requesens refuses to consider toleration for Protestants and the talks break down.

1576 Antwerp is sacked by Spanish troops mutinying over lack of pay (Nov.). The death of more than 7,000 people in Antwerp unites people against Spanish rule. The Pacification of Ghent, an agreement between the States-General and the provinces of Holland and Zeeland and William of Orange to unite in expelling the Spanish from the Netherlands, is made. Death of Requesens.

1577 Don John of Austria is made Governor General. He signs the Perpetual Edict with the States-General, by which Spanish troops will be withdrawn but Catholic worship will be restored. Holland and Zeeland refuse to accept the Perpetual Edict or the authority of Don John.

1578 Death of Don John. He is replaced as Governor General by Alessander Farnese, Duke of Parma.

1579 The mainly Catholic provinces in the southern Netherlands form the Union of Arras in order to seek an accord with Philip II. The northern provinces form the Union of Utrecht, which is committed to the use of military force to resist the authority of Philip II. As a result William of Orange is proscribed as an outlaw. Parma captures Maastricht and Mechelen.

171

1580	William of Orange defends his actions in his *Apology*, a statement which is subsequently published by the States-General.
1581	In the Edict of Abjuration, members of the Union of Utrecht renounce the sovereignty of Philip II, who is denounced as being a tyrant.
1584	Assassination of William of Orange. Parma captures Bruges and Ghent.
1585	Parma captures Antwerp and Brussels. Elizabeth I of England gives support to the rebels in the Netherlands by the Treaty of Nonsuch. The Earl of Leicester is made lieutenant-general.
1587	Earl of Leicester returns to England when his military campaign ends in failure.
1588	Maurice of Nassau (son of William of Orange) is appointed captain-general of the rebel forces and begins introducing a series of military reforms. Defeat of the Spanish Armada reduces the ability of Philip II to crush his enemies in England and the Netherlands.
1590	Breda captured by Maurice of Nassau.
1591	Rebel forces recover lost territory and towns, including Nijmegen, Zutphen and Deventer.
1592	Death of Parma.
1594	Capture of Groningen by Maurice of Nassau.
1596	Archduke Albert is made Governor General by Philip II.
1607	A cease-fire is negotiated between Archduke Albert and the Dutch rebels.
1608	Twelve Year Truce is agreed between Spain and the Dutch.
1621	War resumes between Spain and the Dutch rebels (United Provinces). Death of Archduke Albert.
1625	Death of Maurice of Nassau. His brother, Frederick Henry, becomes captain-general. Spanish troops capture Breda.
1628	Dutch fleet captures Spanish treasure ships.
1629	Dutch capture 'sHertogenbosch.
1632	Dutch capture Maastricht.
1639	Battle of the Downs, in which the Spanish fleet is defeated by the Dutch.
1647	Cease-fire between the Spanish and the Dutch is agreed. Death of Frederick Henry.
1648	Peace of Münster. As part of the agreement, Spain acknowledges the United Provinces as a sovereign independent state.

THE RADICAL REFORMATION

The term radical Reformation covers a large group of separatist churches, sects, conventicles and individuals. These groups proliferated in the period after the Reformation, although the total number of people involved was not particularly great. Radical groups held many differing beliefs, which varied from one group to another, but certain ideas frequently recur. There is an emphasis on separation from the Roman Catholic Church and from churches created by magisterial reform, as radicals emphasised the need for the Church to be free from secular influence. They also stressed that their church should be formed only from those who were true believers, who should keep themselves distinct from others in society. Such views made them appear subversive and a danger to civil society, to the secular and ecclesiastical authorities. Radicals were also treated with suspicion as many rejected worldliness and accepted signs of status and power. In some cases, as with the Hutterites, this led to the formation of communities in which property was held in common. These attitudes have led to the radicals being referred to as the Left Wing of the Reformation. The fears of the authorities concerning the radicals were heightened for, as James Stayer has shown, some of the radicals in the 1520s, men such as Hans Hut, had also been associated with the Peasant War of 1525. An important strand of the radical Reformation was Anabaptism, which held that baptism was the sign of true believers accepting Christ. Since infants were unable to make this decision, baptism should be administered only to adults. Another important strand of radicalism was apparent in mysticism. This emphasised the importance of direct inner enlightenment of the human soul by God. This approach valued mystical experience over biblical study and outward signs of Christian witness. Within the radical Reformation there were many who held strong apocalyptical beliefs, and in some cases endorsed the need for the godly to use violence against their enemies. These ideas were evident in the teaching of Müntzer, and were most clearly seen in the events in Münster, but pacifism generally prevailed after 1534.

Anabaptism

1524   Some erstwhile supporters of Zwingli in Zurich, led by Konrad Grebel, begin to question the correctness of infant baptism. The secular authorities in Zurich order that infants must be baptized. In Saxony, Karlstadt ceases to baptize infants in his parish of Orlamünde, but he does not advocate re-baptizing adults.

1525	Disputation between Zwingli and Grebel, after which the city council supports Zwingli over infant baptism. At a meeting in Zurich, Grebel baptizes the former priest Georg Blaurock, who goes on to baptize other adults. The group then celebrate communion together. Hans Denck is expelled from Nuremberg. He was influenced by Müntzer and Karlstadt, and brought together strands of mysticism and Anabaptism.
1526	Arrest of Grebel and Blaurock. Denck baptizes Hans Hut, a former associate of Müntzer. Hut believes in the imminence of apocalypse and spreads his ideas on missionary journeys in south Germany and Austria. An Anabaptist community is established at Nikolsburg in Moravia by Balthasar Hubmaier. Michael Sattler, former prior of the monastery of St Peter im Schwarzwald, travels in Zurich lands and Germany, converting people to Anabaptism.
1527	Execution by drowning of Felix Mantz, one of the original Zurich Anabaptists, in whose house the first baptisms had occurred. Many Anabaptists are arrested in Augsburg, including the leader Hans Hut, who dies in prison. Meeting of Anabaptist leaders at Schleitheim under the presidency of Sattler. They compile the articles of Anabaptist belief (the Schleitheim Confession). This rejects the use of violence against their enemies. Sattler is subsequently arrested and burnt in Rothenburg.
1529	Blaurock is arrested and burnt in Austria. Jacob Hutter joins an Anabaptist community at Auspitz in Moravia, which had separated from the Anabaptists at Nikolsburg. Within the community all goods were held in common but internal division prevails. Hutter eventually becomes the leader of the community and imposes discipline and organisation. The movement becomes known as Hutterites and many new communities are formed. Melchior Hoffman, an apocalyptical lay preacher, joins Anabaptists in Strasbourg and declares the city as the new Jerusalem.
1530	Hoffman is forced to flee from Strasbourg to the Netherlands, where he finds many supporters and carries out mass rebaptism ceremonies.
1533	Arrival in Münster of Anabaptists who are supporters of Hoffman (Melchiorites) from the Netherlands. The Strasbourg clergy, led by Bucer, confront Anabaptists and radicals at the Strasbourg Synod. The council expels those who will not conform to the religious ordinances of the city.
1534	In Münster Melchiorite preachers develop a large following for their apocalyptic preaching. One of the mayors, Bernd Knipperdolling, becomes a supporter, but control of the city passes to the Anabaptist leader Jan Matthys. On the instructions

of Matthys, all opponents of Anabaptism in Münster (including Lutherans and Catholics) are expelled and their property is seized. Matthys considers Münster to be the new Jerusalem. Matthys is killed by hostile troops outside the city and his place taken by Jan Bockelson. He orders the communal ownership of property and the institution of polygamy. Bockelson is declared king by his followers.

1535   Münster is surrounded by troops of the bishop and other princes. After a long siege, it is taken and many Anabaptists are executed. The bodies of the leaders are displayed in cages hanging from the cathedral.

1536   After the events in Münster, Menno Simons begins to re-create an Anabaptist movement which emphasises pacifism and discipline. Hutter is excuted.

1561   Death of Menno Simons. Leadership passes to Dirk Philips but the movement experiences many divisions.

1565–91   Hutterites enjoy a period of expansion and success, described in the *Hutterite Chronicle* as 'The golden years'.

1592–1622   Hutterites experience renewed persecution from the Habsburg rulers, leading to their expulsion from Moravia in 1622. Hutterites move into Hungary and Slovakia.

Spiritualists

1525   Hans Denck, one of the main founders of spiritualist Anabaptism, is expelled from Nuremberg. He had been influenced by the ideas of Karlstadt and Müntzer. He stresses the need for inner enlightenment directly from God, rather than from external acts.

1529   Sebastian Franck, a former priest, resigns his post as a Lutheran pastor near Nuremberg. He believes God communicates with humans by spiritual means. Kaspar von Schwenckfeld, a Silesian nobleman, settles in Strasbourg. He had been a Lutheran, but after receiving visions he becomes one of the most influential spiritualists.

1531   Sebastian Franck publishes *Chronica, Zeytbuch und geschytbibel*, relating the course of history to the working of God in the world.

1534   Franck publishes *Paradoxa Ducenta Octaginta (Two Hundred and Eighty Paradoxes or Wondrous Sayings)*, setting out his spiritual understanding of religion. This makes a sharp distinction between the outer fleshly body and the inner word of God, which has no need of churches or other institutions. Schwenckfeld is forced to leave Strasbourg by the opposition of Bucer. Schwenckfeld believes that Christ retained His divine nature while he was a man. Those who partook in the Eucharist ate divine flesh which transforms the soul.

1540   Schwenckfeldian teaching is condemned by Lutheran theologians meeting at Schmalkalden.

THE REFORMATION AND RELIGIOUS CHANGE IN EARLY MODERN ENGLAND

1489	Statute is promulgated limiting the benefit of the clergy.
1510	John Colet establishes St Paul's school.
1511	Erasmus goes to the University of Cambridge where he teaches Greek.
1514	Death of Richard Hunne (a London Lollard) while in the custody of the bishop of London. This arouses anticlerical sentiments among Londoners. Wolsey is made Bishop of Lincoln.
1515	Cardinal Wolsey is appointed Chancellor of England.
1521	Lutheran books are burnt in public in London. Henry VIII publishes *Assertio Septem Sacramentorum*, attacking Luther's sacramental teaching.
1524	Tyndale flees abroad to avoid arrest.
1525	Publication of the New Testament translated into English by William Tyndale. Foundation of Cardinal College at Oxford by Wolsey.
1529	Negotiations for a divorce between Henry VIII and Catherine of Aragon fail. Cardinal Wolsey is charged with *praemunire* (asserting papal jurisdiction in England which was in conflict with that of the crown). Wolsey is arrested but dies before coming to trial. Reformation Parliament meets.
1532	Submission of the Clergy.
1533	Thomas Cranmer is appointed Archbishop of Canterbury. He annuls the marriage of Henry VIII and Catherine of Aragon. The Act in Restraint of Appeals forbids any appeals being heard at Rome.
1534	Act of Supremacy is passed by Parliament, establishing Henry as supreme head of the Church in England. Act in Restraint of Annates forbids the payment of annates to Rome. Act for the Submission of the Clergy.
1535	More and Fisher are executed for refusing to swear the oath to the Act of Succession. *Valor Ecclesiasticus* is compiled, providing an assessment of clerical income.
1536	Anne Boleyn is executed. The Pilgrimage of Grace, a rebellion in the north of England, is prompted by religious reform and measures against the monasteries. The Ten Articles, a statement

of doctrine allowing for a Protestant understanding of the sacraments, are published. Smaller monasteries are dissolved.

1539	Dissolution of the larger monasteries. Six Articles, asserting Catholic teaching on major points of doctrine, are published. The Great Bible is published.
1547	Death of Henry VIII and accession of Edward VI. Act dissolving chantries is promulgated.
1549	Publication of the Book of Common Prayer.
1552	Publication of the second Prayer Book.
1553	Death of Edward VI, followed by the failed attempt to place Lady Jane Grey on the throne. Accession of Mary I.
1554	Restoration of Catholicism in England.
1555	The Protestant bishops Latimer, Hooper and Ridley are burnt for heresy.
1556	Archbishop Cranmer is burnt for heresy.
1558	Death of Mary and accession of Elizabeth I.
1559	Act of Uniformity and Act of Supremacy restore Protestantism to England. Publication of the revised version of Prayer Book.
1563	Publication by John Foxe of *Acts and Monuments* (*Book of Martyrs*).
1569	Rebellion of northern earls in favour of Catholicism.
1570	Elizabeth I is excommunicated by Pope Pius V.
1571	The Thirty Nine Articles define Anglican beliefs.
1577	Archbishop Grindal is suspended from office for refusing to act against prophesying (a means of instructing Puritan preachers).
1588	The Marprelate tracts attacking bishops are published.
1603	Death of Elizabeth and accession of James I. The Millenary Petition, which seeks greater concessions for Puritans, is presented to James.
1604	Hampton Court Conference is held. James refuses to accept a presbyterian system of church government.
1605	The Gunpowder Plot, an attempt by Catholics to murder James and blow up Parliament, is discovered.
1611	Publication of the Authorized Version of the Bible.
1628	William Laud is made Bishop of London.
1633	Laud is made Archbishop of Canterbury. The *Book of Sports*, defining activities which are permitted on the Sabbath, is published.
1637	Prynne, Burton and Bastwick are mutilated for publishing attacks on bishops.
1638	Riots in Edinburgh are prompted by efforts to impose the Prayer Book on Scotland.

1639	First Bishops' War with the Scots.
1640	Second Bishops' War. The Root and Branch petition calls for the abolition of the episcopacy.
1643	Parliament agrees to the Solemn League and Covenant with the Scots, to harmonise religious observance in Britain.
1645	Use of Prayer Book is prohibited in England. Laud is executed.
1646	Abolition of the episcopacy.
1649	Leveller mutineers in army are arrested.
1660	Restoration of the monarchy and the Church of England.
1662	Revised Prayer Book is published. The Act of Uniformity requires all ministers to conform to Prayer Book services. The Quaker Act imposes punishments on Quakers who attend meetings of more than five people.
1673	Test Act excludes Catholics from public office.
1678	Second Test Act excludes Catholics from membership of the Houses of Parliament.
1685	Death of Charles II. He is succeeded by his brother James II, a Catholic.
1688	Invasion of England by William of Orange and flight of James II to France.
1689	William is declared co-ruler along with his wife Mary (sister of James).

1524 Foundation of the Theatine Order by Thomas de Vio (Cajetan) and Gian Pietro Carafa (later Pope Paul IV), both of whom are members of the Oratory of Divine Love. The Theatines were an order of priests who were dedicated to performing works of charity, preaching, hearing confessions and encouraging the laity to receive communion frequently. They did not wear a distinguishing habit and did not beg. The first house was in Rome.

1528 Foundation of the Capuchins by Matteo da Bascio. They strictly followed the rule of St Francis and were dedicated to spreading the Christian message. The Order began in Italy but grew rapidly and spread to France, Iberia and Central Europe.

1533 Barnabite Order is established in Milan by Antonio Maria Zaccaria. The Order receives papal approval the same year and Zaccaria encourages the establishment of a female order, the Angelic Sisters of Saint Paul the Converted (the Angelics). The Barnabites were treated with hostility by many within the Church, but accusations of heresy against them were not upheld. A Theatine house is established in Naples. After 1550 the Order spreads throughout Italy and elsewhere in Catholic Europe.

1534 Establishment of the Jesuit Order (Society of Jesus) by Ignatius Loyola. Order receives papal approval in 1540. Originally intended for missionary work among heathens, the early focus of the Order became opposition to the spread of Protestantism. Jesuits were required to undergo a long period of education and training, and to be ordained as priests. The focus of the Order was on education and large numbers of colleges were established across Catholic Europe. Loyola's *Spiritual Exercises* had a strong influence on Catholic devotion and spirituality.

Pope Paul III declares his intention to summon a general council of the Church. The Somascans (Clerics Regular of Somasca) are established by Jerome Emiliani. The main focus of the Order was the care of orphans and the establishment of schools. It receives papal approval in 1540. Somascan houses are found only in Italy.

1535 Foundation of the Ursulines (women). The Order receives papal approval in 1536. Following the example of Angela Merici, they were devoted to performing works of charity and education.

Ursulines originally lived in the community, but in the 1560s convents were established. Ursulines spread from Italy to many parts of Catholic Europe.

1536   Pope Paul III establishes a commission to examine the need for reform within the Church. Plans of the Pope to summon a council at Mantua face opposition from Francis I of France.

1537   Papal commission produces the report *Consilium delectorum Cardinalium . . . de Emendanda Ecclesia*, which criticises the conduct of former popes and the quality and conduct of clergy, including monks and friars. Details of this secret report leaked out and were printed by, among others, Luther.

1542   Council of Trent is convened in November. Both France and Spain (which are currently at war) refuse permission for their bishops to attend. Bernadino Ochino, vicar general of the Capuchins, leaves the Order and becomes a Protestant.

1543   Council of Trent is suspended in July.

1544   Peace of Crépy ends the war between Spain and France. The way is open for the resumption of the Council.

1545   Formal opening of the Council of Trent in December. This first phase of the Council was to last until January 1548.

1546   Council of Trent decides to deal with reform of doctrine and reforms to the Church concurrently. The Council decides to attach equal authority to the traditions of the Church and Scripture when considering the reform of the doctrines and institutions of the Church.

1547   Council of Trent condemns Protestant teaching on justification by faith alone and upholds the role of faith and good works in obtaining salvation. The Council upholds the sacramental teaching of the Roman Catholic Church. The Council moves to Bologna from April to avoid a plague epidemic in Trent.

1548   In January the first phase of the Council of Trent ends.

1551   In April the Council of Trent resumes its deliberations. The belief in transubstantiation is upheld. Jesuits establish the Gregorian University in Rome.

1552   In April the second phase of the Council of Trent ends.

1562   Council of Trent resumes for its third and final phase. Some Protestant observers attend the sessions of the Council, but are not allowed to participate. Attempts by the Council to impose residence by all bishops within their diocese are defeated. The Council decides against allowing communion in both kinds to the laity.

1563   Many measures passed by the Council of Trent are designed to uphold discipline and orthodoxy among the clergy and laity.

Bishops are required to conduct visitations of the Church within their dioceses. Final session of the Council of Trent begins in December.

1564   Pope Pius IV confirms all the decrees passed by the Council of Trent.

1566   Roman Catechism is published.

1568   Foundation of Douai College to train priests for work in England.

1582   Death of St Theresa of Ávila, an influential Spanish mystic and founder of the Order of Discalced Carmelites. Her most influential writing is contained in *The Interior Castle*, written in 1577. Establishment of Clerics Regular Ministering to the Sick (Camillans) by Camillus of Lellis. The Order, which remains small, receives papal sanction in 1591. The Order was devoted to helping the sick in mind and body.

1588   Papal Bull *Immensa Dei* establishes fifteen congregations or councils with responsibilities for specific aspects of the government of the Church and the administration of the Papal States. These include congregations to oversee the work of the Inquisition and the Index of forbidden books.

1591   Death of St John of the Cross, a Carmelite who had worked for the reform of his Order. He was famed for his mystical writing, especially *The Ascent of Mount Carmel* and *The Dark Night of the Soul*.

1592   Revised edition of the Vulgate (the Bible in Latin) is published. This supercedes the revision of 1590, which was found to contain many errors.

1595   *Collegium Clementium* is established in Rome for the education of Catholic nobles.

1597   Establishment of the Poor Clerics Regular of the Mother of God of the Pious Schools (Piarists or Scolopi) by José Calaanz. The Order receives papal sanction 1604. They were devoted to providing free education for poor boys. The Order spread rapidly and opened many schools in Italy and in Catholic Europe.

1598   Edict of Nantes restores Catholic worship throughout France but grants limited rights of religious toleration to Huguenots.

1609   Francis de Sales publishes *Introduction to the Devout Life*.

1609–14   Expulsion of Moriscos (Muslims who are at least nominally converted to Christianity) from Spain.

1610   Establishment of the Institute of the Visitation of Our Lady by Francis de Sales and Jeanne-Françoise de Chantal. It was a semi-cloistered congregation for women. By 1618, under pressure from the Church hierarchy, its members were obliged to accept the imposition of a cloistered life.

1611	The Institute of the Blessed Virgin Mary (The English Ladies of Mary Ward), established by Mary Ward, set up their first college for girls. This is followed by many more. Establishment of the Oratory of Jesus and Mary by Pierre de Bérulle in France. This consisted of congregations of priests who lived communal, but not cloistered, lives.
1615	Jesuit Order has expanded to include over 13,000 members.
1617	Vincent de Paul establishes the Congregation of the Mission (Lazarists).
1627	Emperor Ferdinand II declares Catholicism to be the only religion tolerated in Bohemia. (An exception is made for Jews who retained religious privileges.)
1634	First performance of the Oberammergau passion play.
1640	Publication of *Augustinus* by Cornelius Jansen (Bishop of Ypres). In it he questions the emphasis placed by the Catholic Church on free will.
1641	Catholic rebellion in Ireland. Many Protestants are massacred.
1685	Edict of Nantes is revoked by Louis XIV and Huguenots are denied freedom of worship.
1713	The convent of Port-Royal, a centre for the support of Jansenism in France, is destroyed on the orders of Louis XIV. Papal Bull *Unigenitus* condemns the teaching of Jansen.
1717	Work begins on the building of the Karlskirche in Vienna.
1731	Protestants are expelled from the lands of the Archbishop of Salzburg.
1773	The Jesuit Order is suppressed by Pope Clement XIV.

LUTHERANISM FROM 1546

1546	Death of Luther
1547	Wittenberg is occupied by troops of Charles V.
1548	Charles V imposes the Augsburg Interim, allowing Lutherans to keep communion in both kinds and married pastors until a general council settles the religious divisions. Eruption of the Adiaphorist Controversy between Gnesio-Lutherans, led by Flaccius Illyricus, who accepts no changes to Luther's teaching, and the Philippists, led by Melanchthon, who are prepared to accept the Interim.
1550	Publication of *The Confession and Apology of the Pastors and Other Ministers of the Church at Magdeburg* advances the theory of justifiable constitutional resistance against tyrannical rulers.
1555	Melanchthon publishes the final version of the *Loci Communes*. The Peace of Augsburg allows the practice of Lutheranism in the lands of Lutheran rulers.
1557	Division between Lutheran groups intensifies as a result of the Colloquy of Worms.
1560	Death of Melanchthon. Elector Frederick of the Palatinate converts from Lutheranism to Calvinism.
1568	Efforts to restore Lutheran unity are led particularly by Jacob Andreae and Martin Chemnitz.
1580	Formula of Concord provides a statement of belief around which Lutherans unite.
1603	Landgrave Maurice of Hesse-Kassel converts from Lutheranism to Calvinism.
1613	Elector John Sigismund converts from Lutheranism to Calvinism. His subjects refuse to accept his new faith and the Elector is obliged to tolerate both Lutheran and Calvinist worship.
1617	Lutheran territories in Germany celebrate the centenary of the Reformation. Some use the occasion to call for a re-invigoration of the Protestant Church.
1619	Estates of Bohemia offer the throne to Frederick V of the Palatinate and thereby precipitate the Thirty Years' War.
1629	Edict of Restitution. Ferdinand II orders Protestants within the Empire to restore to the Church all the property it held in 1555.

184

1630	Lutheran Gustavus Adolphus of Sweden invades Germany.
1648	Peace of Westphalia.
1670	Philipp Jakob Spener, Lutheran pastor in Frankfurt, establishes regular devotional meetings. The Lutheran Pietist movement, which developed under his influence, aims to strengthen Christian devotion and commitment and increase the role of the laity in spiritual life.
1675	Spener publishes *Pia Desideria*.
1686	Spener made court preacher in Dresden.
1688	Veit Ludwig von Seckendorff publishes *Commentarius historicus et apologeticus de Lutheranismo seu de Reformatione* (*Historical and Apologetic Commentary on Lutheranism or the Reformation*). This is an historical account rather than hagiography and includes some criticism of Luther and his actions.
1691	Spener moves to Berlin where he finds support for his ideas from King Frederick I of Prussia. Pietism spreads through Prussian territory.
1694	Establishment of the University of Halle. Influenced by Spener, it emphasises Pietist values of self-improvement and responsibility for others.
1695	August Hermann Francke, a follower of Spener, establishes a poor school, Latin school, girls' school and orphanage in Halle. He aims at human improvement through education.
1727	Death of Francke.
1722	Count Niklaus von Zinzendorf, godson of Spener and pupil of Francke, establishes the religious community of Herrnhut (Moravian Brethren).
1729	J. S. Bach composes the St Matthew Passion.
1736	Zinzendorf is forced to leave Saxony, accused of religious nonconformity.
1740s	Gradual decline in the influence of Pietism.

THE JEWS IN EARLY MODERN EUROPE

1290	Jews are expelled from England.
1307	Jews are expelled from France.
1475	Jews in Trent (North Italy) are accused of the ritual murder of a Christian boy. Several Jews are executed.
1492	Jews are expelled from Spain.
1497	Portuguese Jews are forced to convert to Christianity.
1503	Konrad Pelikan, a humanist scholar, writes *De Modo Legendi et Intelligendi Hebraea* (*How to Read and Understand Hebrew*).
1505	Johannes Reuchlin, a humanist scholar, publishes a letter in which he offers to help in the conversion of Jews by instruction.
1507	Johannes Pfefferkorn, who is a converted Jew, rebukes Reuchlin and claims the best way to convert Jews is by seizing their religious texts and by forbidding them to practise usury. A long and acrimonious dispute develops between them and their supporters.
1510	Some Jews are executed in Brandenburg, charged with having desecrated a consecrated Host.
1516	Reuchlin writes *De Arte Cabalistica*, a study of the Cabbala and Jewish mystic texts. A Jewish ghetto in Venice is established.
1519	Expulsion of Jews from Ratisbon (Regensburg) in Germany. The site of the synagogue there becomes a place of Christian pilgrimage and of miracles attributed to the Virgin Mary.
1523	Luther writes *That Jesus Christ was Born a Jew*, in which he expresses the hope that Jews will be converted to Christianity by evangelical preaching.
1541	Jews are expelled from Naples.
1543	Luther writes *On the Jews and Their Lies*, calling upon secular authorities to root out Judaism by force.
1553	Pope Julius III declares the *Talmud* to be blasphemous.
1555	Papal Bull requires Christians and Jews to live separately.
1575	Jews are expelled from the Palatinate (Germany).
1614	Emperor Matthias ennobles a Jew, Jacobi Basseri. Fettmilch riots take place in Frankfurt-am-Main, in which the Jewish ghetto is looted. The instigator of the riots is executed by the civic authorities.

1655	Cromwell allows Jews to return to England.
1655–56	Sabbatai Zevi claims to be the Jewish messiah and achieves a large following among Jews in Central Europe.
1672	Amsterdam has a Jewish population of 7,500, drawn to the city by its relative tolerance, for example Jews are not obliged to reside in a ghetto.
1728	Frankfurt Jews are no longer required to wear distinguishing marks on their clothing.
1745	Jews are expelled from Prague.
1750	Prussian General Privilege allows Jews to have their own schools, cemeteries and synagogues but maintains restrictions upon owning property.
1762	Jews are allowed to settle in Munich. Jews are persecuted in Ukraine.

WITCHCRAFT IN THE EARLY MODERN PERIOD

In early modern Europe there was widespread persecution of people accused of witchcraft. Witches were feared as it was believed that they could perform evil acts (*maleficia*) which caused harm to people and property. It was also believed that they gained their magical powers by renouncing God and making a pact with the devil. The worst periods of prosecution were between 1580 and 1650. The prosecution of witches took place throughout Europe but occurred mostly in Germany, France and Switzerland. The exact numbers of those arrested and subsequently executed are not known, but recent estimates suggest that 110,000 were arrested and 60,000 were executed. Of these probably 80 per cent were women.

The fear of witches by the ruling and educated elite prompted the writing of several books which described the crimes committed by witches and identified the means for detecting the perpetrators. This led to witch-hunts which were used by the authorities to root out witches, but the use of torture during interrogations meant that suspects provided false evidence and confessions. Throughout the period there were some who were sceptical of the claims made about the power of witches and by the late seventeenth century prosecutions declined, as the assertions of the Inquisitors were doubted, and governments saw the trials as disrupting order and authority.

c. 1435	Johann Nider writes *Formicarius*, a treatise on witches.
1484	Pope Innocent VIII publishes a Bull against witchcraft, *Summis desiderantes affectibus*.
1486	Publication of *Malleus Maleficarum* by Dominican Inquisitors, Heinrich Kramer (Institoris) and Jacob Sprenger. This brought together many contemporary beliefs about witchcraft and emphasized that female weaknesses and failings meant that most witches were women.
1524	Publication of *Tractatus de Hereticis et Sortilegiis* by Paulus Grillandus which disseminated to prosecutors ideas about the witches' sabbath.
1532	*Lex Carolina* in the Holy Roman Empire requires witches to be punished by death for *maleficia* (black magic). White magic is also to be punished, but not as severely.
1538	Spanish Inquisition warns its officials against accepting statements on witchcraft made in the *Malleus Maleficarum*.
1541	Four witches are burnt in Wittenberg, to the approval of Luther.

1550s and 1560s   Ninety witches are tried in Geneva.

1563   Johann Weyer publishes *De Praestigiis Daemonum*, claiming that witches have no powers, but are merely deranged or deluded. They should not be brought to trial or executed. He supports this idea in *De Lamiis* (1582). Witchcraft statutes are enacted in England and Scotland.

1580s   There is a great upsurge of witch trials in Germany, Sweden, France and England.

1580   Jean Bodin publishes *De la Démonomanie des Sorciers*.

1588   Michel de Montaigne publishes *On Lameness*, criticising belief in diabolism.

1590–91   King James VI of Scotland (James I) takes an active role in the prosecution of witches, whom he believes are plotting his death.

1595   Nicholas Remy publishes *Demonolatreiae*, a comprehensive account of the activities of witches and the dangers they pose to society.

1597   Publication of *Daemonologie* written by James VI.

1602   Henri Boguet publishes *Discours des Sorciers*. The *Parlement* of Paris establishes its right to review all sentences relating to witchcraft. Many of the sentences submitted to it are overturned.

1609–14   Basque witch trials.

1612   First occasion that the evidence of a witches' sabbath is given in a witch trial in England.

1617   Diabolism is made a crime in Denmark.

1623   Pope Gregory XV orders that any who confess to having made a pact with the devil should be executed by the secular authorities.

1624–31   Witch-hunt in Bamberg (Germany). At least 300 people are executed, including the mayor, Johannes Junius.

1626   Sole example of the Portuguese Inquisition ordering the execution of a person for witchcraft.

1631   Friedrich von Spee (a Jesuit) publishes *Cautio criminalis seu de processibus contra sagas liber* which criticised the conduct of the Inquisitors and witchcraft trials.

1634   A priest, Urban Grandier, in Loudon (France) is charged with witchcraft and executed.

1641   The Paris *Parlement* orders that suspect witches should not be subject to ordeal by water.

1645–46   English witch trials are led by Matthew Hopkins. Nineteen people are executed.

1661–62   Scottish witch-hunt and trials.

1669–76   Swedish witch-hunt. About 200 people are executed as witches.

1670	Witch panics in Normandy.
1682	Louis XIV prohibits prosecutions for witchcraft in France.
1692	Salem witch trials in Massachusetts.
1714	Prosecutions for witchcraft are forbidden in Prussia.
1736	Prosecutions for witchcraft are forbidden in England.
1755	Last execution of a witch in Germany.
1776	Witch trials are forbidden in Poland.

THE EXPANSION OF EUROPE

THE AGE OF RECONNAISSANCE

Even prior to the great voyages of exploration which took Europeans to India, China and the New World, there had been a steady exploration of the coast of Africa (mainly by the Portuguese) in the years before 1453. Thus, in 1415 Portugal had conquered the Moroccan port of Ceuta. In 1419 Prince Henry the Navigator was made governor of Algarve and he subsequently sponsored voyages of discovery. In 1427 the Azores were discovered by Diogo de Silves. In 1434 Gil Enneas sailed beyond Cape Bojador, the limit of previous African exploration. By 1444 Portugal had reached the Senegal River.

Principal Voyages of Discovery, 1453–1600

1461	Discovery of Cape Verde islands.
1462	Portuguese round Cape Mensurado and enter the Gulf of Guinea.
1474	Lopo Gonsalves reaches Cape St Catherine (in present-day Gabon).
1482	Start of the voyage of Diogo Cão to Congo and Angola.
1485	Start of the second voyage of Diogo Cão. He eventually reaches present-day Namibia.
1487–88	Outward voyage of Bartholomew Diaz enters the Indian Ocean, having rounded the Cape, and reaches the Great Fish River.
1492–93	Epic voyage of Christopher Columbus. He discovers islands in the Bahamas, the northern coasts of Cuba and Hispaniola, and mistakenly believes he has reached Asia.
1493–94	Second voyage of Columbus explores the south coast of Cuba, believing it to be part of mainland China.
1497	Cabot rediscovers Newfoundland off the coast of Canada. It was first reached by the Norse in the eleventh century. Amerigo Vespucci sails to the Gulf of Mexico and the Florida coast.
1497–99	Voyage of Vasco da Gama. First Portuguese voyage to India which is reached through the navigational efforts of a local pilot. Da Gama makes good use of Atlantic winds to reach the Cape of Good Hope.
1498	Columbus discovers Trinidad and the coast of Venezuela.
1499–1500	Ojeda and Vespucci reach the coast of Guiana and give the first report of the Amazon.

1500	Voyage of Cabral (second Portuguese voyage to India) sights the coast of Brazil.
1501–02	Exploration of the coast of the Gulf of Maracaibo by Bastidas-La Cosa.
1502–05	Columbus explores the coast of Honduras, Nicaragua and the Isthmus. The Comoros Islands are discovered for Portugal.
1508	Expedition of Sebastian Cabot, in search of the North-West Passage, reaches Labrador and possibly Hudson Bay.
1509	The Portuguese reach Malacca in the East Indies.
1512–13	The coast of Florida is explored by Juan Ponce de León, who reveals the strength of the Gulf Current.
1513	Florida is discovered by Juan Ponce de León. Vasco Nuñez de Balboa crosses Panama and the Pacific Ocean is discovered.
1514	The first Portuguese visit to the Canton River in China.
1516	Hernandez de Córdoba explores Yucatan. First reports of the Maya cities reach Europe.
1517–19	Coasts of the Gulf of Mexico are explored in the separate voyages of Grijalba (1517) and Pineda (1519).
1519–22	Epic Magellan voyage. The first circumnavigation of the world. He discovered the Straits of Magellan, crossed the Pacific and reached the Moluccas via the Philippines. Magellan himself was killed on the Philippines.
1523	The Spaniard, Francisco Pizarro, begins a voyage exploring the west coast of South America. The conquest of Peru begins.
1526	The Portuguese land on Papua.
1527	Route from the coast of Mexico across the Pacific to the Moluccas is discovered by Saavedra. Voyage of Alvar Núñez Cadeza de Vaca. He explores the south coast of North America and leads an expedition to the Rio de la Plata region.
1534–35	Exploration of the St Lawrence River and the first sighting of Montreal in 1535 by Jacques Cartier of France.
1539	South-eastern United States is explored by Hernando de Soto.
1540	Exploration of the Colorado River area, Grand Canyon and New Mexico by Francisco Vasquez de Coronado. Francisco de Orellana discovers the source of the Amazon.
1542	Juan Rodriguez Cabrillo and Bartolome Ferrelo of Portugal explore the west coast of Mexico.
1553	An English expedition led by Sir Hugh Willoughby and Richard Chancellor attempts to find the North-East Passage to Asia. Willoughby died trying to winter on the coast of Lapland. Chancellor entered the White Sea and reached what is now Archangel.

1576	Frobisher Bay and Hudson Strait in Canada are discovered during a voyage by Martin Frobisher. The voyage ends in 1578.
1577–80	Francis Drake accomplishes the first circumnavigation by an Englishman. After sailing through the Straits of Magellan and plundering along the South American coast, he crosses the Pacific and reaches Asia in July 1579. He returns to Plymouth in September 1580 and is knighted by the Queen.
1585–93	Voyage of John Davis of England to Baffin Bay via the west coast of Greenland.
1592–93	Thomas Cavendish and John Davis sail to the Straits of Magellan. Cavendish turns back and dies at sea, while Davis goes on to discover the Falkland Islands.
1594–97	Discovery of Novaya Zemlya, Barents Island and the Barents Sea by the Dutchman, Willem Barents.
1595	Sir Walter Raleigh sails to Trinidad and up the Orinoco River in search of 'Eldorado'. On his return he writes his 'Discovery of Guiana'.
1596	Exploration of the west coast of Mexico, San Diego and Monterey Bay by Sebastian Vizcaino of Spain. He completed his voyage in 1603.

THE PORTUGUESE SEABORNE EMPIRE, 1450–1668

For the voyages of exploration which paved the way for conquest and colonisation, see p. 193.

1448	Portuguese fort (*feittoria*) is constructed at Arguin, south of Cape Branco. The pioneering 'factory' which was at the core of their seaborne empire.
1455	Portuguese are confirmed in their African possessions by the Papal Bull *Romanus Pontifex* of Nicholas V.
1471	Tangier is taken by Portugal.
1479	Treaty of Alçacovas confirms Portuguese monopoly of the Guinea trade.
1481	Construction of the fort at Elmina (São Jorge da Mina) on the Guinea coast.
1494	Treaty of Tordesillas (see p. 142).
1497	Vasco da Gama paves the way for Portuguese influence in India.
1507	Ceylon witnesses the first Portuguese landing.
1508	Ormuz (Hormuz) at the mouth of the Persian Gulf is captured by the fleet of Afonso de Albuquerque. It is a major strategic victory.
1509	Albuquerque succeeds Almeida as Viceroy. Maritime dominance of the Portuguese is confirmed by the naval victory at Diu against a combined Egyptian and Gujerati fleet.
1510	Albuquerque captures Goa from the Sultan of Bijapur (Nov.). This marks the beginning of Goa's rise as the location of Portuguese power in India.
1511	Malacca is captured by Albuquerque. A trading post is established.
1518	Construction of a fort in Ceylon.
1531	Daman (on the coast of India) is seized.
1532	First permanent Portuguese settlement in Brazil is established.
1535	Diu (on the coast of India) is ceded to Portugal.
1557	Trading post on Macao is established.
1559	Daman (in India) is formally ceded by Gujerati Sultan Bahadur Shah.
1570	Trading post at Nagasaki (Japan) is established.

1574	Colony is established in Angola.
1580–1640	Portugal (and its empire) comes under Spanish rule.
1648	Muscat is lost to the Arabs, but Luanda and Benguela are recaptured from the Dutch.
1652	Expulsion of the Dutch from north-east Brazil.
1661	Cession of Tangier as part of the dowry of Catherine of Braganza's marriage to Charles II of England (June). Portugal cedes Ceylon to Holland but retains Brazil (Aug.).
1663	All Portuguese possessions in India (except Goa and Diu) are captured by the Dutch.
1665	Military presence in Cabinda is established.
1668	Ceuta is ceded by Portugal to Spain.

THE SPANISH SEABORNE EMPIRE, 1492–1588

1492	Departure of Columbus (1451–1506) from Palos in Andalusia on his first transatlantic voyage (Aug.). He lands in the Bahamas (Oct.), Cuba and then Hispaniola (Dec.).
1493	Spanish claims to the newly-discovered lands are recognised in the Papal Bull *Inter Caetera Eximiae Devotionis*. Spanish crown is required to promote Christianity.
1494	Treaty of Tordesillas (see p. 142).
1495	Subjugation of the interior of Hispaniola.
1496	Foundation of Santo Domingo on Hispaniola (the first European town in the New World, though its site moved after 1502).
1500	First Franciscan mission to the New World.
1503	*Casa de la Contratación* is founded at Seville. It controls all trade to New World and collects the import tax (the royal fifth, *quinto real*).
1508	Papal Bull *Universalis Ecclesiae* gives the Spanish crown rights to found dioceses in the New World. Conquest of Puerto Rico by Juan Ponce de León and of Jamaica by Juan de Esquivel.
1509	First Dominican missions are sent to the New World.
1511	First judicial tribunal (*Audiencia*) in the New World is established at Santo Domingo. Expedition sets out to conquer Cuba.
1512	Baracoa, first Spanish town on Cuba, is founded. Exploitation of native labour in the New World is regulated by the Laws of Burgos (Dec.) but is largely unenforceable.
1513	Vasco Nuñez de Balboa reaches the Pacific Ocean across the Panama isthmus.
1519	Beginning of the conquest of the Aztec empire by Hernando Cortés (1485–1546) and the *conquistadores*.
1521	Conquest of the Aztec empire is achieved.
1525	Santa Marta, the first Spanish settlement in Colombia, is established by Rodrigo de Bastidas.
1532	Francisco Pizarro begins the conquest of Peru.
1533	Spaniards capture Cuzco, the capital of the Inca empire (Nov.). The Inca emperor, Atahualpa, is executed.
1535	Foundation of Lima in Peru marks the end of conquest and the beginning of colonisation.

1536	Buenos Aires is founded by Pedro de Mendoza. Quesada begins the conquest of Colombia.
1537	Asuncion, in Paraguay, is founded by Juan de Salazar.
1538	La Plata (Sucre) is founded in Bolivia.
1539	Creation of the Dominican province in Peru where their missionary work is concentrated.
1541	First Spanish settlement in Chile is established by Pedro de Valdivia.
1565	Part of the Marianas is taken by Spain.
1568	First Jesuit activity in Peru.
1583	Establishment of the Spanish colony at Buenos Aires.
1588	Defeat of Spanish Armada (see p. 124).

THE DUTCH SEABORNE EMPIRE

1588	English and Dutch defeat the Spanish Armada.
1590	Beginning of the great expansion of Dutch seaborne trade, including West Africa and the East Indies.
1597	Dutch trading post on Bali is established.
1598	Mauritius in the Indian Ocean is seized by the Dutch.
1600	First Dutch ship reaches Japan.
1602	Foundation of the Dutch East India Company.
1603	Dutch trading post on Borneo is established.
1604	First Dutch ship arrives at Canton, but is refused permission to trade because of Portuguese influence at Macao.
1605	Amboyna (Amboina) is captured by Dutch. Portuguese are forced out of the Moluccas which are partly recaptured by a Spanish expedition from the Philippines in 1606.
1606	Mozambique and Malacca ward off Dutch attacks.
1607	Spanish fleet is destroyed off Gibraltar by Heemskerk.
1609	Dutch factory at Hirado in Japan begins trading.
1610	Dutch settlers are active in Guiana and Amazon.
1612	Fort Mouree is founded on the Guinea Coast.
1614	Fur-trade activity by the Dutch in Hudson River.
1618	Batavia is founded by the Dutch on the ruins of Jakarta.
1619	Anglo-Dutch rivalry in the East Indies is suspended as a temporary alliance develops.
1621	Banda Islands are conquered by the Dutch. Establishment of the Dutch West India Company.
1622	Dutch fleet attacks Macao, but is repulsed.
1623	The Amboyna massacre.
1624–25	The Dutch capture Bahia and then lose it. New Amsterdam (now New York) is founded on Manhattan Island. Dutch attacks at Puerto Rico and Elmina fail. A Dutch settlement is established on Formosa (Taiwan).
1628	Devastating blow to Spain with the capture of the silver fleet off Cuba by Piet Heyn. Batavia is unsuccessfully besieged by Mataram. Death of Jan Pietersz Coen.
1630	Beginning of the Dutch conquest of Pernambuco in north-east Brazil.

1632	Dutch successes in Caribbean – St Eustatius and Saba are taken.
1634	Curaçao and Aruba are seized by the Dutch.
1637	John Maurice completes the conquest of Pernambuco. The Dutch make an anti-Portuguese alliance with Raja Sinha of Kandy in Ceylon (Sri Lanka).
1638	Coastal areas of Ceylon are conquered by the Dutch. Elmina (on the Guinea coast of West Africa) falls to the Dutch.
1640	Portuguese armada is defeated off Pernambuco by the Dutch.
1641	Malacca is captured by the Dutch (Jan.). Luanda (in Angola) is captured (Aug.). The Dutch become the only Europeans to have trading concessions in Japan (at Nagasaki).
1644	Rebellion erupts in Pernambuco after the departure of John Maurice.
1648	Luanda and Benguela (in Angola) are recaptured by the Portuguese.
1652	Cape Town is founded by Van Riebeeck.
1655	Dutch embassy to Peking is denied trading privileges.
1656	Conquest of the Amboyna islands is completed by Arnold de Vlaming.
1658	Conquest of coastal Ceylon is completed.
1661	Macassar is attacked by the Dutch.
1662	The Dutch are driven from Formosa (Taiwan) by Cheng Cheng-kung (Koxinga).
1664	New Amsterdam (subsequently renamed New York) is lost to the English. Some Gold Coast forts are also lost.
1665	Second Dutch embassy to Peking is denied trading privileges. Beginning of the final subjugation of Macassar by Speelman (completed in 1667).
1677	Dutch suzerainty over Mataram is recognised by treaty. This symbolises the decline of power of Mataram.
1684	Completion of the Dutch subjugation of Bantam (begun in 1682).
1700s	Mataram is embroiled in civil war and the first Javanese War of Succession.
1717	Beginning of the second Javanese War of Succession.
1723	Conclusion of the second Javanese War of Succession.
1740	Chinese in Batavia are massacred. This is followed by war in Java and also in Mataram.
1743	Further territory is ceded by Susuhunan, ruler of Mataram.
1749	Outbreak of the third Javanese War of Succession.

1755   Third Javanese War of Succession is concluded with the division of Mataram into the states of Djogjakarta and Surakarta.

1759   Dutch expedition to Bengal is completely destroyed by the English.

Postscript: On 31 December 1799, the Dutch East India Company was formally dissolved. The Batavian Republic (the creation of Napoleon) took over its possessions and financial liabilities.

THE FIRST BRITISH EMPIRE

1553	Foundation of the Muscovy Company.
1579	The Eastland Company is formed to trade with the Baltic.
1584–91	A new grant for settlement in North America is made to Sir Walter Raleigh. A settlement, which Raleigh named Virginia, is founded on Roanoke Island off the North Carolina coast, but proves short-lived.
1585	The Barbary Company is formed.
1592	The Levant Company is formed from an amalgamation of the Turkey and Venetian Companies.
1600	East India Company is established. Its first fleet sails in 1601 with Sir James Lancaster in command to Achin in Sumatra and Bantam in Java.
1606	Formation of the Royal Council for Virginia.
1607	Foundation of Virginia. The site of Jamestown is chosen by Christopher Newport.
1609	Royal charter is granted to the Virginia Company. Robert Harcourt's colony is founded on the Wiapoco but fails by 1613.
1612	Charter is granted to the North-West Passage Company. Sir Thomas Button discovers the western shore of Hudson's Bay. Bermuda is added to the charter of the Virginia Company.
1613	First shipment of tobacco from Virginia.
1615	Nicholas Downton defeats the Portuguese at Swally Roads, confirming British fortunes in Surat.
1619	Spice Islands Treaty between England and Holland is signed.
1620	Voyage of the *Mayflower* and foundation of Plymouth (America).
1622	The English capture Portuguese fortress of Ormuz in the Persian Gulf.
1623	Dissolution of the Virginia Company; territory henceforth becomes a crown colony. Massacre of Amboyna.
1624	St Kitts is colonised by Sir Thomas Warner.
1625	Barbados is claimed for the British crown by Captain John Powell.
1627	Formation of the Guiana Company. Colonisation of Barbados begins.
1633	Foundation of Connecticut. English factory is established at Balasore (in India).

1635	The French begin to occupy Martinique and Guadeloupe. Convention of Goa, by which the Portuguese concede to the English the right to trade in the ports in Western India.
1639	Acquisition of Madras. Creation of Fort St George.
1640	Introduction of sugar planting to Barbados.
1649	The Colonial Rebellion – Barbados, Antigua, Bermuda, Virginia and Maryland repudiate the Commonwealth and proclaim Charles II as King. Commission for Plantations is established.
1650	Foundation of Hughli. Enactment of the Navigation Act which forbids all foreign ships to trade in any of the colonies.
1652	First Anglo-Dutch War (see p. 130).
1654	Cromwell begins naval harassment of Spanish trade with the West Indies and the Americas.
1655	The 'Western Design' fails at Hispaniola, but Jamaica is subsequently captured and eventually a successful plantation is established there.
1657	Cromwell reorganises the East India Company.
1661	Bombay and Tangier are included in the dowry of Catherine of Braganza on her marriage to Charles II.
1662	Charter is granted to the Royal Adventurers to Africa, with a monopoly to sell slaves to the plantations.
1664	New Amsterdam is taken from the Dutch and renamed New York.
1672	Formation of the Royal African Company, the successor to the Royal Adventurers.
1686	Evacuation of Hughli. First British occupation of Calcutta.
1690	East India Company makes peace with the Mogul Empire. Factory at Calcutta is established.
1696	Establishment of the Board of Trade and Plantations.
1697	Under the Treaty of Ryswick, the Hudson's Bay Company is reduced to only one factory (Fort Albany).
1698	Major attack on the old East India Company in new legislation with an Act creating the New East India Company. Fort William is constructed to protect Calcutta. First Darien expedition by Company of Scotland.
1703	Methuen Treaty with Portugal.
1704	The English capture Gibraltar.
1708	The English capture Minorca.
1709	Fusion of the rival East India Companies is completed. The new body is entitled United Company of Merchants of England trading to the East Indies.

204

1710	Capture of Nova Scotia.
1711	Formation of South Sea Company.
1713	Treaty of Utrecht signed (see p. 149).
1739	War of Jenkins' Ear.
1744	Capture of Annapolis (in Nova Scotia) by the French marks the beginning of an Anglo-French struggle over the colonies.
1748	Peace of Aix-la-Chapelle and the mutual restoration of colonies.
1749	Dupleix's unauthorised war in India. Chanda Sahib is adopted by Dupleix as Nawab of the Carnatic.
1750	British settlement begins on the Gold Coast.
1751	Clive successfully attacks Arcot, the capital of the Carnatic, and is subsequently victorious at the battle of Arni.
1756	Outbreak of Seven Years' War and major colonial conflicts with France. Nawab of Bengal imprisons the British in the 'Black Hole' of Calcutta.
1760	Battle of Windewash ends French power in India (Jan.). Montreal is taken by British forces (Sept.). Under a secret agreement with the East India Company, Mir Kasim becomes Nawab of Bengal.
1761	Shah Alam is defeated by the British at Patna. Pondicherry is taken by Coote. Britain conquers Cuba and the Antilles.
1763	Treaty of Paris. All French possessions in North America east of the Mississippi, Grenada, St Vincent, Tobago, the Windward Islands, Dominica and Senegal are ceded to Britain. Britain returns Guadeloupe to France. Spain cedes Florida to Britain.

THE FRENCH EMPIRE (*FRANCE OUTREMER*)

1604	Settlement begins at Cayenne (the first origins of French Guiana).
1607	First colonisation attempt in Canada fails.
1608	Quebec is founded by Champlain.
1626	Guadeloupe is taken over as a trading post. First settlement on Madagascar begins.
1635	French colony is established on Guadeloupe. Settlement of Fort St-Pierre is founded on Martinique.
1638	French outpost is established at mouth of the Senegal River.
1643	Island of Reunion is annexed by France. Colony of Fort Dauphin is established on Madagascar.
1658	Louis XIV resumes sovereignty over Martinique.
1659	St Louis is founded on an island in the Senegal River.
1664	New French East India Company is established by Colbert.
1666	The French take Montserrat from England.
1668	The first French factory in India is established at Surat.
1671	Foundation of the Senegal Company.
1672	Beginning of the occupation of Pondicherry in India.
1673	French begin settlement of Chandernagore in India. Marquette and Joliet explore along the Wisconsin, Mississippi and Illinois rivers.
1674	Martinique becomes part of the French crown domain.
1677	Gorée is captured from the Dutch. It becomes a naval base in West Africa.
1682	Louisiana is first claimed for France.
1699	Serious colonisation of Louisiana begins (New Orleans is established in 1718).
1725	Mahé, the only important French possession on the west coast of India, is occupied.
1731	Louisiana becomes a French crown colony.
1739	Acquisition of Karikal.
1750	Yanaon is established as a trading post. The Island of Ste Marie in the Indian Ocean is ceded to the French.

1753	Dupleix is recalled (he receives the order in 1754). The French are in effective control of Ohio; Fort Duquesne is established.
1762	Louisiana is ceded to Spain by the Secret Treaty.
1763	Quebec is ceded to Britain under the Treaty of Paris.

Section V

BIOGRAPHIES

Alexander VI, Pope (1431–1503): Pontiff, 1492–1503. Nephew of Pope Calixtus III, who made him head of the papal chancery. He amassed great wealth and experience which he used to achieve his own election as pope. While a cardinal he fathered seven children, and a further two when he was pope. He openly acknowledged his children, granting them titles, money and lands. His son Cesare was made Duke of the Romagna and seized lands for himself within the Papal States, but was driven out after the death of his father. Despite his moral failings, Alexander was an able administrator of the Church.

Alva, Fernando Álvarez de Toledo, Duke of (1507–82): Spanish general. He fought for Charles V in campaigns in Tunis, Provence, Algiers and Germany. He served at the court of Philip while he was Regent of Spain, and travelled with him in 1554 to England. He served as viceroy for Philip II in Milan and Naples. In 1566 he was sent by Philip to pacify the political and religious protests in the Netherlands. Even though the violence had ended before he arrived, he arrested those he held to have been the leaders, counts Egmont and Hoorne, and had them executed. He used violence and terror as a way of suppressing rebellion. A new council was established, which became known as the Council of Blood. In 1572 he imposed a new tax, the Tenth Penny. He defeated the leaders of the rebellion but his actions stimulated further opposition to Spanish rule. He returned to Spain in 1573 and in 1580 he led the Spanish invasion of Portugal.

Arminius, Jacobus (Jacob Hermanszoon) (1559–1609): Born in Oudewater in Holland, he was educated in Marburg, Leiden, Geneva (under Théodore de Bèze) and Basle (under Thomas Erastus). He was a pastor in Amsterdam, 1588–1603 and was appointed professor of theology at Leiden in 1603. He caused controversy by his criticism of the Calvinist teachings on predestination. He rejected the belief that God foreordained some for salvation (the 'elect') and others for damnation (the 'reprobate'). Instead, he believed that the 'elect' could fall from grace, and that God could give His grace to all who persevered with faith. His views were contained in the Remonstrance of 1610 which called for the freedom of pastors in Holland to hold these views. Arminian teachings were influential in the Netherlands, England and France.

Bach, Johann Sebastian (1685–1750): German composer and musician. From a musical family, he was appointed organist in Arnstadt at the age of 18. By 1708 he was court organist in Weimar and later moved to be musical director at the court in Käthen. In 1721 he was placed in charge of music at the St Thomas church in Leipzig, for which he composed some of his most famous church music. These included the *St Matthew Passion*, the *Christmas Oratorio* and the *St John Passion*. He also wrote much secular music, including the Brandenburg Concertos and the *Well-tempered Clavier*.

Bodin, Jean (1529–96): French scholar and writer. He studied in Paris and Toulouse and became a lawyer. He first entered royal circles as a companion of Henry III and later served his brother, the Duke of Anjou. A *politique*, he favoured granting toleration in order to end the religious wars in France. The most important of his writings were *Six livres de la république* (1576), a significant early work on political philosophy, in which he established that sovereignty was necessary, and opposition to a sovereign could not be justified even if that sovereign were a tyrant. He believed rulers who offended against divine and natural law would be punished by God. In *De la démonomanie des sorciers* (1580) he stressed the need to prosecute witches vigorously in order to eradicate witchcraft.

Borromeo, Charles (1538–84): Italian churchman and reformer. He studied at Padua. He was the nephew of Pope Pius IV, who promoted him within the papal administration and made him a cardinal and Archbishop of Milan. In his archdiocese he introduced Tridentine reforms and attempted to improve standards in monastic houses. He encouraged the work of the new Orders and was noted for his acts of charity towards the sick and the poor. He tried to impose higher moral standards and improve spiritual conduct among the population, by such measures as a ban on dancing on Sundays and religious festivals.

Botticelli, Sandro (Alessandro Filipepi) (1444?–1510): Italian artist and a leading figure in the Renaissance in Florence. He was born in Florence, where he spent most of his working life. He was patronized by the Medici and other leading families in the city. He painted many pictures on religious themes, including *The Adoration of the Magi, The Annunciation* and the *Madonna of the Magnificat.* He also completed pictures on secular themes, especially mythological ones, including *Primavera, The Birth of Venus* and *Pallas and the Centaur.* Following the expulsion of the Medici from Florence, the demand for his work declined and he spent his later years neglected and in poverty.

Bucer, Martin (Butzer, Martin) (1491–1551): German theologian and Protestant reformer. A Dominican friar, he was educated in Heidelberg where he encountered Luther at the disputation in 1518. He left his Order and went eventually to Strasbourg where he became a pastor and assisted in the introduction of religious reform. He was influenced by Zwingli's teaching and emphasised the need for an ordered godly community for Christian belief and practice to flourish. He was present at the Colloquy of Marburg and the 1530 Imperial Diet in Augsburg. He was a staunch opponent of religious radicals and contributed to their expulsion from Strasbourg in 1533. He devised the Strasbourg Church Order in 1534 and assisted in the composition of religious legislation in several other cities. He was a crucial mediator in the negotiations between Luther and the South German Zwinglians in the 1530s, which culminated in the accord known as the Wittenberg Concord of 1536. He also participated in negotiations aimed at reconciliation between Protestants and Catholics in Ratisbon (Regensburg) in 1541. He refused to accept the Interim in 1548 and moved to England. He taught at Cambridge University and assisted Cranmer with the revision of the Prayer Book.

Canisius, Peter (1521–97): Born in the Netherlands, he was educated at Cologne and joined the Jesuit Order. He came to prominence at the Council of Trent and on his return to Germany he played a major role in the Counter Reformation in South Germany and Austria. In 1549 he was appointed to teach theology at the University of Ingolstadt. During the 1550s and 1560s he served as Cathedral preacher in Augsburg, and during that period he assisted in the establishment of many Jesuit colleges, including those in Augsburg, Fribourg, Dillingen, Innsbruck, Mainz, Prague and Vienna. He gained fame as a preacher and a writer of catechisms.

Catherine de Medici (1519–89): Queen of France (1547–59), Regent of France (1560–74). Three of her sons succeeded as kings of France (Francis II, Charles IX, Henry III). The instability caused by the death of her husband, Henry II, at a time of religious and political conflict, caused her to seek moderate religious policies which would preserve peace and the authority of the crown. She tried to counteract the influence of the powerful Catholic Guise family by organising the Colloquy of Poissy (1561), which tried to reconcile Huguenots and Catholics, and by passing the Edict of Amboise (1563) which granted some measures of toleration. Hopes of reconciliation were destroyed by the Massacre of St Bartholomew's Day (1572) which occurred at the time of the wedding of her daughter to Henry of Navarre (Henry IV). She was widely believed to have been implicated in instigating the violence and her influence subsequently declined.

Charles V (1500–58): Holy Roman Emperor (1519–58), King of Spain (1515–56). Born in Ghent and educated in the Netherlands, he was heir to the Habsburg and Burgundian lands and titles through his father, and to the Castilian and Aragonese lands and possessions through his mother. He was never able to centralise the government within his Empire and spent most of his adult life fighting rebellion from his subjects and attacks from outside. In Spain there was resentment about the absence of the king, the use of foreigners to govern the land, and heavy taxation. This culminated in a revolt by towns and the aristocracy, the *communeros* in 1520, which was put down by force the following year. He secured his election as Emperor in 1519 after bribing the electors, but faced the problems created by the Reformation. At the Diet of Worms (1521) he announced his opposition to Luther and his determination to destroy heresy, but he was forced to leave to defend his interests in Italy before he could take action. In Italy he gained victory at the battle of Pavia and took Francis I prisoner. To gain his freedom Francis promised to abandon his claims in Italy and Burgundy (Treaty of Madrid), but reneged on this when he was freed, fearing the encirclement of France by Habsburg lands. Charles returned to Germany and, at the Diet in Augsburg (1530), he rejected the Augsburg Confession. In 1532 a further Ottoman attack on Vienna (the Ottomans had unsuccessfully besieged Vienna in 1529) forced Charles to conciliate with the Protestants. Charles, who saw himself as the champion of Christendom against the Ottomans, led an army in North Africa where he successfully captured Tunis in 1535, but his naval forces were defeated at the major battle of Prevesa in 1538. To free himself to deal with German Protestants and the Ottomans, he made peace with Francis I at

Crépy in 1544. Protestant forces of the Schmalkaldic League were defeated at the battle of Mühlberg in 1547. Charles tried to impose the religious Interim on the German Protestants in 1548. The defection of his former ally Moritz of Saxony prompted a further outbreak of war and Charles abandoned his attempt to impose the Interim. At the Peace of Augsburg, (1555) Charles disliked the formula of *cuius regio, eius religio* which was conceded by his brother Ferdinand. He abdicated in 1556, leaving the Netherlands, Spain, his Italian lands and non-European territories to his son Philip, and his lands in Germany and Central Europe to his brother Ferdinand.

Charles I (1600–49): King of Great Britain and Ireland (1625–49). After an attempt to form a marriage alliance with Spain, Charles married Henrietta Maria of France (1625). He was under the influence of the Duke of Buckingham, who had been the favourite of his father, until his murder in 1628. Charles was frequently at odds with Parliament, especially over taxation. The refusal of Parliament to grant revenues to cover the cost of his ambitious foreign policy prompted him to rule without calling Parliament between 1629 and 1640. Instead he collected taxes, including Ship Money, without Parliamentary consent. He also provoked opposition by his religious policies, which aimed at restoring ritual in the church and reducing the influence of Puritans. In Scotland his efforts to impose the use of the Prayer Book led to rebellion. The rising in Scotland forced him to call Parliament twice in 1640, which led to efforts to restrict the powers of the king and his ministers. His failed attempt to arrest opponents in Parliament in 1642 led to civil war. He was ultimately defeated and arrested in 1646 but managed to escape. This caused a resumption of civil war, which was ended by the defeat and arrest of the king in 1648. He was tried for treason and in 1649 he was executed. He was a great patron of the arts and established a superb collection of pictures.

Charles II (1630–85): King of Great Britain and Ireland (1660–85). He fled into exile in 1645 with the defeat of his father Charles I in the Civil War. He attempted to invade Scotland and England in 1651, but lack of support led to his defeat and second period in exile. Following the death of Oliver Cromwell (1658) he negotiated with Parliament a restoration of the monarchy, which occurred in 1660. He was crowned in 1661. The Anglican church was restored but the opposition of his government, led by Lord Clarendon, meant that Charles was unable to honour his promises concerning religious toleration. War was waged against the Dutch Republic in 1665–66 and 1672–74, but his negotiations with Louis XIV for an alliance against the Dutch were viewed with suspicion. In 1673 he was forced by Parliament to accept the Test Act, which effectively barred Catholics from public office and limited the power of the king to appoint whoever he wished as advisers. This included his brother James, who in 1672 had become a Catholic. Charles was always short of money, but was a patron of the arts and sciences.

Charles XII (1682–1718): King of Sweden (1697–1718). An able military leader, he was called upon to defend the Swedish possessions in the Baltic lands against an alliance of Russia, Denmark and Poland. In the Great Northern War which ensued, he quickly defeated Denmark and inflicted a crushing defeat on the Russians at Narva in 1700. His army then conquered Poland. His attempt to conquer Russia led to total defeat at Poltava (1709) and he was forced to flee into Turkish territory. He encouraged the Sultan to attack Russia but with little success. He eventually returned to Sweden and died in action fighting in Norway.

Cisneros, Francisco Jiménez de (Ximénez) (1436–1517): Spanish churchman and statesman. Educated at Salamanca, he became an Observant Franciscan friar. In 1492 he was made the confessor to Queen Isabella of Castile. He used his influence at court and within his Order to institute reforms of Franciscan houses. In 1495 he was made Archbishop of Toledo and gained papal authority to force reform upon other monastic Orders. He encouraged policies of forced conversions or expulsion for Muslims in Spain. In 1507 he was made Inquisitor General and became a Cardinal. On the death of King Ferdinand (1516) he served as Regent until the heir to the throne (Charles V) arrived in Spain. He founded the University of Alcalá (1508) where scholars completed the Complutensian Polyglot Bible (1513–17).

Colbert, Jean-Baptiste (1619–83): French statesman who entered government service and rose to prominence under Mazarin. He encouraged Louis XIV to arrest his *surintendant*, Nicolas Fouquet, for corruption and eventually was made *contrôleur-général* of finances (1669). He attempted to improve the economy of France and the finances of the government by using protectionist tariffs, monopolies and state subsidies, and he closely regulated industry and trade. He encouraged the building of roads and canals and the development of the navy. He was successful in introducing some fiscal reforms and reducing the state debts, but the costs of Louis XIV's wars undermined his achievements.

Copernicus, Nicolas (1473–1543): Polish astronomer, educated at Cracow, Padua, Bologna and Ferrara. During his stay in Italy he developed an interest in mathematics and astronomy. He returned from Italy in 1506 and in 1512 took up his duties as canon of Frauenburg Cathedral in East Prussia, but he spent much time in the study of astronomy. Between 1506 and 1530 he wrote *De Revolutionibus Orbium Coelestium* (*On the Revolutions of the Celestial Spheres*), but the work was not published until 1543. In it he challenged the belief that the earth was at the centre of the universe, with the other planets orbiting round it. While not rejecting all aspects of existing astronomy, he was the first to maintain that the planets orbited the sun (i.e. a heliocentric system), that the earth rotated on its axis, and that the position of stars was fixed. Copernicus was unable to prove his theories mathematically or by observations and his ideas were condemned by the Church and largely rejected. His ideas were vindicated by the work of the Danish astronomer Tycho Brahe, the German Johannes Kepler, and Galileo.

215

Cranmer, Thomas (1489–1556): English theologian and reformer, he served as Archbishop of Canterbury from 1533 to 1556. He first came to prominence when assisting in the divorce of Henry VIII from Catherine of Aragon. By the early 1530s he had become a supporter of evangelical teaching and his nomination as Archbishop by the King in 1533 came as a surprise. In 1533 he granted a divorce to Henry. He compiled the Prayer Book of 1549, which he subsequently revised in 1552. Following the death of Edward VI, he supported the unsuccessful bid to place Lady Jane Grey on the throne. With the accession of Mary I, he was arrested for treason. He recanted while under arrest, but then affirmed Protestant teaching. He was executed by burning.

Cromwell, Oliver (1599–1658): Rose to prominence as a Member of Parliament in the Long Parliament (1642), and in the Civil War which ensued he raised his own mounted regiment, known as Ironsides. They played a significant part in the Parliamentary victories at the battle of Marston Moor (1644) and the battle of Naseby (1645). After 1648 he was convinced of the need for the king to be tried for treason, and he defended the interests of the army against Parliament. Cromwell defeated rebellions in Ireland at Drogheda and Wexford, and in Scotland at the battle of Dunbar (1650). He was critical of the Rump Parliament which he dissolved using soldiers in 1653. It was followed by the short-lived Barebones Parliament, after which he was made Lord Protector by the Instrument of Government. He introduced some measures of religious toleration, and followed a successful foreign policy, but his rule rested on the threat of force rather than consent. He named his son as his successor, but in 1660 the Stuart monarchy was restored.

Descartes, René (1596–1650): French scientist and philosopher, who lived for most of his adult life in the Netherlands. In his most famous book, *Discours de la méthode*, he applied a rigorous deductive approach to philosophy, questioning every proposition except that of his own existence, 'I think, therefore I am'. As a scientist he made great advances in the study of the reflection of light. He was a distinguished mathematician who introduced new methods for understanding and using mathematical equations.

Dürer, Albrecht (1471–1528): German artist famous for his paintings and prints. He integrated the styles of German and Flemish art with the innovations of the Italian Renaissance. He was born and worked in Nuremberg where he originally trained as a goldsmith. He travelled extensively, visiting Italy in 1494–95 and 1505–07. He also spent time in the Netherlands (1520–21). From his large output some of his most significant works were his prints of the theme of the Apocalypse and his portraits, including self-portraits. He was an early supporter of the Reformation and associated with humanist scholars in Nuremberg. He also wrote extensively on the theory of painting.

Elizabeth I (1533–1603): Queen of England (1558–1603). Daughter of Henry VIII and Anne Boleyn. Brought up a Protestant, on her accession she restored the Anglican church following the reign of her Catholic sister Mary.

She was determined to resist the demands by Puritans for further reforms to the church. She faced threats to her authority, especially from Catholic conspiracies such as the Revolt of the Northern Earls (1569) and plots associated with Mary Queen of Scots, who was held prisoner in England from 1568 until her execution in 1587. In the 1560s she gave support to rebels against Spain in the Netherlands, and in 1588 English ships fought off a threatened invasion by the Spanish Armada. She was highly educated and an astute politician.

Erasmus, Desiderius (1467?–1536): Born in Rotterdam as the illegitimate son of a priest, he was educated in the schools of the Brethren of Common Life at Deventer and 'sHertogenbosch. He became an Augustinian at the monastery of Steyn (1486?) and was ordained a priest in 1492. Discontented in the monastery, he was allowed to leave and study theology in Paris. In 1499 he visited England where he became a friend of Thomas More. He travelled to Italy and was made a doctor of theology at Turin, and while in Venice he worked for the printer Aldo Manuzio. In 1509 he returned to England and taught at Cambridge. He returned to the Netherlands in 1514 and settled in Louvain. In 1515 he was made a councillor to the future Charles V. Following the outbreak of the Reformation he moved to Basle and subsequently to Freiburg. Erasmus had an international reputation and was considered the foremost Christian humanist of his time. He wrote educational books including *De pueris instituendis* (*On the Education of Children*) (1529), *De ratio studii* (*The Method of Study*) (1512) and *Adagia* (1500). In 1516 he produced a version of the New Testament in the original Greek (*Novum instrumentum*) and he translated works by patristic writers, including Ambrose, Origen and Augustine, along with translations of classical texts by Cicero, Euripides and Plutarch among others. Erasmus was perhaps most famous for his devotional works, especially *Enchiridion militis Christiani* (*Handbook of the Christian Soldier*) (1503) and for his satirical attacks on the failings of the Church and secular society, including *Moriae encomium* (*Praise of Folly*) (1511), *Colloquia* (1519) and *Julius Exclusus* (*Julius Excluded*) (1517). Erasmus attacked Luther's denial of free will in *De libero arbitrio* (*On the Freedom of the Will*) (1524). As a result he was distrusted by reformers but also held responsible by many in the Catholic Church for provoking the Reformation. In 1531 some of his writings were condemned as being heretical by the theology faculty of the University of Paris, and after his death some books by Erasmus were placed on the Index of Prohibited Books.

Ferdinand I (1503–64): King of Hungary and Bohemia (1526–64), King of the Romans (1531–58), Holy Roman Emperor (1558–64). The younger brother of Charles V, he was born and brought up in Spain. In 1522 he was made Archduke of Austria and was established as governor to control Imperial affairs during the absences of Charles. With the death of his brother-in-law at the battle of Mohács in 1526 he assumed the crowns of Hungary and Bohemia. He failed to recover Hungarian territory lost to the Turks, but prevented further losses. He was a firm supporter of the Catholic Church

217

but was prepared to take a more flexible approach than Charles in negotiations with Protestants. He played a major role in establishing peace in Germany in 1555 on the basis of *cuius regio, eius religio*. Relations between Ferdinand and Charles were frequently strained and in the 1550s Ferdinand was aggrieved by the plans for succession established by Charles and his failure to give him more help in fighting the Turks in Hungary.

Ferdinand II (1578–1637): Holy Roman Emperor (1619–37). He was a devout Catholic, who before becoming Emperor had successfully imposed the Counter Reformation in the duchy of Styria. He had also subjected the representative estates there to his control. His efforts to achieve the same in Bohemia led to the Defenestration of Prague (1618). The Bohemians repudiated the rule of Ferdinand and elected the Protestant Frederick of the Palatinate to be their king. The forces of Frederick were defeated at the battle of the White Mountain in 1620. Restored to his lands, Ferdinand consolidated his power and the Counter Reformation in Bohemia, and used force to do the same in Germany. This culminated in the Edict of Restitution (1629) which ordered the return to the Church of lands secularized since 1552. This measure provoked Protestant and Catholic opposition to Ferdinand and encouraged Gustavus Adolphus to enter the war. Despite prolonged war, Ferdinand was unable to enforce his demands and his successor was forced to make concessions to obtain peace in 1648.

Ferdinand II (1452–1516): King of Aragon (1479–1516), King of Sicily (1468–1516), King of Naples (1504–16). In 1469 he married Isabella of Castile (1451–1504), with whom he established a joint monarchy over the two Spanish kingdoms. He helped in the restoration of order and royal authority in Castile and led the forces in the conquest of Granada (1482–92). In 1506, on the death of Philip I, who had succeeded Isabella in Castile, he served as Regent until his own death.

Francis I (1494–1547): King of France (1515–47). Much of his reign was spent in conflict with Charles V over claims to Italian and Burgundian lands. In 1515 he invaded the duchy of Milan which was secured by victory at the battle of Marignano. He offered himself as a candidate in the Imperial election in 1519 but was defeated by Charles V. In order to resist Charles he sought alliances with England, the Papacy, Protestants in Germany and the Turks. He met with Henry VIII at the Field of the Cloth of Gold in 1520. In 1525 he was defeated at the battle of Pavia and taken prisoner by Charles. He promised to abandon his claims in Italy and to cede lands to Charles, but failed to fulfil them once he was free. By the Treaty of Cambrai in 1529, he again promised to abandon his Italian claims. In 1537 he invaded Piedmont. Francis formed an alliance with the Ottomans and allowed their fleet to use Toulon harbour in 1543. He finally made peace with Charles by the Treaty of Crépy in 1544. By the Concordat of Bologna, he gained the right to nominate candidates for the major ecclesiastical benefices in France. He proved to be hostile to the Reformation in France, especially following the

Affair of the Placards in 1534, after which French Protestants were persecuted. Francis attempted to deal with the weaknesses of French government and finances, and created a centralised treasury, but he increasingly relied upon the revenue from selling offices and on loans.

Frederick II (1712–86): King of Prussia (1740–86). Known as Frederick the Great. When young his interest in the arts had led him into conflict with his father (Frederick William I), who for a while had placed him under arrest. They were reconciled when Frederick showed greater interest in the army and his state responsibilities. When he succeeded in 1740, he used the death of Emperor Charles VI to seize the rich lands of Silesia from Maria Theresa. In the fighting which ensued (1740–45), Frederick was able to hold on to his gains. Fearing an alliance was forming against him, he provoked war again in 1756 with the invasion of Saxony (Seven Years' War). During the course of the war his lands were invaded and devastated, but as the coalition against him disintegrated after 1762, he was able to reassert his power and at the Peace of Hubertusberg (1763) he managed to keep all his lands, including Silesia. He then introduced many projects to restore the economy. He was interested in the Enlightenment and introduced legal and educational reforms. He encouraged religious toleration but he was not prepared to compromise his own authority.

Frederick III (1463–1525): Elector of Saxony (1486–1525). Known as 'The Wise', he was noted for his piety and for being an effective ruler of his lands. He reformed the administrative systems within his own lands and was active in the efforts to achieve reform of the constitution of the Empire in 1495. In 1500 he was made head of the short-lived *Reichsregiment* (Regency Council). In 1519 he was considered to be a likely candidate to stand for election as Emperor, but he refused to stand against Charles V. He established the University of Wittenberg and protected Luther from arrest and persecution. He secured safe conduct for Luther to attend the Diet of Worms and arranged for his protective incarceration in the Wartburg castle. He nevertheless had virtually no direct contact with Luther.

Frederick William (1620–88): Elector of Brandenburg (1640–88). Known as the Great Elector. He succeeded to widely dispersed lands which had suffered badly as a result of the ongoing Thirty Years' War. From 1643 he created a substantial standing army funded by forced levies from his subjects. In 1648 he gained the secularized bishoprics of Halberstadt, Minden and Kammin. In 1675 his army defeated the Swedes at the battle of Fehrbellin, and he went on to eject them from Pomerania and Stettin, which he then occupied. His main achievements were to create a standing army for all his domains, along with a centralised treasury (*Generalkriegskasse*) to support it.

Frederick William I (1688–1740): King in Prussia (1713–40). His major interest was the army, which he increased from 40,000 in 1713 to 80,000 in 1740. In 1721 he recovered Stettin and lands in Pomerania which had been occupied by Sweden since the Thirty Years' War, but made little use of his forces. In

219

1733 he established the cantonal system of recruitment for the army which placed levies for men on each area. He reorganised provincial and central government, and by the terms of the 1722 *Generaldirektorium* brought the control of finances and war under one administration. This, coupled with his parsimony, allowed him to accumulate large financial surpluses. He was a supporter of the ideals of Pietism. To foster economic development within his lands he enforced protectionist policies. He maintained a regiment of tall grenadiers at Potsdam for drill and show.

Galileo (Galileo Galilei) (1564–1642): Italian scientist and astronomer. He was educated in Pisa, where he became professor of mathematics. He began experiments on gravitation and inertia, and these were continued after he was appointed professor of mathematics at Padua in 1592. In 1609 he made improvements to the new invention, the telescope, which he used for astronomical study. He discovered the satellites around Venus, mountains on the moon and several stars, and published his findings in *Sidereus Nuncius* (1610). In 1611 he went to Florence as mathematician to the Grand Duke of Tuscany, but his astronomical findings were denounced by some in the Church as showing support for the Copernican interpretation of the universe. He defended himself against attacks from the Inquisition and was forced to accept that Copernican views were heretical. In 1632 he published *Dialogue on the World Systems* which vindicated Copernican theories. All copies of the book were seized by the Inquisition and he was tried for heresy. He was forced to abjure the views in his book and was placed under house arrest. He continued to work and wrote *Two New Sciences*, which he smuggled out of Italy for publication in the Netherlands in 1638. His significance rested on his discoveries, on his use of experimentation and observation as the basis of science, and his opposition to the imposition of theological and philosophical preconceptions upon scientific research.

Gustavus Adolphus (Gustav II Adolph) (1594–1632): King of Sweden (1611–32). He fought campaigns against Russia (1613–17) and Poland (1621–29) which gave Sweden dominance within the Baltic region. Fearing the growth of Habsburg influence in Northern Germany, he entered the Thirty Years' War in 1629 and revived the flagging Protestant and anti-Imperial cause. Following his victory at the battle of Breitenfeld in 1631, Swedish forces occupied Bavaria and Bohemia. In 1632 his army was victorious at the battle of Lützen, but he was killed in the fighting. In Sweden he reformed the system of justice, local government, the royal chancery, and he introduced fiscal reforms. He was an astounding military commander and introduced many reforms to his navy and army, including the use of conscription, the use of muskets, the adoption of light mobile artillery pieces, and an emphasis upon drill and training. He was ably assisted by his Chancellor, Axel Oxenstierna, who continued to direct the government after the death of the king.

Gutenberg, Johannes (1395?–1468): Little is known about his early life, but he was probably born in Mainz, where he was later apprenticed as a goldsmith.

He was exiled in 1430 following political conflict in the city, and moved to Strasbourg where he conducted experiments in printing. He discovered an alloy which allowed him to cast stamps of individual letters from moulds. These formed the moveable type which could be put together to form blocks of type which could be printed on a press. He returned to Mainz in 1448 and in 1454 he began to produce a printed version of the Bible. The first edition ran to three hundred copies and it was the first book printed using moveable type. He did not benefit from his invention as he was forced to surrender his press to repay debts.

Handel (Händel), George Frederick (1685–1759): German composer and musician. Born in Halle, he joined an orchestra in Hamburg at the age of seventeen. Shortly after he travelled to Italy where he became famous for his keyboard skills. He was also influenced by Italian musical fashion. On returning to Germany he became musical director at the court of the then Elector of Hanover. In 1716 he moved to England and was employed at the court of Queen Anne and later George I. He was a prolific composer and wrote many operas, *concerti grossi* and oratorios. His most famous work was *The Messiah* of 1742.

Henry IV (1553–1610): King of France (1589–1610) and founder of the Bourbon dynasty. The son of Antoine de Bourbon, he was a prince of the blood. His mother, Jeanne d'Albret, was a Huguenot and he also converted to Calvinism. In 1572 he married Marguerite de Valois, the sister of the king. The wedding celebrations degenerated into the Massacre of St Bartholomew's Day. He was held captive and forced to recant his Calvinist beliefs, but having escaped in 1576, he became the Huguenot leader. With the death of the Duke of Anjou he became heir to the throne, and the murder of Henry III in 1589 made him king. Members of the Guise faction and the Catholic League refused to accept him as king and civil war ensued. In 1593 he converted to Catholicism and was crowned king in 1594, ending the civil wars in France. He granted limited toleration to Huguenots by the Edict of Nantes (1598). He worked to restore order and unity in France, and under his minister Sully, the finances of the state recovered. His marriage was annulled in 1599 and in 1601 he married Marie de Médicis. He was assassinated in 1610.

Henry VIII (1491–1547): King of England (1509–47). In 1509 he married the widow of his deceased older brother. He gained a victory over the French at the battle of the Spurs in 1513, but gained little from the peace settlement. He appointed Thomas Wolsey as his first minister in 1515. He met Francis I at the Field of the Cloth of Gold in 1520, but their negotiations had no outcome. He opposed the teachings of Luther and refuted them in the *Assertio Septem Sacramentorum* in 1521 (although he probably wrote no more than a small part of it), for which he was rewarded by Pope Leo X with the title Defender of the Faith. Being without a son, he proposed in 1527 a divorce from Catherine of Aragon. The refusal of the pope to grant him a divorce prompted Henry to dismiss Wolsey. In 1531 he rejected papal authority and was proclaimed 'Protector and Supreme Head of the English Church'. In 1533 Henry's marriage to Catherine was annulled by Thomas Cranmer, Archbishop of Canterbury, and he married Anne Boleyn. In 1534 Parliament passed the legislation which established the English Reformation. In 1536 Henry divorced Anne Boleyn (who was executed) and married Jane Seymour (d. 1537). He subsequently married Anne of Cleves in 1540 but swiftly divorced her. He married Catherine Howard in 1540 but she was executed for her adultery in 1542. In 1543 he married Catherine Parr who outlived him. In 1539 Henry supported the Act of Six Articles, which repudiated evangelical teaching and emphasised the catholic doctrines of the Church of England. Military campaigns against the French and Scots in the 1540s gained victories but their cost absorbed the money the crown had gained from the secularisation of monastic property.

Hoffman, Melchior (1495?–1543): A radical lay preacher who emphasised the imminence of the Second Coming of Christ. In 1523 he had become a follower of Luther and spread evangelical ideas in Estonia. He soon parted company with Lutheranism with calls for control of churches by the congregation and by his denial of the Real Presence. Over the next few years he went to Sweden, Lübeck and Schleswig-Holstein, and wherever he went his preaching provoked disorder. After a disputation in Flensburg in 1529, his teaching was condemned by Lutherans. He went to Strasbourg where he was re-baptized and became convinced that the city would be the new Jerusalem in the anticipated apocalypse. He was arrested but escaped to Frisia where he found strong support for his beliefs and re-baptized many. On his return to Strasbourg in 1533 he was arrested and spent the rest of his life in prison. Some of his followers from the Netherlands went to Münster and were the leaders of the Anabaptist kingdom established there in 1533–34. His followers were known as Melchiorites.

Hume, David (1711–76): Scottish philosopher and historian. He was born and educated in Edinburgh. He studied for five years in France, where he started work on his *Treatise on Human Nature*. His work initially had little impact and he was unable to secure a university appointment. He published *Essays Moral and Political* in 1741, *An Enquiry Concerning Human Understanding* and the *Essay on Miracles* in 1748, and *Political Discourses* in 1752. In the 1750s he also began work on his *History of England*. Hume questioned the existing views on causality and challenged the emphasis given to reason, which he believed could not provide an explanation of events and conduct. He believed the mind tried to find explanations for the unconnected impression caused by events. He was sceptical of divine involvement in the world and of humankind having a spiritual nature.

Jansen, Cornelius (1585–1638): Flemish theologian and bishop. In his posthumously published book *Augustinus*, he advanced the belief in predestination and challenged Catholic teaching on free will and the efficacy of works in achieving salvation. He and his followers remained loyal to Catholicism, but his views were treated with suspicion of being heretical by many in the Church, especially the Jesuits. His ideas gained a wide following, especially in France, where support was centred upon the convent of Port-Royal-des Champs. Louis XIV was particularly hostile as he believed many of his opponents were Jansenists. In 1710 Louis had Port-Royal destroyed and in 1713 he persuaded the pope to declare Jansenism heretical in the Bull *Unigenitus*.

Josquin Des Prés (Desprez) (1440?–1521): French composer, perhaps the most influential composer of his day. He served at the papal court from 1486 to 1499. He also served as music director at the courts in Milan, Ferrara and the French court of Louis XII. In 1505 he returned to the church of Condé in Burgundy where he remained until his death. His church music made innovative use of all the contemporary musical styles to create a rich and powerful sound. He wrote many secular songs, often having parts for several singers. One of his most famous compositions is his *Missa Pange Lingua*.

Karlstadt, Andreas Bodenstein von (1486–1541): German theologian and religious reformer. He studied at Erfurt and Cologne and was professor of theology at Wittenberg from 1505 to 1522. He initially opposed Luther's reforms to the curriculum and theological changes, but in 1517 became a firm supporter. He accompanied Luther to the Leipzig Disputation (1519) where he spoke in his support. While Luther was secreted in the Wartburg, he became a leader of the evangelical movement in Wittenberg. He gave communion in both kinds to the laity (1521) and married early the following year. He opposed religious images and encouraged acts of iconoclasm. His radicalism prompted a rift with Luther, and Karlstadt left the university to work in a rural parish at Orlamünde. Luther attacked his radical views in the pamphlet, *Against the Heavenly Prophets*, and in 1524 he was forced to leave Saxony. In 1530–34 he served as a deacon in Zurich and in 1534 was made a professor of theology in Basle.

Leibniz, (Leibnitz) Gottfried Wilhelm (1646–1716): German mathematician and philosopher. He studied at Leipzig, Jena and Altdorf, and travelled widely in Europe. His early career was as a diplomat, but he increasingly devoted his time to scholarship. In 1675 he discovered calculus. His work was independent of that of Newton, and Leibniz published his findings in 1684, twenty years before Newton made his discovery public. His main philosophical works were *Théodicée* (1710), and *Monadologie* (1714). He believed that all aspects of the universe existed in harmony, following a divine plan. Evil existed within this system, but God had created the best that was possible. His views were subsequently criticised by Voltaire for their excessive optimism.

Louis XIV (1638–1715): King of France (1643–1715). Known as *le roi soleil* (the Sun King). He succeeded to the throne as a child and the government was initially in the hands of his mother, Anne of Austria, and Cardinal Mazarin, who was to remain as Chief Minister until his death in 1661. Louis then took control of government and was concerned to improve order within France and to increase French power in Europe. Through war he hoped to extend and strengthen the boundaries of France, but his aggressive foreign policy prompted the hostility of other states and left France isolated. During his reign France fought in the War of Devolution (1667–68), the Dutch War (1672–79), the War of the League of Augsburg (the Nine Years' War) (1689–97), the War of Spanish Succession (1701–13). As a result, France gained parts of the Spanish Netherlands, Strasbourg and some colonial lands, but at a huge cost to the economy and people of France. At home he was determined to remove all challenges to his authority or threats to unity and order. He suppressed the Jansenist movement within the French church, and in 1685 withdrew the Edict of Nantes which had granted limited religious toleration to Huguenots. As a result, many thousands were forced into exile. He was a great patron of the arts and used his patronage to enhance the power of the monarch. He built an enormous palace at Versailles where he established an elaborate court.

Louis XV (1710–74): King of France (1715–74). He succeeded to the throne as a child and until 1723 France was governed by the duke of Orléans who acted as Regent. He made his tutor, Cardinal Fleury, into his Chief Minister until his death in 1743. France participated in the War of the Austrian Succession (1740–48) and the Seven Years' War, but her forces performed poorly and the country lost possessions in India and North America to the British. His ministers Maupeou and Choiseul attempted to reform government and state finances, but achieved little.

Loyola, Ignatius (1491?–1556): Spanish theologian and religious reformer. As a young man he was a soldier, but while recovering from injury in 1521 he underwent a religious conversion. He began writing his devotional work, the *Spiritual Exercises*, and went on to study at Alcalá, Salamanca and Paris. In Spain the Church initially viewed his ideas with suspicion, but in Paris he formed a small group of followers, including Francis Xavier and Diego Laínez, who were to play an influential role in the Jesuit Order. They planned to carry out missionary work in Palestine, but instead formed a new Order, the Society of Jesus, or Jesuits, with Loyola as its head. The Order, based in Italy, received papal sanction in 1540. He spent the rest of his life organising the Order and compiled its *Constitutiones* which were approved in 1558. He also continued to work on the *Spiritual Exercises*. By 1556 there were a thousand Jesuits, and by 1580 there were five thousand, who were engaged in combating Protestantism in Europe and in missionary work in colonial lands. He stamped his character on the Jesuit Order, emphasising discipline, high academic achievement and religious fervour.

Luther, Martin (1483–1546): German religious reformer and theologian. He was educated at the University of Erfurt where he gained a masters degree in 1505. He abandoned study of the law to become an Augustinian friar in 1505. He achieved positions of responsibility within his Order, but suffered from spiritual doubts over how salvation might be achieved. In 1512 he became a doctor of theology and was made Professor of Biblical Studies at Wittenberg. He came to believe that salvation could be achieved only when a sinner sought God's mercy, and not by any human action, a teaching which he eventually expressed as salvation by God's grace through faith. He rose to national prominence when he produced his *Ninety Five Theses* (1517) which attacked the sale of indulgences. Between 1517 and 1521 he wrote treatises which revolutionised teaching on the sacraments, papal and clerical authority, and salvation. These included *The Address to the Christian Nobility of the German Nation, The Babylonian Captivity of the Church, On the Freedom of the Christian.* In 1521 Luther was excommunicated and subsequently summoned by Charles V to the Diet of Worms, but refused to recant his teachings. After the Diet he was taken in secret to the Wartburg castle on the orders of his ruler, to protect him from arrest. While he was there he translated the New Testament into German. He returned to Wittenberg in 1522 to restore order, which had been threatened by the radical reforms of Karlstadt. Luther's ideas spread quickly throughout Germany and beyond, but he was soon concerned that his teachings were used to justify radical religious reforms, which he deemed inappropriate, and to support demands for social and political change. This problem was emphasised in the 1525 Peasant War in Germany, which prompted Luther to write *Against the Robbing and Murdering Hordes of Peasants*, which called upon the princes to use force to put down the rebellion. He insisted subjects did not have the right of rebellion against their rulers, even when rulers obstructed his teachings. After 1525 he became involved in a conflict with Zwingli and his followers over the correct understanding of sacraments and their significance. During the 1520s Charles V failed to summon the promised council to settle religious disputes in Germany, and in 1530 he reaffirmed his opposition to Lutheran teaching. As a result Luther was persuaded to relax his views on opposing Charles when he was attempting to eradicate Protestant teaching. He wrote many works defending and explaining his views against his Catholic and radical critics, and proved to be an astute publicist, who used the printing press to reach a wide audience.

Machiavelli, Niccolò (1469–1527): Italian politician, political theorist and historian. He rose to prominence in the Florentine republic established after the expulsion of the Medici in 1494. He was appointed head of the second chancery and secretary to the Council of Ten in 1498. His work involved him serving as an envoy to foreign governments, and in this capacity he had the opportunity to visit and observe many rulers. These included Julius II, Louis XII of France and Cesare Borgia. He also was made responsible for the creation of a Florentine civic militia, for he firmly believed that it would be a more effective way of defending the city than relying upon mercenary soldiers. In 1513 the Medici were restored to power in Florence and he was dismissed. He spent the following years using his classical knowledge and his experience in government to write on the theory and practice of politics, on the history of Florence and on warfare. In 1513 he began work on *The Prince*, in which he argued that a successful ruler must control his own forces and be prepared to use them ruthlessly, in order to establish his power. To achieve this he acknowledged that princes might disregard normal restraints of morality and justice. In *The Discourses* he examined the nature of political change and the importance of creating strong constitutional institutions.

Maria Theresa (1717–80): Archduchess of Austria, Queen of Hungary and Bohemia. She was the heir to the lands of Emperor Charles VI, who had gained international agreement to the succession of a female by the terms of the Pragmatic Sanction. On the death of Charles VI in 1740, the Habsburg province of Silesia was seized by Frederick II, in violation of the Pragmatic Sanction. This prompted other states to contest the rights of Maria Theresa in the War of the Austrian Succession. Showing great fortitude, she rallied her support and held on to her lands, with the exception of Silesia. In order to strengthen her government and power she introduced a series of reforms, with the help of ministers Kaunitz and Haugwitz. These involved reform of the state finances, changes to local and central government and restricting the power of local estates. She also undertook a change in the traditional alliances of Austria. One result of the changes was that Austria was able to maintain a standing army. When Frederick II precipitated the Seven Years' War with an attack on Saxony, Maria Theresa tried to regain Silesia, but failed. From 1765 she ruled with her son (the future Joseph II) as co-regent. Her husband, Francis of Lorraine, was Emperor from 1745 until his death in 1765.

Maximilian I (1459–1519): Holy Roman Emperor (1493–1519). In 1477 he married Mary (d. 1482) heiress to the Duke of Burgundy. This involved him in many conflicts to defend the lands of his wife. In 1490 he took control of the Tyrol and in 1493 he inherited the Habsburg Austrian and Upper Rhineland territories. The Ottomans were repelled at Villach in 1492, and in 1493 he recovered the Burgundian lands of Artois and Franche-Comté. He joined the Holy League in 1495 which aimed at expelling the French from Italy, but in this and future Italian campaigns he gained little. He was defeated by the Swiss at Dorneck in 1499 and was obliged to concede Swiss independence from the Empire. This and other military campaigns were hampered by a lack of money and resources. His attempt to impose a Common Penny tax within the Empire to pay for military and defensive measures was a failure as the Estates feared it would increase the power of the Emperor. The marriage alliances he negotiated for his family proved to be spectacularly successful. His son Philip married Juana (Joanna), the daughter of Ferdinand and Isabella of Spain, and his granddaughter Mary married King Louis of Hungary. The lands inherited as a result of these marriages formed the Empire of Charles V, the grandson of Maximilian, who succeeded him as Holy Roman Emperor. Despite being frequently short of money, Maximilian was a patron of many artists and scholars.

Mazarin, Jules (Giulio Mazarini) (1602–61): An Italian who became Chief Minister of Louis XIV of France. He came to the attention of Richelieu when, as a papal diplomat, he helped in the negotiations for peace at the end of the War of the Mantuan Succession in 1631. He went to France from 1634 as papal envoy and became a French citizen. On the recommendation of Louis XIII he was made a Cardinal in 1641. On the death of the king (1643) he became Chief Minister to the Regent, Anne of Austria, mother of Louis XIV. He continued the war policies of Richelieu and at the end of the Thirty Years' War made territorial gains for France, including Metz, Verdun, Alsace and Breisach. In 1648 his demands for increased taxation prompted rebellion (the Fronde) and he was forced from office and into exile until 1653. He returned as Chief Minister to Louis XIV and spent much time educating him in matters of statecraft. With the Treaty of the Pyrenees in 1659 Mazarin brought the war with Spain to a conclusion, with significant territorial gains for France.

Medici, Lorenzo de (1449–92): Florentine banker and political leader. He inherited control of the Medici bank and the political power exercised by the Medici family in Florence. He controlled Florence through manipulation of office-holding and the republican institutions of the city. Although he was generally popular, there was some opposition to him within the ruling elite, and this became apparent in the Pazzi conspiracy of 1473, which was supported by Pope Sixtus IV. He escaped an attempt on his life but Florence was plunged into war with the pope and his allies. He personally negotiated peace during a visit to the King of Naples and, as a consequence, his authority in Florence was enhanced. He was a generous patron of the arts and scholarship, commissioning many paintings, statues and buildings. He was also an accomplished poet but less astute in business, and the affairs of the Medici bank declined during his period of control.

Melanchthon, Philipp (1497–1560): German religious reformer and educational reformer. Born in Baden, he was educated at Heidelberg and Tübingen. In 1518 he was made Professor of Greek at Wittenberg, where he collaborated with Luther. In 1521 he composed the *Loci Communes* which subsequently passed through several additions and was greatly expanded. It provided a systematic investigation and explanation of evangelical theological thought and was highly influential. He attempted to follow a moderate view in disputes and was frequently called upon to represent Luther in discussions. He played a major role in settling disputes between Luther and South German Zwinglians in the 1530s. After the death of Luther (1546) he became the leader of the Lutheran church. He rejected the Interim of Charles V (1548), but was prepared to make concessions over religious issues he considered to be of little consequence (adiaphora), a position which led to divisions within the Lutheran church. He was frequently called upon to assist governments in the establishment of schools and in the design and reform of the curricula for schools.

Monteverdi, Claudio (1567–1643): Italian composer. In 1607, while at the court in Mantua, he wrote *Orfeo*, one of the earliest operas, and was the first to use a combination of recitative, solo and chorus. He went on to write other operas, including *L'incoronazione di Poppea* (1642), by which time the popularity of opera was established. Many other composers imitated his style. He was appointed director of music at St Mark's in Venice in 1613, and composed much liturgical music, including his *Vespro della Beata Vergine*. His music was characterised by striking and innovative use of harmony.

Müntzer, Thomas (1490?–1525): German religious reformer, theologian and revolutionary leader. Born in Saxony, he was educated at Leipzig and Frankfurt an der Oder. He was ordained in 1514 and became a chantry priest. Probably by 1518 he was a supporter of Luther, but he was also influenced by mysticism and stressed the need for divine revelation. He was a preacher in Zwickau in 1520, but left in 1521 for Prague and by 1523 he was a preacher in Allstedt. By this stage he emphasised the importance of revelation through dreams over biblical study, and he criticised the doctrine of justification by faith alone by stressing the need for faith to be put to the test through suffering. Luther considered him to be a fanatic and warned the Saxon rulers against him. Müntzer was called to preach before Duke John and his son, and he warned them of the coming apocalypse, insisting that if they did not assist in the movement they risked being deposed. Shortly after he fled, but by 1524 he was pastor in Mühlhausen. There he persuaded the populace to join peasant rebels in 1525, but their forces were savagely defeated by the princes at the battle of Frankenhausen. Müntzer was captured and executed.

Newcomen, Thomas (1663–1729): British inventor and engineer. Although not the inventor of steam power, he was the first person to produce efficient and reliable engines, which could be used for industrial purposes. They were widely used for pumping water from mine workings.

Newton, Sir Isaac (1642–1727): English scientist and mathematician. In 1666 he wrote a paper which established the basic principles of calculus, or what he called the 'fluxional method'. He did not publish his work until 1704, by which time Leibniz, who made the same discovery in 1675, had already published his findings. In 1669 he was appointed as Lucasian Professor of Mathematics at Cambridge, but during the 1670s he spent most of his time studying theology and alchemy. Stimulated in 1684 by a visit from the astronomer Edmund Halley, he began work which led him to discover his laws on motion and gravitation. These were expounded in his book *Principia*, which was published in 1687. In 1703 he was elected as President of the Royal Society and in 1704 he published his book *Opticks*, in which he described his findings on the study of light and colour.

Olivares, Gasper de Guzmán, Conde Duque de (1587–1645): Chief Minister of Philip IV of Spain (1622–43). He aimed to restore Spanish power by domestic reforms and military campaigns. The Twelve Year Truce with the Netherlands ended in 1621 and Olivares decided to renew the war, leading to vast expenditure on the navy and army. In 1626 he introduced the Union of Arms which spread the cost of supporting the Spanish army among all parts of Spain instead of relying on Castilian contributions. The scheme led to rebellion in Catalonia (1640–52) and Portugal (1640–43). In 1628–31 Olivares involved Spain in the War of the Mantuan Succession against France, but gained nothing. In 1636 Spain attempted unsuccessfully to invade France. In 1639 a Spanish fleet was defeated by the Dutch at the battle of the Downs. The problems caused by defeats abroad were made worse by rebellions in Portugal and Catalonia in 1640. In 1643 the failure of his policies led to the dismissal of Olivares from office.

Peter I (1672–1725): Tsar of Russia (1682–1725). Known as Peter the Great. His reign was characterised by the enactment of reforms aimed at introducing the technological, military, cultural and administrative practices of Western Europe to Russia. Change was driven mainly by the desire of Peter to increase his military power. Between 1697 and 1698 he visited Western Europe to view the technology and institutions he wished to emulate. He created a substantial army and the first Russian navy. In 1696 he captured Azov from the Turks, but in 1700 he engaged in war against the Swedes, seeking to remove Swedish dominance over the eastern Baltic region. His army was heavily defeated by Swedish forces at the battle of Narva (1700). In 1711 his army was defeated by the Ottomans at the battle of Pruth. At the battle of Poltava (1709) the Russian army defeated their Swedish opponents and by the Treaty of Nystad (1721) Peter gained several Baltic provinces from Sweden. In 1703 he began the construction of a new capital of St Petersburg which had direct access to the Baltic. From 1708 he introduced reforms to local government, and in 1711 he improved the efficiency of central government with the creation of a Senate, followed in 1718 with the introduction of government departments. In 1722 he instituted the Table of Ranks which established that rank in society came not through birth, but by civil or military service to the state.

Philip of Hesse (1504–67): Ruled as Landgrave (1509–67). Known as Philip the Magnanimous, he succeeded his father at the aged of four and came to his majority at fourteen. He faced internal opposition, which he ended by crushing the Knights' Revolt in 1523 and suppressing rebellious peasants in 1525. In 1524 he became a supporter of Luther and established the Lutheran church in his lands. He played a major role in efforts to create a Protestant alliance to resist the Habsburgs and their defence of Catholicism, notably by calling the Colloquy of Marburg in 1529, which aimed at settling the differences between Luther and Zwingli. He was influential in the Protestant Schmalkaldic League, but after the defeat of its forces by Charles V he was held prisoner from 1547 to 1552. After his release, his power and influence were diminished but he assisted in the 1555 peace settlement at Augsburg. In 1540 he persuaded Luther, Bucer and Melanchthon to give their agreement to his bigamous marriage to Margarethe von der Sale, an action which did much to harm the reputation and unity of the Protestant cause.

Philip II (1527–98): King of Spain (1556–98). He acted as Regent in Spain from 1543. In 1543 he married Maria of Portugal (d. 1545), in 1554 he married Mary Tudor (d. 1558). He married Elizabeth de Valois in 1560 (d. 1568) and Anna of Austria in 1570 (d. 1580). During much of his reign Spain was at war against the enemies of the Habsburgs, Protestants and the Ottomans. Against France his armies were successful at the battles of St Quentin (1557) and Gravelines (1558). Fighting against the Ottomans, his troops were defeated at the battle of Djerba (1560), but fought successfully to relieve the besieged island of Malta (1565). His navy won a decisive victory over the Ottomans at Lepanto (1571). His forces were unsuccessful in suppressing the Revolt of the Netherlands, although some territory was recovered from the rebels in the 1580s. To prevent the English from aiding the Dutch rebels, and to punish English support for privateers who attacked his possessions and ships in the Americas, Philip dispatched the Armada to assist in the invasion of England in 1588. The venture proved to be a disaster and of the 130 ships which set sail only 60 returned to Spain. He commissioned and collected many works of art, and ordered the construction of the Escorial Palace (1563–84). In 1561 Philip established Madrid as the capital of Spain. The cost of his military campaigns left his successors burdened with debt.

Philip IV (1605–65): King of Spain (1621–65). During his reign Spain was debilitated by the wars advocated by his Chief Minister Olivares. They also prompted rebellions in Catalonia and Portugal. By the Treaty of Westphalia (1648) Spain acknowledged the independence of the United Provinces, and the war with France was ended by the Treaty of the Pyrenees (1659), by which Spain lost Artois and Roussillon. Spain experienced state bankruptcies in 1647 and 1653. Philip IV was an important patron of the arts.

Pius IV, Pope (Giovanni Angelo de Medici) (1499–1565): Pope (1559–65). He was not related to the Medici of Florence, but was of a noble family. He was educated in law at Pavia and Bologna. On becoming pope he reconvened the Council of Trent in 1562. When the Council concluded in 1563 he confirmed the decrees which had been passed and showed he was determined to enforce their observance by the Church. All bishops and secular clergy were obliged to accept the confession of faith formulated at Trent. He promoted his nephew Charles Borromeo to be Archbishop of Milan. He was a patron of the arts and scholarship.

Pombal, Sebastião José de Carvalho e Mello (1699–1782): Portuguese diplomat and statesman. He served as Ambassador in London (1739–45) and in Vienna (1745–49). In 1749 he was appointed Secretary of State for Foreign Affairs and in 1756 he became Chief Minister. He espoused the ideas of the Enlightenment and pursued reform vigorously and ruthlessly. King Joseph had little interest in government and Pombal held almost total control over the country. He showed his skills following the catastrophic earthquake which destroyed much of Lisbon in 1755, organising relief and rebuilding. He reformed education, finances and trade, especially with the colony of Brazil.

He used an attempt on the life of the king to accuse opponents among the aristocracy and the Jesuits of conspiracy. This resulted in the execution of opponents and the expulsion of the Jesuit Order. On the death of the king he was removed from office and accused of abusing his powers. He was found guilty but not punished.

Richelieu, Armand Jean du Plessis, Cardinal Duc de (1585–1642): Chief Minister of Louis XIII of France. Made Bishop of Luçon in 1606, he was a representative of the clergy at the Estates-General of 1614. He became a secretary of state in 1616, a Cardinal in 1622 and Chief Minister in 1624. As part of his plan to end resistance to royal authority by the Huguenots, he led the siege of La Rochelle in 1627, which was eventually forced to surrender to him in 1628. By the Peace of Alais in 1629, the Huguenots lost most of their privileges but retained the right of public worship. Richelieu led France into war against Spain over the Mantuan Succession dispute in 1629, and although successful he was criticised at home for weakening the fight of Spain against Protestantism. This led to a plot at court to have him removed from office (Day of the Dupes) in 1630, but Louis XIII refused to dismiss him. He continued to give support to the enemies of Spain and in 1631 made the Treaty of Bärwalde with Gustavus Adolphus. In 1635 France declared war on Spain. Richelieu suppressed rebellions against royal authority, notably that led by the Duke of Montmorency and the brother of the king in 1632, and the popular 'Nu-Pieds' rebellion in Normandy in 1639. Richelieu was successful in increasing the authority of the ruler and French power in Europe, but his efforts to improve the economy were sacrificed to the need to finance wars.

Rousseau, Jean Jacques (1712–78): Swiss philosopher. Despite having only limited formal education he wrote on a wide range of topics. He had an itinerant existence and benefited from the generosity of wealthy patronesses. At the invitation of Diderot, he contributed to the *Encyclopédie*. His most important work was *Du Contrat Social* (1762) in which he examined social and political relations and responsibility within the state. He advanced the idea of civil liberty, and of the General Will which embodied popular sovereignty. This notion was later criticised for providing justification for totalitarian regimes. In *Emile* (1762) he advanced his ideas on education. He believed a young child unaffected by society was near to nature and therefore enjoyed a state of happiness. For this reason children should be allowed to develop freely without systematic efforts to inculcate knowledge and the values of the world. His ideas became influential in the early stages of the French Revolution.

Rudolf II (1552–1612): King of Hungary (1572–1612), King of Bohemia (1575–1612), Holy Roman Emperor (1576–1612). An ineffective ruler, he increasingly withdrew from public affairs during the course of his reign. He supported the Counter Reformation, but opposed religious oppression, and in 1609 he granted the Letter of Majesty, which upheld religious toleration for Protestants in Bohemia. He gathered an enormous collection of art and was renowned for his patronage of artists and scientists. He was fascinated by the occult and alchemy.

Sattler, Michael (1490?–1527): Prior of the Benedictine monastery of St Peter im Schwarzwald, he left during the Peasant War in 1525. By 1526 he had become an Anabaptist and was making missionary journeys and re-baptizing in Switzerland. He played a leading role in the meeting of Anabaptists at Schleitheim and drafted the Schleitheim Confession, a general statement of Anabaptist beliefs. This rejected the violent apocalyptical beliefs expounded by Hans Hut. Sattler was arrested in 1527 and executed by burning.

Savonarola, Girolamo (1452–98): Born and educated in Ferrara, he became a Dominican friar in 1475. His preaching was noted for its apocalyptic content and after a period in Florence he moved to Bologna, before being recalled to Florence after the intervention of Lorenzo de Medici. His apocalyptic message drew much support from all sections of society and he became an outspoken critic of greed and the exploitation of power. He prophesied the imminent punishment of the Church and Italy as retribution for their failings. The French invasion of 1494 appeared to confirm his words, and with the expulsion of the Medici from Florence, he played an influential political role. In particular, he advocated the need for constitutional reform, but the failures of the new republic caused public opinion to turn against him. He was accused of being a false prophet, executed, and his body was burnt.

Schwenckfeld, Kaspar von (1489–1561): Theologian and spiritualist leader. A nobleman from Silesia, he was educated at Cologne and at Frankfurt on Oder. He served at the court of the rulers of Liegnitz and Oels, but in 1519 was converted to Luther's teachings and left court life. Although a layman, he became a leading Lutheran in Silesia, but in 1525 had a religious experience which led him to reject Luther's doctrines on justification and the sacraments. He emphasised instead the importance of mystical experience and denied belief in the ubiquity of Christ's body. He was forced to leave Silesia and moved to Strasbourg in 1529. Opposition by Bucer forced him to leave in 1534 and he spent his remaining years moving from town to town. He established a small but devoted group of followers.

Shakespeare, William (1564–1616): English dramatist and poet. Born in Stratford-upon-Avon, by 1592 he was in London, where his plays were successful. By 1594 he was associated with an acting company known as the Lord Chamberlain's Men. His plays included several based on English history, such as *Henry IV (Parts I and II)*, *Richard III* and *Henry V*. He also wrote several tragedies, including *Macbeth*, *Othello* and *Romeo and Juliet*. He produced many comedies, including *Comedy of Errors* and *A Midsummer Night's Dream*. On several occasions his plays were performed before Queen Elizabeth I and James I. There has been much inconclusive speculation as to whether all the plays attributed to Shakespeare were written by him or were all his own work. He is also famed for his sonnets which express idealised notions of love.

Spener, Philipp Jakob (1635–1705): Lutheran theologian and an early leader of the Pietist movement. He was keen to restore the evangelical enthusiasm of Lutheranism and when he was made a pastor in Frankfurt in 1666 he began twice weekly meetings known as the *Collegia Pietatis* at his home, aimed at stimulating spiritual life and acts of devotion and charity. In 1686 he was appointed court preacher in Dresden, but his teachings were attacked by theologians at the University of Leipzig. In 1691 he became pastor of the Nikolaikirche in Berlin, where he gained the support of King Frederick William I. He was influential in the establishment of the University of Halle and his ideas had a considerable impact on Lutheranism.

Suleiman (1494–1566): Sultan (1520–66). Known in Europe as 'The Magnific-ent' and known to his subjects as *kanuni* (law giver). He was an able military leader who extended Ottoman control in Central Europe and the Mediter-ranean. In 1521 he captured Belgrade and in 1526 his forces were victorious at the battle of Mohács, killing King Louis of Hungary. Suleiman occupied much of Hungary and established suzerainty over Transylvania. In 1529 he besieged Vienna without success and in 1536 he formed an alliance against the Habsburgs with Francis I of France. In the Mediterranean he captured Rhodes in 1522. His ships defeated the Christian fleet at the battle of Prevesa in 1538, which allowed him to remove the Venetians from their remaining possessions in the eastern Mediterranean. In 1565 he launched a massive and unsuccessful siege against Malta. On the other borders of his Empire he fought campaigns in Asia Minor in 1534, 1548 and 1554, which established his control of Iraq. In 1538 he captured Aden as part of a campaign to prevent the Portuguese trading in the Indian Ocean. At home he was noted for his efforts to prevent corruption within the government and administration.

Titian (Tiziano Vecellio) (1488?–1576): Italian artist. Of a noble family, he was apprenticed in Venice to the artist Gentile and also studied with Giovanni Bellini. Some of his earliest work was done in collaboration with Giorgione, from whom he assimilated the latest techniques of oil painting. He com-pleted many important commissions in Venice after 1513, including the *Assunta* (*Assumption of the Virgin*) in the Frari church. These works established him as the leading artist in Venice. He also became a master of portrait painting and was in demand from the rulers of Italy, painting the portraits of Charles V, Philip II, Pope Paul III, Alfonso d'Este and Federico Gonzaga. He enjoyed the patronage of the Habsburgs and was held in particularly high regard by Charles V, who granted him a patent of nobility. His later years were spent in Venice where he completed many paintings on religious and mythological themes.

Vivaldi, Antonio (1678–1741): Italian composer and musician. Born in Venice, he became a priest but spent most of his career in the city, working at *Ospedale della Pietà*, an orphanage for girls, where he taught music. He was a noted violinist and a prolific composer, and his operas became highly pop-ular. Late in life he sought alternative employment at the court of Charles VI in Vienna but he died soon after his arrival. His most famous composition is *The Four Seasons*.

Voltaire (Arouet, François-Marie) (1694–1778): French writer and philosopher, who became one of the leading figures in the Enlightenment. He was an opponent of religious and political oppression. In 1717 he was imprisoned in the Bastille for a satirical attack on the Regent of France. After his release, he changed his name to Voltaire and his play *Œdipe* was performed. He was imprisoned briefly in 1726 and then spent two years in exile in England. In 1734 he published *Lettres anglaises ou philosophiques*, which attacked political and religious institutions in France, and which were condemned by the *Parlement* of Paris. Between 1745 and 1747 he served as a royal historiographer and moved in 1749 to the court of Frederick II of Prussia. Although the king was interested in the ideas of the Enlightenment, Voltaire doubted his sincerity in the light of his bellicose actions, and left the court in 1753. He eventually settled at Ferney in Switzerland and wrote some of his major works. These included *Essai sur l'histoire générale et sur les moeurs et l'esprit des nations* (1756), the novel *Candide* (1759) and the *Dictionnaire philosophique* (1764).

Wallenstein, Albrecht Eusebius Wenzel von (1583–1634): Bohemian military leader who commanded the imperial forces in the Thirty Years' War. He raised an army for Ferdinand II in 1618, and after the battle of the White Mountain (1620) he was rewarded with property confiscated from the defeated enemies of the Habsburgs. In 1625 he provided an army of 20,000 men for use in Germany. An effective commander, he won several battles and was made Duke of Friedland and Mecklenburg in 1628. By this time Ferdinand had grown suspicious of Wallenstein's ambitions and believed he opposed the Edict of Restitution. He was dismissed in 1630 and began negotiations with the enemies of the Emperor. In 1632 he was recalled and initially led a successful campaign against Gustavus Adolphus, but his army was defeated by the Swedes at the battle of Lützen. Ferdinand, aware that Wallenstein was negotiating with the Swedes and the French, dismissed him in 1634. He was assassinated by some of his own men.

Wesley, John (1703–91): British theologian and founder of the Methodist movement. He was educated at Oxford and was an ordained clergyman. At Oxford he established the Holy Club which encouraged piety among its members. He went to Georgia in America in 1735 but met with little success and he returned to England. He had met members of the Moravian Brethren on the journey and had been attracted by their faith and piety. He visited meetings of the Moravian Brethren in England and went to their community of Herrnhut. As a result of these contacts, he experienced a conversion and was convinced by the doctrine of justification by faith alone. He began travelling the country, preaching to large audiences. As he was often forbidden to use local churches, his sermons were frequently given in the open. It is estimated that he preached over 40,000 sermons and travelled 200,000 miles.

In 1739 he established the first Methodist society in London and these societies soon proliferated over all Great Britain and beyond. In many cases laymen were appointed as preachers. He opposed Calvinist teaching on predestination and split with one of his earliest supporters, George Whitfield and his followers, over this issue.

William I (of Orange) (1533–84): Known as William the Silent. Born a prince of Nassau, he inherited lands in the Netherlands and the principality of Orange in France. From 1555 he served on the Council of State in the Netherlands and he was made Stadtholder of Holland, Zealand and Utrecht in 1559. Although he was a Catholic, he opposed the oppression of Protestants in the Netherlands by Philip II and he became a leader of the opponents of Spanish rule. When Philip II sent the Duke of Alva to pacify the Netherlands, William fled abroad. He led two invasion forces in 1568 and 1572 but both were defeated. A successful invasion began in 1573, at which time he converted to Calvinism. He was a reluctant rebel and agreed to the Union of Utrecht unwillingly. When he was declared an outlaw by Philip II, he published his *Apology*, a justification for his actions. He died by assassination.

Wolff, Christian von (1679–1754): German philosopher and mathematician. He modified and popularised the ideas of Leibniz and established a system of rationalist thought based on natural law. Educated at Jena, he was appointed professor at Halle in 1706. He was expelled in 1723, accused of atheism for holding that Christianity and Confucianism could produce in humans similar views on morality. He taught at Marburg until 1743, when he accepted the invitation of Frederick II to return to Halle. His major work was *Vernünftige Gedanken von den Kräften des menschlichen Verstandes* (1712).

Wolsey, Thomas (1473?–1530): Cardinal (1515–29) and first minister of Henry VIII of England. In 1509 he was made Almoner to Henry VIII. In 1511 he became a Privy Councillor and from 1512–13 directed preparations for war against France. He became Archbishop of York in 1514, and in 1515 he was made Lord Chancellor and a Cardinal. In 1518 he was made papal legate and thus held simultaneously the highest offices in church and state in England. He improved the working of the Courts of Star Chamber and Chancery, over which he presided, but was generally disliked for his General Proscription of 1522 and 1523, which was used to raise forced loans for the crown. His diplomacy was initially successful and he organised talks between Francis I and Henry VIII at the Field of the Cloth of Gold in 1520. In 1521 he organised negotiations between Charles V and Francis I, but his failure to negotiate a divorce for Henry VIII from Catherine of Aragon led to his dismissal in 1529. He was arrested for treason in 1530, but died before he was brought to trial. Although himself a pluralist on a massive scale, he attempted to improve clerical standards among the regular and secular clergy. He established schools and a new college at Oxford. He organised opposition to the infiltration of Lutheran teachings into England.

Zwingli, Huldrych (1484–1531): Born in Toggenburg in Switzerland, he studied in Basle and Vienna before becoming a parish priest in Glarus. He continued to study and was strongly influenced by the work of Erasmus and other humanists. In 1516 he served as a chaplain to Swiss mercenary soldiers in Italy and became an opponent of mercenary service. On his return he continued to study and was made priest at the pilgrimage church of Einsiedeln in 1516. He became preacher at the Grossmünster in Zurich in 1518 and concentrated on expounding Scripture in his sermons. By 1522 he was openly criticising indulgences, the veneration of saints and other aspects of Catholic worship, and he found much support in Zurich. In 1523 the city staged a disputation, in which Zwingli justified his attacks on works theology, monasticism and Purgatory and upheld the primacy of Scripture. The city council supported his views and in a further disputation later in 1523 Zwingli attacked the mass and religious images. The mass was abolished in Zurich in 1525. He believed that the Eucharist was a memorial service in which the bread and wine symbolised the body and blood of Christ without their substance being changed. This view brought him into conflict with Luther, and when they met at Marburg in 1529 they were unable to agree on Eucharistic teaching. Zwingli was challenged by Anabaptists, who wished to abolish child baptism, but he resisted and supported severe punishments for Anabaptists. He believed in the need for the civil and spiritual authorities to cooperate in the creation of a godly community, and to this end a marriage court was established in Zurich in 1525. Religious disputes aggravated political conflict within the Swiss Confederation and eventually led to war in 1531 in which Zwingli was killed at the battle of Kappel.

GLOSSARY OF TERMS

Abbreviators   Papal officials responsible for preparing papal Bulls (see p. 243). These venal offices were abolished during the pontificate of Paul III.

Abhorrers   Alternative name given to the Tory party in England in the seventeenth century during the reign of Charles II.

absolutism   A key concept of *ancien régime* Europe which stressed unlimited, centralised authority and sovereignty vested in a single person (particularly the monarch). In such a system, based on the divine right of kings, there were no checks (except for the traditional liberties of the subject and natural law) on the power of the sovereign. Rulers aspired to exercise unrestricted powers, but in reality they had to rule with the consent of their most powerful subjects. For this reason, absolutism can be misleading as in practice unrestrained powers were exercised with limits. It was best expressed by Louis XIV's dictum *'L'état, c'est moi'*. Absolutism developed rapidly in the sixteenth century and reached its best illustrations in France, Spain, Prussia and Austria.

Age of Greatness   The period in Swedish history, usually dated from the accession of Gustavus Adolphus in 1611 and ending with the Peace of Nystad of 1721, which ended the Great Northern War. It was a period of efficient government, military prowess and much territorial expansion, including Livonia, western Pomerania, Bremen, Verden, Wismar as well as Danish and Norwegian provinces.

Age of Liberty   The period in Swedish history, from the death of Charles XII in 1718 until the *coup d'état* of Gustav III in 1772, marked by constitutional government and the emergence of rival parties.

aides   Indirect taxes imposed in France.

Alascans   Foreign Protestant refugees in England in the reign of Edward VI (1547–53) named after Laski, the superintendent of foreign church communities.

alcabala   A sales tax on all commodities that was originally imposed in Spain in 1341. Although the *alcabala* was the single most important source of crown revenue, it greatly hampered trade. Attempts to impose it in the Netherlands in 1569 were so bitterly opposed that it had to be postponed for two years and when it was introduced, it resulted in a cessation of trade. In Spain's colonies an *alcabala* of 2–6 per cent was imposed on all commercial transactions (except those between Indians) between 1575 and 1591.

alcalde   Spanish system of judiciary established between 1492 and 1550, by which time it had taken the definitive form it kept up to the late eighteenth century. Its officers wielded judicial, political and administrative authority, and were also chairmen of the town councils. The word derived from the Arabic for judge (*al-qādi*).

alteration Term for the switch of loyalties by Amsterdam in 1578 during the Revolt of the Netherlands. Having previously supported Catholic Spain, the city joined the rebels and became staunchly Protestant. The term derives from the Dutch *alteratie*.

alumbrados Groups of mystics which emerged in Spain *c.* 1510 and were persecuted by the Inquisition. They were the forefathers of the better-known Illuminati in parts of Germany.

amicable grant A tax imposed in England in 1525 by Henry VIII's Chief Minister, Thomas Wolsey (*c.* 1473–1530), to finance war against France. The tax, which was levied at a third of clergy's property and a sixth of laymen's, was withdrawn following protests.

Anabaptists An extreme religious sect which arose in Switzerland and Germany and became famous for their seizure of the city of Münster (see pp. 174–5).

ancien régime The governmental and social structure which prevailed in Europe prior to the French Revolution of 1789. It was centred on absolutism, based on the divine right of kings, and the rigid division of society into three orders – the aristocracy, the Church and the third estate.

annates Fees or taxes payable by clerics to the Papacy in respect of ecclesiastical preferment, consisting originally of the whole of the first year's income from the office. They were a constant source of acrimony.

antinomianism The belief that the law expounded in the Old Testament is no longer relevant and binding upon Chrtistians.

Apostle of Rome Title given to St Philip Neri (1515–95), the founder of the Oratorians. He was canonised in 1622.

appanages In *ancien régime* France, the provision made from the thirteenth to the sixteenth centuries for the younger sons of kings, consisting of feudal lands owned by the crown. In 1790 they were reduced to pensions and rents and later abolished.

Arbitistras A term for the economic experts who tried (unsuccessfully) to halt the economic decline of Imperial Spain in the seventeenth century with their diagnoses of Spanish ills.

Armada The name of the great Spanish fleet sent against England (see p. 124).

Armatoli Greek mercenaries in the employ of the Sultans of Turkey from the fifteenth to the early nineteenth centuries.

Arminians The followers of Jacob Arminius (1560–1609), a Leyden professor who in the early seventeenth century dissented from the strict Calvinism of Dutch Protestantism (see p. 170). They rejected the doctrine of predestination, emphasising instead the teachings of the early Church on free will. In 1618 the Synod of Dort issued a decree banishing the Arminian preachers. Oldenbarneveldt, their chief lay supporter, was executed.

Arrabiati   The party of the Medici at the time of the Florentine Republic, established in 1493.

asiento   A contract, usually one made between financiers and the crown. It was also often used of the 33-year monopoly to sell black slaves to the Spanish colonies, secured for England by the Treaty of Utrecht in 1713 and managed by the South Sea Company. In 1748 the monopoly was renewed for four years by the Treaty of Aachen. It was abandoned for a lump sum settlement in 1750.

Assembly of Notables (*Assemblé des notables*)   In *ancien régime* France, the consultative national assembly called by the personal summons of the crown. Its membership was drawn from the nobility, the Church, the municipalities and the holders of judicial and fiscal office.

Ataman   A military title of the sixteenth century used by the Zaporozhian Cossacks of Ukraine. It was also the title given to the prince of the area east of the River Dnieper in the seventeenth and eighteenth centuries and to the elected commander of Russia (after 1723 only the lesser village *ataman* was elected). The term was related to *hetman*.

audiencias   Higher courts in Spain and subsequently in colonial South America. The three most significant domestic *audiencias* were Valladolid (established 1452), Ciudad Real (1494) and Granada (1505), and their task was to act as a final court of appeal in civil and criminal cases. In colonial South America they discharged an administrative and political function as the equivalent of regional parliaments in areas far removed from the seat of the Viceroy.

Austrian lands   Part of the Habsburg dynastic inheritance, the Austrian lands are traditionally divided into three areas: *Upper Austria* (Oberösterreich), comprising the Tyrol; *Inner Austria* (Innerösterreich), comprising eastern Austria, Carinthia, Styria and Carniola; and *Lower Austria* (Niederösterreich).

auto-de-fé   The ceremony which accompanied the execution of condemned heretics during the Inquisition in Spain and Portugal. Pope Sixtus IV first authorised the Spanish monarchy to name Inquisitors in a Bull of 1478. In Spanish, the term means 'act of faith'.

bailli   In *ancien régime* France, the representative of the king in a *bailliage*. The *bailli* was responsible for military matters and the maintenance of law and order. The *baillis* were always members of the hereditary nobility of the sword.

ban   A title used in the Ottoman Empire for a ruler or governor of a large province (e.g. Bosnia and elsewhere in the Balkans).

banalités   In *ancien régime* France, the minor feudal obligations of the peasantry, for example, the requirement to use the seigneur's mill.

241

Bandes d'Ordonnance A body of 3,000 cavalrymen which formed the standing army of the Netherlands in the mid-sixteenth century.

Barbary The term for the North African coastline, formerly the home of the corsairs. Known as Barbary pirates, the corsairs collaborated with Ottoman regular troops during the struggle between the Ottoman Empire and Spain in the sixteenth century. They established bases at Algiers, Tunis and Tripoli which became the capitals of new Ottoman states in 1518 when the corsair Khairredin Barbarossa placed himself and his bases under the protection of the Ottoman sultan, Selim I. These new provinces became effectively independent in the seventeenth century, though piracy continued.

Barbons In early seventeenth-century France, the name given to the veteran counsellors of Louis XIII, namely Sillery, Jeannin and Villeroy.

Barrier treaties A series of treaties signed by the Dutch Republic with Spain (1697), England (1709), and Austria and England (1715) giving the Republic the right to garrison towns in the southern Netherlands to protect the area against France. The towns were captured by France in the 1740–48 War of the Austrian Succession and the treaties were declared void by Emperor Joseph II of Austria in 1781.

beard tax A tax imposed by Peter the Great of Russia in 1698 and 1701 as part of his programme to modernise the country. He ordered the removal of beards by all but the Orthodox clergy and the wearing of Western-style clothes, but allowed those who paid the tax to retain facial hair. The tax was on a sliding scale depending on the wealth of the individual.

Beggars of the Sea (Sea Beggars) The Dutch privateers led by William de la Marck and commissioned by the Prince of Orange in the 1570s to attack Spanish merchant shipping.

Belski One of two factions of nobles, the other being the Choviski, who between them ruled Russia _c._ 1530 during the minority of Ivan IV ('the Terrible').

benevolences In England, an arbitrary form of taxation, introduced by Edward IV in 1473, that was imposed without the consent of Parliament. They were made illegal under Richard III in 1484 but Henry VII sought to reintroduce them in 1495. Henry VIII sought to reintroduce them in 1528 and 1545 and James I in 1614, 1615, 1620 and 1622. The last, unsuccessful, attempt to raise them was made by Charles I in 1633.

bey In the Ottoman Empire, the ruler of a province with his own flag. In Tunis, after 1705, the office was hereditary. Gradually the title became one merely of courtesy.

black bands German mercenaries enlisted for service in the Italian Wars of the sixteenth century by Louis XII of France.

Black Legend The term used for the cruelty and exploitation of the Spanish conquest and subjugation of the New World, by opponents of Spain. The term grew popular partly from the accounts of Spanish missionaries such as Bartolomé de las Casas, the champion of the local peoples who was named Protector of the Indians in 1516.

Bohemian Brethren   *See Unitas Fratrum.*

Bourbons   Members of the Bourbon dynasties which reigned in Spain, France and Naples. The older French line was overthrown by the Revolution of 1789. The Neapolitan Bourbons were a branch of the Spanish family who ruled Naples and Sicily from 1738 to 1860.

boyars   Members of the nobility which emerged in Russia. In the fifteenth and sixteenth centuries the boyars declined as a class and a new nobility of service was created. By the eighteenth century the boyars and the new nobility were indistinguishable, since the boyars had also accepted obligations of service.

Braganza   The ruling house of Portugal from the reign of John IV, Duke of Braganza (1640–56) to the abdication in 1910 of Manuel II.

buccaneers (Deriv. Fr. *boucanier*, 'to smoke meat')   English, French and Dutch adventurers who preyed on Spanish colonies and shipping in the Caribbean and off the Pacific coast of America in the seventeenth century. They were also known as privateers, the French termed them *filibustiers* and the Dutch *zeerovers*. Their Spanish victims called them *corsarios*.

Bull (*bulla*, 'seal')   The seal affixed to a papal edict, hence, by extension, the common term for the edict itself.

Byzantine Empire   The eastern half of the Roman Empire which, when it fell to the Turks in 1453, had survived the Western Empire by a thousand years.

cabinet noir   Government department established by Louis XIV for the surveillance of the correspondence of suspected persons.

Calvinism   A branch of Protestantism founded on the teaching of the French reformer Jean Chauvin (1509–64) known as Calvin from the Latin form of his name (see pp. 164–5).

campanilismo (Deriv. It. *campanile*, 'bell tower')   In the Italian city states, term for extreme devotion and allegiance to a person's own town or city.

cantons   The territorial units into which the Swiss Confederation was divided. As early as 1513 they numbered sixteen.

Capetian   A member or supporter of the royal house of France. The main line of the dynasty came to an end in 1328 with the death of Charles IV when the throne passed to the related house of Valois until 1589.

capitation   A poll tax imposed in France in 1695–97 and 1701 onwards.

Caps and Hats   Rival political parties in eighteenth-century Sweden. The pro-French Hats dominated Swedish politics from the 1730s until 1765 when the Caps took power with the aim of attacking the privileges of the nobility.

243

Capuchin   A member of a mendicant Order of Franciscans founded in the sixteenth century with the aim of restoring the primitive and stricter observance of the rule of St Francis.

carnets   The notebooks compiled by Mazarin, often on his journeys. Historians see them as providing an insight into his private thoughts and preoccupations.

Carreira da Índia   The Portuguese term (lit. 'roadway') for the maritime route established by Vasco da Gama to India, and hence the term for Portuguese trade with India and the rest of Asia.

Casa da Índia   The principal body in Lisbon which administered Portuguese trade with Asia. The 'House of Trade' was the equivalent of the Spanish *Casa de contratación* at Seville (see below).

Casa de contratación (also known as the Council of Seville)   The principal body responsible for the organisation and regulation of Spanish colonial commerce, founded by Ferdinand and Isabella in Seville in 1503. All trade from the colonies was required to pass through the customs house at Seville, the *Casa* dispensing licences for all shipping to and from the colonies and for migration there. It collected duties on trade and received the precious metals that accrued to the Spanish crown. It was moved to Cadiz in 1718 and abolished in 1790.

Catholic Majesties   The titles continuously used of the Spanish monarchs from the time of Ferdinand the Catholic (see p. 218).

Cavalier   A member of the Royalist party during the English Civil War (1642–49) (see p. 128).

Cavalier Parliament   The parliament in England which met on 8 May 1661 and was dissolved in 1679. It succeeded the Convention Parliament and took its name from its strongly Royalist and Anglican complexions which led to its passing the Clarendon Code.

Chambres de Réunion   Those special courts (established as part of the *réunion* policy of Louis XIV) which decided on the annexation of territories along France's eastern frontier. They were established in 1680 at Besançon, Breisach, Metz and Tournai.

Chambre Ardente   The Court of devout Roman Catholics, charged with the trial of heretics, established by Henry II in the *Parlement* of Paris in 1551.

Cinquecento   The sixteenth century (It.) (see p. 289).

Circles (*Reichskreise*)   Administrative sub-divisions within the Holy Roman Empire. The original six Circles were organised in 1495. In 1512 the number was increased to ten. They were mainly concerned with issues relating to defence.

Cleves-Jülich   The two duchies where a disputed succession caused a crisis (from 1609 to 1614). Both were situated within the Holy Roman Empire.

The crisis was eventually defused with a compromise whereby Jülich and Berg went to a Catholic (Wolfgang William of Neuberg) while Cleves and Mark went to a Protestant (John Sigismund of Brandenburg).

Clubmen Bands of armed men who assembled in various parts of England in 1644, mainly in the West Country, for the purpose of protecting their districts and property from the ravages of the Civil War. They attacked both Royalists and Parliamentarians impartially.

Code Noir The 'Black Code' issued by Louis XIV in 1685. The Edict regulated the French Caribbean colonies and the treatment of, for example, black slaves.

Commonwealth Generally, the period in England between the execution of Charles I on 30 January 1649 and the restoration of the monarchy on 8 May 1660; specifically, the period from the declaration of the English Republic on 19 May 1649 to the establishment of the Protectorate by the Instrument of Government on 16 December 1653, which made Cromwell Lord Protector.

compagnies d'ordonnance The companies of heavy cavalry created in France after 1439. With captains appointed by the crown, and troops paid by the government, they became the core of a standing army.

condottieri Mercenary captains who hired themselves out to various warring Italian states (where in the absence of standing armies mercenary warfare had become the norm) in the fifteenth and sixteenth centuries. The most successful, the Sforzas, rose from humble origins to become Dukes of Milan.

Congregationalism In England, the oldest tradition of nonconformism, originating with the Barrowists and represented in the ranks of the Independents. Congregationalists were finally given liberty of worship under William III in 1689.

conquistadores The Spaniards who participated in the conquest of America between 1492 and the 1550s.

Consistorium The Tribunal established by Calvin in Geneva in 1541 to maintain religious and moral standards. It acted with great severity, proscribing all amusements and vigorously repressing criticism of Calvinist doctrine. Within five years it was responsible for 58 executions and 800 imprisonments.

Consubstantiation The belief of German Protestant reformer Martin Luther (1483–1546) that although the bread and wine remain unchanged at the Eucharist, Christ's body and blood are physically present, a concept that divided the reform movement.

consulados Merchant gilds in Spain and, from the sixteenth century onwards, in Spain's South American colonies.

Consulta The Committee of three members – the Bishops of Arras, Berlaymont and Viglius – which was part of the Council of State of the Netherlands in the Regency of Margaret of Parma (1559–67).

contado   The area around an Italian city that is ruled by the city.

Contra-remonstrants   Opponents of the Arminians in early seventeenth-century Netherlands. The name is derived from their presentation to the States-General of a counter-remonstrance against the five articles set out in the 1610 Arminian Remonstrance. They were also known as Gomarists.

conversos   A term applied in Spain to those Jews who had converted.

cortes   The various parliaments of Spain. The earliest were in León and Castile. Later cortes were established in Catalonia (1218), Aragon (1274), Valencia (1283) and Navarre (1300). The cortes consisted of three estates: the nobility, clergy and *procuradores* (town clerks or attorneys elected by fortified boroughs and given written instructions by the electorate). The *procuradores* became the dominant estate as it was only they who could consent to the extraordinary taxes required by the crown. The cortes did not meet as of right, but were convened when and where the king wished. Their power declined in the sixteenth and seventeenth centuries as Spain's Empire overseas relieved the monarchy of the need for extraordinary taxes. By the early eighteenth century their authorising of royal actions was merely a formality.

corvée   A French term which, from the fifteenth century onwards, became synonymous with forced labour on public projects, periodically revived when state revenues were too low to hire sufficient labour. From 1726 the *corvée* was used in France to provide free labour on roads. It was finally abolished following the Revolution of 1789.

Council of Blood   The notorious court established in the Netherlands by the Duke of Alva to suppress religious and political opposition to Philip II. From its opening session on 20 September 1567, it became a byword for tyranny. Among its most prominent victims were the Counts of Egmont and Hoorne in 1568.

Council of Seville (*Consejo de Sevilla*)   *See Casa da contratación.*

Council of Ten   In the Venetian Republic, the secret council which exercised power over the supervision of internal and external affairs. Established in 1310, it grew from ten to seventeen members. Its powers were often used oppressively. It was abolished in 1797.

Council of Trent   The great Council of the Catholic Church which met at Trent (in the Tyrol) from 1545 to 1563 (see pp. 181–2). The adjective Tridentine derives from Trent.

Croquants (Lit. 'a clod-hopper')   The term was used of the peasants who participated in the 1637 rebellion (see p. 127).

cruzado   The main Portuguese money of account during the sixteenth and seventeenth centuries. Each *cruzado* consisted of 400 *reis* (approximately equal to ten Spanish *reals*).

cuius regio, eius religio   The principle provided for at the religious Peace of Augsburg of 1555 (see p. 184). It provided that, within the Holy Roman Empire, in the secular territories of princes and Imperial knights, the ruler had the right to determine the religion of his subjects.

Dauphin   The title borne by the eldest sons of the French kings from 1349 until the Revolution of 1830.

Defenestration of Prague   The incident that started the Thirty Years' War (see p. 126). When Ferdinand II threatened the religious liberties of Bohemian Protestants, Count von Thürn led Protestant nobles to the palace in Prague on 23 May 1618. Two Roman Catholic governors and a secretary were thrown out of a window but their fall was broken by a rubbish heap.

Defensor Fidei (Defender of the Faith)   The title conferred on Henry VIII of England by Pope Leo X in 1521 for his defence of the seven sacraments in opposition to Luther. After Henry broke with Rome and assumed headship of the Church of England in 1534, Pope Paul III withdrew the title but Parliament confirmed it in 1544.

dévots   The term for those zealous Catholics who opposed any toleration for Huguenots and who opposed Richelieu's foreign policy. *Dévots* wanted a pro-Spanish, pro-Catholic policy.

devshirmeh   The 'tribute of children', established by Bayezid I (1389–1403), which was levied on Christian people, particularly the Slavs in the Balkans who were subject to Ottoman rule. It lapsed after the battle of Ankara (1401) but was revived by Murad II (1421–51). Many of the children became Janissaries and the most able were trained for high administrative posts. The *devshirmeh* was only intermittently applied in the sixteenth and seventeenth centuries and was last imposed in 1705.

Diet   In the Holy Roman Empire, the assembly of dignitaries and delegates called to decide important political or ecclesiastical questions. The most famous Diets were those held at Worms (1521), Speyer (1529) and Augsburg (1530) to settle matters of religious conflict arising from the Reformation. After 1663, until the dissolution of the Empire in 1806, the Diet was permanently in session at Ratisbon (Regensburg).

Diplomatic Revolution   The term used by historians for the dramatic reversal of alliances in the period 1749 to 1756 (i.e. from the end of the War of the Austrian Succession to the beginning of the Seven Years' War). Although the chief protagonists were the same, Britain was now the ally of Prussia (not Austria) while France was allied to Austria (not Prussia). The revolution was the result of colonial rivalries overseas (between France and Britain) and a changed balance of power in Europe (with the rise of Prussia and Russia).

Divine Right of Kings   The doctrine which holds that monarchs in direct line of succession have a divine or God-given right to the throne and that rebellion against their will is a sin. The doctrine originated in France where it reached its apogee in the seventeenth century. In England the doctrine was most prevalent during the reign of Charles I (1625–49).

dixième A French tax of 10 per cent of all gross incomes imposed by Louis XIV in 1710 to finance the War of the Spanish Succession. Regarded as an attack on their financial privileges by the nobility, it was opposed and abandoned in 1717. It was revived as a wartime emergency measure in 1733 and again in 1741 and 1746.

Doge (Deriv. Lat. *dux*, 'leader') Chief magistrate in, and ruler of, the former republics of Venice (prior to 1797) and Genoa (1339–1797, 1802–05).

Dragonnades The persecution of the Huguenots in Poitou and other parts of France in 1684 by the brutal dragoons of the minister, Louvois. The persecution culminated in the revocation of the Edict of Nantes on 22 October 1685.

Edict of Nantes The Edict issued on 13 April 1598 by Henry IV of France which ended the religious wars (see p. 122). Its grant of toleration to the Huguenots lasted until the famous revocation of the Edict by Louis XIV on 22 October 1685. (For further details, see pp. 166–9.)

Edict of Restitution The Edict issued on 6 March 1629 by the Emperor Ferdinand II which ordered Protestants to restore to Roman Catholics the sees and ecclesiastical property taken since the 1552 Treaty of Passau. The Protestant reaction to this Edict was a major factor in the Thirty Years' War. (See p. 126.)

Electors In the Holy Roman Empire, the Electors were members of the Electoral College regulated after 1356 by the Golden Bull of the Emperor Charles IV. At the beginning of the sixteenth century the seven members (in the order in which they cast their vote) were the Archbishop of Trier, the Archbishop of Cologne, the King of Bohemia, the Count Palatine of the Rhine, the Duke of Saxony-Wittenberg, the Margrave of Brandenburg and the Archbishop of Mainz.

Eleven Years' Tyranny The period of autocratic rule by King Charles I (from 1629 to 1640) which helped precipitate the English Civil War (see p. 128).

encomiendas In Spain, in the middle ages, a grant of land made by the king in return for military service. Also, in colonial Spanish America, concessions of the labour services of Indians granted by the Spanish crown to colonists, who were in theory to care for their welfare and Christianize them. In practice, the system, which was common in the early sixteenth century as a means of supplying labour on *haciendas* and for the mines, caused abuses and hardship for the Indians. A moral crusade by the Dominicans led the crown to decree new laws to abolish the system in 1542 but the laws were revoked when the colonists threatened revolt. The system was finally abolished in 1720.

Enfants de Dieu   The name used by the Camisards, the Protestants of the Cévennes, whose 1702 rebellion against the French crown was suppressed in 1704.

enlightened despotism   A form of absolutism in which the government claimed to act for the good of the governed rather than for its own self-interest. In the eighteenth century some rulers used criticisms of feudalism and existing political and social institutions to justify the introduction of reforming programmes (e.g. Maria Theresa, Frederick II).

Enlightenment, the   A broad term for the eighteenth-century philosophical movement in which the power of human reason was stressed and obscurantist religious and political practices were criticised. Its influence can be seen in both the French and American revolutions. (See p. 292.)

entrada   The term used in Spain's South American colonies to denote a military expedition into previously unexplored or unconquered regions. In Portuguese Brazil, the term specifically meant any exploratory expedition into the interior and also, occasionally, the conversion of Indians to Christianity by military force.

Erastians   The followers of Thomas Erastus (1524–83), the German author of works on excommunication. These ideas were usually associated with the subjection of ecclesiastical power to national secular control.

escalade   The term applied to the failure in 1602 of the Duke of Savoy's attempt to conquer Geneva.

Estado da Índia   The Portuguese term ('State of India') for the Portuguese Empire in Asia – not only the settlements along the Indian Coast, but also the East Indies, Macao and the administration of the Portuguese viceroy based at Goa.

Estates-General   The national assembly in which the chief 'estates' of the realm were represented in separate bodies. In pre-Revolutionary France, the Estates-General consisted of three estates of nobility, clergy and commons. It was first summoned in 1302 by Philip IV to gain support from the bodies represented in his quarrel with Pope Boniface VIII. It met rarely as the French monarchy became more powerful and not at all between 1614 and 1789.

Exclusion Crisis   The English political crisis (1679–81) which grew out of the movement arising from the popish plot to exclude the Catholic James, Duke of York (brother of Charles II) from the succession to the throne. Various Exclusion Bills were proposed by Parliament. With French financial support, Charles II was able to resist.

Familia   In Poland, this was the name given to the politically-important Czartoryski family.

feitoria   These were trading posts, or compounds, in fifteenth- and sixteenth-century Portugal during its early period of overseas expansion. The largest were in Brazil and such Asian centres as Goa and Macao.

fermiers généraux   A system of gathering taxes initiated by Francis I whereby persons, often royal favourites, obtained the right to collect taxes in return for payment of a fixed sum. The *gabelle* was farmed out in this way in 1546. The system lasted until the Revolution.

Field of the Cloth of Gold   The site near Calais where, in June 1520, Henry VIII of England met Francis I of France in an extravagant, expensive, but insincere show of friendship. Only a year later England signed an alliance against France with the Emperor Charles V.

Fifth Monarchy Men   Members of a seventeenth-century extremist sect with great influence among the supporters of Cromwell in the English Civil War.

firman   An official edict of the government of the Ottoman Empire, issued in the sultan's name.

Five Members   These were the members of parliament and leaders of parliamentary agitation for reform in England, whom Charles I tried to arrest on 4 January 1642. They were John Pym, John Hampden, Denzil Holles, Sir Arthur Heselrig and William Strode. The episode, in uniting Lords and Commons against the king, was instrumental in bringing nearer the Civil War.

Flight of the Earls   The self-exile in France in September 1607 of 99 people, including Hugh O'Neill, Earl of Tyrone, and Rory O'Connell. The flight followed the failure of O'Neill's rebellion in 1603, leading to the successful imposition of English administration in the area.

francs archers   A French militia first raised by Charles VII in 1448. Every parish was forced to select and equip one man who was relieved of all taxation in return for military service.

French Fury   The attack by French soldiers on Antwerp on 17 January 1583. The attackers (numbering around 4,000) were repulsed by the citizens with very heavy casualties.

Fronde, the   The great rebellion which convulsed seventeenth-century France (see also p. 129).

fueros   The charters and special privileges granted by the crown to individuals and corporate bodies in Spain (e.g. town guilds or the Church) in return for services. The earliest known *fuero* was granted to the town of León by Alfonso V in 1020. *Fueros* related to the parts of the Spanish kingdom *outside* Castile. They were revoked in the nineteenth century.

gabelle   A French tax on salt, first levied in the fourteenth century. Nobility, clergy and certain towns and provinces were exempt while elsewhere it was strictly imposed. The *gabelle* proved both burdensome and unpopular. It was abolished in 1791. *Gabeleur* became a popular name for a tax collector.

Gallicanism   A term in French religious history with three main strands: the assertion of the independence of the French king from the Papacy; the collaboration of clergy and secular powers to limit papal intervention in the French state; and the superiority of an ecumenical council over the Papacy. In 1438 Charles VII issued the Pragmatic Sanction of Bourges, stating that the pope's secular jurisdiction was dependent on the king and that the pope was subject to a general council of the Church. The Papacy secured its revocation in 1516. The best exposition of Gallicanism was the 'Gallican Articles' issued by a synod of the French clergy in 1682. The Articles were condemned by Pope Alexander VIII in 1690 and revoked by Louis XIV in 1693. However, not all the French clergy (e.g. the Jesuits) accepted the Gallican position.

Germanía   The name given to the association of rebels in the revolt in the kingdom of Valencia in 1519 against the privileges of the nobility (see p. 120).

Gevey, Les   A confederacy formed in 1566 by patriotic nobles and gentry of the Netherlands, led by Count Louis of Nassau and Brederode. It was broken up in 1567 and many of its members were executed.

Glippers   Netherlanders who supported the party of the Spanish king *c.* 1570.

Glorious Revolution   *See* p. 136.

Golden League   The League formed by the Catholic states of Switzerland in 1655 in the civil wars known as the Villmergen Wars.

Gomarists   The followers of Gomarus, professor of theology at Utrecht University, and opponents of the Arminians.

Grand Remonstrance   The famous protest passed by the English House of Commons on 22 November 1641 setting out the unconstitutional acts of the reign of Charles I.

Grand Siècle ('the Great Century')   The period of the reign of Louis XIV (1643–1715), symbolised in the classical age of French literature.

Great Elector   The popular title for Frederick William, Elector of Brandenburg (1620–88) (see p. 219).

Great Privilege   The *'Groote Privilegie'* granted at Ghent by the Regent Mary on 3 February 1477 at the first regular assembly of the States-General of the Netherlands. This charter, restoring ancient rights, is known as the Dutch 'Magna Carta'.

Great Rebellion   A term commonly used of the Civil War in England between the Royalists and Parliamentarians after 1642.

Gregorian Calendar   The modern calendar introduced by Pope Gregory XIII (1502–85) on 24 February 1582 to replace the Julian Calendar.

Gueux, Les (French 'Beggars') The league of Flemish nobles organised in 1566 to resist the introduction of the Inquisition into the Low Countries by Philip II. The name was previously given to them in contempt, and was borne by their followers in the succeeding war.

Gunpowder Plot The Catholic conspiracy in England against James I which aimed to blow up Parliament in November 1605. The leading conspirators were Catesby, Percy, Digby, Winter, Guy Fawkes and others.

Habsburg The Austrian royal dynasty (originally of Swiss origin) which ruled from 1282 to 1918. The family held the title of Holy Roman Emperor (1438–1740 and 1745–1806). When the Empire was dissolved the dynasty took the title Emperor of Austria. Its rise to power was based on a series of fortunate marriages and reached its zenith with the Emperor Charles V, who divided his empire into two branches, part ruled by the Austrian Habsburgs and part by the Spanish Habsburgs. In 1526 the Hungarian and Bohemian crowns were united with the Austrian crown to form the Habsburg Danubian Monarchy.

Hanoverians The royal dynasty which ruled Great Britain and Ireland from 1714 to 1901 (under the terms of the 1701 Act of Succession). From the Brunswick-Lüneburg branch of the Guelph family, they took their name from the German state of Hanover where they were Electors of the Holy Roman Empire.

Hanseatic League The confederation of North German towns established to promote trade. Dating from 1241, by the mid-seventeenth century its decline was evident. Its last meeting was in 1669.

Hermandad The confederation of the major cities of medieval Castile. It gradually usurped the functions of a legislative body and used force to secure obedience to its rule.

Hetman See *Ataman*.

Hohenzollern The Prussian ruling house. The Hohenzollerns were rulers of Brandenburg from 1415 and provided the kings of Prussia from 1701.

Holy Synod The Council created by Peter the Great (1672–1725) in 1720 to exercise state control over the Orthodox Church. It was closely based on the Lutheran model.

Hospitalers, Knights The military monks of the Order of St John of Jerusalem. In 1309 they captured Rhodes, which they held until expelled by the Ottomans in 1522. In 1530 Emperor Charles V gave them the island of Malta which, as Knights of Malta, they held until 1798.

Huguenots French Protestants of the sixteenth and seventeenth centuries. On 24 August 1572 thousands were killed in the Massacre of St Bartholomew. In 1598 Henry IV, their former leader, who had become a Catholic, granted them religious toleration by the Edict of Nantes. When this was revoked by Louis XIV in 1685, thousands left France for exile.

Humanism   The scholarly movement seeking to restore the learning of the classical past (especially Greek learning and the writings of Plato). It paved the way for such Christian humanists as Erasmus, who sought the reform of the existing Church to accord with the true principles of the Scriptures.

Hutterites   An anabaptist sect named after Jacob Hutter. They were distinguished by their withdrawal from the world and the establishment of communities in which all property was held in common.

Imperial Free Cities   Those cities within the Holy Roman Empire which owed their allegiance directly to the Emperor (with no obligation to any intermediary prince). Among their number were Aachen, Augsburg, Bremen, Lübeck, Münster, Speyer, Ulm and Worms.

Imperial knights   Military members of the feudal order in Germany who held their lands directly from the emperor. By the sixteenth century, their military role had declined, and their power and independence was being eroded by territorial rulers. In an attempt to resist this, Franz von Sickingen and Ulrich von Hutten, both imperial knights, led an unsuccessful rebellion by the knights in 1522.

Index expurgatorius (*Index of expurgations*)   The list of books which the Roman Catholic Church forbids its members to read on grounds of immorality or heresy. The first papal *Index* was commissioned by Pope Paul IV in 1559 but was largely ignored by the Council of Trent (1545–63). Pope Pius IV commissioned a new list in 1564. Originally part of the Counter-Reformation, the *Index* attempted to halt the diffusion of heretical opinions.

indulgences   The remission granted by an ecclesiastical authority of the temporal punishment due to a repentant sinner. Indiscriminate and corrupt sale of indulgences by Tetzel and other papal agents in the sixteenth century was one of the grievances against the Catholic Church which fuelled the Reformation.

Infanta   The title given to a royal princess in Spain or Portugal.

Infante   The title of the legitimate male issue of a reigning monarch, except the heir to the throne.

Inquisition   The ecclesiastical court of the Roman Catholic Church made into a very formidable weapon for stamping out heresy by Pope Innocent III in the thirteenth century. It was established in various Catholic countries in Europe but obtained its most extensive power and organisation in Spain under the rule of Ferdinand V of Aragon (1452–1516) and his wife Isabella of Castile (1451–1504). The Grand Inquisitor Torquemada exercised its duties with terrible cruelty and harshness (see *auto-de-fé*). Not until the eighteenth century did the Inquisition's authority and influence start to decline.

Intendants   In France, the special commissioners despatched by the crown into the provinces. By the seventeenth century they had become the most powerful of royal agents.

Interregnum In England, the term usually refers to the period of the Commonwealth and Protectorate, that is between the execution of Charles I on 30 January 1649 and the restoration of Charles II on 5 May 1660. A shorter interregnum occurred between the flight of James II in December 1688 and the accession of William III and Mary II on 23 February 1689.

Jacobites The adherents of the Stuart cause after the abdication of James II of England in 1688. The Stuart cause was finally defeated in 1746 by the Duke of Cumberland at Culloden. Scottish Jacobitism was then ruthlessly suppressed. (See p. 138.)

Janissaries The elite band of Ottoman foot soldiers who acted as the sultan's bodyguard, they were first recruited under Bayezid I in the fourteenth century from Christian children taken from the conquered countries of Serbia and Albania (see *devshirmeh*). They were brought up as Muslims and were not allowed to marry. They gained great power in the Ottoman Empire.

Jansenists Members of a Roman Catholic sect in seventeenth-century France, whose doctrines were based on the *Augustinus* of Cornelius Jansen, Bishop of Ypres, published posthumously in 1638 (see p. 222). They supported teaching, stressing the role of predestination.

Jesuits The members of the 'Society of Jesus', founded by Ignatius Loyola in 1534 and confirmed by the pope in 1540. They played a crucial role in the revival of Catholicism (see p. 180). They were expelled from France in 1594, restored in 1603 and again expelled in 1764. The Order was suppressed by Clement XIV in 1773 but subsequently revived.

Landrecht (Ger.) Also known as the *Codex Fredericamus*, this was the codification of Prussian law published under the auspices of Frederick the Great in 1751.

Landsknecht Mercenary infantry soldiers first raised by Emperor Maximilian in Germany in 1492 and employed by France, Italy and England in the sixteenth century. Like their Swiss counterparts, they fought with pikes and halberds.

Laudian A supporter of the policies of William Laud, Archbishop of Canterbury (1633–45), in the seventeenth-century Church of England. Laudians favoured the restoration of ceremony and ritual.

legatus a latere In the Roman Catholic Church, a Cardinal Legate with plenipotentiary powers, for example Thomas Wolsey under Henry VIII of England.

lettre de cachet In pre-Revolutionary France, a warrant of arrest issued by the king or his ministers by which persons incurring the Court's disfavour might be imprisoned indefinitely without trial.

Levellers A radical democratic group existing during the English Civil War and under the Commonwealth. Stressing the birthright of freeborn Englishmen, they advocated the extension of the suffrage, republicanism, the abolition of the House of Lords and religious toleration. A heterogeneous party, they were led by, among others, John Lilburne. From 1647 to 1649 they were a significant element in the New Model Army.

Libertins A term in Switzerland for those who opposed the extreme stringency of Calvinism in Geneva in 1541. They were repressed by the Consistory.

liberum veto (Lat.) In Poland, the nobility's right of dissent or veto in the national assembly. The basis of an obstructive technique which was often detrimental to national interests, it was abolished by the constitution of 1791.

Ligueur A supporter of the anti-Huguenot Catholic Party in France in the 1570s.

lit de justice In pre-Revolutionary France, a sitting of the *parlement* with the king in attendance to enforce by edict an ordinance or law to which they had previously denied their consent. The mechanism was usually used only after parliamentary refusal to accept a bill, although extensive use was made of it in the eighteenth century.

Long Parliament The Parliament in England which met on 3 November 1640 and sat, with intermissions, until 16 March 1660.

Magnificat The term applied during the Golden Age of Amsterdam in the seventeenth century to the ruling clique of powerful families in the city.

Major Generals Officers appointed to command the twelve military districts into which Cromwell divided England in 1655.

Malcontents Catholic nobles in the Netherlands, opposed to William of Orange after 1578, who desired the supremacy of the Catholic religion. They placed themselves under the leadership of the French Duke of Alençon; their ranks included Montigny, Hèze and Lalaing. Originally anti-Spanish, their dislike of Calvinism caused them to return to allegiance to Spain.

marranos A term used offensively of those Jews in Spain and Portugal who, although they were converted to Christianity (*conversos*), secretly continued to practise their Jewish beliefs.

Massacre of St Bartholomew The massacre of the Huguenots in Paris on the night of 23–24 August 1572 (see chronology, p. 167).

Medici The powerful ruling family of Florence (see p. 7). Their power was aided by the fact that they also produced two popes.

Mennonites Anabaptists who followed the teachings of Menno Simons, they were distinguished by their pacifism and separation from secular authority.

mercenaries Soldiers fighting for another country in return for payment.

Merchant Adventurers The trading company incorporated in 1407 which came to supplant the Hanseatic League. It was based first in Bruges, then moved to Antwerp in 1446, Calais in 1493, Antwerp again in 1496, Hamburg in 1567 and back to the Netherlands in the 1580s. By 1550 it had control of more than three-quarters of English foreign trade. Its monopoly status provoked great criticism and in 1689 its charter was withdrawn.

Mestnichestvo   The Russian system under which the appointment to high offices of state was based on hereditary rank and status. The system was abolished in 1682 when genealogical records were burned.

Metropolitan   The title bestowed in Russia on the Orthodox bishops in the historic capitals of Moscow, St Petersburg, Kiev, Minsk and Novosibirsk. More generally, the title of any archbishop.

Millenary Petition   The Puritan appeal to James I in 1603 for changes in the liturgy and form of worship. James promised to consider the matter at the 1604 Hampton Court Conference, but by then he had allied himself with the Anglican bishops.

millones   The tax voted by Castile in 1590.

mita   The system of forced labour used in New Spain.

Moravians   Members of the Moravian Church, a revival of the 'Bohemian Brethren' (see *Unitas Fratrum*) in 1722. As a Protestant sect it was persecuted by Emperor Ferdinand II but survived.

Moriscos   Muslims (Moors) in Spain who converted to Christianity.

Muscovy   A general term for Russia. The last tsar of Muscovy was Peter the First (the Great), the first Emperor of Russia.

New Christians   In Portugal, after the royal decree of 1499, those Jews and their descendants who were forcibly converted to Christianity.

New Model Army   The name given to the reformed Parliamentary army during the English Civil War. The New Model Army was established by parliamentary ordinance in February 1645 and the armies of Waller and Essex were reorganised into a single force of 22,000 men. Thomas Fairfax was appointed head of the army and Oliver Cromwell was made Lieutenant General.

New Style   The Gregorian calendar, which replaced the Julian calendar or old style. It was introduced by Italy in 1582 but not adopted in Britain until the 1752 Calendar Act, by which date Britain was eleven days behind the rest of western Europe.

New World   The term used for the Americas once it was realised in Europe that Columbus had discovered a previously unknown continent in 1492 and not a passage to the East. It fell out of general use in the late seventeenth century.

Nineteen Propositions   The series of parliamentary demands presented to Charles I on 1 June 1642. Civil war was by this time almost inevitable, though Charles's rejection of the demands marked the final breakdown in negotiations between Parliament and the crown.

Noblesse d'épée In *ancien régime* France, the old nobility of the sword, performing military service to the king as his feudatories. The term contrasted with *noblesse de robe*, those whose nobility derived from judicial or administrative office.

Noces Vetmeilles ('the blood red wedding') The marriage between the Protestant Henry of Navarre and the Catholic Marguerite de Valois in August 1572, which was followed by the massacre of Huguenots on the feast of St Bartholomew.

Noche Triste (sad night) The night of 20 June 1520, when the Spaniards, led by Cortes, suffered very heavy losses in an attack by Mexican Indians and were almost annihilated.

North-east Passage The sea route between the Atlantic and Pacific Oceans, navigable through Siberian waters. The Muscovy Company, founded in England in 1555 to trade with Russia, was responsible for most of the earlier attempts to find the route (see pp. 194–5).

Northern War *See* p. 137.

North-west Passage The sea route from the North Atlantic to the Pacific Ocean, much sought in the sixteenth century as a short way from Europe to the East. In 1497 the Genoese explorer John Cabot (1425–1500) sailed in the service of Henry VII of England to find it. Instead he discovered Newfoundland and Nova Scotia and believed them to be part of Asia (see pp. 194–5).

nu-pieds The peasant revolt, so called because of the 'bare feet' of the peasants (see also p. 127).

Nueva Planta The term used of the new constitution of 1716 in Catalonia.

Nuevas Ordenanzas ('new laws') The code of laws promulgated at Madrid in 1543 which was designed to ameliorate the condition of the Indians in the Spanish colonies.

Nuncio The title of papal envoys to foreign courts.

octroi In pre-Revolutionary France, this was a tax levied on articles brought into towns. It was also the name of the customs station at which the tax was collected.

octrooi In Holland, the charter which created the United Dutch East India Company in 1602.

Official Reformation The term used to describe the process by which Henry VIII in England broke with the jurisdiction of Rome, as opposed to the wider reforms of doctrine and worship undertaken by the Protestant Reformation.

Old Believers The Russian dissenters who in the seventeenth century refused to accept the Patriarch Nikon's reforms of the Russian Orthodox Church.

ordonnances In France, the laws enacted by French monarchs beginning with 'In the name of the King' and ending 'Such is our pleasure'.

Ormée (Deriv. Fr. *orme*, 'elm') The insurrectionary government established at Bordeaux in 1652 and known during the civil wars also as the Fronde (see p. 129).

Ottoman The name given to the Turkish Empire from *c.* 1300 onwards. The expansion of the Ottoman state, based on the morale of *Jihad* and the administrative skills acquired by Islam, reached a peak in the late sixteenth and early seventeenth centuries, when the Empire stretched north-westwards from Asia Minor to the Danube (see p. 68).

Pacta Conventa In Poland, the conditions drawn up in 1573 which severely restricted the rights and powers of future Polish kings.

Palatinate An important principality on the Rhine that was elevated to an Imperial Electorate in 1356. It was the leading Protestant state after the introduction of Calvinism and the head of the Protestant Union in 1608. It was divided and devastated in the Thirty Years' War.

Pale, the That portion of Ireland first subdued and settled by the English during the 1170s in the reign of Henry II. The original area of English rule gradually shrank under Irish encroachment, and was only re-established by Henry VIII's reconquest of Ireland in the sixteenth century.

Parlement The judicial body which replaced the *Cours Plénières* or Baronial Courts of the early French kings. In 1302, in the reign of Philip the Fair, it was established in Paris and became known as the *Parlement de Paris.* It was composed of two prelates, two nobles, thirteen clerics and thirteen laymen. Later, similar bodies, also known as *Parlements*, were organised in the leading provincial centres (e.g. Bordeaux, 1462; Dijon, 1477; Rouen, 1515; Rennes, 1553).

pashalic In the Ottoman Empire, the territory governed by a pasha.

patriciate The term for the urban elite in such major Italian cities as Florence and Venice.

patronato real (Sp., 'royal patronage') The right granted to Spanish kings by the Papacy to appoint candidates to ecclesiastical benefices in colonial possessions such as South America, placing the Latin American Church effectively under the crown's control. The equivalent Portuguese term was *padroado real.*

Patroon The title given from 1629 to members of the Dutch West India Company in the New Netherlands (Dutch North America).

pays d'élections In *ancien régime* France, provinces in which *taille* tax was collected. They were supervised by royal officials known as *élus*, who were first appointed in 1355 and increased in numbers in 1386. They formed the core of the kingdom. At the end of the sixteenth century, *élus* were superseded by *Intendants* who, with their greater powers, exercised untrammelled control over the *pays d'élections* until the Revolution.

pays d'états In *ancien régime* France, those provinces, annexed to the crown on a semi-contractual basis, which in theory kept a measure of fiscal and general autonomy. Many of the estates of the *pays d'états* had disappeared by the seventeenth century and in the eighteenth century only the more recently annexed provinces such as Brittany, Languedoc, Corsica and Burgundy retained effective estates and fiscal privileges.

Peasants' Revolt *See* p. 121.

Periwig Period The period of stagnation and decline in the Netherlands in the eighteenth century following the great period of Dutch expansion in the 'golden age' of the previous two centuries.

Petition of Right The declaration of the 'rights and liberties of the subject' that was presented to Charles I by Parliament in 1628. Largely drafted by the lawyer and MP Sir Edward Coke (1552–1634), it marked an important stage in the development of opposition to royal prerogative.

Phanariots Greeks in the Ottoman Empire to whom the imperial authorities devolved administrative powers over Christian subjects. The term derived from the Phanar area of Constantinople.

Physiocrats Adherents of an eighteenth-century French school of economics known at the time as *Les Économistes* but later renamed by DuPont de Nemours, one of their number. Other members were Turgot, Quesnay and Mirabeau. They held the common eighteenth-century view of the bounty of nature and the goodness of man in his natural state. They pressed for agricultural and fiscal reforms in France.

Piagnoni ('the weepers') The name given to the followers of Savonarola, the guiding spirit of the Florentine Republic which was established during a temporary eclipse of the power of the Medicis in 1494.

Pilgrim Fathers The 101 English Puritans and other Congregationalists who, after living for some years in exile in Holland, sailed for America in the *Mayflower* on 6 September 1620. They landed at Plymouth, Massachusetts, on 4 December, where they founded a settlement and are thus regarded as the pioneers of American colonisation.

Pilgrimage of Grace The name given to insurrections in Cumberland, Durham, Lincolnshire, Lancashire, Northumberland, Westmoreland and Yorkshire in 1536–37 against the ecclesiastical and other reforms of Henry VIII. The rebellions failed.

Placards The Affair of the Placards was an attempt by French Protestant evangelicals in October 1534 to force Francis I to take up a defined religious position. The attempt went badly wrong and the leading reformers were arrested. Others (including Calvin) fled from Paris.

places de sûreté Towns in France that were allowed, under the Edict of Nantes, to have a Huguenot garrison (see p. 169).

Politiques   The French Catholic party, led by the Montmorency family and formed after the St Bartholomew's Day Massacre of Parisian Huguenots in 1572, which wished to put an end to such religious persecution and bigotry.

Pragmatic Army   An army organised in the Netherlands by Britain in the 1740–48 War of the Austrian Succession, with contingents from Austria, Britain, Holland, Hanover and Hesse and which, commanded by George II, marched up the Rhine and defeated the French at Dettingen on 27 June 1743.

Pragmatic Sanction   The law announced by Emperor Charles VI on 19 April 1713 to ensure that the Habsburg succession would pass to his daughter Maria Theresa, his male heir having died. Though acknowledged by most European powers by 1738, Frederick II of Prussia's rejection of the agreement on Charles's death in 1740 brought about the War of the Austrian Succession (see p. 139).

Predestination   An important doctrine stressed by Calvinism and other Protestant faiths which holds that God has destined some souls for salvation and others for damnation and that nothing individual people can do will change their allotted destinies.

Preobajensky   The regiment of royal bodyguards formed by Peter I of Russia. During the eighteenth century, the regiment was active in palace coups which led to the succession first of the Tsarina Anna in 1730, then of Elizabeth in 1741 and finally of Catherine II in 1762.

Presbyterianism   A system of Church government by presbyters. Based on the model of church government established by Calvin in Geneva, it provided a means of imposing discipline on pastors and members of the church.

Protector of the Indians   The title bestowed on Bartolomé de las Casas, a Spanish Dominican (1474–1566) in 1516.

Protectorate   The period in the Interregnum, from 16 December 1653 to 25 May 1659, when England was governed by a Protector. Parliament's powers were transferred to Oliver Cromwell (1599–1658). The Instrument of Government was drafted and Cromwell was appointed Lord Protector.

Protestantism   *See* p. 159 *et seq.*

Puritans   Extreme Protestants of the sixteenth and seventeenth centuries, including Presbyterians and Independents. The Puritans pressed for Calvinist reform in the Anglican church, had a strict code of morality, a high sense of public duty and were opposed to certain forms of art and amusement.

Quadruple Alliance   The league against Spain, formed in 1718 by Great Britain, France, Austria and the Netherlands.

quinto (Sp., 'fifth')   The royalties derived by the crown of Spain from the mines in her American colonies. They totalled about one-fifth of the yield.

Ranters   In Commonwealth England, a fanatical sect of pantheists and 'antinomians' who did not believe that Christians were bound to keep the law of God.

Raskol   The great religious schism in the seventeenth-century Russian Church which arose because of attempts by Patriarch Nikon to introduce innovations in ritual. Dissenters were excommunicated and thousands fled the country.

Reconquísta (Sp. 'reconquest')   The 800-year Christian struggle to drive the Moorish occupiers from Spain. The final Arab kingdom in Spain, that of Granada, was defeated and the Moors were expelled in a campaign waged from 1482 to 1492 by Ferdinand and Isabella. It left the whole of the Spanish peninsula under their control (see also p. 118).

recusants   In England, those who refused to attend the services of the Church of England, most commonly Roman Catholics. Recusants were first fined under the Acts of Uniformity of 1552 and 1559. Elizabeth fined both Catholics and recusant Protestants.

reductions   Those villages in colonial South America established for Christianised Indians (*reducciones*). Such villages were a notable feature of Spanish missionary activity in New Spain.

Reformation   *See* p. 159 *et seq.*

régale   The right claimed by French kings to present benefices that fell vacant when the bishop's see of the same diocese was also vacant and to collect the revenues of vacant sees. The Papacy disputed the claim and a conflict arose between Louis XIV and Pope Innocent XI in 1678.

Reichskammergericht   The standing high court of justice of the Holy Roman Empire that was reorganised from the Imperial Council in 1495 by Maximilian I. The Emperor nominated the president who was assisted by eight nobles and eight doctors of law approved by the *Reichstag*.

Remonstrants   A term in the Netherlands for those Arminians who, in 1610, presented a remonstrance to the States-General against the charges of heresy made against them. The document contained the *Five Articles of Arminianism*.

Restoration   The restoration of the English monarchy, secured in 1660 by the accession of Charles II to the throne. It ended the period of the Commonwealth which had followed the Civil War.

Réunion (Fr., 'reunion')   The territorial expansion policy of Louis XIV. With his potential enemies preoccupied, Louis XIV was successful in extending France to the largest extent yet achieved.

Rohosz   In old Poland, a self-constituted assembly of nobles which took the lead in calling the nobility to arms if it became necessary to force the king to accede to their demands.

Roi Soleil (Fr., 'sun king')   The soubriquet of Louis XIV of France.

Romanov   The family of German or Prussian-Lithuanian origins which ruled Russia from 1613 to 1917.

Roundhead   The term of derision given during the English Civil War by Royalists, who usually wore ringlets, to Puritans and members of the parliamentary party, who wore their hair cut short.

Royalists   The supporters of Charles I during the English Civil War (1642–49). They were also known as Cavaliers.

Rump   Members of the Long Parliament not expelled in Pride's Purge, who voted to try Charles I and who declared the Commonwealth in England.

sanbenito (Sp.)   The name of the long garment of yellow cloth enforced on penitent heretics by the Spanish Inquisition.

Schmalkaldic League   The League of the Protestant princes which was formed in 1531 (see p. 121).

Sea Beggars   *See* Beggars of the Sea.

Sea Dogs   English privateers of the early Elizabethan period who preyed on French commercial shipping in the Channel. They sailed under *Lettres de Marque* granted by Condé and the French Huguenots. These were withdrawn after the reconciliation of the Huguenots and Catholics and the sea-dogs then joined the Dutch 'Beggars of the Sea' in attacking Spanish shipping instead.

'Second Reformation'   The term, from the German '*Zweite Reformation*', for the spread of Calvinism in the years after 1555 in some German principalities and cities.

Sectaries   Puritan extremists in the fragmented church during the English Civil War, (see p. 128), they stressed their inner light and the hearing of divine voices. They included Antinomians, Baptists, Fifth Monarchy Men and Ranters.

seigneurie   In *ancien régime* France, the basic economic unit in the countryside. A complex variety of dues and services was owed to each *seigneur* by his tenants.

sejm   The national parliament of old Poland which met at Warsaw, although once every three years it met at Grodno in Lithuania. It was divided into 68 constituencies for electoral purposes.

Serene Republic   A title often bestowed on the Venetian Republic in the heyday of its power.

Socinians   The followers of Laelius Socinus, who founded a sect in 1560 with doctrines similar to those of the later Unitarians. They attracted many adherents in Poland and in 1658 the Diet of Warsaw proscribed them, after which they gradually declined.

sol pour livre   The 5 per cent sales tax introduced in France in 1640.

solidité (Fr.)   The system of taxation in seventeenth-century France whereby a peasant was held responsible for his neighbour's taxes even if he had paid all his own.

South Sea Bubble   The overvaluation and subsequent slump in the value of the shares of the South Sea Company in 1720. This joint-stock company was floated in 1711 with the intention of trading largely in slaves with the Spanish colonies of South America. The rapid collapse of the shares left many bankrupt, and involved three government ministers in charges of corruption. The political skill of the paymaster-general, Walpole (1676–1745), averted a royal scandal.

Spanish Fury   The name given to the sack of Antwerp by Spanish troops in 1576.

Spanish Main   Correctly the mainland between the Orinoco River and the Isthmus of Panama, the term is often used incorrectly to refer to the Caribbean.

Spanish Road   The term coined for the route down the Rhine which was used by Spain to move its troops and supplies during, for example, the Thirty Years' War.

Stadtholder   The office in the Low Countries introduced in the fifteenth century by the ruling Burgundian dukes and retained by their Habsburg successors. Stadtholders, who were initially noblemen, acquired wide powers in the United Provinces of the Netherlands, including presiding over assemblies and commanding provincial armies. The office was abolished by French Revolutionary armies in 1795.

streltsy   The military force stationed by Ivan IV in Moscow and other major Russian towns to repel Tatar incursions. Their revolt against Peter was ruthlessly suppressed (see p. 135).

Stuart   The Scottish dynasty which provided England with its monarchs from 1603 to 1688 (James I, Charles I, Charles II and James II) during a period of great political upheaval.

Sublime Porte   The high gate in the wall of the main governmental building in Constantinople. The name was used, by extension, to refer to the government of the Ottoman Empire.

Sumperk   The location in Moravia of the infamous witch-trials of 1679 when around 100 people were burnt alive. The Inquisition, approved by the Church, was led by a publican who selected wealthy merchants and seized their property.

Supremacy, Acts of   The Act of 1534 which established Henry VIII as head of the Church of England in place of the pope and gave him control of Church doctrine, ecclesiastical appointments and Church income. It was repealed during the Catholic 'reaction' in the reign of Queen Mary (1553–58) but was followed by the Act of 1559 which established Elizabeth I as supreme head of the Church of England.

Swiss Guard (1) The Papal Swiss Guard is the corps that has provided a special military force for popes and the Vatican palace continuously since 1505. (2) The body of Swiss mercenaries that constituted 'Gardes' by French Royal decree in 1616. The Swiss Guard provided a loyal bodyguard to successive French monarchs.

szlachta The Polish term for the noble caste in the country. The *szlachta* enjoyed exemption from taxation and full political rights. In return they were supposed to be prepared to fight on Poland's behalf. They were estimated to number nearly 10 per cent of the population.

Table of Ranks A system of social stratification in Tsarist Russia formulated by Peter the Great in 1722 which involved 14 parallel grades in the civil service, court, army and navy. Progress depended on rising from the bottom grade by ability and length of service, and it was theoretically possible for those of the lowest birth to rise to the nobility. The Table of Ranks remained in existence until 1762.

taille An important direct tax in France which took two main forms: personal (*personelle*) and property (*réelle*). Personal *taille*, a direct tax levied from the fifteenth century to 1789, was assessed on personal possessions at a rate determined by the tax collector. Because the First and Second Estates, together with many of the Third Estate, were exempt, it bore heavily on the peasantry. The *taille réelle* was levied over a similar period in the Midi and south-west of France and fell on common land. Less arbitrary than personal *taille*, it raised more revenue.

Tenth Penny The name of a tax imposed by the Spanish Duke of Alva to help raise money for his army of occupation in the Netherlands in 1573. The tax was levied at 10 per cent on all sales but was resisted by Netherlands' merchants and was never collected.

tercio A regiment in the Spanish army, comprising *c.* 2500 infantrymen.

Test Acts In England, the Test Acts were designed to exclude members of churches other than the Church of England from certain positions of authority. For example, the 1673 Test Act excluded Catholics and nonconformists from military and civil office.

Testament Politique The general plan or philosophy of Richelieu. Written or dictated by him, it provides raw material for the historian on Richelieu's ideas and strategy.

Teutonic Knights The crusading knights engaged in the conversion of the pagan peoples of the Baltic, eastern Germany and Poland. From 1309 they were based at Marienburg, south-east of Danzig (Gdansk). Their territorial losses increased as a result of wars with Poland.

Thorough   In the reign of Charles I (1623–49), the policy of Strafford and Laud, who were determined to carry through their schemes whatever obstacles were placed in their way.

tiers état (Fr. 'third estate')   In *ancien régime* France, it comprised all the social classes other than the aristocracy, the higher clergy and the privileged magistracy.

tithe   The right of a clerical incumbent to collect a tenth of agricultural produce.

toisée   The much-hated tax proposed in 1643 by Louis XIV's finance minister, Emery, on houses in the suburbs of Paris. Resistance to the tax was quelled.

Tsar (also Czar)   The title (emperor) of the Russian rulers adopted by Ivan IV in 1547 and meant to express the highest form of domination. It was equivalent to that of the Holy Roman Emperor in the West. The Tsar's eldest son was known as the Tsarevitch and his wife as the Tsarina.

Uniformity, Acts of   A series of Acts in England that were designed to provide the legal and doctrinal bases on which the Church of England stands. The first two were passed in the reign of Edward VI (in 1549 and 1552). Both Acts were repealed in the reign of Queen Mary I (1553–58). However, in 1559, a third Act was introduced following the accession of Queen Elizabeth I. This required the use of a modified version of the 1552 Prayer Book. In 1662 a fourth Act was passed.

Unitas Fratrum   The Bohemian Brethren, a small, rigorous Hussite sect that was influenced by the pacifist ideas of Peter Chelčický. It split from the Utraquists in 1467.

United Provinces   The seven Dutch-speaking provinces of Friesland, Gelderland, Gröningen-Drente, Holland, Utrecht, Zeeland, and Overijssel which, in alliance with other European states, fought a war of independence from 1568 until their independence as the Dutch Republic was recognised in 1648.

Utraquists   A religious movement in Hungary, Bohemia and Poland in the fifteenth century which evolved from the moderate wing of the Hussites. Their main demand was for communion in both kinds (*sub utraque specie*) for the laity, from which they take their name.

Valois   The French royal dynasty which reigned from 1328 to 1589. It was a branch of the Capetian family.

Valor Ecclesiasticus   The tax book in which all the ecclesiastical property in England was valued by commissioners appointed by Thomas Cromwell as a prelude to the dissolution of the monasteries in 1535.

Valtelline   Alpine valley area (enclosing the valley of the Upper Adda from its source to Lake Como) of great strategic importance for troops and communications from Milan to Vienna and Brussels.

vingtième (Fr. 'twentieth')   A direct tax in France based on the earlier *dixième* ('tenth') that was introduced in 1710. The *vingtième* was levied by Machault in 1749 as a universal tax of 5 per cent on incomes derived from rents, property, feudal rights and business. The privileged classes attempted to restrict its operation and to evade it but it proved the most efficient and just form of taxation available. Further *vingtièmes* were levied in 1756 and 1760–63, both times of financial stringency.

voivodes   The name given to the princes of Moldavia and Wallachia during this period.

Zweite Reformation   *See* Second Reformation.

ECONOMY AND SOCIETY

POPULATION, URBANISATION AND HEALTH

It is difficult to produce reliable figures for the population of Europe before the nineteenth century. In the early modern period few territories held regular and systematic censuses of their population; although there were some exceptions, notably the Grand Duchy of Tuscany and the Republic of Venice. Even then the figures may mislead, as those exempt from taxation might be excluded from the total. Historians have estimated the level of population using many indicators and whatever forms of evidence are available. These include tax assessments and returns, baptismal and burial records, muster lists for military service, and techniques of 'family reconstitution', which provide insight into the size of households, marriage patterns and fertility. As a result, estimates made by different historians vary considerably. The figures given below are not accurate but give some indication of probable population levels and demographic fluctuations.

Population of Early Modern Europe by country (in millions)

	1500	1550	1600	1650	1700	1750
Scandinavia	1.5	1.7	2	2.6	2.9	3.4
England and Wales	2.6	3.2	4.4	5.6	5.8	6.5
Scotland	0.8	0.9	1	1	1	1.3
Ireland	1	1.1	1.4	1.8	2.8	3.1
Germany	12	14	16	12	16	19
France	16.4	19	19	20	20	24.6
Italy	10.5	11.4	13.1	11.3	13.4	15.5
Spain	6.8	7.4	8.1	7.1	8	9
Austria/Bohemia/Moravia	3.5	3.6	4.3	4.1	4.6	5.7
Portugal	1	1	1.4	1.5	2.3	2.8
Netherlands	0.95	1.25	1.5	1.9	1.9	1.9
Belgium	1.4	1.65	1.6	2	2	2.2
Poland	1	1.2	1.1	1.2	2	2.3
Switzerland	0.65	0.8	1	1	1.2	1.3
Russia	9		15.5		17.5	
Balkans	7		8		8	

Sources: J. de Vries, *European Urbanization 1500–1800* (London, 1984), p. 36; R. Mols, 'Population in Europe 1500–1700', in C. Cipolla, ed., *The Fontana Economic History of Europe: The Sixteenth and Seventeenth Centuries* (London, 1974), p. 38; H. Moller, ed., *Population Movements in Modern European History* (London, 1964), p. 5.

Population of Early Modern European cities (in thousands)

	1500	1550	1600	1650	1700	1750
London	50	120	200	375	490	675
Constantinople					700	
Paris		250	250	450	530	570
Naples		80	289	265	232	315
Marseilles		30	45	65	75	88
Lisbon		100			188	
Amsterdam					172	
Rome			102	121	142	158
Rouen	40	75	60	82	64	67
Seville			150			
Venice		158	139	120	138	149
Moscow					130	
Bordeaux	20	33	35	40	45	60
Milan		130	109	120	124	
Palermo		80	105	100	100	107
Antwerp					66	43

Sources: T. Chandler and G. Fox, *3000 Years of Urban Growth* (New York, 1974), pp. 11–20; P. Benedict, 'French cities from the sixteenth century to the Revolution: An overview', in P. Benedict, ed., *Cities and Social Change in Early Modern France* (London, 1989), p. 24; R. Finlay and B. Shearer, 'Population growth and suburban expansion', in A. Beier and R. Finlay, eds, *London 1500–1700: The Making of the Metropolis* (London, 1986), p. 39; G. Felloni, 'Italy', in C. Wilson and G. Parker, eds, *An Introduction to the Sources of European Economic History* (London, 1977), pp. 5–6.

Number of cities with at least 10,000 inhabitants, by territory

	1500	1550	1600	1650	1700	1750
Scandinavia	1	1	2	2	2	3
England and Wales	5	4	6	8	11	21
Scotland	1	1	1	1	2	5
Ireland	0	0	0	1	3	3
Netherlands	11	12	19	19	20	18
Belgium	12	12	12	14	15	15
Germany	23	27	30	23	30	35
France	32	34	43	44	55	55
Switzerland	1	1	2	2	3	4
Italy	44	46	59	50	51	65
Spain	20	27	37	24	22	24
Portugal	1	4	5	5	5	5
Austria/Bohemia/Moravia	3	3	3	3	4	6
Poland	0	1	1	1	1	2

Source: J. de Vries, *European Urbanization 1500–1800* (London, 1984), p. 29.

Total population of all cities with at least 10,000 inhabitants (in thousands)

	1500	1550	1600	1650	1700	1750
Scandinavia	13	13	26	63	115	167
England and Wales	80	112	255	495	718	1,021
Scotland	13	13	30	35	53	119
Ireland	0	0	0	17	96	161
Netherlands	150	191	364	603	639	580
Belgium	295	375	301	415	486	432
Germany	385	534	662	528	714	956
France	688	814	1,114	1,438	1,747	1,970
Switzerland	10	12	25	22	39	60
Italy	1,302	1,498	1,973	1,577	1,761	2,159
Spain	414	639	923	672	673	767
Portugal	30	138	155	199	230	209
Austria/Bohemia/Moravia	60	67	90	100	180	294
Poland	0	10	15	20	15	36

Source: J. de Vries, *European Urbanization 1500–1800* (London, 1984), p. 30.

Urban population as a percentage of total population

	1500	1550	1600	1650	1700	1750
Scandinavia	0.9	0.8	1.4	2.4	4.0	4.6
England and Wales	3.1	3.5	5.8	8.8	13.3	16.7
Scotland	1.6	1.4	3.0	3.5	5.3	9.2
Ireland	0	0	0	0.9	3.4	5.0
Netherlands	15.8	15.3	24.3	31.7	33.6	30.5
Belgium	21.1	22.7	18.8	20.8	23.9	19.6
Germany	3.2	3.8	4.1	4.4	4.8	5.6
France	4.2	4.3	5.9	7.2	9.2	9.1
Switzerland	1.5	1.5	2.5	2.2	3.3	4.6
Italy	12.4	12.8	14.7	14.0	13.4	14.2
Spain	6.1	8.6	11.4	9.5	9.0	8.6
Portugal	3.0	11.5	14.1	16.6	11.5	9.1
Austria/Bohemia/Moravia	1.7	1.9	2.1	2.4	3.9	5.2
Poland	0	0.3	0.4	0.7	0.5	1.0

Source: J. de Vries, *European Urbanization 1500–1800* (London, 1984), p. 39.

Infant mortality rate in Fiesole (Tuscany), 1621–61 (infants dying in the first year of life per 1,000 christened)

Year	Deaths	Year	Deaths
1621	141	1642	192
1622	238	1643	287
1623	119	1644	224
1624	258	1645	369
1625	177	1646	234
1626	278	1647	118
1627	216	1648	363
1628	148	1649	514
1629	186	1650	296
1630	164	1651	223
1631	140	1652	236
1632	228	1653	222
1633	224	1654	355
1634	243	1655	273
1635	213	1656	411
1636	257	1657	310
1637	319	1658	496
1638	193	1659	736
1639	315	1660	162
1640	322	1661	303
1641	205		

Source: C. Cipolla, *Before the Industrial Revolution: European Society and Economy 1000–1700*, 3rd edition (London, 1993), p. 285.

Distribution of population according to age in Carpi and Pesaro (as a percentage)

The survival of rare census material, in which the population was divided into age-groups, enables historians to identify the age profile of the population of two communities in Italy.

Ages	Carpi (1591)		Pesaro (1689)	
	Men	Women	Town	Country
81 and over	0.3	0.1	0.5	0.7
71–80	0.6	0.4	2.4	2.7
61–70	1.8	1.4	5.9	5.9
56–60	3.1	3.5	3.9	3.8
51–55	2.8	2.4	6.7	5.4
46–50	5.1	5.7	5.8	5.5
41–45	4.1	4.1	8.2	6.6
36–40	7.1	8.7	6.0	5.0
31–35	5.9	5.9	7.1	6.6
26–30	8.1	9.1	8.4	7.7
21–25	8.2	8.6	10.4	8.2
16–20	9.8	11.0	9.1	9.5
11–15	14.4	12.5	8.7	9.7
6–10	15.5	13.8	8.2	10.4
0–5	13.0	12.8	8.7	11.3

Source: R. Mols, 'Population in Europe 1500–1700', in C. Cipolla, ed., The Fontana Economic History of Europe: The Sixteenth and Seventeenth Centuries (London, 1974), p. 49.

Baptisms, burials and weddings in Esslingen

The evidence from Esslingen in Germany indicates a situation which was apparent in most towns and cities of Europe, that the annual number of deaths regularly exceeded the number of births. For a town or city to maintain its level of population or to grow, migration from outside was necessary.

Year	Baptisms	Burials	Weddings
1631	207	145	35
1632	170	137	60
1633	173	171	39
1634	268	598	37
1635	177	1,985	46
1636	162	113	237
1637	149	156	63
1638	204	656	67
1639	195	234	61
1640	211	86	48
Decade total	1,916	4,281	693
Decade average	192	428	69

Source: C. Friedrichs, *The Early Modern City 1450–1750* (London, 1995), p. 118.

Plague and Epidemics

The great plague outbreak known as the Black Death had arrived in Europe in 1347 and, beginning in Messina in Sicily, it had gradually spread across the continent, arriving in England in 1348. Between one-third and a half of the population of Europe died as a result of the Black Death in those years, and the level of the population was slow to recover. Plague and other epidemics continued to ravage Europe and outbreaks of disease acted as a check on the growth of the population.

Mortality in selected Italian cities during plague epidemics in 1630–31 and 1656–57

Date	City	Population before epidemic (000s)	Deaths during epidemic (000s)	Deaths as % of population
1630–31	Bergamo	25	10	40
	Bologna	62	15	24
	Brescia	24	11	45
	Milan	130	60	47
	Monza	7	4	57
	Padua	32	19	59
	Parma	30	15	50
	Prato	6	1.5	25
	Venice	140	46	33
	Verona	54	33	61
	Vicenza	32	12	38
1656–57	Genoa	75	45	60
	Naples	300	150	50
	Rome	123	23	19

Source: C. Cipolla, *Before the Industrial Revolution: European Society and Economy 1000–1700*, 3rd edition (London, 1993), p. 133.

Major epidemics in London, 1563–1665

Year	All burials	Plague burials	Estimated total population	Gross mortality as %
City and Liberties				
1563	20,372	17,404	85,000	24.0
1593	17,893	10,675	125,000	14.3
1603	31,861	25,045	141,000	22.6
1625	41,312	26,350	206,000	20.1
City, Liberties and Outparishes				
1636	23,359	10,400	313,000	7.5
1665	80,696	55,797	459,000	17.6

Source: P. Slack, 'Metropolitan government in crisis: the response to the plague', in A. Beier and R. Finlay, eds, *London 1500–1700: The Making of the Metropolis* (London, 1986), p. 62.

The size of London's population of aliens

Year	Number of aliens	Total population	% of aliens in population
1567	4,700	100,000	4.7
1571	4,850	100,000	4.9
1573	5,315	100,000	5.3
1593	5,450	150,000	3.6
1635	3,600	350,000	1.0

Source: R. Finlay, *Population and Metropolis: The Demography of London 1580–1650* (Cambridge, 1981), p. 68.

WAGES AND PRICES

Average yields of grain for each one sown in various areas in Europe

Florence		Imola		Romagna		Russia/Poland/Bohemia	
1611–20	9.4	1515–24	7.3	1550–59	5.9	1500–49	2.4
1621–30	7.6	1525–34	6.3	1560–69	5.6	1550–99	4.5
1631–40	7.4	1535–44	6.7	1570–79	5.7	1600–49	4.2
1641–50	7.5	1545–54	6.3	1580–89	5.9	1650–99	3.7
1651–60	6.7	1555–64	5.2	1590–99	4.8	1700–49	3.7
1661–70	6.1	1565–74	6.0	1600–09	5.9	1750–99	3.4
1671–80	5.9	1585–94	5.6	1610–19	6.2		
1681–90	6.7	1595–1604	5.1	1620–29	5.4		
1691–1700	6.0	1605–14	6.4	1630–39	5.5		

Sources: C. Cipolla, *Before the Industrial Revolution: European Society and Economy 1000–1700*, 3rd edition (London, 1993), p. 102; G. Felloni, 'Italy', in C. Wilson and G. Parker, eds, *An Introduction to the Sources of European Economic History 1500–1800* (London, 1977), p. 10; C. Wilson, 'The British Isles', in C. Wilson and G. Parker, eds, *An Introduction to the Sources of European Economic History 1500–1800* (London, 1977), p. 121.

The growth in the size of the population which occurred across Europe, especially from the late fifteenth century, increased the demand for food, especially grain. The inability of agriculture to increase grain production in line with demand, led to a rise in prices.

Price paid for rye by the Augsburg Hospital, 1455–1750

Prices in Augsburg Pfennig per Schaff (1 Schaff = 205.3 litres).

Year	Price	Year	Price
1455	172	1605	804
1460	176	1610	1,196
1465	–	1615	1,344
1470	–	1620	1,153
1475	134	1625	2,604
1480	180	1630	1,089
1485	138	1635	3,320
1490	374	1640	695
1495	198	1645	525
1500	313	1650	–
1505	168	1655	399
1510	243	1660	701
1515	272	1665	711
1520	210	1670	371
1525	–	1675	1,128
1530	533	1680	1,322
1535	306	1685	576
1540	552	1690	1,132
1545	492	1695	802
1550	704	1700	1,789
1555	373	1705	959
1560	607	1710	1,446
1565	494	1715	1,182
1570	1,563	1720	1,161
1575	630	1725	940
1580	854	1730	1,062
1585	845	1735	1,157
1590	1,339	1740	3,150
1595	836	1745	1,327
1600	1,379	1750	1,362

Source: M. J. Elsass, *Umriss einer Geschichte der Preise und Löhne in Deutschland*, Vol. 1 (Leiden, 1936), pp. 593–6.

The early modern period witnessed a marked increase in prices, especially those of basic foodstuffs. As abundant labour was available, the level of wages, particularly those of unskilled labourers, did not rise at the same rate as prices.

Wages paid to unskilled building workers by the Augsburg Hospital, 1510–1748
(wages paid in Augsburg Pfennig per day)

Year	Summer rate	Winter rate
1510	10.5	
1513	10.5	
1553	21.0	
1563	21.0	
1564	–	21.0
1571	28.0	
1575	28.0	
1580	28.0	
1584	28.0	21.0
1590	31.5	
1595	31.5	
1600	28.0	
1605	24.5	
1612	29.7	
1617	35.0	
1625	42.0	
1630	42.0	
1644	56.0	
1652	42.0	
1672		35.0
1675	49.0	
1681	52.5	
1685	52.5	
1690	49.0	
1695	49.0	
1700		49.0
1705	49.0	
1710		49.0
1716	52.5	45.5
1721	52.5	
1726	52.5	42.0
1730	52.5	45.5
1737	42.0	35.0
1741	42.0	35.0
1748	52.5	42.0

Source: M. J. Elsass, *Umriss einer Geschichte der Preise und Löhne in Deutschland*, Vol. 1 (Leiden, 1936), pp. 733–4.

Daily wages of building and agricultural workers in Italy, 1500–1759
(all wages are in soldi)

	Monferrat agricultural labourer	Milan master mason	Modena master mason	Genoa master mason	Florence master mason	Florence agricultural labourer
1500–09				8		
1510–19				9		
1520–29				9	15–20	8
1530–39			14	11–12	21	
1540–49				13		10
1550–59			14	13	21–28	
1560–69			14–15	14		10
1570–79	?10		18	15	35–40	10
1580–89			20	18–20	35	10
1590–99	10		24	22	40	10
1600–09	10	35	27	24	40	10
1610–19	?12	40	27	24	40–50	
1620–29	12	40	27	26		
1630–39	?10	40	35	30		
1640–49		40	38	34		
1650–59	12	40	43	34		
1660–69	12	40	43	36		
1670–79	12	40	43	40		
1680–89	12	40	45	40		
1690–99	12	35	50	36		
1700–09	12	35		36		
1710–19	12	32.5		36–40		
1720–29	12	32.5		36		
1730–39	12	32.5		40		
1740–49	12	32.5		38		
1750–59	12	32.5		40		

Source: G. Felloni, 'Italy', in C. Wilson and G. Parker, eds, *An Introduction to the Sources of European Economic History 1500–1800* (London, 1977), p. 26.

Price and wage movements in Western and Central Europe during the sixteenth century (25-year averages, silver content of coinage, 1501–25 = 100)

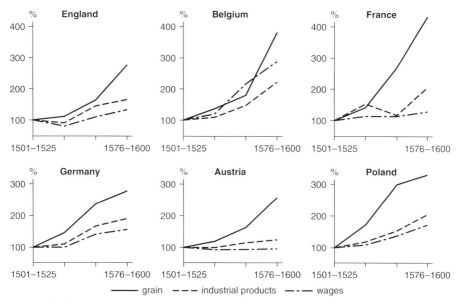

Source: W. Abel, *Agricultural Fluctuations in Europe: From the Thirteenth to the Twentieth Centuries* (1966; Engl. trans., London, 1980), p. 120.

The decline in real wages of a day labourer in Halliwil (Aargau), 1476–1700

	Real wages expressed in kilogrammes of spelt	*Indices*
1476–1500	4.77	100.0
1501–25	6.51	136.7
1526–50	4.27	89.7
1551–75	3.16	66.5
1576–1600	2.94	61.8
1601–25	2.07	43.6
1626–50	2.14	45.1
1651–75	3.47	73.0
1676–1700	2.34	49.3

Source: B. H. Slicher van Bath, *The Agrarian History of Western Europe, A.D. 500–1850* (1960; Engl. trans., London, 1963), p. 199.

281

TRADE, COMMERCE AND INDUSTRY

The early modern period experienced a gradual shift of economic activity away from the Mediterranean region, especially Italy, towards the Atlantic seaboard countries, particularly to the United Provinces in the seventeenth century and Great Britain in the eighteenth century.

The number of cloths produced in Venice, 1520–1710

1520	3,639	1620	23,000
1530	6,065	1630	13,275
1540	7,000	1640	11,719
1550	11,558	1650	10,082
1560	17,569	1660	7,861
1570	9,492	1670	5,226
1580	21,387	1680	3,820
1590	20,607	1690	2,009
1600	24,719	1700	2,033
1610	17,129	1710	2,057

Source: D. Sella, 'The rise and fall of the Venetian woollen industry', in B. Pullan, ed., *Crisis and Change in the Venetian Economy in the Sixteenth and Seventeenth Centuries* (London, 1968), pp. 109–10.

The size and destination of the Hungarian copper trade of the Fuggers, 1497–1529 (annual averages in tons and percentages)

	Tonnage of total exports	Exports to Antwerp via Danzig and Stettin as %	Exports to Venice and Trieste as %
1497–1503	1390.4	12.3	32.1
1507–09	1476.8	49.3	13.3
1510–18	1625.2	55.8	2.6
1519–26	1367.3	35.2	4.5
1527–29	1099.1	53.9	10.2

Note: The remaining exports went mainly to Nuremberg, Leipzig, Hamburg, Frankfurt and Lüneburg but many of these would probably have had Antwerp as their ultimate destination.

Source: P. Kriedte and H. van der Wee, *The Growth of the Antwerp Market and the European Economy*, Vol. 1 (Louvain, 1963), p. 523.

Trade between Spain and America, 1600–1710

| | *Outgoing* | | *Incoming* | |
| | Ships | Tonnages | Ships | Tonnages |
	(*annual averages*)		(*annual averages*)	
1600–40	55	19,800	56	21,600
1640–50	25	8,500	29	9,850
1670–80	17	4,650	19	5,600
1701–10	8	2,640	7	2,310

Source: F. Mauro, 'Spain', in C. Wilson and G. Parker, eds, *An Introduction to the Sources of European Economic History 1500–1800* (London, 1977), p. 46, using material from J. Vicens Vives, ed., *Historia de España y América Social y Económica*, 2nd edition, Vol. III, p. 282.

Manpower employed in Dutch shipping (estimates), 1610–1725

	1610	*1635*	*1670*	*1725*
European trade	20,000	21,500	25,000	20,000
Fisheries (except whaling)	6,500	7,000	5,500	4,000
Whaling	0	1,000	8,000	8,000
VOC	2,000	4,000	9,000	11,000
Navy	3,000	7,000	11,000	3,500
New World Trade	1,000	2,500	3,000	2,000

Note: VOC = *Verenigde Oostindische Compagnie* (Dutch East India Company).

Source: J. Israel, *The Dutch Republic: Its Rise, Greatness and Fall, 1477–1806* (Oxford, 1998), p. 623.

The balance of trade between France and the United Provinces, 1635–1750 (in livres tournois)

Dutch exports to France	1635–45	%	1750	%
Spices	3,193,130	14.9	3,482,000	15.5
Sugar, tea, cocoa, tobacco	1,885,150	8.75	1,446,000	6.4
Drugs, dyes, colours	1,877,300	8.75	2,390,000	10.6
Precious stones, wool, cotton, ivory, silk, hair	1,835,200	8.55	1,820,000	8.1
Cloth, serges, etc.	6,889,960	32.1	2,327,000	10.3
Metal	1,500,000	7.0	2,137,000	9.5
War-materials	1,235,000	5.8	–	–
Linen, hemp, wood, masts, leather, skins, furs	2,375,470	11.05	1,636,000	7.3
Fishing products, oil, lime	454,300	2.1	2,180,000	9.7
Dairy-products	200,010	0.95	770,000	3.4
Cereals	–	–	1,960,000	8.6
Others	–	–	c. 2,238,000	c. 10.6
Total	**21,445,520**	**100**	**22,386,000**	**100**

French exports to the United Provinces	1635–45	%	1750	%
Wine, brandy	6,192,632	39.5	4,702,000	19.1
Cereals	3,450,450	21.9	–	–
Linen	1,583,432	10.1	1,450,000	5.9
Salt, fruits, oil of Provence	3,203,927	20.35	922,000	3.7
Textiles, paper, glass	915,525	5.8	1,794,000	7.3
Fruit, honey, woad, etc.	355,500	2.3	–	–
Colonial products	–	–	12,447,000	50.7
Others	–	–	3,205,000	13.3
Total	**15,701,466**	**100**	**24,520,000**	**100**

Source: J. A. van Houtte and L. van Buyten, 'The Low Countries', in C. Wilson and G. Parker, eds, An Introduction to the Sources of European Economic History 1500–1800 (London, 1977), p. 94.

Exports of manufactures from England, 1699–1754 (in £000s)

	1699–1701	1722–24	1752–54
Woollen goods:			
Continental Europe	2,745	2,592	3,279
Ireland and Channel Islands	26	19	47
America and Africa	185	303	374
India and Far East	89	72	230
Other manufactures:			
Continental Europe	456	367	647
Ireland and Channel Islands	60	40	168
America and Africa	290	376	1,197
India and Far East	22	15	408

Source: R. Davis, 'English foreign trade, 1700–1774', *Economic History Review*, 2nd series, Vol. XV (1962–63), p. 108.

The English balance of trade, 1530–1700 (£s sterling)

Year	Exports	Imports
1530s	721,117	686,352
1613	2,487,435	2,141,151
1622	2,320,436	2,619,315
1663–69	4,100,000	4,400,000
1669–1701	6,419,000	5,849,000

Source: C. Wilson, 'The British Isles', in C. Wilson and G. Parker, eds, *An Introduction to the Sources of European Economic History 1500–1800* (London, 1977), p. 125.

An important element within the trade surplus enjoyed by England was the re-export of goods from non-European countries.

Imports into Europe, 1591–1600 (annual averages)

Region of origin	Type of goods	Weight (in tons)	Value (in tons of silver)
Baltic	Grain	*c.* 126,109.4	*c.* 87.5
Asia	Spices	*c.* 2,712	*c.* 136.8
America	Precious metals	*c.* 287.7	*c.* 309.4

Source: P. Kriedte, *Peasants, Landlords and Merchant Capitalists: Europe and the World Economy 1500–1800* (1980; Engl. trans., Leamington Spa, 1983), p. 41.

In the early modern period large quantities of precious metals were required for the growing trade with the Far East as spices, silks, porcelain and other luxury goods had to be purchased with bullion.

Exports of silver to Asia by the Dutch East India Company (Verenigde Oostindische Compagnie) in kilogrammes of fine silver, 1602–1769

Decades	Kilogrammes of fine silver
1602–09	6,959.7
1610–19	10,382.9
1620–29	12,610.8
1630–39	8,994.0
1640–49	8,892.9
1650–59	8,488.7
1660–69	11,563.1
1670–79	11,854.6
1680–89	18,847.0
1690–99	27,720.9
1700–09	37,392.9
1710–19	37,108.1
1720–29	63,104.0
1730–39	40,656.8
1740–49	38,171.9
1750–59	52,584.3
1760–69	52,171.4

Source: C. Cipolla, *Before the Industrial Revolution: European Society and Economy 1000–1700*, 3rd edition (London, 1993), p. 221, using material from F. Gaastra, 'The export of precious metal from Europe to Asia by the Dutch East India Company, 1602–1795', *Proceedings on Pre-Modern Monetary History* (Wisconsin, 1977).

CULTURE AND SOCIETY

THE RENAISSANCE

1374	Death of Petrarch. A scholar and poet, his writing and study of classical texts helped revive interest in classical literature. He is considered to be one of the originators of humanism.
1375	Salutati is made Chancellor of Florence. He uses his humanist knowledge to enhance the status of his post and of the city.
1401	Competition is held in Florence for an artist to design bronze doors for the Baptistery. It is won by Ghiberti.
1407	Poggio Braccioloni discovers 'lost' classical texts in the library of the monastery of Montecassino.
1416	Poggio discovers more 'lost' classical texts at the monastery of St Gall in Switzerland.
1420	Brunelleschi begins the building of the dome of Florence cathedral.
1427	Bruni is made Chancellor of Florence. He wrote narrative histories of Florence in the classical style, which emphasised its republican values.
1434	Jan van Eyck paints *John Arnolfini and his Wife.*
1436	Alberti publishes *Della pittura* (*On Painting*), describing how artists could achieve the impression of linear perspective in their art.
1440	Lorenzo Valla proves the *Donation of Constantine* (the document by which the Emperor Constantine granted the Papal States to the Papacy) to be a forgery.
1446	Work begins on the reconstruction of the Tempio Malatestino in Rimini.
1453	Fall of Constantinople to the Ottomans.
	Death of John Dunstable, English composer renowned for his innovatory use of harmony.
1468	Cardinal Bessarion bequeaths his vast library, including many Greek texts, to the Republic of Venice.
1475	The humanist Bartolomeo Platina is appointed as the first librarian of the Vatican library.
1478	Pazzi Conspiracy against the Medici in Florence, in which Lorenzo de' Medici (Lorenzo the Magnificent) narrowly avoids an attempt on his life.
	Botticelli paints *Primavera.*

c. **1480**	Piero della Francesca publishes his study of perspective.
1483	Leonardo da Vinci paints the *Virgin of the Rocks.*
1484	Botticelli paints the *Birth of Venus.*
1486	Pico della Mirandola writes *De hominis dignitate oratio* (*Oration on the Dignity of Man*).
1492	Death of Lorenzo de Medici.
1493	Publication of the *Weltchronik* by Hartmann Schedel, which includes more than 1,800 illustrations.
1495	Aldine Press is established in Venice, concentrating on publishing works in Greek.
1496	Dürer begins work on a series of woodcuts known as the *Apocalypse.*
1497	Leonardo da Vinci completes his painting of the Last Supper.
	Michelangelo begins work on the *Pietà.*
1500	Erasmus publishes his *Adagia.*
1503	Belvedere gardens are laid out in the Vatican by Bramante.
1504	Michelangelo carves his statue of David, which was placed in the Piazza della Signoria in Florence.
1506	Leonardo paints *Mona Lisa.*
	Reuchlin publishes *De rudimentis hebraicis,* allowing biblical scholars to learn Hebrew.
	Work begins on the re-building of St Peter's in Rome to designs by Bramante.
1512	Michelangelo completes painting the ceiling of the Sistine Chapel.
	Jacques Lefèvre d'Étaples publishes his translation and commentary on the Epistles of St Paul.
1513	Machiavelli begins work on *The Prince.*
	Raphael paints *The School of Athens.*
1515	Grünewald paints the Isenheim altarpiece.
	Work begins on the construction of Hampton Court palace for Wolsey.
1516	Erasmus publishes the New Testament in Greek.
	Thomas More publishes *Utopia.*
	Ludovico Ariosto writes *Orlando Furioso,* a narrative poem which has great influence on writers.
1517	Ulrich von Hutten is named as poet laureate by Emperor Maximilian. Hutten and others publish *Epistolae obscurorum virorum* (*Letters of obscure men*), an attack on those seeking to suppress the work of the scholar of Hebrew, Johann Reuchlin.

1519	Erasmus publishes *Colloquia*.
	Construction begins of the château at Chambord for Francis I of France.
1520	Machiavelli begins his *History of Florence* (*Istorie fiorentine*).
1523	Hans Sachs writes *Die Wittenbergisch Nachtigall* (*The Wittenberg Nightingale*), in praise of Luther.
1527	Sack of Rome by the troops of Charles V.
1528	Castiglione publishes *The Courtier*.
	Francis I begins the re-building of the château at Fontainebleau in the style of the Italian Renaissance.
1531	Beatus Rhenanus publishes *Rerum Germanicarum libri tres*, which includes a history of Germany in classical times.
1533	Titian completes his portrait of Charles V. The Emperor grants him a patent of nobility.
	Hans Holbein the Younger paints *The Ambassadors*.
	Michelangelo begins work on the painting of *The Last Judgement* in the Sistine Chapel.
1534	Guicciardini begins work on his *History of Italy* (*Storia d'Italia*).
1550	Vasari writes *Lives of the Artists*.
1555	Work begins on the gardens of the Villa d'Este, Tivoli.
1559	Pieter Brueghel the Elder paints *Carnival and Lent*.
1562	Palestrina composes the *Missa Papae Marcelli*, considered by the Church authorities to be the ideal model for church music.
1563	Work begins on the construction of the Escorial for Philip II of Spain.
1566	Work begins on the Villa Rotunda at Vicenza by Palladio.
1570	Palladio publishes *I quattro libri dell' architettura* (*The Four Books on Architecture*).
1577	El Greco paints *The Assumption of the Virgin*.
c. **1588**	Christopher Marlowe begins work on *Dr Faustus*.
1596	Performance of Shakespeare's *Henry VI, Part I*.
1598	Performance in Florence of *La Dafne*, probably the first opera.
1599	Shakespeare begins to write *Hamlet*.
1600	Opening of the Globe Theatre in London.
1604	Caravaggio paints *The Deposition*.
1605	Cervantes writes *Don Quixote*.
1607	First performance of Monteverdi's *L'Orfeo*.

THE ENLIGHTENMENT

1652	Descartes publishes *Discourse on Method,* arguing for reasoning based on discernable propositions rather than unquestioned authorities.
1667	Pufendorf publishes *De statu imperii germanici.*
1672	Pufendorf publishes *De iure naturae et gentium.*
1686	Leibniz writes *Discours de métaphysique.*
1687	Newton publishes *Principia.* The discovery of laws governing natural phenomena will later stimulate thinkers during the Enlightenment to seek laws which govern society.
1690	Locke publishes *Essay Concerning Human Understanding,* arguing that the human character is formed by experience in the world rather than supernatural forces.
1710	Leibniz publishes *Théodicée.*
1712	Christian Wolff publishes *Vernünftige Gedanken von den Kräften des menschlichen Verstandes.*
1714	Leibniz publishes *Monadologie.*
1718	Performance of *Œdipe,* the first play by Voltaire.
1721	Montesquieu publishes *Lettres persanes* which offer thinly veiled criticism of French society.
1723	Wolff is accused of atheism, removed from his post of professor at Halle University and is banished from Prussia on pain of execution.
1727	Establishment of chairs of cameral studies at the universities of Halle and Frankfurt on Oder.
1734	Voltaire publishes *Lettres philosophiques* which attack the methods of Descartes and praise a Newtonian approach to philosophical issues.
	Alexander Pope publishes the *Essay on Man.*
	Montesquieu publishes *Considérations sur les Causes de la Grandeur des Romains et de leur Décadence.*
1737	Moser begins work on *Teutsches Staatsrecht.*
1738	Hume publishes his *Treatise of Human Nature* (later revised as *Inquiry Concerning Human Nature*). It rejects the notion of divine causation regulating human affairs. Instead, it emphasises the role of experience rather than reason in shaping human conduct.

1740	Use of judicial torture is forbidden in Prussia.
	Wolff returns to Halle following an invitation from Frederick II.
1746	Condillac publishes *Essai sur l'origine des connaissances humaines* (*Essay on the Origins of Human Understanding*).
	Frederick II writes *Histoire de mon temps*.
1748	Montesquieu publishes *L'Esprit des lois* (*The Spirit of the Laws*), an analysis of different forms of government. He calls among other things for checks on the power of the executive.
	Hume publishes *Essay on Miracles* which attacks belief in religious miracles as being contrary to reason.
	La Mettrie publishes *L'Homme Machine* which expresses atheistic opinions.
1749	Buffon publishes the first volume of *Histoire naturelle*, an account of natural history based on the observation of geological and other evidence, rather than on the biblical account of creation. (It is completed in 1778.)
1750	Voltaire visits Frederick II in Berlin but becomes disillusioned and leaves in 1753.
1751	Diderot and d'Alembert publish the first volume of the *Encyclopédie*. (It is completed in 28 volumes in 1772).
1752	Hume publishes *Political Discourses*.
1755	Rousseau publishes *Discourse on the Origins of Inequality Among Mankind*.
1756	Voltaire publishes *Essai sur l'histoire générale sur les moeurs et l'esprit des nations*.
1758	Helvétius publishes *Of Mind*.
1759	Adam Smith publishes *Theory of Moral Sentiments*.
1762	Rousseau publishes *Du Contrat Social* (*The Social Contract*). Rousseau publishes his novel *Emile*, advancing his view that the minds of children are corrupted by existing forms of education. He recommends that children be taught to express themselves free from the constraints of formal learning.
	Execution of Jean Calas, a French Protestant, who is charged with murdering his son to prevent him from converting to Catholicism.
1763	Inspired by the Calas execution, Voltaire publishes *Traité sur la tolérance*, in which he calls for limited religious toleration to be granted in France.
	General Education Act in Prussia (*General-Landschulreglement*) establishes compulsory education for 5–13 year-old children. This is widely ignored.

1764   Beccaria publishes *Della delitti e delle pene* (*Of Crimes and Punishment*) which denounces the use of torture to extract evidence and advances the idea of uniform justice and punishment for all society.

Voltaire publishes *Dictionnaire philosophique.*

ENLIGHTENED DESPOTISM TO *c.* 1763

1729   Victor Amadeus II of Piedmont introduces a new law code which restricts feudal powers.

1737   Establishment of the university of Göttingen.

1740   Accession of Frederick II as King of Prussia.

1740s   Cocceji and other jurists begin codification of the laws in Prussia for Frederick II.

1749   Completion of new tax assessments in Milan which allow fairer taxes to be levied on property.

Administrative reforms are introduced into the Habsburg lands by Haugwitz. He introduces the collection of taxes in Bohemia and Moravia directly by the central government rather than the local estates. The extra revenue raised is used to support a standing army.

1750   Pombal is appointed Minister of State in Portugal.

1753   Kaunitz is placed in charge of foreign affairs in Austria.

1755   Pombal takes charge of re-building of Lisbon following the destruction of much of the city in an earthquake. Pombal establishes *Junta do Comercio* to supervise trade and commerce.

All internal tolls and tariffs are abolished within the hereditary lands of the Habsburgs.

1756   Pombal is made Chief Minister of Portugal.

1757   Riots in Oporto against the regulation of the port wine trade by the *Junta do Comercio*. They are put down with considerable force by Pombal.

1759   Pombal orders the expulsion of Jesuits from Portugal.

Accession of Charles III as King of Spain.

1760   Creation of a State Council in Austria by Maria Theresa.

Creation of a centralized treasury for Portugal by Pombal.

1761   Reform of government administration in Portugal by Pombal.

Spanish crown assumes control of the *excusado*, a tax paid by the clergy, resulting in a great increase in its yield.

1762   Accession of Catherine as Empress of Russia. Catherine invites d'Alembert to Russia. Nobles in Russia are relieved of the duty to serve the state as established by the Table of Ranks of Peter I (1722).

1763   Serfdom is abolished on royal domain lands in Prussia.

1764   Jesuits are expelled from France.

Catherine II begins a reform of the civil administration in Russia.

1765   Leopold (the future Emperor Leopold II) is made Grand Duke of Tuscany.

1766   Frederick II creates a new government department (*Régie*) to collect taxes.

Charles III of Spain orders the Inquisition to seek his permission before acting on any instructions received from Rome.

SCIENCE AND TECHNOLOGY

1455	Gutenberg prints the first book using moveable type.
1476	Caxton establishes the first printing press in England.
1493	Martin Behaim produces a globe depicting the world.
1495	First use of mercury to cure syphilis.
	Aldus Manutius establishes the Aldine Press in Venice, which is renowned for producing texts in Greek.
c. **1500**	European ships begin to use jib sails.
1502	Henlein invents the pocket watch.
1505	Publication of *Ein nützlich Bergbüchleyn* in Augsburg, describing how to smelt copper.
1520	Completion of the first *trace Italienne* fortification system at Civitavecchia.
1540	Biringucci publishes *Pirotechnia*, a treatise on metallurgy.
1543	Copernicus publishes *De Revolutionibus*, advancing a heliocentric theory of the universe.
1545	Paré describes how to cauterise wounds effectively.
1547	Girolamo Cardano publishes *De subtilitate*, establishing the organic origin of fossil remains.
1552	Röhrerbühel mines produce 6,430 kilogrammes of silver and 361 tons of copper.
1556	Agricola publishes *De re metallica*, a treatise on mining.
1569	Publication of Mercator's world map, which aids navigation by making allowances for the curvature of the surface of the world.
1571	Thomas Digges invents the theodolite.
1573	Thomas Tusser publishes *Five hundreth good points of husbandry*.
1578	Tycho Brahe publishes *Nova Stella*. Based on astronomical observations, this account of the appearance of a new star disproves Aristotelian theories of the universe.
	Publication of *Théâtre des Instruments*, an illustrated handbook providing details on how to construct a range of machinery, including pumps and cranes.
1582	Adoption of the Gregorian calendar in Catholic lands of Europe.
1586	Invention of a mechanical loom in Danzig by Anton Möller.

1589	Invention of a stocking frame for knitting stockings by William Lee.
1592	In Holland Cornelius Cornelisz uses a windmill to power a sawmill.
1593	Johan Coler publishes *Oeconomia ruralis et domestica* concerning farming techniques and household management.
1595	First *fluit* merchant ships are built in the Netherlands.
c. 1605	Invention of the flintlock musket.
1608	Invention of the telescope by Hans Lippershey.
1609	Galileo improves the telescope and uses it for astronomical research.
	Kepler publishes *Astronomia Nova*, establishing laws of planetary motion.
1612	Antonio Neri publishes *Arte Vitraria*, describing the process of glass-making.
1614	Napier publishes the first logarithmic tables, which assist in making complex calculations.
1617	Simon Stevin publishes *Nieuwe maniere van sterctebou door Spils-luysen*, describing the construction of drains and sluices.
1628	Harvey publishes *On the Motion of the Heart*, which describes the circulation of blood.
1630	Galileo publishes *Dialogue on the World Systems*, establishing the movement of the earth round the sun.
1637	Descartes publishes *Discourse on Method*, applying algebra to geometric calculations.
1642	Completion of Briare Canal, connecting the rivers Seine and Loire.
1652	Walter Blith publishes *English Improver Improved*, describing methods of agricultural improvement, especially concerning the drainage of the soil.
1665	*Metallum Martis* is published in England, describing experiments in the use of coal in smelting.
1666	Newton discovers calculus but does not publish the discovery until 1704.
c. 1670	Invention of the 'hollander', a pulverising device used in the manufacture of paper.
	George Ravenscroft discovers how to manufacture lead crystal.
1675	Leibniz discovers calculus independently of Newton and publishes his discovery in 1684.
1687	Newton publishes *Principia*, establishing the law of gravity.

1704   Newton publishes *Optiks*, expounding his theories on light.

1705   Newcomen builds a steam engine suited for industrial use.

1708   Johann Böttger discovers how to manufacture porcelain.

1711   A Newcomen engine is used to drive pumps in Warwickshire mine workings.

1713   Abraham Darby of Coalbrookdale is the first to use coke successfully to smelt iron.

1742   In Sheffield, Benjamin Huntsman discovers how to manufacture cast steel.

1751   Carolus Linnaeus publishes *Philosophia botanica*, expounding a system for classifying all plant species.

BIBLIOGRAPHY

Topics

1. General
2. Population
3. Economy
4. Society
   (a) Rural Society
   (b) Towns
   (c) Ruling Elites
   (d) The Poor and the Imposition of Social Discipline
   (e) Gender Issues
   (f) The Family
   (g) Witchcraft and Society
5. Religion
6. War
7. Renaissance
8. Enlightenment
9. Popular Culture
10. Science and Technology
11. France
12. Iberia
13. Great Britain
14. Germany
15. The Netherlands
16. Central Europe
17. Russia and the Baltic
18. The Ottomans and the Balkans
19. European Expansion Overseas

List of abbreviations

ARG	*Archiv für Reformationsgeschichte*
AHR	*American Historical Review*
CH	*Church History*
EcHR	*Economic History Review*
ESR	*European Studies Review*
FHS	*French Historical Studies*
HJ	*Historical Journal*
HWJ	*History Workshop Journal*
J. Eccles Hist.	*Journal of Ecclesiastical History*
JMH	*Journal of Modern History*
P & P	*Past and Present*
SCJ	*Sixteenth Century Journal*
SH	*Social History*
TRHS	*Transactions of the Royal Historical Society*

1. General

There are several good surveys of the early modern period, but particularly useful are: H. Kamen, *Early Modern European Society* (London, 2000); and E. Cameron, ed., *Early Modern Europe* (Oxford, 1999), a collection of studies written by leading authorities on the subjects. The early part of the period is covered in R. Bonney, *The European Dynastic States, 1494–1660* (Oxford, 1991), and the later period in W. Doyle, *The Old European Order, 1660–1800*, 2nd edition (Oxford, 1992). An older, but still useful account of the fifteenth and sixteenth centuries is given by A. G. Dickens, *The Age of Humanism and Reformation* (London, 1977). There are many general accounts of European history covering parts of the early modern period: D. Hay, *Europe in the Fourteenth and Fifteenth Centuries*, 2nd edition (London, 1989); J. Hale, *Renaissance Europe, 1480–1520* (London, 1971); H. G. Koenigsberger, G. Mosse and G. Bowler, *Europe in the Sixteenth Century*, 2nd edition (London, 1989); G. R. Elton, *Reformation Europe, 1517–1559*, 2nd edition (London, 1999); J. Elliott, *Europe Divided, 1559–1598* (London, 1968); J. Mackenney, *Sixteenth-Century Europe: Expansion and Conflict* (New York, 1993); and D. Maland, *Europe in the Sixteenth Century* (London, 1973). For the seventeenth century see: D. Pennington, *Europe in the Seventeenth Century*, 2nd edition (London, 1989); G. Parker, *Europe in Crisis, 1598–1648* (London, 1979); V. G. Kiernan, *State and Society in Europe, 1550–1650* (Oxford, 1980); and T. Munck, *Seventeenth-Century Europe, 1598–1700: State, Conflict and the Social Order in Europe* (London, 1990). For the eighteenth century see: M. S. Anderson, *Europe in the Eighteenth Century*, 3rd edition (London, 1987); J. Black, *Eighteenth Century Europe, 1700–1789* (London, 1990); O. Hufton, *Europe: Privilege and Protest, 1730–1789* (London, 1980); and I. Woloch, *Eighteenth-Century Europe: Tradition and Progress, 1715–1789* (London, 1982). A useful reference resource for the fifteenth and sixteenth centuries is T. Brady, H. Oberman and J. Tracy, eds, *Handbook of European History, 1400–1600: Late Middle Ages, Renaissance and Reformation*, 2 vols (Leiden, 1994). Still useful for reference are the first seven volumes of *The New Cambridge Modern History*, although the interpretation given in some of the older volumes has been superceded by more recent scholarship.

2. Population

For general surveys see: E. A. Wrigley, *Population and History* (London, 1969); M. W. Flinn, *The European Demographic System 1500–1800* (London, 1981); D. Grigg, *Population Growth and Agrarian Change* (Cambridge, 1980); D. V. Glass and D. Eversley, eds, *Population in History* (London, 1965); and R. A. Houston, *The Population Growth of Britain and Ireland, 1500–1750* (Cambridge, 1995). Also see section 4(*f*).

Essay topics

What were the most significant social causes of the growth of population in Europe in the late fifteenth and early sixteenth centuries?

What were the main causes and consequences of population migration in early modern Europe?

3. Economy

A useful collection of source material is found in C. Wilson and G. Parker, eds, *An Introduction to the Sources of European Economic History 1500–1800* (London, 1977). There are several excellent surveys of the European economy of the period, including: C. Cipolla, *Before the Industrial Revolution*, 3rd edition (London, 1993); H. Miskimin, *The Economy of Early Renaissance Europe, 1300–1460* (Englewood Cliffs, NJ, 1969); H. Miskimin, *The Economy of Later Renaissance Europe, 1460–1600* (Cambridge, 1977); H. Kellenbenz, *The Rise of the European Economy: An Economic History of Continental Europe* (London, 1976); C. Cipolla, *The Middle Ages* (Fontana Economic History of Europe, vol. 1) (London, 1972); C. Cipolla, *The Sixteenth and the Seventeenth Centuries* (Fontana Economic History of Europe, vol. 2) (London, 1977); C. Cipolla, *The Industrial Revolution* (Fontana Economic History of Europe, vol. 3) (London, 1973); and *The Cambridge Economic History of Europe*, vol. 4, E. Rich and C. H. Wilson, eds, *The Economy of Expanding Europe in the Sixteenth and Seventeenth Centuries* (Cambridge, 1967) and vol. 5, *The Economic Organization of Early Modern Europe* (Cambridge, 1977). The development of capitalism is examined in R. Duplessis, *Transitions to Capitalism in Early Modern Europe* (Cambridge, 1997), and P. Kriedte, *Peasants, Landlords and Merchant Capitalists: Europe and the World Economy 1500–1800* (1980; Engl. trans. Leamington Spa, 1983).

The debate is set in a global perspective by F. Braudel in his trilogy *Civilization and Capitalism 15th–18th Century*: F. Braudel, *The Structures of Everyday Life* (1979; Engl. trans. London, 1982); F. Braudel, *The Wheels of Commerce* (1979; Engl. trans. London, 1982); F. Braudel, *The Perspective of the World* (1979; Engl. trans. London, 1984). The role of Europe in the development of a world economy in the early modern period is examined by I. Wallerstein, *The Modern World System I: Capitalist Agriculture and the Origins of the European World Economy in the Sixteenth Century* (London, 1974), and I. Wallerstein, *The Modern World System II: Mercantilism and the Consolidation of the European World Economy 1600–1750* (London, 1980). The role of agriculture in the economy is investigated in W. Abel, *Agricultural Fluctuations in Europe from the Thirteenth to the Twentieth Centuries* (1966; Engl. trans. London, 1980), and the debate surrounding the origins of capitalist agriculture in England is summarised in T. Aston and C. Philpin, eds, *The Brenner Debate: Agrarian Class Structure and Economic Development in Pre-Industrial Europe* (Cambridge, 1985). The significance of the rural economy is emphasised in H. Kellenbenz, 'Rural industries in the West from the end of the Middle Ages to the eighteenth century', in P. Earle, ed., *Essays in European Economic History 1500–1800* (Oxford, 1974). The wider debate on the impact of proto-industrialisation is covered in: P. Kriedte, H. Medick and J. Schlumbohm, eds, *Industrialization before Industrialization: Rural Industry in the Genesis of Capitalism* (Cambridge, 1981);

S. Ogilvie and M. Cerman, eds, *European Proto-Industrialization* (Cambridge, 1996); and L. Clarkson, *Proto-Industrialization: The First Phase of Industrialization* (London, 1985). For the growth of trade and commerce see: R. Davis, *The Rise of the Atlantic Economies* (London, 1973); J. Ball, *Merchants and Merchandise: The Expansion of Trade in Europe 1500–1630* (London, 1977); and J. D. Tracy, *The Rise of Merchant Empires: Long-Distance Trade in the Early Modern World, 1350–1750* (Cambridge, 1990). For prices and wages see H. Phelps-Brown and S. Hopkins, *A Perspective of Prices and Wages* (London, 1981) and R. Outhwaite, *Inflation in Tudor and Early Stuart England*, 2nd edition (London, 1982).

There are many studies of the economic history of individual countries. For the Netherlands see: J. de Vries and A. van der Woude, *The First Modern European Economy: Growth, Decline and Perseverance of the Dutch Economy, 1500–1815* (Cambridge, 1996); J. Israel, *Dutch Primacy in World Trade, 1585–1740* (Oxford 1989); M. Bogucka, 'Amsterdam and the Baltic in the first half of the seventeenth century', *EcHR* 2nd Series 26 (1973). For Germany see Bob Scribner, ed., *Germany: A New Social and Economic History 1450–1630* (London, 1996) and T. Scott, 'Economic conflict and co-operation on the Upper Rhine, 1450–1600', in E. I. Kouri and T. Scott, eds, *Politics and Society in Reformation Europe* (London, 1987). For England see: D. C. Coleman, *The Economy of England, 1450–1750* (Oxford, 1977); C. G. Clay, *Economic Expansion and Social Change: England 1500–1700*, 2 vols (Cambridge, 1984); D. C. Coleman, *Industry in Tudor and Stuart England* (London, 1975).

Essay topics

To what extent, and why, did the economic centre of Europe shift away from the Mediterranean region in the sixteenth and seventeenth centuries?

What were the most significant effects of price inflation in the sixteenth century?

4. Society

(a) Rural Society

An excellent overview of early modern agriculture is contained in B. H. Slicher van Bath, *The Agrarian History of Europe A. D. 500–1850* (New York, 1963). In recent years our knowledge and understanding of peasant life and society has increased considerably. Much recent research is brought together in T. Scott, ed., *The Peasantries of Europe from the Fourteenth to the Eighteenth Centuries* (London, 1998), which contains essays examining rural life in all parts of Europe. There are many detailed studies of the peasantry in various countries. For Germany see: T. Robisheaux, *Rural Society and the Search for Order in Early Modern Germany* (Cambridge, 1989); D. Sabean, *Power in the Blood: Popular Culture and Village Discourse in Early Modern Germany* (Cambridge, 1984); P. Blickle, *The Revolution of 1525: The German Peasants' War from a New Perspective* (1977; Engl. trans. Baltimore, MD, 1981); W. Rösener, 'The agrarian economy, 1300–1600', in B. Scribner, ed., *Germany: A New Social and Economic History. Vol. 1, 1450–1630* (London, 1996); T. Scott, *Freiburg and the Breisgau:*

Town–Country Relations in the Age of the Reformation and the Peasant War (Oxford, 1986); T. Robisheaux, 'Peasant unrest and the moral economy in the German southwest, 1560–1620', *ARG* 77 (1987). The peasantry of Central Europe is discussed in: H. Rebel, *Peasant Classes: The Bureaucratization of Property and Family Relations under Early Habsburg Absolutism, 1511–1636* (Princeton, NJ, 1983); W. Hagen, 'How mighty the Junkers? Peasant rents and seigneurial profits in sixteenth-century Brandenburg', *P & P* 108 (1985). For France see: E. Le Roy Ladurie, *The Peasants of Languedoc* (1966; Engl. trans. Urbana, IL, 1976); E. Le Roy Ladurie, *The French Peasantry, 1450–1660* (1977; Engl. trans. Berkeley, CA, 1987); P. Goubert, 'The French peasantry of the seventeenth century: a regional example', *P & P* 10 (1956). N. Z. Davis, *The Return of Martin Guerre* (Cambridge, MA, 1983) provides an insight into French rural life by recounting the events surrounding the trial of an imposter who fraudulently obtained property and a wife by convincing the peasants of Artigat that he was a long-lost inhabitant of the village. For Spain see D. Vassberg, *Land and Society in Golden Age Castile* (Cambridge, 1984), and for Russia, J. Blum, *Lord and Peasant in Rural Russia from the Ninth to the Nineteenth Century* (Princeton, NJ, 1961). For England there is much material available, but particularly useful is M. Spufford, *Contrasting Communities: English Villages in the Sixteenth and Seventeenth Centuries* (London, 1974); K. Wrightson and D. Levine, *Poverty and Piety in an English Village: Terling, 1525–1700* (London, 1979); D. Hey, *An English Rural Community: Myddle under the Tudors and Stuarts* (Leicester, 1974), an account of life in a Shropshire village. For the role of the rural workforce in manufacture see P. Kriedte, H. Medick and J. Schlumbohm, *Industrialization before Industrialization: Rural Industry in the Genesis of Modern Capitalism* (Cambridge, 1981).

(b) Towns

Excellent surveys of the development of early modern urban life are provided by A. Cowan, *Urban Europe, 1500–1700* (London, 1998) and C. Friedrich, *The Early Modern City, 1450–1750* (London, 1995). P. Clark, ed., *Small Towns in Early Modern Europe* (Cambridge, 1995) contains a collection of essays focusing on the characteristics of individual small towns, much the most common form of urban community in the period. In contrast, P. Clark and B. Leppett, eds, *Capital Cities and their Hinterlands* (London, 1996) considers the functions of capitals and the networks needed to sustain their growth. There are many studies of government, society and the economy in individual towns and cities across Europe, of which the following are particularly to be recommended: G. Strauss, *Nuremberg in the Sixteenth Century* (Bloomington, IN, 1976); C. Friedrichs, *Urban Society in an Age of War, Nördlingen, 1580–1700* (Princeton, NJ, 1979); M. Walker, *German Home Towns: Community, State and General Estate* (Ithaca, NY, 1971); P. Benedict, *Rouen during the Wars of Religion* (Cambridge, 1980); J. K. Thompson, *Clermont-de-Lodève, 1633–1789: Fluctuations in the Prosperity of a Languedocian Cloth-making Town* (Cambridge, 1982); C. Dolan, 'The artisans of Aix-en-Provence in the sixteenth century: a micro analysis of social relationships', in P. Benedict, ed., *Cities and Social Change in Early Modern France* (London, 1989); C. Phythian-Adams, *Desolation of a City: Coventry and the Urban Crisis of the Late Middle Ages* (Cambridge, 1979); A. L. Beier and R. Finlay, eds, *London 1500–1700: The Making of the Metropolis* (London, 1986); P. Burke, *Venice and Amsterdam: A Study of Seventeenth Century Élites*, 2nd edition (Cambridge, 1994); D. V. Kent and F. W. Kent, *Neighbours and Neighbourhood in Renaissance Florence: The District of the Red Lion in the Fifteenth Century* (New York, 1982); J. R. Hale, ed., *Renaissance Venice* (London, 1973).

(c) Ruling Elites

For the nobility of Europe see J. Dewald, *The European Nobility 1400–1800* (Cambridge, 1996) and H. M. Scott, ed., *The European Nobility in the Seventeenth and Eighteenth Centuries*, 2 vols (London, 1995). A useful brief discussion of some of the issues raised in these books is found in M. L. Bush, 'An anatomy of nobility', in M. L. Bush, ed., *Social Orders and Social Classes in Europe since 1500: Studies in Social Stratification* (London, 1992). One of the most important works on the English aristocracy is L. Stone, *The Crisis of the Aristocracy, 1558–1642* (Oxford, 1965). H. Miller, *Henry VIII and the English Nobility* (Oxford, 1986) shows the ruthlessness of a ruler in curtailing the power and independence of his nobles, while H. van Nierop, *The Nobility of Holland* (1984; Engl. trans. Cambridge, 1993), reveals the ability of the nobility to adapt in order to survive in the United Provinces.

(d) The Poor and the Imposition of Social Discipline

The problem of how to deal with the effects of poverty concerned governments throughout the early modern period. The best survey of the problems and the measures taken to deal with them is R. Jütte, *Poverty and Deviance in Early Modern Europe* (Cambridge, 1994). C. Lis and H. Soly, *Poverty and Capitalism in Pre-industrial Europe* (London, 1979) draws on examples from France, England and the Netherlands, and places the problems created by the growth of poverty and destitution in the context of structural changes in the economy. There are many studies of various systems of poor relief which were introduced in the early modern period. For England see: E. M. Leonard, *The Early History of English Poor Relief* (Cambridge, 1990); P. Slack, *Poverty and Policy in Tudor and Stuart England* (London, 1988); A. L. Beier, *Masterless Men: The Vagrancy Problem in England, 1560–1640* (London, 1985). For France see N. Z. Davis, 'Poor relief, humanism and heresy', in N. Z. Davis, ed., *Society and Culture in Early Modern France* (London, 1975) and O. Hufton, *The Poor of Eighteenth-Century France, 1750–1789* (Oxford, 1974). For Italy, B. Pullan, 'Catholics and the poor in early modern Europe', *TRHS* 26 (1976) shows that Protestant and Catholic states shared a common aim to regulate begging and control the poor. See also B. Pullan, *Rich and Poor in Renaissance Venice: The Social Institutions of a Catholic State to 1620* (Oxford, 1971) and C. Black, *Italian Confraternities in the Sixteenth Century* (Cambridge, 1989). For Switzerland see L. P. Wandel, *Always Among Us: Images of the Poor in Zwingli's Zurich* (Cambridge, 1990). For Germany see W. Wright, 'A closer look at house poor-relief through the common chest and indigence in sixteenth-century Hesse', *ARG* 70 (1979). For Spain see L. Martz, *Poverty and Welfare in Habsburg Spain: The Example of Toledo* (Cambridge, 1983) and M. Flynn, *Sacred Charity: Confraternities and Social Welfare in Spain, 1400–1800* (London, 1989).

Social disciplining, seen as an effort to force the poor and those at the margins of society to accept the authority of government and the norms of society, has recently received considerable attention. The debate was prompted by G. Oestreich, *Neostoicism and the Early Modern State* (1969; Engl. trans. Cambridge, 1982). The best survey is R. Po-Chia Hsia, *Social Discipline in the Reformation: Central Europe 1550–1750* (London, 1989). See also: T. Robisheaux, *Rural Society and the Search for Order in Early Modern Germany* (Cambridge, 1989); W. Monter, *Enforcing Morality in Early Modern Europe* (London, 1987); L. Roper, 'Discipline and respectability: prostitution and the Reformation in Augsburg', *HWJ* 19 (1985); M. Valeri, 'Religion, discipline and economy in Calvin's Geneva', *SCJ* 28 (1997).

(e) Gender Issues

Issues concerning the role of women, women at work and the exercise of patriarchal powers have all been researched in great detail. A good introduction is given in M. Wiesner, *Women and Gender in Early Modern Europe* (Cambridge, 1994). For the working role of women see: M. Wiesner, *Working Women in Renaissance Germany* (New Brunswick, NJ, 1986); L. Roper, *The Holy Household: Women and Morals in Reformation Augsburg* (Oxford, 1989); P. Hudson and W. Lee, eds, *Women's Work and the Family Economy in Historical Perspective* (Manchester, 1990); B. Hanawalt, *Women and Work in Preindustrial Europe* (Bloomington, IN, 1980); J. Quataert, 'The shaping of women's work in manufacturing: guilds, households and the state in Central Europe', *AHR* 90 (1985). For changing attitudes towards marriage and the role of women in the family see: S. Ozment, *When Fathers Ruled: Family Life in Reformation Europe* (Cambridge, MA, 1983); A. Fletcher, *Gender, Sex and Subordination in England 1500–1800* (New Haven, CT, 1995); T. M. Safley, *Let No Man Put Asunder: The Control of Marriage in the German Southwest* (Kirksville, MO, 1984); M. Ingram, *Church Courts, Sex and Marriage in England 1570–1640* (Cambridge, 1987); L. Roper, 'Going to church and street: weddings in Reformation Augsburg', *P & P* 106 (1985); L. Roper, *The Holy Household. Women and Morals in Reformation Augsburg* (Oxford, 1989); J. Watt, *The Making of Modern Marriage: Matrimonial Control and the Rise of Sentiment in Neuchâtel, 1550–1800* (Ithaca, NY, 1992); J. Harrington, *Reordering Marriage and Society in Reformation Germany* (Cambridge, 1995). U. Rublack, in 'Pregnancy, childbirth and the female body in Early Modern Germany', *P & P* 150 (1996), examines how women and their families coped with the dangers and anxieties surrounding childbirth. For the impact of religious change on women and the role played by women in the Reformation and Counter-Reformation see: M. Wiesner, *Gender, Church and State in Early Modern Germany* (London, 1998); S. Marshall, ed., *Women in Reformation and Counter-Reformation Europe: Public and Private Worlds* (Bloomington, IN, 1989); S. Karant-Nunn, 'Kinder, Küche, Kirche: social ideology in the wedding sermons of Johannes Mathesius', in S. Karant-Nunn and A. Fix, eds, *Germania Illustrata: Essays Presented to Gerald Strauss* (Kirksville, MO, 1991); J. L. Thompson, *John Calvin and the Daughters of Sarah: Women in Regular and Exceptional Roles in the Exegesis of Calvin, His Predecessors and His Contemporaries* (Geneva, 1992); P. Matheson, *Argula von Grumbach: A Woman's Voice in the Reformation* (Edinburgh, 1995).

(f) The Family

Research in recent years has deepened our understanding of family life in early modern times. Important contributions have been made by: P. Laslett and R. Wall, eds, *Household and Family in Past Time* (Cambridge, 1972); J. Goody, J. Thirsk and E. P. Thompson, *Family and Inheritance: Rural Society in Western Europe, 1200–1800* (Cambridge, 1976); J. L. Flandrin, *Families in Former Times: Kinship, Household and Sexuality* (1976; Engl. trans. Cambridge, 1979); M. Mitterauer and R. Seider, *The European Family: Patriarchy to Partnership from the Middle Ages to the Present* (Oxford, 1982); M. Anderson, *Approaches to the History of the Western Family, 1500–1914* (London, 1980); R. Houlbrooke, *The English Family, 1450–1700* (London, 1984); D. Sabean, *Property, Production and Family in Neckarhausen, 1700–1870* (Cambridge, 1990). On the life and development of children, one of the earliest works written on the subject, P. Ariès, *Centuries of Childhood: A Social History of Family Life* (London, 1960) is still useful, although his views on the relationship between parent and infant have been challenged. A sound recent survey is H. Cunningham, *Children and Childhood in Western Society since 1500* (London, 1995).

(g) Witchcraft and Society

The best general survey of the subject is B. Levack, *The Witch-hunt in Early Modern Europe*, 2nd edition (London, 1994), but the briefer account, G. Scarre, *Witchcraft and Magic in Sixteenth- and Seventeenth-Century Europe* (London, 1987), is also useful. A classic study is K. Thomas, *Religion and the Decline of Magic: Studies in Popular Belief in Sixteenth- and Seventeenth-Century England* (London, 1971). N. Cohn, *Europe's Inner Demons* (London, 1975) traces the belief in witchcraft from medieval antecedents. Essential reading which brings together some of the latest research on witches is J. Barry, M. Hester and G. Roberts, eds, *Witchcraft in Early Modern Europe: Studies in Culture and Belief* (Cambridge, 1996). There are many studies which examine the social and cultural background of the persecution of witches, including: S. Clark, *Thinking with Demons: The Idea of Witchcraft in Early Modern Europe* (Oxford, 1999); R. Briggs, *Witches and Neighbours: The Social Context of European Witchcraft* (London, 1996); C. Ginzburg, *The Night Battles: Witchcraft and Agrarian Cults in the Sixteenth and Seventeenth Centuries* (1966; Engl. trans. London, 1983); C. Ginzburg, *Ecstasies: Deciphering the Witches' Sabbath* (1989;

Engl. trans. London, 1990); D. Purkiss, *The Witch in History: Early Modern and Twentieth-Century Representations* (London, 1996).

There are many studies which place witchcraft and the persecution of witches in national and local contexts. For Germany see: W. Behringer, *Witchcraft Persecutions in Bavaria: Popular Magic, Religious Zealotry and Reason of State in Early Modern Europe* (1987; Engl. trans. Cambridge, 1997); L. Roper, *Oedipus and the Devil: Witchcraft, Sexuality and Religion in Early Modern Europe* (London, 1994); H. C. E. Midelfort, *Witch Hunting in Southwestern Germany, 1562–1684: The Social and Intellectual Foundations* (Stanford, CA, 1972). For France see: chapters one to four in R. Briggs, *Communities of Belief: Cultural and Social Tensions in Early Modern France* (Oxford, 1989); W. Monter, *Witchcraft in France and Switzerland: The Borderlands during the Reformation* (Ithaca, NY, 1976); E. Le Roy Ladurie, *Jasmin's Witch* (1983; Engl. trans. New York, 1987); E. W. Monter, 'Toads and Eucharists: the male witches of Normandy, 1546–1660', *FHS* 22 (1997). For Spain see G. Henningsen, *The Witches' Advocate: Basque Witchcraft and the Spanish Inquisition, 1609–14* (Reno, NV, 1980). For England see J. Sharpe, *Instruments of Darkness: Witchcraft in England, 1550–1750* (London, 1996) and I. Bostridge, *Witchcraft and its Transformations, c. 1650–1750* (Oxford, 1997). For Scotland see C. Larner, *Witchcraft and Religion: The Politics of Popular Belief* (Oxford, 1984) and J. Goodare, 'Women and the witch-hunt in Scotland', *SH* 23 (1998). There is good material on witch trials in Scandinavia in B. Ankarloo and G. Henningsen, eds, *Early Modern European Witchcraft: Centres and Peripheries* (Oxford, 1993). For Central Europe consult chapters ten and eleven of R. Evans, *The Making of the Habsburg Monarchy 1550–1700: An Interpretation* (Oxford, 1979).

Essay topics

How effective were the measures of poor relief which were introduced in early modern Europe in dealing with the problem of widespread poverty?

To what extent, and why, did the employment opportunities of women decline in the sixteenth and seventeenth centuries?

How can one account for the widespread fear of the power of witchcraft in the sixteenth and seventeenth centuries?

5. Religion

The best account of religious life in late medieval Europe is, R. N. Swanson, *Religion and Devotion in Europe, c. 1215–1515* (Cambridge, 1995). For popular religious practices and beliefs before the Reformation see: R. Scribner, 'Cosmic order and daily life: sacred and secular in pre-industrial German society', in K. von Greyerz, ed., *Religion and Society in Early Modern Europe, 1500–1800* (London, 1984), also published in R. Scribner, ed., *Popular Culture and Popular Movements in Reformation Germany* (London, 1987); R. Scribner, 'Ritual and popular belief in Catholic Germany at the time of the Reformation', *J. Eccles. Hist.* 35 (1984), also in R. Scribner, *Popular Culture and Popular*

Movements; C. Zika, 'Hosts, processions, and pilgrimages in fifteenth-century Germany', *P & P* 118 (1988); M. Rubin, *Corpus Christi: The Eucharist in Late Medieval Culture* (Cambridge, 1991). A good survey of late medieval theology is contained in S. Ozment, *The Age of Reform, 1250–1550* (New Haven, CT, 1980). The significance of anticlericalism in prompting the outbreak of the Reformation is examined in P. Dykema and H. A. Oberman, eds, *Anticlericalism in Late Medieval and Early Modern Europe* (Leiden, 1993). Useful documents are translated in G. Strauss, *Manifestations of Discontent in Germany on the Eve of the Reformation* (Bloomington, IN, 1971).

There are many good general books on the Reformation. Much useful material is provided by M. Greengrass, *The Longman Companion to the European Reformation, c. 1500–1618* (London, 1998), and an invaluable source of reference is H. J. Hillerbrand, ed., *The Oxford Encyclopedia of the Reformation*, 4 vols (Oxford, 1996). É. Cameron, *The European Reformation* (Oxford, 1991) provides a readable and authoritative account which is particularly good on the medieval antecedents of the Reformation. For general accounts see also C. Lindberg, *The European Reformations* (Oxford, 1996) and L. Spitz, *The Protestant Reformation* (New York, 1985). S. Ozment, *Protestants: The Birth of a Revolution* (London, 1993) focuses on investigating the impact of the Reformation on ordinary people. Useful collections of essays are: C. S. Dixon, ed., *The German Reformation* (Oxford, 1999), which brings together some of the most influential articles which have been published on the subject in recent years; O. P. Grell and R. Scribner, eds, *Tolerance and Intolerance in the European Reformation* (Cambridge, 1996); H. Robinson-Hammerstein, ed., *The Transmission of Ideas in the Lutheran Reformation* (Dublin, 1989). Country-by-country accounts are given in A. Pettegree, ed., *The Early Reformation in Europe* (Cambridge, 1992) and R. Scribner, R. Porter and M. Teich, eds, *The Reformation in National Context* (Cambridge, 1994). The way in which the Reformation became rooted in the cultures and identities of different nations in Europe is examined in B. Gordon, ed., *Protestant History and Identity in Sixteenth Century Europe*, 2 vols (Aldershot, 1996). For source material by Luther see J. Pelikan and H. Lehman, eds, *Luther's Works: American Edition*, 55 vols (Philadelphia, PA, 1955–87) and E. G. Rupp and B. Drewery, eds, *Martin Luther* (London, 1970). There are many biographies of Luther but not all can be recommended. The best are: M. Brecht, *Martin Luther: His Road to Reformation, 1483–1521* (1981; Engl. trans. Philadelphia, PA, 1985); M. Brecht, *Martin Luther: Shaping and Defining the Reformation, 1521–1532* (1986; Engl. trans. Philadelphia, PA, 1990); M. Brecht, *Martin Luther: The Preservation of the Church, 1532–1546* (1987; Engl. trans. Philadelphia, PA, 1993); H. Bornkamm, *Luther in Mid-Career, 1521–1530* (1979; Engl. trans. London, 1983); H. Oberman, *Luther: Man between God and the Devil* (1982; Engl. trans. New Haven, CT, 1989). Two sound, although more basic accounts of Luther's life are J. Todd, *Luther: A Life* (London, 1982) and J. Kittelson, *Luther the Reformer: The Story of the Man and His Career* (Minneapolis, MN, 1986). A useful guide to Luther's thought is contained in B. Lohse, *Martin Luther: An Introduction to His Life and Work* (1980; Engl. trans. Edinburgh, 1986) and

J. Estes, 'The role of the godly magistrates in the church: Melanchthon as Luther's interpreter and collaborator', *CH* 67 (1998). For Luther's political ideas see W. Cargill Thompson, *The Political Thought of Martin Luther* (Brighton, 1984).

For Zwingli see: G. Potter, *Zwingli* (Cambridge, 1976); U. Gäbler, *Huldrych Zwingli: His Life and Work* (1983; Engl. trans. Edinburgh, 1986); G. Locher, *Zwingli's Thought: New Perspectives* (Leiden, 1981). For a collection of source material on Zwingli see G. R. Potter, *Huldrych Zwingli* (London, 1978). For Calvin see: F. Wendel, *Calvin: The Origins of His Development and Thought* (1950; Engl. trans. London, 1963); T. H. L. Parker, *John Calvin: A Biography* (London, 1975); D. Steinmetz, *Calvin in Context* (Oxford, 1995); A. E. McGrath, *A Life of John Calvin* (Oxford, 1990). For documents on Calvin and Calvinism see G. Potter and M. Greengrass, *John Calvin* (London, 1983) and A. Duke, G. Lewis and A. Pettegree, *Calvinism in Europe, 1540–1610* (Manchester, 1992).

Only a representative sample can be given of the vast numbers of books and articles which have been published on the Reformation in various countries. For Germany see: R. Scribner, *The German Reformation* (London, 1986); R. Po-Chia Hsia, ed., *The German People and the Reformation* (Ithaca, NY, 1988); A. G. Dickens, *The German Nation and Martin Luther* (London, 1974); S. Karant-Nunn, *Reformation of Ritual: An Interpretation of Early Modern Germany* (London, 1997). For the role of towns and cities in the German Reformation see: B. Moeller, *Imperial Cities and the Reformation: Three Essays* (Philadelphia, PA, 1972); T. Brady, *Ruling Class, Regime and Reformation at Strasbourg, 1520–1555* (Leiden, 1978); L. Abray, *The People's Reformation: Magistrates, Clergy and Commons in Strasbourg, 1500–1598* (Oxford, 1985); P. Broadhead, 'Guildsmen, religious reform and the search for the common good: the role of the guilds in the early Reformation in Augsburg', *HJ* 39 (1996); G. Strauss, *Nuremberg in the Sixteenth Century: City Politics and Life between the Middle Ages and Modern Times* (New York, 1966); S. Karant-Nunn, *Zwickau in Transition, 1500–47: The Reformation as an Agent of Change* (Columbus, OH, 1987). For the debate on the extent of change brought about by the Reformation see: G. Strauss, 'Success and failure in the German Reformation', *P & P* 67 (1975); G. Strauss, *Luther's House of Learning: Indoctrination of the Young in the German Reformation* (Baltimore, MD, 1978); G. Parker, 'Success and failure during the first century of Reformation', *P & P* 136 (1992). A valuable collection of essays which examines changing popular religious attitudes in the region is B. Scribner and T. Johnson, eds, *Popular Religion in Germany and Central Europe, 1400–1800* (London, 1996). Also relevant is R. Bottigheimer, 'Bible reading, "Bibles" and the Bible for children in early modern Germany', *P & P* 139 (1993). The impact of the Reformation in the German countryside is examined in C. S. Dixon, *The Reformation and Rural Society: The Parishes of Brandenburg-Ansbach-Kulmbach, 1528–1603* (Cambridge, 1996); C. S. Dixon, 'The Reformation and parish morality in Brandenburg-Ansbach-Kulmbach', *ARG* 87 (1996); and B. Tolley, *Pastors and Parishioners in Württemberg during the Late Reformation* (Stanford, CA, 1995). See also L. Schorn-Schütte, 'The Christian clergy in the early modern Holy Roman Empire: a comparative social study', *SCJ* 29 (1998). For the German Peasant War of 1525 see: P. Blickle, *The Revolution of 1525: The German Peasants' War from a New Perspective* (1977; Engl. trans. Baltimore, MD, 1981); P. Blickle, *Communal Reformation: The Quest for Salvation in Sixteenth Century Germany* (1985; Atlantic Heights, NJ, 1992); T. Scott, 'The Peasants' War: a historiographical review' and 'The common people in the German Reformation', both in *HJ* 22 (1979); H. Cohn, 'Anticlericalism in the German Peasants' War', *P & P* 83 (1979). There is an excellent collection of documents on the Peasants' War in T. Scott and B. Scribner, *The German Peasants' War: A History in Documents* (Atlantic Heights, NJ, and London, 1991).

For Switzerland see the entries above for Zwingli and Calvin, and also: B. Gordon, *Clerical Discipline and the Rural Reformation: The Synod in Zurich, 1532–80* (Bern, 1992); L. P. Wandel, *Voracious Idols and Violent Hands: Iconoclasm in Zurich, Strasbourg and Basel* (Cambridge, 1995); E. W. Monter, *Calvin's Geneva* (New York, 1967); W. Naphy, *Calvin and the Consolidation of the Genevan Reformation* (Manchester, 1994).

For the French Wars of Religion and their aftermath see the section on France. Also useful is J. Bergin, *The Making of the French Episcopate, 1589–1661* (New Haven, CT, 1996) and, for the eighteenth century, J. McManners, *Church and Society in Eighteenth Century France*, 2 vols (Oxford, 1998).

For the religious conflict in the Netherlands see section 15 and the entries above on Calvin. Also relevant are: A. Duke, *Reformation and Revolt in the Low Countries* (London, 1991); P. Mack-Crew, *Calvinist Preaching and Iconoclasm in the Netherlands, 1549–1569* (Cambridge, 1978); A. Pettegree, *Emden and the Dutch Revolt: Exile and the Development of Reformed Protestantism* (Oxford, 1992).

For the Reformation in Scandinavia see O. P. Grell, *The Scandinavian Reformation: From Evangelical Movement to the Institutionalization of Reform* (Cambridge, 1995).

The religious history of the British Isles has been studied in intense detail, and because so much has been published on the subject, only a small selection can be included here. *See also section 13.* For Lollards see A. Hudson, *The Premature Reformation: Wycliffe Texts and Lollard History* (Oxford, 1988). For the early Reformation in England see: E. Duffy, *The Stripping of the Altars: Traditional Religion in England, 1400–1580* (New Haven, CT, 1992); C. Haigh, *English Reformations: Religion, Politics and Society under the Tudors* (Oxford, 1993); R. Rex, *Henry VIII and the English Reformation* (London, 1993); D. MacCulloch, *Thomas Cranmer: A Life* (New Haven, CT, 1996). For Puritanism see: P. Collinson, *The Elizabethan Puritan Movement* (London, 1967); P. Collinson, *The Religion of the Protestants: The Church in English Society, 1559–1625* (Oxford, 1982); P. Lake, *Moderate Puritans and the Elizabethan Church* (Cambridge, 1982). A controversial and influential account of the impact of Laud and the Arminians on religious stability in Britain is given in N. Tyacke, *Anti-Calvinists: The Rise of English Arminianism, c. 1590–1640* (Oxford, 1987). A useful collection of documents is D. Cressy and L. Ferrell, *Religion and Society in Early Modern England: A Sourcebook* (London, 1996).

Religious revival in the Catholic Church has received extensive attention by historians. A good general account is given in M. Mullett, *The Catholic Reformation* (London, 1999). A valuable collection of some of the most significant articles on the subject is D. Luebke, ed., *The Counter-Reformation: The Essential Readings* (Oxford, 1999). Other useful general surveys are: N. Davidson, *The Counter Reformation* (Oxford, 1987); A. Wright, *The Counter-Reformation: Catholic Europe and the Non-Christian World* (London, 1982); D. Fenlon, *Heresy and Obedience in Tridentine Italy: Cardinal Pole and The Counter Reformation* (Cambridge, 1972); J. Delumeau, *Catholicism between Luther and Voltaire* (1971; Engl. trans. London, 1977), which presents the Counter-Reformation as introducing Christian teaching in place of medieval superstition, although his thesis may underestimate the religious knowledge of the medieval laity. L. Châtellier, *The Europe of the Devout: The Catholic Reformation and the Formation of a New Society* (1987; Engl. trans. Cambridge, 1989) shows how the spiritual values preached in the Counter-Reformation were absorbed by the laity. For the social and religious roles played by confession see J. Bossy, 'The social history of confession in the age of the Reformation', *TRHS* 26 (1976).

There are books and articles of particular relevance for the Counter-Reformation in individual countries. For Spain see: H. Kamen, *Inquisition and Society in Spain* (London, 1985); W. Christian, *Local Religion in Sixteenth-Century Spain* (Princeton, NJ, 1981). For Italy see: N. Davidson, 'Rome and the Venetian Inquisition in the sixteenth century', *J. Eccles. Hist.* 39 (1988); C. Black, 'Perugia and post-Tridentine church reform', *J. Eccles. Hist.* 35 (1984); C. Ginzburg, *The Cheese and the Worms: The Cosmos of a Sixteenth Century Miller* (1976; Engl. trans. London, 1980). For France see: A. L. Martin, *The Jesuit Mind: The Mentality of an Elite in Early Modern France* (Ithaca, NY, 1988); A. N. Galpern, *The Religions of the People in Sixteenth-Century Champagne* (Cambridge, MA, 1976). For the Holy Roman Empire see R. Bireley, *Religion and Politics in the Age of the Counter Reformation: Emperor Ferdinand II, William Lamormaini, S.J., and the Formulation of Imperial Policy* (Chapel Hill, NC, 1981). For the new Orders see: W. Bangert, *A History of the Society of Jesus*, 2nd edition (St Louis, MO, 1986); P. Caraman, *St Angela: The Life of Angela Merici, Foundress of the Ursulines 1474–1540* (New York, 1964); H. O. Evennett, 'The New Orders', in *The New Cambridge Modern History*, vol. 2 (Cambridge, 1965).

For the Radical Reformation the best recent general survey is H.-J. Goertz, *The Anabaptists* (1980; Engl. trans. London, 1996). Also important is C.-P. Clasen, *Anabaptism: A Social History, 1525–1618* (Ithaca, NY, 1972). G. Williams, *The Radical Reformation* (Philadelphia, PA, 1962) is a detailed study of the various radical groups and remains an important source of reference, but its tendency to separate the violent from the peaceable groups obscures the relationship between the different strands in the radical movement. A good collection of documents on the early development of radicalism is M. G. Baylor, *The Radical Reformation* (Cambridge, 1991). For Müntzer see T. Scott, *Thomas Müntzer: Theology and Revolution in the German Reformation* (London, 1989) and A. Friesen, *Thomas Muentzer, a Destroyer of the Godless: The*

Making of a Sixteenth-Century Religious Revolutionary (Berkeley, CA, 1990), and for a splendid translation of Müntzer's writings see P. Matheson, *The Collected Works of Thomas Müntzer* (Edinburgh, 1988). A work of major significance for demonstrating the connection between radical religious movements and demands for social and political reform is J. M. Stayer, *The German Peasants' War and the Anabaptist Community of Goods* (Montreal, 1991). For the growth of apocalyptic belief see K. Deppermann, *Melchior Hoffman: Social Unrest and Apocalyptic Visions in the Age of the Reformation* (1979; Engl. trans. Edinburgh, 1987), and for the events in Münster in 1533–34 see R. Po-Chia Hsia, 'Münster and the Anabaptists', in R. Po-Chia Hsia, ed., *The German People and the Reformation* (Ithaca, NY, 1988). For later developments in Anabaptism see W. O. Packull, *Hutterite Beginnings: Communitarian Experiments during the Reformation* (Baltimore, MD, 1995), and an illuminating source is *The Chronicle of the Hutterian Brethren*, Vol. 1, (Rifton, NY, 1987) [no named editor]. For the origins of spiritualism in the Reformation see R. E. McLaughlin, *Caspar Schwenckfeld, Reluctant Radical: His Life to 1540* (New Haven, CT, 1986) and the texts in G. Williams and A. Mergal, eds, *Spiritual and Anabaptist Writers* (Philadelphia, PA, 1957).

For the role of radical religious movements during the English Civil War see J. McGregor and B. Reay, eds, *Radical Religion in the English Revolution* (Oxford, 1984) and C. Hill, *The World Turned Upside Down: Radical Ideas during the English Revolution* (London, 1972).

Essay topics

How important were anticlerical sentiments in promoting support for the Reformation?

Why was reform of the moral conduct of the laity an important objective of Protestant religious reformers?

Why were the towns and cities of Germany attracted by evangelical teaching in the 1520s and 1530s?

How successful was the Counter-Reformation in generating lay support for the Roman Catholic Church?

6. War

There are several good introductions to wars and warfare in the early modern period, including: F. Tallett, *War and Society in Early Modern Europe, 1495–1715* (London, 1992); J. Hale, *War and Society in Renaissance Europe, 1450–1620* (London, 1985); M. S. Anderson, *War and Society in Europe of the Old Regime, 1618–1789* (London, 1988); J. Black, *European Warfare 1660–1815* (London, 1994); J. Childs, *Armies and Warfare in Europe, 1648–1789* (New York, 1982); G. Parker, ed., *The Thirty Years' War* (London, 1984). The debate on whether there was a military revolution was begun by M. Roberts, *The Military Revolution, 1560–1660* (London, 1956), reprinted in M. Roberts, ed., *Essays in Swedish History* (London, 1967). The original thesis has stimulated much discussion, such as in: G. Parker, 'The Military Revolution, 1560–1660 – a myth?', *JMH* 48

(1976), reprinted in G. Parker, ed., *Spain and the Netherlands, 1559–1659* (London, 1979); G. Parker, *The Military Revolution: Military Innovation and the Rise of the West, 1500–1800* (London, 1988); J. Black, *A Military Revolution? Military Change and European Society, 1550–1800* (London, 1991); and D. Eltis, *The Military Revolution in Sixteenth-Century Europe* (London, 1995). Evidence from the Thirty Years' War plays a crucial role in the evaluation of the arguments both for and against a military revolution, and the best study of this is G. Parker, ed., *The Thirty Years' War* (London, 1984). More brief, but including documents, is P. Limm, *The Thirty Years' War* (London, 1984).

Changes in military technology are evaluated in B. Hall, *Weapons and Warfare in Renaissance Europe* (London, 1997), and the best study of military and logistical problems facing an army on campaign is G. Parker, *The Army of Flanders and the Spanish Road, 1567–1659: The Logistics of Spanish Victory and Defeat in the Low Countries' War* (Cambridge, 1972). Also for these aspects see M. van Creveld, *Supplying War: Logistics from Wallenstein to Patton* (London, 1977). The causes of conflict are examined in J. Black, ed., *The Origins of War in Early Modern Europe* (Edinburgh, 1987).

For discussion of the changes in naval warfare see: J. Guilmartin Jr, *Gunpowder and Galleys: Changing Technology and Mediterranean Warfare at Sea in the Sixteenth Century* (Cambridge, 1974); C. Martin and G. Parker, *The Spanish Armada* (London, 1988); J. Black and P. Woodfine, eds, *The Royal Navy and the Use of Naval Power in the Eighteenth Century* (London, 1988); N. Rodger, *The Wooden World: An Anatomy of the Georgian Navy* (London, 1986); J. Bruijn, *The Dutch Navy of the Seventeenth and Eighteenth Centuries* (Columbia, SC, 1993). Material on military changes in the eighteenth century is found in C. Duffy, *The Army of Frederick the Great* (London, 1974) and C. Duffy, *The Army of Maria Theresa* (London, 1977).

Essay topics

What were the most important consequences for European society of changes in warfare in the early modern period?

How compelling is the evidence for a 'military revolution' having occurred between 1560 and 1660?

7. Renaissance

Good reference works on the Renaissance are S. Fletcher, *The Longman Companion to Renaissance Europe, 1390–1530* (London, 2000) and P. Grendler, ed., *Encyclopedia of the Renaissance*, 6 vols (New York, 1999). Two good introductory studies are P. Burke, *The Renaissance* (London, 1987) and A. Brown, *The Renaissance*, 2nd edition (London, 1999). More detailed works are: R. Porter and M. Teich, eds, *The Renaissance in National Context* (Cambridge, 1992); A. Goodman and A. MacKay, eds, *The Impact of Humanism on Western Europe* (London, 1990); P. O. Kristeller, *Renaissance Thought: The Classic, Scholastic and Humanist Strains* (New York, 1955); P. Burke, *The Renaissance*

Sense of the Past (London, 1969); J. Kraye, ed., *The Cambridge Companion to Renaissance Humanism* (Cambridge, 1996). For the visual arts see: M. Baxandall, *Painting and Experience in Fifteenth-Century Italy* (Oxford, 1972); M. Wackernagel, *The World of the Florentine Artists* (Princeton, NJ, 1981); P. Murray, *The Architecture of the Italian Renaissance*, 2nd edition (London, 1986); P. Burke, *The Italian Renaissance: Culture and Society in Italy*, 2nd edition (Cambridge, 1986).

The origins and development of the Renaissance in Italy are examined in: D. Hay and J. Law, *Italy in the Age of the Renaissance, 1380–1530* (London, 1989); D. Hay, *The Italian Renaissance in its Historical Background*, 2nd edition (Cambridge, 1977); J. Stephens, *The Italian Renaissance: The Origins of Intellectual and Artistic Change before the Reformation* (London, 1990).

There are many works available on the Renaissance in Florence, but especially useful are: J. Hale, *Florence and the Medici: The Pattern of Control* (London, 1977); N. Rubinstein, *The Government of Florence under the Medici, 1434–1494*, 2nd edition (Oxford, 1997); F. Gilbert, *Machiavelli and Guicciardini: Politics and History in Sixteenth-Century Florence* (Princeton, NJ, 1965); Q. Skinner, *Machiavelli* (Oxford, 1981). For Venice see D. S. Chambers, *The Imperial Age of Venice, 1380–1580* (London, 1970) and E. Muir, *Civic Ritual in Renaissance Venice* (Princeton, NJ, 1981). For the effects of the Renaissance upon the Papacy, the Papal States and the Church in general see: J. A. F. Thomson, *Popes and Princes, 1417–1517: Politics and Polity in the Late Medieval Church* (London, 1980); P. Partner, *Renaissance Rome, 1500–59: A Portrait of a Society* (London, 1976); P. Prodi, *Papal Prince, One Body and Two Souls: The Papal Monarchy in the Early Modern Period* (Cambridge, 1988), K. J. P. Lowe, *Church and Politics in Renaissance Italy: The Life and Career of Cardinal Francesco Soderini, 1453–1524* (Cambridge, 1993). For the Renaissance in Northern Europe see: L. Spitz, *The Religious Renaissance of German Humanism* (Cambridge, MA, 1963); J. McConica, *Erasmus* (Oxford, 1991); M. M. Phillips, *Erasmus and the Northern Renaissance* (London, 1959); R. Marius, *Thomas More: A Biography* (London, 1985). For the impact of printing on the spread of ideas see M. Chrisman, *Lay Culture, Learned Culture: Books and Social Change in Strasbourg, 1480–1599* (New Haven, CT, 1982) and E. L. Eisenstein, *The Printing Revolution in Early Modern Europe* (Cambridge, 1983). *Also see section 10.*

Essay topics

What, if anything, was new about the Renaissance?

Why did Italy play a prominent role in the development of Renaissance art and ideas?

8. Enlightenment

Good general surveys of the Enlightenment are: N. Hampson, *The Enlightenment* (London, 1968); D. Outram, *The Enlightenment* (Cambridge, 1995); U. Im Hof, *The Enlightenment* (1993; Engl. trans. Oxford, 1994); R. Porter and M. Teich, eds, *The Enlightenment in National Context* (Cambridge, 1981). For the social impact of the Enlightenment see: R. van Dülmen, *The Society of the Enlightenment: The Rise of the Middle Class and Enlightenment Culture in Germany* (London, 1992); M. Jacob, *The Radical Enlightenment, Pantheists, Freemasons and Republicans* (London, 1981). For enlightened despotism see: H. M. Scott, ed., *Enlightened Absolutism* (1989); F. Szabo, *Kaunitz and Enlightened Absolutism, 1753–1780* (Cambridge, 1994); K. Maxwell, *Pombal: Paradox of the Enlightenment* (Cambridge, 1995); J. Gagliardo, *Enlightened Despotism* (London, 1968); C. B. A. Behrens, *Society, Government and the Enlightenment: The Experiences of Eighteenth-Century France and Prussia* (London, 1985).

Essay topics

What were the most radical achievements of the Enlightenment?

Why did the ideas of the Enlightenment prove attractive to despotic rulers?

9. Popular Culture

The best general book is P. Burke, *Popular Culture in Early Modern Europe*, 2nd edition (Aldershot, 1994). A major contribution towards understanding early modern popular culture is made by E. Muir, *Ritual in Early Modern Europe* (Cambridge, 1997). See also: R. Muchembled, *Popular Culture and Elite Culture in France, 1400–1750* (Baton Rouge, LA, 1985); R. Chartier, *Cultural History: Between Practices and Representations* (Oxford, 1988); N. Z. Davis, 'The reasons of misrule', in N. Z. Davis, ed., *Society and Culture in Early Modern France* (London, 1975) (this was also published in *P & P* 50 (1971)); D. Sabean, *The Power in the Blood: Popular Culture and Village Discourse in Early Modern Germany* (Cambridge, 1984); M. Ingram, 'Ridings, rough music and the "reform of popular culture" in Early Modern England', *P & P* 105 (1984). One of the most significant forces for cultural change was the spread of literacy and this is admirably covered in R. Houston, *Literacy in Early Modern Europe: Culture and Education, 1500–1800* (London, 1988).

Essay topics

How successful were efforts by ruling elites to reform popular culture in early modern Europe?

What were the most important consequences of the discovery of printing using moveable type?

10. Science and Technology

There have been several good accounts of the Scientific Revolution produced in recent years. See: J. Henry, *The Scientific Revolution and the Origins of Modern Science* (London, 1997); R. Porter and M. Teich, eds, *The Scientific Revolution in National Context* (Cambridge, 1992); A. R. Hall, *The Revolution in Science, 1500–1750* (London, 1983); D. Linberg and R. Westman, eds, *Reappraisals of the Scientific Revolution* (Cambridge, 1990); W. Clark, J. Golinski and S. Schaffer, eds, *The Sciences in Enlightened Europe* (Chicago, IL, 1999);

J. Field and F. James, eds, *Renaissance and Revolution: Humanist Scholars, Craftsmen and Natural Philosophers in Early Modern Europe* (Cambridge, 1993); A. G. R. Smith, *Science and Society in the Sixteenth and Seventeenth Centuries* (London, 1972). Early modern scientists often had an interest in alchemy and benefited from practical experience accumulated by alchemists. The connection is examined in C. Webster, *From Paracelsus to Newton: Magic and the Making of Modern Science* (Cambridge, 1992). The development of scientific methods and ideas is also examined in M. Hunter, *Archives of the Scientific Revolution: The Formation and Exchange of Ideas in Seventeenth-Century Europe* (Woodbridge, 1998). For the practical consequences of scientific discovery see A. E. Musson, ed., *Science, Technology and Economic Growth in the Eighteenth Century* (London, 1972).

Essay topics

How can one account for the growth of scientific knowledge in the early modern period?

What were the most important consequences for early modern society of scientific discoveries?

11. France

There are several good surveys of French history of the period, including: D. Potter, *A History of France, 1460–1560: The Emergence of a Nation State* (London, 1995); R. Briggs, *Early Modern France, 1560–1715*, 2nd edition (Oxford, 1998); D. Parker, *The Making of French Absolutism* (London, 1983); Y.-C. Bercé, *The Birth of Absolutism: A History of France 1598–1661* (1992; Engl. trans. London, 1996); P. Campbell, *The Ancien Régime in France* (Oxford, 1988). P. Goubert, *The Ancien Régime: French Society 1600–1750* (1969; Engl. trans. London, 1973) provides important insights into French society and contains many useful documents. For the development of the French Renaissance monarchy see: R. Knecht, *Francis I* (Cambridge, 1982); R. Knecht, *Renaissance Warrior and Patron: The Reign of Francis I* (Cambridge, 1994); R. Knecht, *French Renaissance Monarchy: Francis I and Henry II*, 2nd edition (London, 1996).

There are many good studies of the political ideas and institutions in early modern France, including: E. Le Roy Ladurie, *The Royal French State, 1460–1660* (1987; Engl. trans. London, 1994); J. Collins, *The State in Early Modern France* (Cambridge, 1995); J. R. Major, *Representative Government in Early Modern France* (London, 1980); H. A. Lloyd, *The State, France and the Sixteenth Century* (London, 1983); R. Harding, *Anatomy of a Power Elite: The Provincial Governors of Early Modern France* (New Haven, CT, 1978); J. H. Shennan, *Government and Society in France, 1461–1661* (London, 1969).

There are many studies of the French Wars of Religion. Particularly useful ones are: M. P. Holt, *The French Wars of Religion, 1562–1629* (Cambridge, 1995); J. H. M. Salmon, *Society in Crisis: France in the Sixteenth Century* (London, 1975); R. Knecht, *The French Wars of Religion, 1559–1598*, 2nd edition (London, 1996); D. Kelley, *The Beginning of Ideology: Consciousness and Society in the French Reformation* (Cambridge, 1981); D. Potter, *The French Wars of Religion: Selected Documents* (London, 1997). For the impact of the wars on French society see: N. Z. Davis, *Society and Culture in Early Modern France* (London, 1975); B. Diefendorf, *Beneath the Cross: Catholics and Huguenots in Sixteenth-Century Paris* (Oxford, 1991); P. Benedict, *Rouen during the Wars of Religion* (Cambridge, 1981); J. Wood, *The King's Army: Warfare, Soldiers and Society during the Wars of Religion in France, 1562–1576* (Cambridge, 1996); M. P. Holt, 'Wine, community and Reformation in sixteenth-century Burgundy', *P & P* 138 (1993). For the conclusion of the wars and the accession of Henry IV see: M. P. Holt, *The Duke of Anjou and the Politique Struggle during the Wars of Religion* (Cambridge, 1986); M. Greengrass, *France in the Age of Henri IV: The Struggle for Stability* (London, 1984); M. Greengrass, 'The sixteen: radical politics in Paris during the League', *History* 69 (1984); S. A. Finley-Croswhite, *Henry IV and the Towns: The Pursuit of Legitimacy in French Urban Society, 1589– 1610* (Cambridge, 1999).

Much material is available on the recovery of French power and the establishment of royal absolutism in the first half of the seventeenth century. Especially useful are: R. Bonney, *Society and Government in France under Richelieu and Mazarin* (London, 1988); D. Buisseret, *Sully and the Growth of Centralized Government in France, 1598–1610* (London, 1968); R. Bonney, *Political Change in France under Richelieu and Mazarin, 1624–1661* (London, 1976); G. Treasure, *Richelieu and Mazarin* (London, 1998); O. Ranum, *Richelieu and the Councillors of Louis XIII* (Oxford, 1963); J. Bergin, *Cardinal Richelieu: Power and the Pursuit of Wealth* (New Haven, CT, 1985); J. H. Elliott, *Richelieu and Olivares* (Cambridge, 1984); G. Treasure, *Mazarin: The Crisis of Absolutism in France* (London, 1995); D. Parker, *La Rochelle and the French Monarchy: Conflict and Order in Seventeenth-Century France* (London, 1980). For an assessment of the significance of the Fronde consult: A. L. Moote, *The Revolt of the Judges: The Parlement of Paris and the Fronde, 1643–52* (London, 1971); R. Bonney, 'The French Civil War, 1649–1653', *ESR* 8 (1978); P. J. Coveney, ed., *France in Crisis, 1620–1675* (London, 1977), although some of the articles translated here are now rather dated. For the personal reign of Louis XIV there is much to recommend P. Goubert, *Louis XIV and Twenty Million Frenchmen* (1966; Engl. trans. London, 1970). Also valuable are R. Mettam, *Power and Faction in Louis XIV's France* (Oxford, 1988) and R. Mettam, ed., *Government and Society in Louis XIV's France* (London, 1977), which contains a useful selection of documents. Further material can be found in P. Campbell, *Louis XIV* (London, 1994); R. Hatton, ed., *Louis XIV and Absolutism* (London, 1976); V. Mallia-Milanes, *Louis XIV and France* (London, 1986); D. Sturdy, *Louis XIV* (London, 1998); J. H. Shennan, *Louis XIV* (London, 1986); J. Lynn, *The Wars of Louis XIV, 1667–1714* (London, 1999). P. Burke, *The Fabrication of Louis XIV* (New Haven, CT, 1992) uses contemporary depictions of Louis XIV to evaluate the use of art in consolidating royal power in the minds of his subjects. For the reign of Louis XV see: P. Campbell, *Power and Politics in Old Regime France, 1720–1745* (London, 1996); F. L. Ford, *Robe and Sword: The Regrouping of the French Aristocracy after Louis XIV* (London, 1953);

J. Rogister, *Louis XV and the Parlement of Paris, 1737–1755* (Cambridge, 1995); J. H. Shennan, *Philippe, Duke of Orléans, Regent of France, 1715–23* (London, 1979); C. B. A. Behrens, *The Ancien Régime* (London, 1967).

Essay topics

How successful was the French monarchy in overcoming obstacles to the establishment of absolute power?

How important was the role of religion in the French Civil Wars of 1562–98?

12. Iberia

Good general histories of Spain in this period are: H. Kamen, *Spain 1469–1714: A Society in Conflict* (London, 1983); J. Elliott, *Imperial Spain 1469–1716* (London, 1963); and H. Kamen, *The Golden Age of Spain* (London, 1988). Also useful are J. Lynch, *Spain 1516–1598: From Nation State to World Empire* (London, 1991) and J. Lynch, *The Hispanic World in Crisis and Change, 1598–1700* (London, 1992). For the reigns of Ferdinand and Isabella and the climax of the defeat of the Moors see, N. Hillgarth, *The Spanish Kingdoms, 1410–1516: Castilian Hegemony* (Oxford, 1978). For the reign of Charles V in Spain see M. F. Álvarez, *Charles V* (London, 1975) and M. Rodríguez-Salgado, *The Changing Face of Empire: Charles V, Philip II and Habsburg Authority, 1551–1559* (London, 1988). There is much material available in English on the reign of Philip II: G. Parker, *Philip II* (London, 1979); G. Parker, *The Grand Strategy of Philip II* (New Haven, CT, 1998); I. A. A. Thompson, *War and Government in Habsburg Spain, 1560–1620* (London, 1976); G. Woodward, *Philip II* (London, 1992). For debate on the decline of Spain see: J. Elliott, 'The decline of Spain', *P & P* 20 (1961); J. Elliott, 'Self-perception and decline in early seventeenth-century Spain', *P & P* 74 (1977); H. Kamen, 'The decline of Spain: a historical myth', *P & P* 81 (1978); R. Stradling, 'Seventeenth-century Spain: decline or survival?', *ESR* 9 (1979); R. Stradling, *Europe and the Decline of Spain* (London, 1981); R. Stradling, *Philip IV and the Government of Spain, 1621–1665* (Cambridge, 1988); J. Elliott, *The Revolt of the Catalans* (Cambridge, 1963); and G. Darby, *Spain in the Seventeenth Century* (London, 1994). The character and the work of Olivares are examined in detail in J. Elliott, *The Count-Duke of Olivares: The Statesman in an Age of Decline* (London, 1984), and are summarised in J. Elliott, *Richelieu and Olivares* (Cambridge, 1984). For the later period see H. Kamen, *Spain in the Later Seventeenth Century* (London, 1980) and H. Kamen, *The War of Succession in Spain, 1700–1715* (London, 1969). Spain in the eighteenth century is examined in J. Lynch, *Bourbon Spain, 1700–1808* (London, 1989).

Although the role of Portugal in the voyages of discovery is well covered, especially in C. Boxer, *The Portuguese Seaborne Empire, 1415–1825* (London, 1969), there is little on the internal history of the kingdom which is available in English. The best account is in D. Birmingham, *A Concise History of Portugal* (Cambridge, 1993).

Essay topics

How can one account for Spanish military domination in Europe in the sixteenth century?

When did the 'decline of Spain' occur, and why?

13. Great Britain

There is copious material available on politics and society within the British Isles. General surveys are provided in: D. Loades, *Politics and the Nation: England 1450–1660*, 5th edition (Oxford, 1999); D. M. Palliser, *The Age of Elizabeth. England under the Later Tudors, 1547–1603*, 2nd edition (London, 1992); K. Wrightson, *English Society, 1580–1680* (London, 1982); J. Sharpe, *Early Modern England: A Social History, 1550–1760*, 2nd edition (London, 1997). For the end of the Wars of the Roses and the early Tudors see R. Britnell, *The Closing of the Middle Ages? England 1471–1529* (Oxford, 1997) and J. R. Lander, *Government and Community 1450–1509* (London, 1980). For the Tudor rulers, a useful reference work is R. O'Day, *The Longman Companion to the Tudor Age* (London, 1994). See also: M. Nicholls, *A History of the Modern British Isles, 1529–1603: The Two Kingdoms* (Oxford, 1999); S. Guy, *Tudor England* (Oxford, 1988); S. Guy, ed., *The Tudor Monarchy* (London, 1997); D. M. Palliser, *Henry VII*, 2nd edition (London, 1983); J. Scarisbrick, *Henry VIII*, 2nd edition (New Haven, CT, 1997); R. Tittler, *The Reign of Mary I* (London, 1991); W. MacCaffrey, *Elizabeth I* (London, 1993). Much work has been published on Tudor government and parliaments. The main issues are considered in: P. Williams, *The Tudor Regime* (Oxford, 1979); D. Loades, *Tudor Government: Structures of Authority in the Sixteenth Century* (Oxford, 1997); M. Graves, *Early Tudor Parliaments, 1485–1558* (London, 1990); M. Graves, *The Tudor Parliaments: Crown, Lords and Commons, 1485–1603* (London, 1985); J. Loach, 'The function of ceremonial in the reign of Henry VIII', *P & P* 142 (1994); M. Graves, *Elizabethan Parliaments, 1559–1601*, 2nd edition (London, 1996); D. L. Smith, *Stuart Parliaments 1603–1689* (London, 1999). The best general account of opposition and rebellion against the rule of the Tudors is A. Fletcher and D. MacCulloch, *Tudor Rebellions*, 4th edition (London, 1997). The best general history of Britain in the seventeenth century is D. L. Smith, *A History of the Modern British Isles 1603–1707: The Double Crown* (Oxford, 1998). For the early reign of James I see M. Lee, *Great Britain's Solomon: James VI and I in his Three Kingdoms* (Urbana, IL, 1990) and J. Wormald, 'James VI and I: Two kings or one?', *History* 68 (1983).

The events leading to the outbreak of the Civil War are covered in: A. Hughes, *The Causes of the English Civil War* (London, 1991); C. Russell, *Parliaments and English Politics, 1621–1629* (Oxford, 1979); and K. Sharpe, *The Personal Rule of Charles I* (New Haven, CT, 1992). Of the numerous works available on the Civil War, some of the most useful are: C. Russell, *The Fall of the British Monarchies, 1637–1642* (Oxford, 1991); G. E. Aylmer, *Rebellion or Revolution? England 1640–1660* (Oxford, 1986); A. Fletcher, *The Outbreak of the English*

Civil War (London, 1981); J. Morrill, *The Revolt in the Provinces: The People of England and the Tragedies of War, 1630–1648*, 2nd edition (London, 1999); M. Bennett, *The Civil War in Britain and Ireland, 1638–51* (Oxford, 1997).

For the aftermath of the Civil War see: R. Hutton, *The British Republic, 1649–1660* (London, 1990); D. Hirst, 'The failure of Godly Rule in the English Republic', *P & P* 132 (1991); B. Coward, *Oliver Cromwell* (London, 1991). Good accounts of the reign of Charles II are given in R. Hutton, *Charles II: King of England, Scotland and Ireland* (Oxford, 1989). The reign of James II is examined in J. Miller, *James II: A Study in Kingship*, 2nd edition (London, 1989), and his overthrow in J. Miller, *The Glorious Revolution*, 2nd edition (London, 1997) and W. Speck, *Reluctant Revolutionaries: Englishmen and the Revolution of 1688–9* (Oxford, 1989).

The best account of England in the eighteenth century is F. O'Gorman, *The Long Eighteenth Century: British Political and Social History, 1688–1832* (London, 1997). L. Colley, *Britons: Forging the Nation, 1707–1832* (London, 1992) is a stimulating interpretation, and also useful is G. Holmes and D. Szechi, *The Age of Oligarchy: Pre-industrial Britain* (London, 1993).

Essay topics

How secure was the control exercised by Tudor rulers over England?

Were political conflicts more important than religious divisions in prompting the outbreak of the Civil War?

14. Germany

Also see sections 5, 6 and 16. General accounts of the history of early modern Germany are: M. Hughes, *Early Modern Germany, 1477–1806* (London, 1992); B. Scribner, ed., *Germany: A New Social and Economic History, 1450–1630* (London, 1996); S. Ogilvie, ed., *Germany: A New Social and Economic History, 1630–1800* (London, 1996); H. Holborn, *A History of Modern Germany*, vols 1–2 (Princeton, NJ, 1959–65); E. Sagarra, *A Social History of Germany, 1648–1914* (London, 1977); J. Gagliardo, *Germany under the Old Regime, 1600–1700* (London, 1991).

For political changes see: F. R. Du Boulay, *Germany in the Later Middle Ages* (London, 1983); T. Brady, *Turning Swiss: Cities and Empire, 1450–1550* (Cambridge, 1985); T. Brady, *Protestant Politics (1489–1553) and the German Reformation* (Atlantic Highlands, NJ, 1995); H. Cohn, *The Government of the Rhine Palatinate in the Fifteenth Century* (Oxford, 1965); F. L. Carsten, *Princes and Parliaments in Germany from the Fifteenth to the Eighteenth Century* (Oxford, 1959); G. Benecke, *Society and Politics in Germany 1500–1750* (London, 1974); J. Harrington and H. Smith, 'Confessionalization, community and state building in Germany, 1555–1870', *JMH* 69 (1997); R. Vierhaus, *Germany in the Age of Absolutism* (1978; Engl. trans. Cambridge, 1989). The way in which economic interest transcended political divisions is examined in T. Scott, *Regional Identity and Economic Change: The Upper Rhine, 1450–1600* (Oxford, 1997).

For the Habsburgs in the fifteenth and sixteenth centuries see: G. Benecke, *Maximilian I, 1459–1519: An Analytical Biography* (London, 1982); M. Rady, *The Emperor Charles V* (London, 1988); K. Brandi, *The Emperor Charles V* (London, 1939); P. S. Fichtner, *Ferdinand I of Austria: The Politics of Dynasticism in the Age of the Reformation* (New York, 1982). For the events leading up to the Thirty Years' War see: C.-P. Clasen, *The Palatinate in European History, 1559–1660* (London, 1963); R. Bireley, *Religion and Politics in the Age of the Counter-Reformation: Emperor Ferdinand II, William Lamormaini, S.J., and the Formation of Imperial Policy* (Chapel Hill, NC, 1981). For documents which reveal the impact of the Thirty Years' War on Germany see G. Benecke, *Germany in the Thirty Years' War* (London, 1978). For the functioning of Imperial institutions after the Thirty Years' War see J. Gagliardo, *Reich and Nation: The Holy Roman Empire as Idea and Reality, 1763–1806* (Bloomington, IN, 1980) and M. Hughes, *Law and Politics in Eighteenth-Century Germany: The Imperial Aulic Council in the Reign of Charles VI* (Woodbridge, 1988). Much has been written on the growth of Prussian power after 1648. See: F. L. Carsten, *The Origins of Prussia* (Oxford, 1954); R. A. Dorwart, *The Prussian Welfare State before 1740* (Cambridge, MA, 1971); R. A. Dorwart, *The Administrative Reforms of Frederick William I of Prussia* (Cambridge, MA, 1953); H. Rosenberg, *Bureaucracy, Aristocracy, and Autocracy: The Prussian Experience, 1660–1815* (Cambridge, MA, 1958). For the influence of Pietism upon the Lutheran church and society in general, consult: M. Fulbrook, *Piety and Politics: Religion and the Rise of Absolutism in England, Württemberg and Prussia* (Cambridge, 1983); R. Gawthorp, *Pietism and the Making of Eighteenth-Century Prussia* (Cambridge, 1993); K. J. Stein, *Philipp Jakob Spener: Pietist Patriarch* (Chicago, IL, 1986); F. E. Stoeffler, *German Pietism during the Eighteenth Century* (Leiden, 1973). For Frederick II see G. Ritter, *Frederick the Great: A Historical Profile* (1936; Engl. trans. London, 1968) and H. Johnson, *Frederick the Great and His Officials* (New Haven, CT, 1975). For other principalities in Germany see: J. A. Vann, *The Making of a State: Württemberg, 1593–1793* (Ithaca, NY, 1985); R. H. Thompson, *Lothar Franz von Schönborn and the Diplomacy of the Electorate of Mainz* (The Hague, 1974); T. C. W. Blanning, *Reform and Revolution in Mainz, 1743–1803* (Cambridge, 1974); J. Whaley, *Religious Toleration and Social Change in Hamburg, 1529–1819* (Cambridge, 1985); C. Ingrao, *The Hessian Military State, 1760–85* (Cambridge, 1987).

Essay topics

Why were the Habsburgs unable to assert their dominance over Germany?

How can one account for the rise of Prussian power in Germany from the late seventeenth century onwards?

15. The Netherlands

Also consult section 3. A general survey of events in the Netherlands and their wider significance for Europe is given in H. van der Wee, *The Low Countries in the Early Modern World* (London, 1993). There are many studies of the rebellion against Spain, including: P. Limm, *The Dutch Revolt, 1559–1648* (London, 1989); G. Parker, *The Dutch Revolt* (London, 1977); G. Parker, *Spain and the Netherlands 1559–1659* (London, 1979); H. G. Koenigsberger, 'Orange, Granvelle and Philip II', in E. Kouri and T. Scott, eds, *Politics and Society in Reformation Europe* (London, 1987); M. Gutmann, *War and Rural Life in the Early Modern Low Countries* (Assen, 1980); and J. Tracy, *Holland under Habsburg Rule, 1506–66* (Oxford, 1990) also provides useful material on the effectiveness of the governments of Charles V and Philip II. The institutions and the economy of the United Provinces are examined in: J. Israel, *The Dutch Republic: Its Rise, Greatness and Fall, 1477–1806* (Oxford, 1995); J. Israel, *The Dutch Republic and the Hispanic World* (Oxford, 1982); J. Price, *The Dutch Republic in the Seventeenth Century* (London, 1998); J. de Vries, *The Dutch Rural Economy in the Golden Age* (New Haven, CT, 1974); and J. van Houtte, *An Economic History of the Low Countries* (London, 1977). Much valuable material on society and culture in the Dutch Republic is contained in A. T. van Deursen, *Plain Lives in a Golden Age: Popular Culture, Religion and Society in Seventeenth-Century Holland* (1978; Engl. trans. Cambridge, 1991) and S. Schama, *The Embarrassment of Riches: An Interpretation of Dutch Culture in the Golden Age* (London, 1987).

Essay topics

How can one explain the economic prosperity of the United Provinces in the seventeenth century?

Why was Spain unable to suppress the Revolt of the Netherlands?

16. Central Europe

Also consult section 14. The most illuminating surveys are R. J. W. Evans, *The Habsburg Monarchy, 1550–1700* (Oxford, 1979) and R. A. Kann, *A History of the Habsburg Empire, 1526–1918* (Berkeley, CA, 1974). See also: R. J. W. Evans, *Rudolf II and His World: A Study in Intellectual History, 1576–1612* (Oxford, 1973); C. Ingrao, *The Habsburg Monarchy, 1618–1815* (Cambridge, 1994); R. Evans and T. Thomas, eds, *Crown, Church and Estates: Central European Politics in the Sixteenth and Seventeenth Centuries* (London, 1991); J. Bérenger, *A History of the Habsburg Empire, 1700–1918* (1990; Engl. trans. London, 1997). For later rulers see: J. Spielman, *Leopold I of Austria* (London, 1977); C. Ingrao, *In Quest and Crisis: Emperor Joseph I and the Habsburg Monarchy* (West Lafayette, IN, 1979); E. Crankshaw, *Maria Theresa* (New York, 1970).

For Poland see: N. Davies, *God's Playground: A History of Poland*, Vol. 1, *Origins to 1795* (Oxford, 1981); J. Lukowski, *Liberty's Folly: The Polish-Lithuanian Commonwealth in the Eighteenth Century, 1697–1795* (London, 1991); K. Friedrich, *The Other Prussia: Royal Prussia, Poland and Liberty, 1569–1772* (Cambridge, 2000); R. Frost, *After the Deluge: Poland and the Second Northern War, 1655–1660* (Cambridge, 1993).

For economic change in the region see: Z. P. Pach, *Hungary and the European Economy in Early Modern Times* (Aldershot, 1994); F. Carter, *Trade and Urban*

Development in Poland: An Economic Geography of Cracow from its Origins to 1795 (Cambridge, 1994); J. Topolski, *The Manorial Economy in Early Modern East-Central Europe* (Aldershot, 1994).

Essay topics

How important was the Counter-Reformation in the efforts of the Habsburgs to establish their control over their Central European lands?

How can one account for the increase in serfdom in eastern Europe from the sixteenth century onwards?

17. Russia and the Baltic

There are several general accounts of the history of early modern Russia: P. Dukes, *The Making of Russian Absolutism* (London, 1982); R. Pipes, *Russia under the Old Regime*, 2nd edition (London, 1995); L. Kochan and J. Keep, *The Making of Modern Russia from Kiev and Rus' to the Collapse of the Soviet Union*, 3rd edition (London, 1997). The period of reform initiated by Peter the Great is covered in: L. Hughes, *Russia in the Age of Peter the Great* (London, 1998); M. Anderson, *Peter the Great*, 2nd edition (London, 1995); W. Marshall, *Peter the Great* (London, 1996). For Russia in the eighteenth century and the impact of efforts to reform Russian society see: I. de Madariaga, *Russia in the Age of Catherine the Great* (London, 1981); S. Dixon, *The Modernization of Russia* (Cambridge, 1999); and a collection of essays, I. de Madariaga, *Politics and Culture in Eighteenth-Century Russia* (London, 1998).

The history of the Baltic region is surveyed in D. Kirby, *Northern Europe in the Early Modern Period: The Baltic World, 1492–1772* (London, 1990) and J. Lisk, *Struggle for Supremacy in the Baltic, 1600–1725* (London, 1967). Rural life in the region is examined in D. Gaunt, 'The peasants of Scandinavia, 1300–1700', in T. Scott, ed., *The Peasantries of Europe* (London, 1998). There is some material on political change in Denmark in E. L. Petersen and K. J. V. Jespersen, 'Two revolutions in early modern Denmark', in E. I. Kouri and T. Scott, eds, *Politics and Society in Reformation Europe* (London, 1987). Much has been written on the rise and decline of Swedish power in the early modern period. On the sixteenth century see M. Roberts, *The Early Vasas: A History of Sweden, 1523–1611* (Cambridge, 1968). For the growth of Swedish power in the seventeenth century see M. Roberts, *Gustavus Adolphus*, 2nd edition (London, 1992) and M. Roberts, ed., *Sweden's Age of Greatness, 1632–1718* (London, 1973). A detailed study of the consolidation of royal power in the seventeenth century is contained in A. Upton, *Charles XI and Swedish Absolutism* (Cambridge, 1998). The events surrounding the eclipse of Swedish military power are examined in R. M. Hatton, *Charles XII of Sweden* (London, 1968).

Essay topics

How successful were measures to 'modernise' Russia in the eighteenth century?

Why was Sweden able to dominate the Baltic region in the seventeenth century?

18. The Ottomans and the Balkans

A good general survey is provided by H. Inalcik, *The Ottoman Empire: The Classical Age, 1300–1600* (London, 1973). Good accounts of Suleiman (Süleyman) the Magnificent and the impact of his military campaigns on Europe are found in M. Kunt and C. Woodhead, eds, *Süleyman the Magnificent and His Age: The Ottoman Empire in the Early Modern World* (London, 1995) and A. Clot, *Suleiman the Magnificent: The Man, His Life, His Epoch* (London, 1992). The significance of Ottoman attacks in Central Europe for the development of the Reformation in Germany is examined in S. Fischer-Galati, *Ottoman Imperialism and German Protestantism 1521–55* (New York, 1972). See also C. Kortpeter, *Ottoman Imperialism during the Reformation: Europe and the Caucasus* (London, 1973). An interesting study of the Ottoman invasions is C. Finkel, *The Administration of Warfare: The Ottoman Military Campaigns in Hungary, 1593–1606* (London, 1988). An account of economic change is given in B. McGowan, *Economic Life in Ottoman Europe: Taxation, Trade and the Struggle for Land, 1600–1800* (Cambridge, 1981). Useful material on rural life and agriculture is in F. Adanir, 'The Ottoman peasantries, *c.* 1360–*c.* 1800', in T. Scott, ed., *The Peasantries of Europe from the Fourteenth to the Eighteenth Centuries* (London, 1998). For the later conflicts between the Ottomans and the Habsburgs see D. McKay, *Prince Eugene of Savoy* (London, 1977) and J. Stoye, *The Siege of Vienna* (London, 1964).

For the Balkan lands see: J. Fine, *The Late Medieval Balkans* (Ann Arbor, MI, 1987); C. Woodhouse, *Modern Greece: A Short History,* 5th edition (London, 1991); A. Vacalopoulos, *The Greek Nation, 1453–1669* (New Brunswick, NJ, 1976); S. Pollo, *The History of Albania* (London, 1981).

Essay topic

How great was the threat posed to Western Europe by the rise of Ottoman power in the fifteenth and sixteenth centuries?

19. European Expansion Overseas

The cultural impact of the European conquest and settlement is examined in: A. Pagden, *European Encounters with the New World* (New Haven, CT, 1992); A. Pagden, *Lords of All the World: Ideologues of Empire in Spain, Britain and France, c. 1500–c. 1800* (New Haven, CT, 1995); J. H. Elliott, *The Old World and the New, 1492–1560* (Cambridge, 1970); U. Bitterli, *Cultures in Conflict: Encounters between European and Non-European Cultures, 1492–1800* (Stanford, CA, 1989). A detailed but readable account of the voyages of discovery and the establishment of colonial empires is given in G. V. Scammell, *The World Encompassed: The First European Maritime Empires, c. 800–1650* (London, 1981). The impact of expansion overseas in the later seventeenth and eighteenth centuries is covered in: J. H. Parry, *Trade and Dominion: The European Overseas Empires in the Eighteenth Century* (London, 1971); J. H. Parry, *The Spanish*

Seaborne Empire (London, 1966); and G. Williams, *The Expansion of Europe in the Eighteenth Century* (London, 1966).

Essay topics

Were overseas empires more of a liability than an asset for the states of Europe?

What impact did overseas discoveries have on European culture and society in the early modern period?

GENEALOGIES

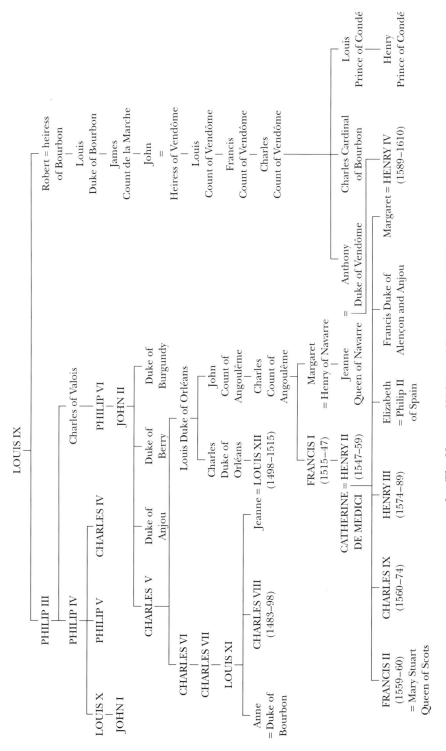

1. The Houses of Valois and Bourbon (to 1610)

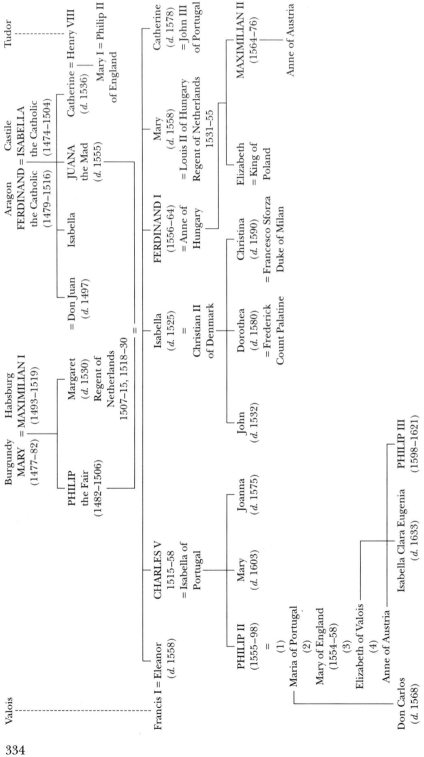

2. The Family of Charles V

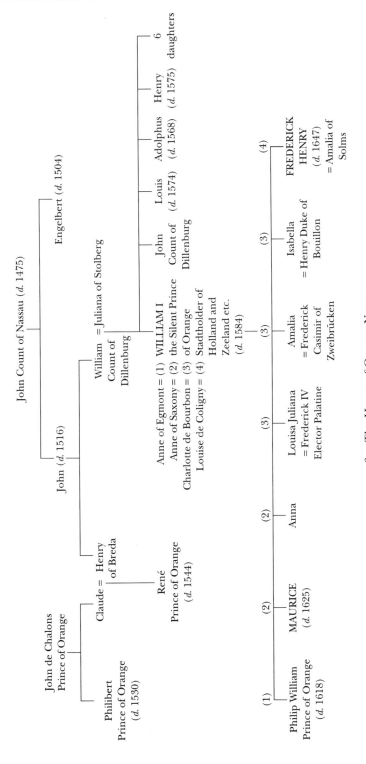

3. The House of Orange-Nassau

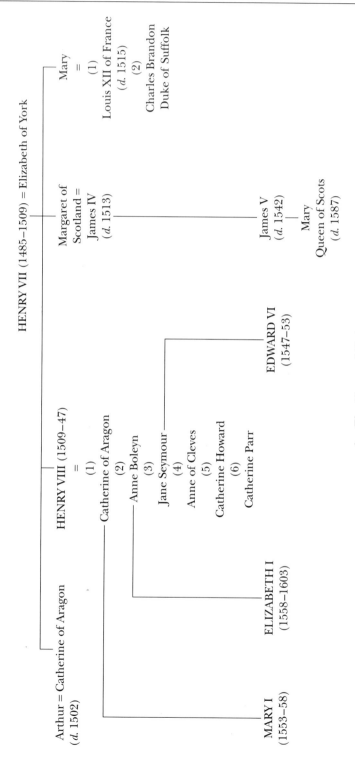

HENRY VII (1485–1509) = Elizabeth of York

Arthur = Catherine of Aragon
(d. 1502)

HENRY VIII (1509–47)
=
(1)
Catherine of Aragon
(2)
Anne Boleyn
(3)
Jane Seymour
(4)
Anne of Cleves
(5)
Catherine Howard
(6)
Catherine Parr

Margaret of
Scotland =
James IV
(d. 1513)

Mary
=
(1)
Louis XII of France
(d. 1515)
(2)
Charles Brandon
Duke of Suffolk

James V
(d. 1542)

Mary
Queen of Scots
(d. 1587)

MARY I
(1553–58)

ELIZABETH I
(1558–1603)

EDWARD VI
(1547–53)

4.   The House of Tudor

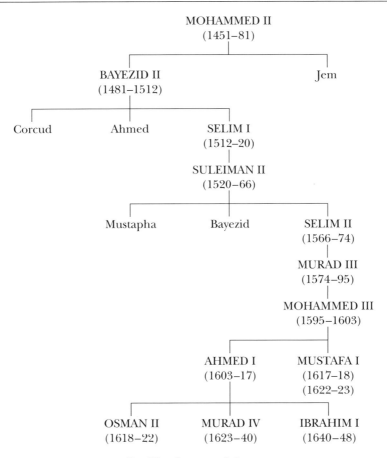

5. The Ottoman Sultans

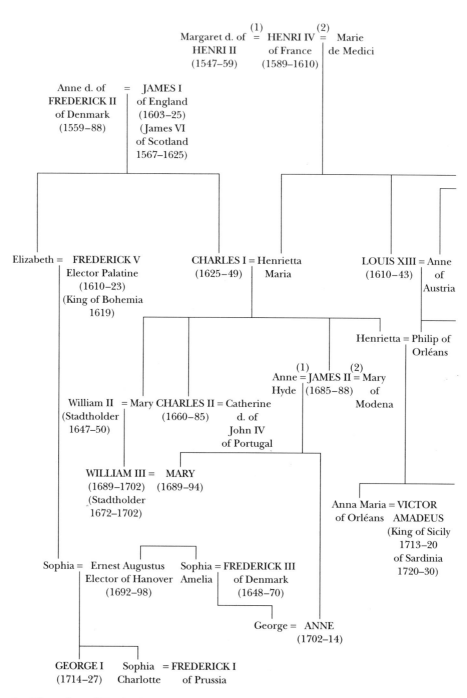

6. The rulers of England, France, Spain and the Empire

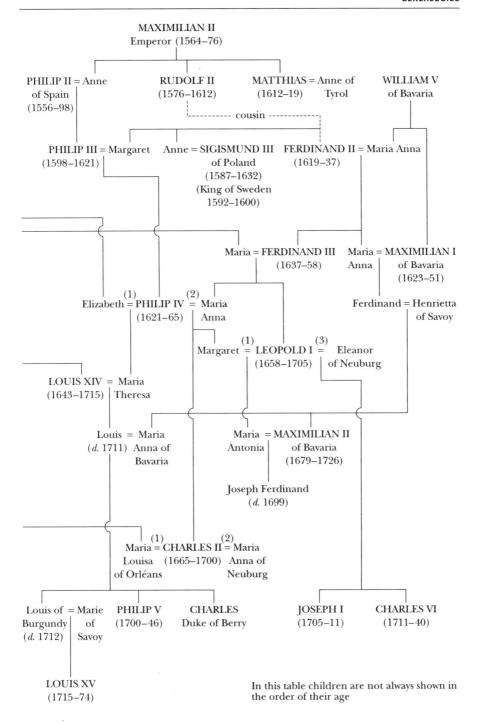

MAXIMILIAN II
Emperor (1564–76)

PHILIP II = Anne
of Spain
(1556–98)

RUDOLF II
(1576–1612)

MATTHIAS = Anne of
(1612–19)   Tyrol

WILLIAM V
of Bavaria

cousin

PHILIP III = Margaret
(1598–1621)

Anne = SIGISMUND III
of Poland
(1587–1632)
(King of Sweden
1592–1600)

FERDINAND II = Maria Anna
(1619–37)

Maria = FERDINAND III
(1637–58)

Maria = MAXIMILIAN I
Anna   of Bavaria
(1623–51)

Ferdinand = Henrietta
of Savoy

(1)
Elizabeth = PHILIP IV = Maria
(1621–65)   Anna

(2)

Margaret = LEOPOLD I = Eleanor
(1)   (1658–1705) (3) of Neuburg

LOUIS XIV = Maria
(1643–1715) Theresa

Louis = Maria
(d. 1711) Anna of
Bavaria

Maria = MAXIMILIAN II
Antonia   of Bavaria
(1679–1726)

Joseph Ferdinand
(d. 1699)

(1)
Maria = CHARLES II = Maria
Louisa   (1665–1700) Anna of
of Orléans   Neuburg
(2)

Louis of = Marie
Burgundy   of
(d. 1712) Savoy

PHILIP V
(1700–46)

CHARLES
Duke of Berry

JOSEPH I
(1705–11)

CHARLES VI
(1711–40)

LOUIS XV
(1715–74)

In this table children are not always shown in
the order of their age

339

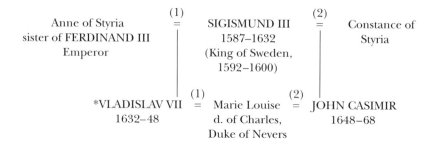

	(1)		(2)	
Anne of Styria	=	SIGISMUND III	=	Constance of
sister of FERDINAND III		1587–1632		Styria
Emperor		(King of Sweden,		
		1592–1600)		

	(1)		(2)	
*VLADISLAV VII	=	Marie Louise	=	JOHN CASIMIR
1632–48		d. of Charles,		1648–68
		Duke of Nevers		

MICHAEL = Eleanor Maria
WÍSNOWIECKI sister of Leopold I
1669–73 Emperor

JOHN SOBIESKI = Marie d'Arquien
1674–96

AUGUSTUS II
1697–1704 and 1709–33

STANISLAW LESZCZYŃSKI
1704–09

* Also known, by counting only Jagiellon kings, as Vladislav IV.

7. The rulers of Poland

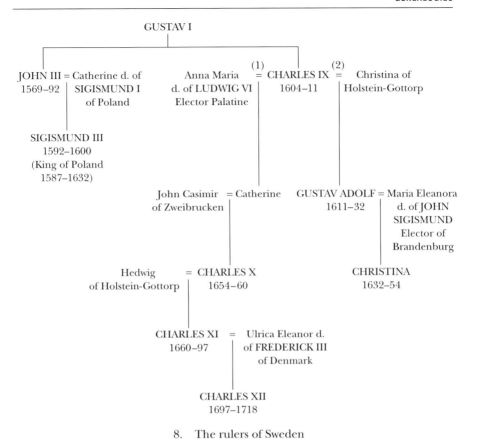

8.   The rulers of Sweden

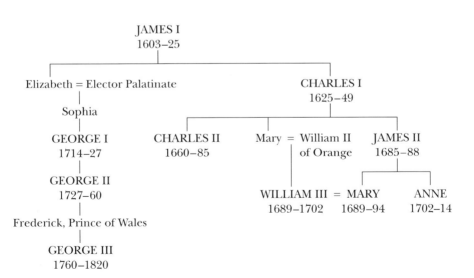

9.   The rulers of England (1603–1820)

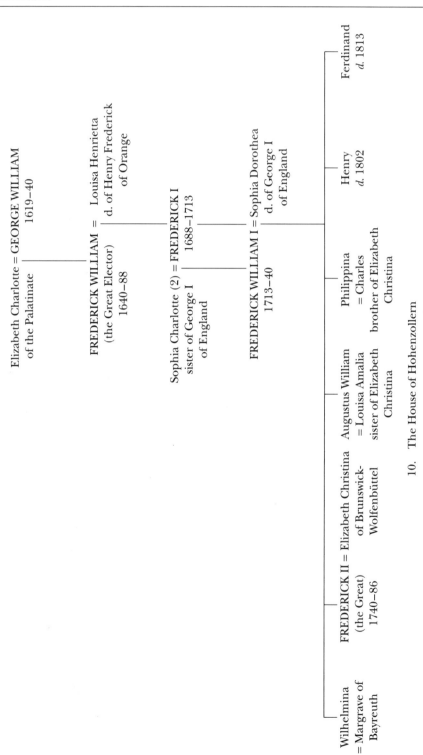

Elizabeth Charlotte = GEORGE WILLIAM
of the Palatinate   1619–40

FREDERICK WILLIAM = Louisa Henrietta
(the Great Elector)   d. of Henry Frederick
1640–88   of Orange

Sophia Charlotte (2) = FREDERICK I
sister of George I   1688–1713
of England

FREDERICK WILLIAM I = Sophia Dorothea
1713–40   d. of George I
of England

Wilhelmina   FREDERICK II = Elizabeth Christina   Augustus William   Philippina   Henry   Ferdinand
= Margrave of   (the Great)   of Brunswick-   = Louisa Amalia   = Charles   d. 1802   d. 1813
Bayreuth   1740–86   Wolfenbüttel   sister of Elizabeth   brother of Elizabeth
                                            Christina   Christina

10.   The House of Hohenzollern

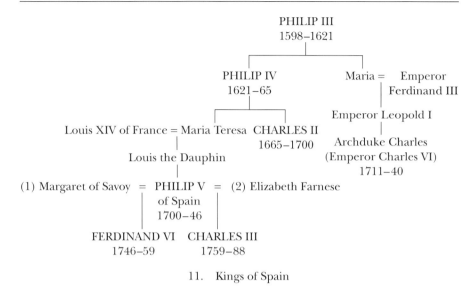

11.   Kings of Spain

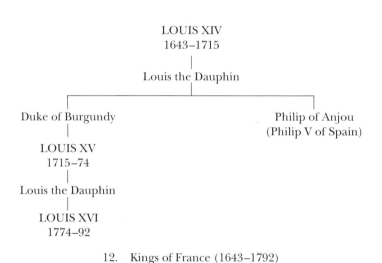

12.   Kings of France (1643–1792)

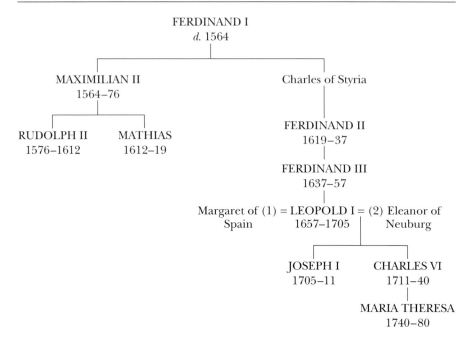

FERDINAND I
d. 1564

MAXIMILIAN II
1564–76

Charles of Styria

RUDOLPH II   MATHIAS
1576–1612   1612–19

FERDINAND II
1619–37

FERDINAND III
1637–57

Margaret of (1) = LEOPOLD I = (2) Eleanor of
Spain   1657–1705   Neuburg

JOSEPH I   CHARLES VI
1705–11   1711–40

MARIA THERESA
1740–80

13.   The Austrian Habsburgs

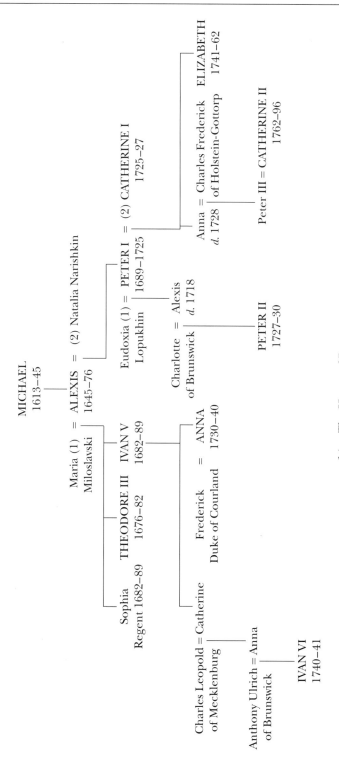

14. The House of Romanov

MAPS

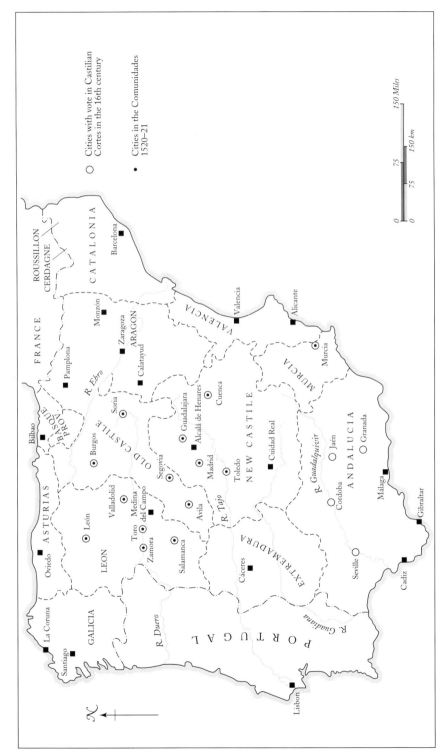

Cities with vote in Castilian Cortes in the 16th century

Cities in the Comunidades 1520–21

Map 1 Spain, 1469–1714

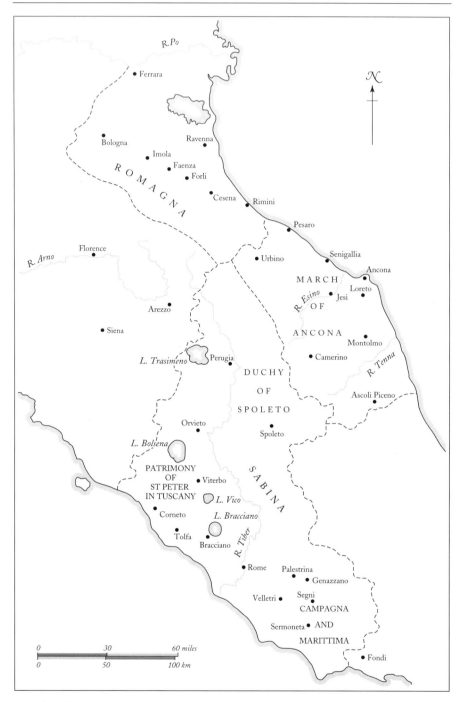

Map 2   The states of the Catholic Church

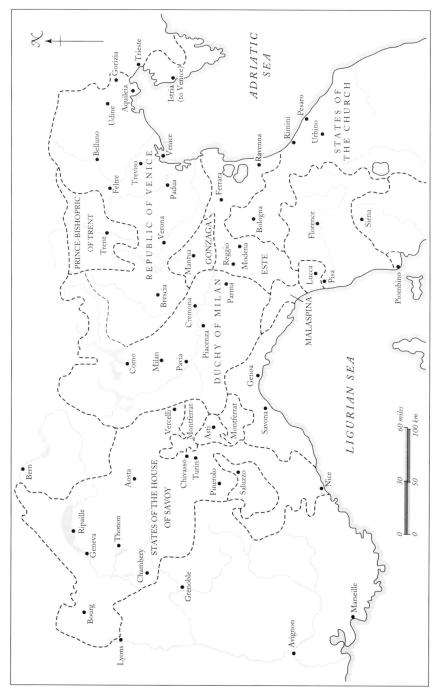

Map 3 Northern Italy in the mid-fifteenth century

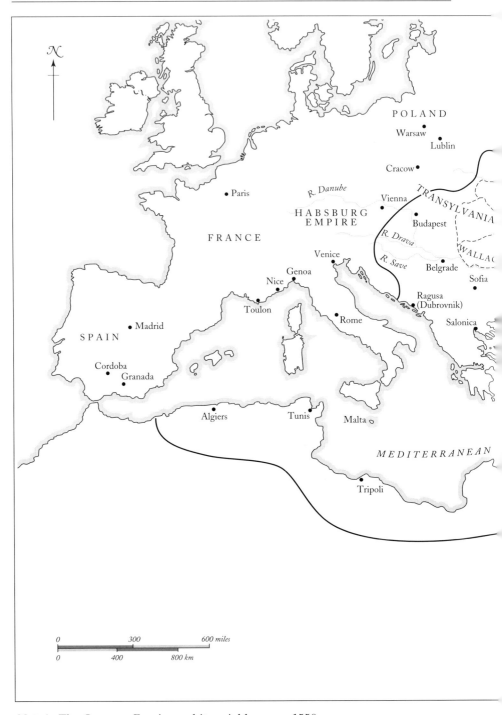

Map 4 The Ottoman Empire and its neighbours, *c.* 1550

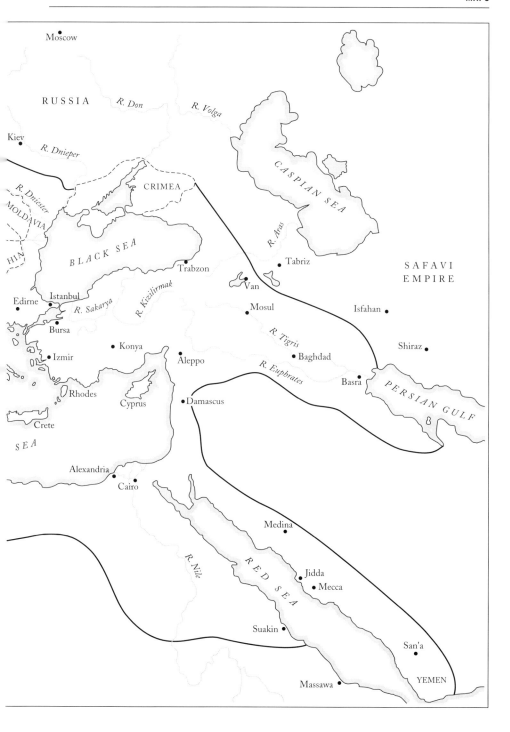

Moscow

RUSSIA   *R. Don*   *R. Volga*

Kiev   *R. Dnieper*

R. Dniester

MOLDAVIA   CRIMEA   *CASPIAN SEA*

HIN   BLACK SEA   *R. Aras*   Tabriz   SAFAVI
EMPIRE

Trabzon

Edirne   Istanbul   *R. Sakarya*   *R. Kızılırmak*   Van   Mosul   Isfahan

Bursa

Konya   Aleppo   *R. Tigris*   Baghdad   Shiraz

Izmir   *R. Euphrates*   Basra   PERSIAN GULF

Rhodes   Cyprus   Damascus

Crete

SEA

Alexandria   Cairo

Medina

R. Nile   RED SEA   Jidda   Mecca

Suakin   San'a

Massawa   YEMEN

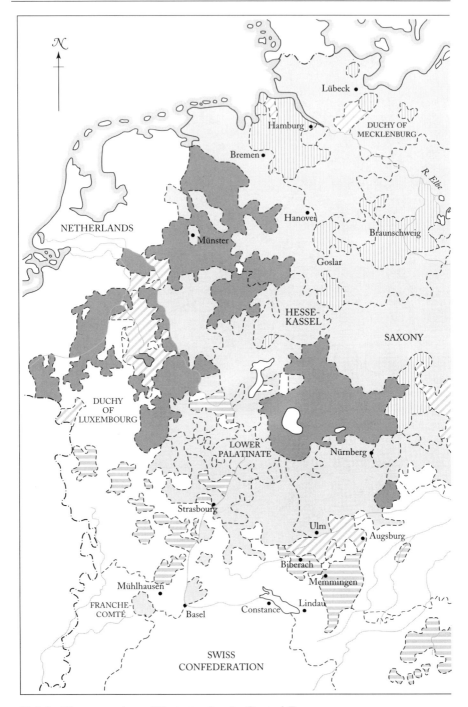

Map 5   The expansion of Protestantism in Central Europe

DUCHY OF
POMERANIA

ELECTORATE OF
BRANDENBURG

POLAND

DUCHY OF
SILESIA

KINGDOM
OF
BOHEMIA

MARGRAVATE
OF
MORAVIA

DUCHY
OF
BAVARIA

HUNGARY

AUSTRIA

Areas affected by Protestantism

Ecclesiastical territories affected
by Protestantism

Other ecclesiastical territories

Areas where the Reformation
was legally adopted

Secularised ecclesiastical
territories

Holy Roman Empire

0   60   120 miles
0   100   200 km

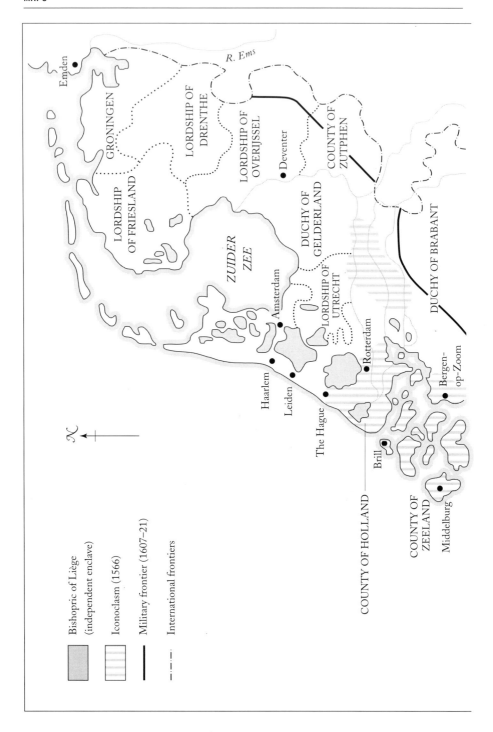

Bishopric of Liège
(independent enclave)

Iconoclasm (1566)

Military frontier (1607–21)

International frontiers

R. Ems

Emden

GRONINGEN

LORDSHIP
OF FRIESLAND

LORDSHIP OF DRENTHE

LORDSHIP OF OVERIJSSEL

Deventer

COUNTY OF
ZUTPHEN

DUCHY OF
GELDERLAND

DUCHY OF BRABANT

ZUIDER
ZEE

Amsterdam

LORDSHIP OF
UTRECHT

Rotterdam

Bergen-
op-Zoom

Haarlem

Leiden

The Hague

Brill

COUNTY OF HOLLAND

COUNTY OF
ZEELAND

Middelburg

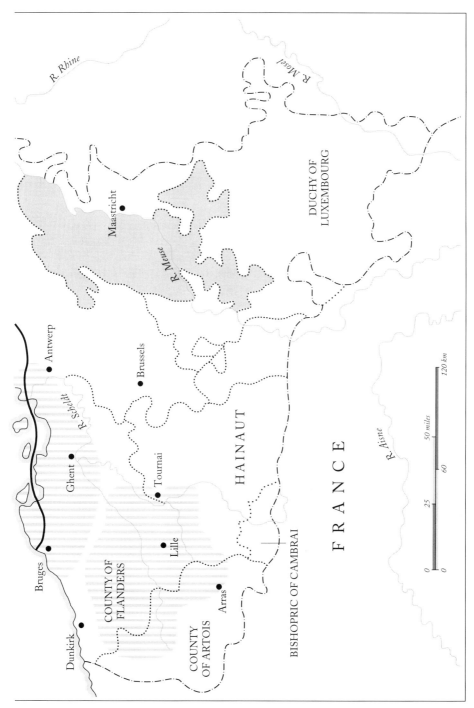

Map 6 The Netherlands during the Dutch Revolt

Map 7 Sites associated with the Thirty Years' War, 1618–48

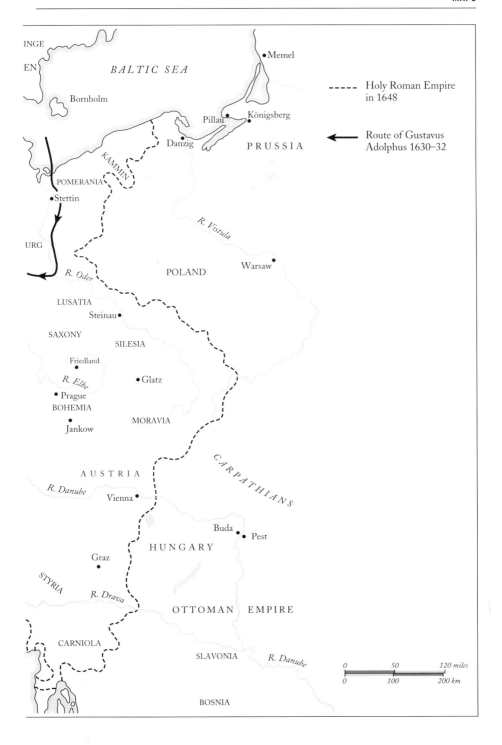

INGE

EN

BALTIC SEA

Memel

Bornholm

Pillau   Königsberg

Danzig

PRUSSIA

KAMMIN

POMERANIA

Stettin

URG

R. Vistula

R. Oder

POLAND

Warsaw

LUSATIA

Steinau

SAXONY

SILESIA

Friedland

R. Elbe

Glatz

Prague

BOHEMIA

Jankow

MORAVIA

CARPATHIANS

AUSTRIA

R. Danube

Vienna

Buda   Pest

HUNGARY

Graz

STYRIA

R. Drava

OTTOMAN EMPIRE

CARNIOLA

SLAVONIA

R. Danube

BOSNIA

- - - - - Holy Roman Empire in 1648

◄—— Route of Gustavus Adolphus 1630–32

| 0 | 50 | 120 miles |
| 0 | 100 | 200 km |

359

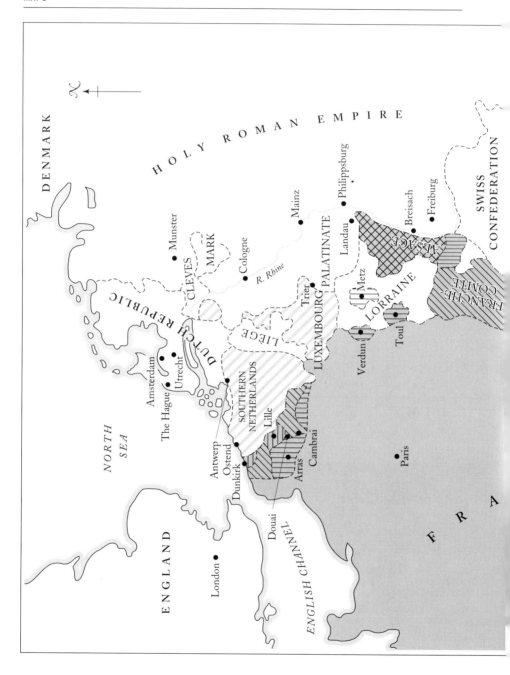

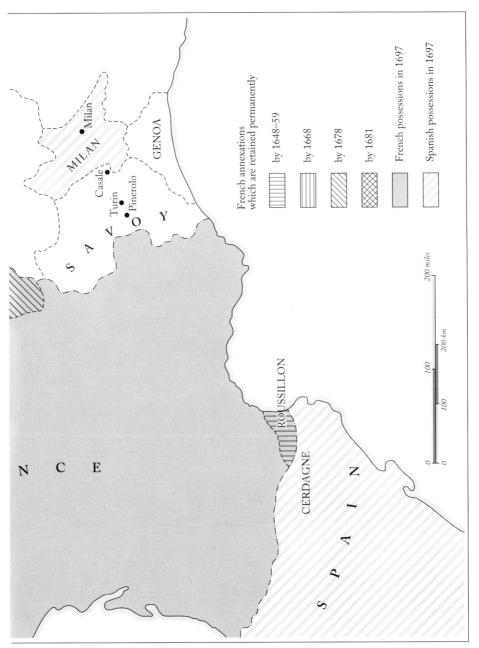

French annexations
which are retained permanently

by 1648–59

by 1668

by 1678

by 1681

French possessions in 1697

Spanish possessions in 1697

MILAN

• Milan

Casale •

Turin •
• Pinerolo

S A V O Y

GENOA

N C E

ROUSSILLON

CERDAGNE

S P A I N

0   100   200 km
0   100   200 miles

Map 8 Western Europe, 1648–97

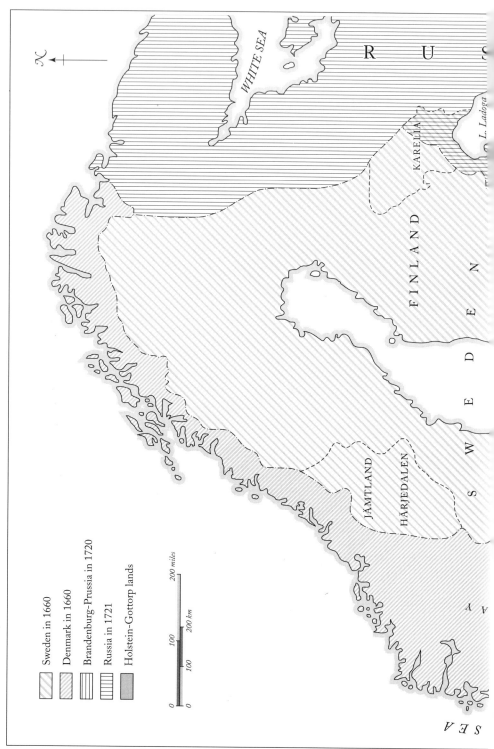

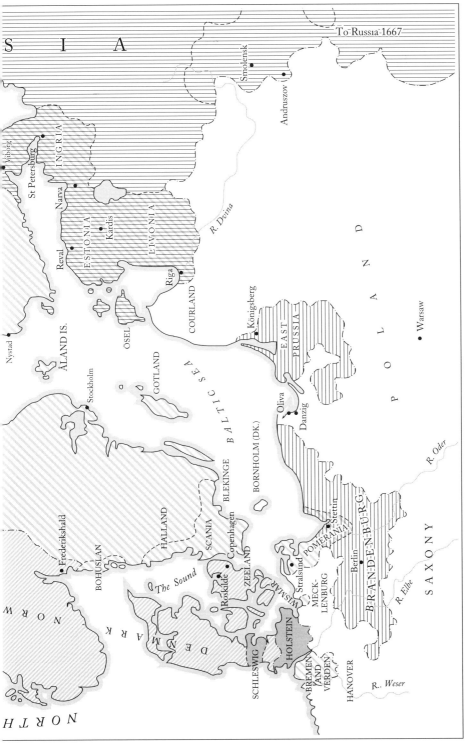

Map 9   The Baltic, 1648–1721

Map 10 Brandenburg-Prussia, 1640–1786

BALTIC SEA

Memel

Tauroggen
1691(1793)

R. Memel

Tilsit

Königsberg

1657

Lauenburg

Danzig

Kolberg

Kammin

1772

Marienburg

Allenstein

1679

Neustettin

Konitz

Gollnow

ettin

1772

Bromberg

Thorn

chwedt

Landsberg

R. Vistula

Küstrin

Schwiebus
1742

Posen

Gnesen

Warsaw

rankfurt

Krossen

ottbus

R. Oder

Glogau

Kalisch

Lodz

Liegnitz

Görlitz

Breslau

Czenstochau

Sandomierz

1742

Oppeln

Neisse

R. Vistula

Cracow

Ratibor

Tarnow

R. Elbe

Königgratz

R. Moldau

Teschen

Olmütz

Acquired by Prussia, 1742, 1744, 1772

0   75   150 miles

0   75   150 km

365

Map 11 Austria in the eighteenth century

IC SEA

Danzig

PRUSSIA

NEW
EAST
PRUSSIA

WEST
PRUSSIA

Bialystok

Schwiebus

SOUTH
PRUSSIA

Warsaw

RUSSIAN

EMPIRE

R. Oder

Görlitz Liegnitz Breslau

SILESIA to
Prussia 1742

Czenstochau

Lubin

WEST GALICIA
from Poland 1795

Königgratz

Cracow

R. Vistula

GALICIA
from Poland 1722

Przemysl

Lemberg

IA

Olmütz

MORAVIA

Brünn

Kaschau

Czernowitz

Vienna Pressburg

BUKOVINA
1775

IA

Budapest

Debrecen

Graz

Klausenburg

IA

KINGDOM OF
HUNGARY

TRANSYLVANIA

LA

Agram

Temesvar

Kronstadt

CROATIA

SLAVONIA

B A T S C H K A

BANAT

WALLACHIA
1718-39

EMPIRE

R. Save

Belgrade

Passarowitz

Krajowa

R. Danube

OTTOMAN

NORTH-SERBIA
1718-39

═╪═╪═╪═╪═ Boundary of the Holy Roman Empire

0   75   150 miles

0   75   150 km

367

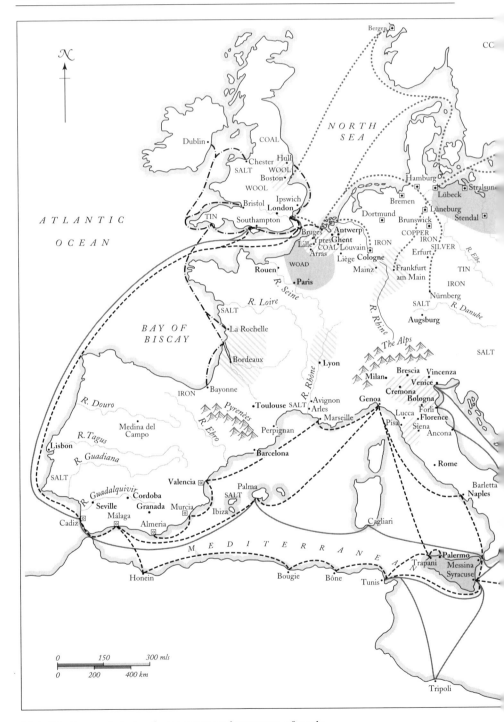

Map 12 Europe's natural resources and patterns of trade

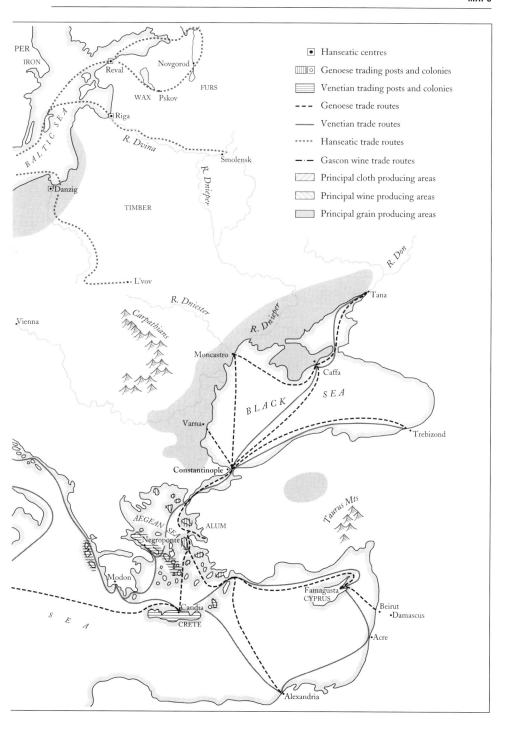

Hanseatic centres

Genoese trading posts and colonies

Venetian trading posts and colonies

Genoese trade routes

Venetian trade routes

Hanseatic trade routes

Gascon wine trade routes

Principal cloth producing areas

Principal wine producing areas

Principal grain producing areas

PER
IRON

Reval
Novgorod

FURS

WAX Pskov

Riga

R. Dvina

Smolensk

BALTIC SEA

Danzig

TIMBER

R. Dnieper

L'vov

Vienna

R. Dniester

Carpathians

R. Dnieper

R. Don

Tana

Moncastro

Caffa

BLACK   SEA

Varna

Trebizond

Constantinople

Taurus Mts

AEGEAN SEA ALUM

Negroponte

Modon

Famagusta
CYPRUS

Beirut
Damascus

S E A

Candia
CRETE

Acre

Alexandria

369

INDEX

Page numbers in bold denote major section devoted to entry. Page numbers in italic denote a glossary entry.